An Introduction to Sustainability

An Introduction to Sustainability provides students with a comprehensive overview of the key concepts and ideas which are encompassed within the growing field of sustainability.

The fully updated second edition, including new figures and images, teases out the diverse but intersecting domains of sustainability and emphasises strategies for action. Aimed at those studying the subject for the first time, it is unique in giving students from different disciplinary backgrounds a coherent framework and set of core principles for applying broad sustainability principles within their own personal and professional lives. These include: working to improve equality within and across generations; moving from consumerism to quality of life goals; and respecting diversity in both nature and culture.

Areas of emerging importance such as the economics of prosperity and wellbeing stand alongside core topics including:

- Energy and society
- Consumption and consumerism
- Risk and resilience
- Waste, water and land.

Key challenges and applications are explored through international case studies, and each chapter includes a thematic essay drawing on diverse literature to provide an integrated introduction to fundamental issues.

Housed on the Routledge Sustainability Hub, the book's companion website contains a range of features to engage students with the interdisciplinary nature of sustainability. Together these resources provide a wealth of material for learning, teaching and researching the topic of sustainability.

This textbook is an essential companion to any sustainability course.

Martin Mulligan is associate professor and senior lecturer in the Sustainability and Urban Planning teaching programme, and senior researcher within the Centre for Urban Research in the School of Global, Urban and Social Studies (GUSS) at RMIT University in Melbourne, Australia.

'This is a timely and much-needed book, written by experienced university educators who know how to engage with students and spark and sustain their interest. This involves being engaging and hopeful – and having the skill to explain quite complex ideas in a lucid, meaningful way. The second edition builds on the many strengths of the first, with updated information, figures and photos capturing the dynamism of sustainability thinking and practice.'

Allan Johnstone, Murdoch University, Australia

'This is a clear, well-pitched introduction to sustainability issues for undergraduate students. The book combines analysis of contemporary environmental concerns and their interwoven social dynamics with a real sense of the personal dimension of sustainability. Built on a decade's worth of teaching experience, this book encourages a wide-ranging and accessible approach to the subject for students from a diversity of academic backgrounds. I would happily recommend this as a core introductory text for a 1st year undergraduate module on environmental issues as it covers so many of the most important issues with critical appreciation while retaining a sense of optimism too.'

Sam Randalls, University College London, UK

'Sustainability is a "wicked problem," in which everyone is enmeshed; deep systemic change, rather than a cookbook of simple solutions, is required. The immensity of facing such a problem leads some of us to despair, others to complacent denial; Mulligan avoids both. The emergence of enviro-hatred as a mode of power, especially in the US, means that hope for any future requires champions, well-informed, critically thoughtful, and emotionally prepared. This book is excellent preparation on all three fronts.'

Kim Sorvig, University of New Mexico, USA

'In this new edition, Martin Mulligan adds a renewed emphasis on systems thinking, the "triple bottom line" concept of corporate responsibility, and provides a series of global challenges framed as "wicked" problems to illustrate the magnitude of the transition to the sustainability paradigm. And yet the book retains the hopeful element that made the original edition such a worthy addition to the sustainability literature. This mix of reality and hope creates a compelling story about humans, our social and economic needs, and the health of the planet on which we dwell.'

Thomas Theis, Director of the Institute for Environmental Science and Policy, University of Illinois, USA

An Introduction to Sustainability

Environmental, Social and Personal Perspectives

Second Edition

MARTIN MULLIGAN

With Michael Buxton, Ruth Lane,
Melissa Neave and Anthony Richardson

Routledge
Taylor & Francis Group
LONDON AND NEW YORK

earthscan
from Routledge

Second edition published 2018
by Routledge
2 Park Square, Milton Park, Abingdon, Oxon OX14 4RN

and by Routledge
711 Third Avenue, New York, NY 10017

Routledge is an imprint of the Taylor & Francis Group, an informa business

First edition published by Routledge 2015

British Library Cataloguing-in-Publication Data
A catalogue record for this book is available from the British Library

Library of Congress Cataloging-in-Publication Data
Names: Mulligan, Martin, author.
Title: An introduction to sustainability : environmental, social and personal perspectives / Martin Mulligan.
Description: Abingdon, Oxon ; New York, NY : Routledge, 2018. | Earlier edition: 2015. | Includes bibliographical references and index.
Identifiers: LCCN 2017019707| ISBN 9781138698291 (hardback) | ISBN 9781138698307 (pbk.) | ISBN 9781315519456 (ebook)
Subjects: LCSH: Sustainability.
Classification: LCC HC79.E5 M856 2018 | DDC 338.9/27–dc23
LC record available at https://lccn.loc.gov/2017019707

ISBN: 978-1-138-69829-1 (hbk)
ISBN: 978-1-138-69830-7 (pbk)
ISBN: 978-1-315-51945-6 (ebk)

Typeset in Akzidenz Grotesk and Eurostile
by Keystroke, Neville Lodge, Tettenhall, Wolverhampton

Printed and bound by CPI Group (UK) Ltd, Croydon, CR0 4YY

This book is dedicated to the youngest in my clan – Indu, Roshan, Amelie and Baxter – because your future is at the forefront of my mind.

Contents

Visual tour

KEY CONCEPTS AND CONCERNS

At the beginning of each chapter, a number of key issues are set out so it is clear what is to be covered in the forthcoming chapters.

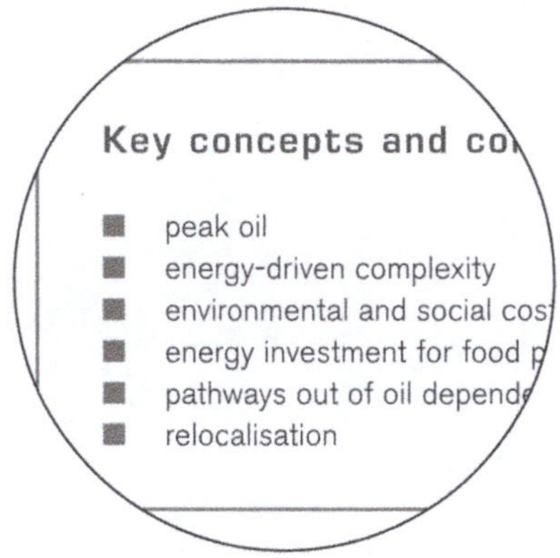

Key concepts and co
peak oil
energy-driven complexity
environmental and social cos
energy investment for food
pathways out of oil depend
relocalisation

MARGINAL GLOSSARY TERMS

A glossary at the back of the book helps with new terms and their definitions. Where these terms are used for the first time in the book they can be found in bold and their definitions located in the margin nearby.

Worldwatch Institute is an environmental research organisation in Washington, DC, founded by Lester Brown in 1974 and famous for producing an annual State of the World report since 1984.

MARGINAL KEY TITLES

Where the author makes references in the text to key titles, the biographical details can be located nearby in the margin to make it easier to read beyond the text.

Rachel Carson (1907–64) trained as a zoologist before becoming editor-in-chief of US Fish and Wildlife Service publications and a newspaper columnist. Before the publication of Silent Spring in 1962 her main publication was

DISCUSSION QUESTIONS

Towards the end of each chapter there are a number of discussion questions that students can undertake inside or outside the class. These give students an opportunity to further consider the topics arising in the chapter.

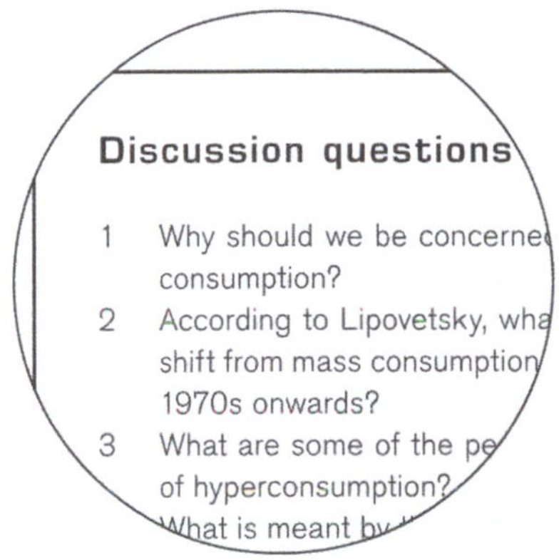

THEMATIC ESSAY

After the main text of each chapter you will find a 'thematic essay' which explores a theme emerging from the main text. These articles can be used as an extended case study, a platform for class discussion or assignments or simply as a 'postscript' for the chapter main.

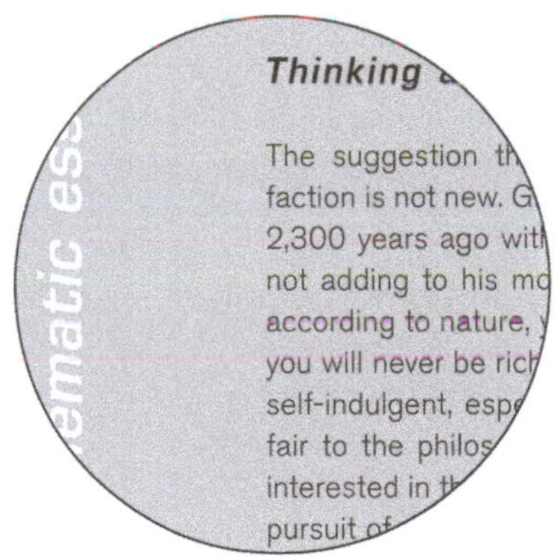

Photos

Figures

Tables

Preface

A survey of academics using the first edition of this book suggested a number of amendments and improvements. For example, it was suggested that the significance of the 'triple bottom line' model introduced by John Elkington in 1994 needed to be acknowledged and that the concept of 'ecosystem services' deserved more attention. One respondent suggested that more attention should be given to the influence of 'systems thinking' on the emergence of sustainability discourses. In general it was suggested that less emphasis should be placed on the way the introduction to sustainability subject has been taught at the author's university.

Amendments have been made to almost all chapters to make the suggested improvements. The introduction of the 'triple bottom line' model, seven years after the publication of the landmark *Brundtland Report*, has been acknowledged (see Figure 2.1), although the book continues to work with the view that it has not been helpful in the longer term to separate economic policies and practices from the domain of social sustainability. For pedagogical reasons, the book still features the 'Social Ecology' model introduced by Professor Stuart Hill at the University of Western Sydney because it brings the 'personal dimensions' of sustainability challenges into play.

The author is grateful for the opportunity to work on a second edition of the book because it is always possible to make improvements. In reworking almost all the chapters, key ideas have been highlighted, information updated and influential concepts explained better. New references and source materials have been used and many items have been added to the marginal glossary. Discussion questions have been revised and new figures and photos have been included.

Sustainability is such a broad-ranging topic that it is not easy to decide what should be included in an introductory text and other authors would structure such a book differently. Even with amendments, there is still a strong influence in the book on the way the introductory subject is taught at RMIT University because the approach has been developed and refined for teaching diverse cohorts of students for more than 15 years. However, the book also aims to go beyond the scope of a single introductory subject and Chapters 13–16 were added for those who may prefer to approach sustainability through a range of contemporary socio-environmental challenges. Hopefully the revised book, and the companion website housed on the Routledge Sustainability Hub, provide flexible resources for teaching sustainability to a wide range of student cohorts.

Martin Mulligan
April, 2017

Acknowledgements

The seed for the first edition of this book was planted when Earthscan/Routledge senior commissioning editor Khanam Virjee visited me at RMIT University in early 2012 to ask if I was working on anything that could be turned into a book proposal. At the time, I had just assumed responsibility for teaching a 'foundational' introduction to sustainability subject to 300–500 first year students in RMIT's School of Global, Urban and Social Studies and I said that it was hard to find suitable introductory texts for such a subject. Khanam said that an extensive Earthscan/Routledge review of academics teaching sustainability in the UK, North America and Australia had reached the same conclusion and she encouraged me to develop a proposal based on the survey responses. Khanam and production editor Alexandra McGregor backed my proposal enthusiastically and both played active roles in developing the first edition of the book. No author could wish for more support than I received from Khanam and Alex. When Khanam moved to another publishing house, Rebecca Brennan stepped in as a strong advocate for the book and it was Rebecca who proposed a second edition and conducted a survey of academics using the first edition to suggest improvements. Rebecca has continued the outstanding service I have received from Earthscan/Routledge. I must also acknowledge the diligent support I have received from Leila Walker as the editorial assistant and Hannah Ewing as the production editor for this second edition; wonderful!

The introductory subject that I took over at RMIT in 2012 had very strong foundations and I acknowledge the work of those who had developed it for nearly ten years before it fell into my hands; they include Ian Thomas, Kathryn Hegarty, Nicole Cook and Cathryn Kriewaldt. Several of the tutors who worked with me in 2012 had taught the subject before I arrived and some were still with me in 2017. I was fortunate to have experienced tutor Anthony Richardson as my Head Tutor in 2012 because he helped me develop ideas for the book; including the development of the composite 'RMIT Principles' which serve an important pedagogical role in teaching an introduction to sustainability course to a very wide range of students. Anthony offered a lecture on the topic of 'Energy and Society' which became the basis for Chapter 5 in both editions of this book. Others who have helped me in the role of Head Tutor are Laurel Mackenzie, Anne-Lise Ah-Fat and Arley Marks. At the time of writing I had worked with Arley as Head Tutor for three consecutive years and her diligent and creative work on our teaching pedagogy is reflected in changes made for the second edition of the book. At RMIT I must also acknowledge the support I have been given by Professor Jean Hillier, who first asked me to teach the subject, and Professor Robin Goodman in her role as head of the Sustainability and Urban Planning teaching programme within the School of Global, Urban and Social Studies. I also received wonderful support from the Dean of the school, Professor David Hayward. I am blessed to be able to work in a supportive and innovative academic environment. Raven Cretney, at RMIT, helped to locate some better photos for the second edition.

Because 'sustainability' is such a broad-ranging topic it is very hard to know how to best carve it up for an introductory subject. The focus on unsustainable human impacts on global ecosystems means that it is often seen as a matter for environmental scientists, however the introduction course at RMIT is taught to students undertaking study in areas such as social work and psychology as well as environmental sustainability and so the emphasis is on social sustainability as much as environmental sustainability. I wish to acknowledge Professor Stuart Hill, at the University of Western Sydney, for his work in developing the Social Ecology model which also seeks to bring the personal dimensions of sustainability into view. The first 12 chapters of the book reflect the way we choose to teach introduction to sustainability at RMIT University, although I have taken into account feedback on the need to broaden the scope to some extent. Chapters 13–16 focus on the kinds of topics more commonly found in introductory courses on sustainability (as reflected the Earthscan/Routledge survey which underpinned the development of the first edition). I wish to thank my RMIT colleagues Michael Buxton and Melissa Neave for being willing to take the lead in drafting chapters relevant to their fields of expertise whilst Ruth Lane, from Monash University, agreed to take the lead on writing Chapter 16, knowing that she would get little credit for doing so. I appreciate the generosity of Michael, Mel and Ruth for contributing to a book that would be published in my name. My thanks also go to Kelly Winter and the team at Keystroke for their diligent work on the manuscript.

Finally, I want to thank my wife and life partner Nelum Buddhadasa for her constant support and inspiration after I decided to pursue an academic career at the age of 43. We have shared so many journeys together, in Australia and Sri Lanka, that it is difficult to even imagine life without her and her very strong moral compass. I have also shared many inspirational journeys with my younger children Indu and Roshan and I want to thank my three children – Will, Indu and Roshan – and my grandchildren – Amelie and Baxter – for their constant inspiration. This book is dedicated to the youngest in my clan – Indu, Roshan, Amelie and Baxter – because your future is foremost in my mind.

CHAPTER 1

Introduction

AUTHOR'S INTRODUCTION

When I stepped down as director of **RMIT University's Centre for Global Research** at the end of 2011, I was invited to take responsibility for teaching an introduction to sustainability course for students enrolled in a wide range of degrees within RMIT's School of Global, Urban and Social Studies. It had been more than ten years since I had taught at undergraduate level and I was rather daunted by the prospect of introducing such a complex and contested topic to such a diverse array of students, most of them in their very first year of university study. To make matters worse, I knew that a significant number of the students resented having to take a course on 'environmental issues' when they planned careers in human or social services. How could I convince them that sustainability is about social wellbeing as much as environmental care and that every person on Earth needs to grapple with the dilemmas of sustainability? How could I convince them that the idea of 'sustainability' has not already lost its vitality and relevance? What particular concepts and themes would I select in order to engage the students with the history and enduring relevance of the idea?

RMIT University Centre for Global Research was established in 1992, initially under the name Globalism Institute, to conduct research on sources of insecurity, community sustainability and globalisation and culture.

Fortunately, the course I inherited already had very strong foundations; with a lot of work going into the way it was set up and taught for nearly ten years before it was handed to me. I also inherited a talented team of tutors, most of whom had already worked in the course before my arrival and had figured out ways to make it appeal to diverse cohorts of students. I was confident that I had accumulated enough experience and expertise to add value to what had been done before me. My own career – inside and outside of universities – had taken many twists and turns since I completed an Honours degree in animal ecology at the University of Sydney in the early 1970s. This course gave me a rare opportunity to draw on much of that diverse experience.

After completing my first degree I had decided that life as a scientist was not for me and I left university to become a community development worker in several different Australian cities. I returned to university in the early 1990s to complete a Ph.D. in 'development studies' – with a thesis focusing on environment and development in Latin America. From there I was able to win a position in the very innovative Social Ecology teaching and research programme at the University of Western Sydney. Ten years later I returned to RMIT University, where I had undertaken my Ph.D., to help build what was then called the Globalism Institute (now Centre for Global Research). For another ten years my research focused on challenges facing local communities in Australia and Sri Lanka in the context of global change. My career path might be called opportunistic rather than premeditated and yet it seemed that I had been preparing myself to teach in the area of environmental and social sustainability for a very long time.

THE CONCEPT AS WE NOW KNOW IT

In introducing first-year undergraduate students to the concept of sustainability I argue that we can draw hope from the fact that we humans only really began to think about it as a global challenge in the 1970s. The 1987 report prepared by a special United Nations commission headed by three-times Norwegian prime minister Gro Harlem Brundtland – published under the title *Our Common Future* – drew attention to a growing body of research showing that on a global scale human economic activity had been degrading planetary ecosystems while the majority of people in the world faced worsening conditions for life, often caused by environmental degradation. Reflecting the growth of global awareness that had gathered momentum since the early 1970s, the report argued that we now face 'interlocking crises' because 'the global economy and global ecology' have been 'locked ... together in new ways' (p. 5). The **Brundtland Report** did not coin the term 'sustainability' and nor did it initiate the argument that growing global human impacts on non-human environments cannot be sustained. However, it did give birth to the notion of 'environmentally sustainable development' and it triggered a series of global gatherings and negotiations aimed at giving substance to this headline concept. In an interview marking the 20th anniversary of the report which carries her name, Brundland noted that her commission could have taken the easy option of making recommendations which would have been relatively easy for national governments to adopt.[1] Instead they decided to highlight challenges which are transnational or global in scale and they decided to write a report arguing that sustainability is not a matter to be left to experts or governments because it affects the future of every person living on Planet Earth, and those who are yet to be born. The report argued that sustainable use of the planet's non-human 'resources' cannot be separated from the ongoing need to radically reduce global poverty; i.e. sustainability is about *both* environment and society. While it argued that much more needs to be done to improve equity of opportunity in the present (*intragenerational*) we now need to focus on the even bigger challenge of ensuring equity of opportunity for future generations (*intergenerational*).

Brundtland Report was a report prepared for the United Nations by a World Commissionon Environment and Development headed by Gro Harlem Burndtland. It was published in 1987 under the title *Our Common Future.*

In the context of human history, 25–30 years is a relatively short time to have been grappling with the challenges of global sustainability. We know much more about the challenges we face than ever before and yet this book will make it clear that the challenges are continuing to escalate rather than abate. This is a rather challenging message to present to first-year university students as they embark on the professional development course they have selected. For that reason, I was determined to infuse my teaching with the conviction that there are still reasons for feeling hopeful about the future of humanity. This book does not shy away from the extent and complexity of the global challenges we face; indeed it seeks to counteract all tendencies towards denial or retreat. It argues that we need to work with the rather perplexing concept of 'wicked problems' in order to ensure that action taken in the name of sustainability does not, inadvertently, make things worse.

ARGUMENTS FOR HOPE

At the beginning of the course that I teach at RMIT University, I tell the students that we are embarking on a journey together, noting that it may at times feel like a roller-coaster ride through the ups and downs of hope and despair. Here I refer them to an article I wrote (Mulligan 2008) after a rather challenging journey from Melbourne to Edinburgh which is summarised in the box below. After a series of mishaps along the way I finally enjoyed a relaxing walk around the festive and beautiful city of my apparent destination only to find myself seduced by a thought from the famed Scottish writer Robert Louis Stevenson which continues to prompt me to remember that journeys are never fully completed and that they always hold the hope of new and exciting discoveries.

To travel hopefully ...

In August 2006 I arrived at Melbourne Airport to catch a flight that would take me to London and on to Edinburgh where I was due to present a paper at an international conference on 'art and society'. About a week before my departure Heathrow Airport in London had been thrown into prolonged chaos in the wake of credible threats made to use bombs to bring down undisclosed flights to the USA and I found that extraordinary security measures had been imposed on all passengers travelling to or through Heathrow Airport. A ban had been imposed on all cabin bags and the only thing that each passenger could carry on board was a clear plastic bag with passport and documents; even pens were banned to prevent their potential use as weapons. The early symptoms of a head cold that I felt when the plane took off had blossomed into a raging illness by the time the plane landed, some 24 hours later, at Heathrow.

Because I had travelled with a set of car keys in my pocket, I was plucked out of the line of passengers wanting transit on to Edinburgh and told that I would need to check out through airport security and re-enter the domestic terminal so that my keys could be given a security clearance. It mattered little because all flights to Edinburgh had been cancelled for the day and no intending passengers – transit or otherwise – could get inside the overcrowded domestic terminal. A security guard told me that I needed to head for an information marquee erected outside the terminal to get information about possible flights to Edinburgh. The marquee was too small to cope with the crowds of people wanting to know if or when they might be able to get on a plane and I was obliged to wait in a very long queue. To make matters worse it started to rain. I stood in the rain, clutching my plastic bag and nursing a heavy head, alongside a woman holding an infant; all of us hoping that we would eventually make it inside the tent. I felt I got a small insight into what it might feel like to be a refugee or asylum seeker, although we were blessed by the presence of some cheerful volunteers from the city and by the some amusing running commentary offered by a Scottish joker in the queue. A sense of great frustration slowly transformed into a palpable feeling of camaraderie as people took time to share stories and boost each other's spirits. A volunteer took the mother and her family to the head of the queue inside the tent, amid cheers from those alarmed at her plight.

Edinburgh's festival season occurs in August each year when a range of concurrent festivals are held; perhaps the most famous being the Edinburgh Comedy Festival.

After a night in an expensive Heathrow hotel, I managed to get myself on a flight to Edinburgh although my booked-in luggage would not arrive for more than a week. With only the clothes I was wearing and my small plastic bag I finally arrived at my university accommodation, grateful to see the sun shining for a change. The next day I set out for an exploratory walk around a city in a mood to enjoy its annual **festival season** and high on the hill, before reaching the famed castle, I noticed a sign pointing to a rather quaint old stone building that served as the Edinburgh Writers Centre. In a room dedicated to the work of the celebrated novelist and travel writer Robert Louis Stevenson a quote from his work was prominently displayed, as if designed to catch my attention. It read: 'To travel hopefully is better than to arrive.'

The Stevenson citation spoke directly to my own travel experience because I learnt to enjoy the journey once I stopped worrying about when, or even if, I would reach my destination. I learnt something about my own resilience and about the capacity of my fellow travellers to act with unusual care towards each other. At a global level, humanity is heading into a period of great uncertainty. No one can really be sure what lies ahead of us. However, we will learn a lot about what we are capable of achieving together if we can learn to travel hopefully.

SUCCESSES AND FAILURES SINCE 1987

The Brundtland Report began with a section on 'Successes and Failures' in meeting 'the global challenge'. At the time, the failures clearly outnumbered the successes and that continues to be the case. While some manifestations of environmental degradation that were highlighted in the report – such as 'acid rain' in Europe – have been effectively mitigated, others – such as deforestation and the accumulation of greenhouse gases caused by the burning of fossil fuels – continue to head in the wrong direction. It was never going to be easy to address challenges which transcend the jurisdictions of national governments, and it is important to note successes as well as failures. A gathering of world leaders in Montreal in 1989 agreed on a protocol aimed at phasing out the use of gases known to be causing the dangerous thinning of the atmosphere's ozone layer and action on this global problem has had significant success. The Brundtland Report laid the foundations for the very large and energetic Earth Summit held in Rio de Janeiro in 1992 and its pacesetting *Agenda 21* proposals were adopted by many nations. The Rio Earth Summit, in turn, built momentum for the global convention for 'biological diversity' and other agreements on combatting the spread of deserts and protecting endangered wetlands. Efforts have been made to establish rules to prevent the degradation of marine environments in 'international waters' although these are very hard to enforce. The Rio Earth Summit set wheels in motion for the global summit held in Kyoto in 1997 which aimed to develop an international protocol for reducing emissions of greenhouse gases. Unfortunately, it is much harder to phase out the use of fossil fuels than to replace the use of the gases which thin the ozone layer, and action on reducing greenhouse gases has been much less successful than phasing out the use of the ozone-depleting gases. Ongoing efforts to reach a global agreement on the reduction of greenhouse gas emissions continued to be frustrated by governments prioritising short-term national economic interests until frustrations boiled over at a very disappointing summit held in Copenhagen in 2009. However, the disappointment of Copenhagen stimulated an intensified effort to transcend national differences and the next summit, held in Paris in December 2015, produced much better results. The Brundtland Report's radical call to put global interests ahead of narrowly conceived national interests is finding some success.

Other successes have been racked up at a conceptual level. In particular, English planner, psychologist and sustainability consultant, **John Elkington**, teased out the concept of environmentally sustainable development by introducing the 'triple bottom line' model in 1994, suggesting the need to balance economic development policies and practices with equal concern for environmental impacts and social outcomes. This, in turn, led to the very influential 'three sectors' model for representing the challenges of sustainability (see Figure 1.1). While ecologists have long argued that human wellbeing ultimately depends on the effective functioning of a host of overlapping ecosystems, the concept of 'ecosystem services' has gained considerable momentum as a way of representing this within economic and social development policies and practices. While environmentalists worry that many of the

John Elkington (b. 1949) is an English planner and psychologist, turned sustainability consultant, who invented the 'triple bottom line' concept in 1994.

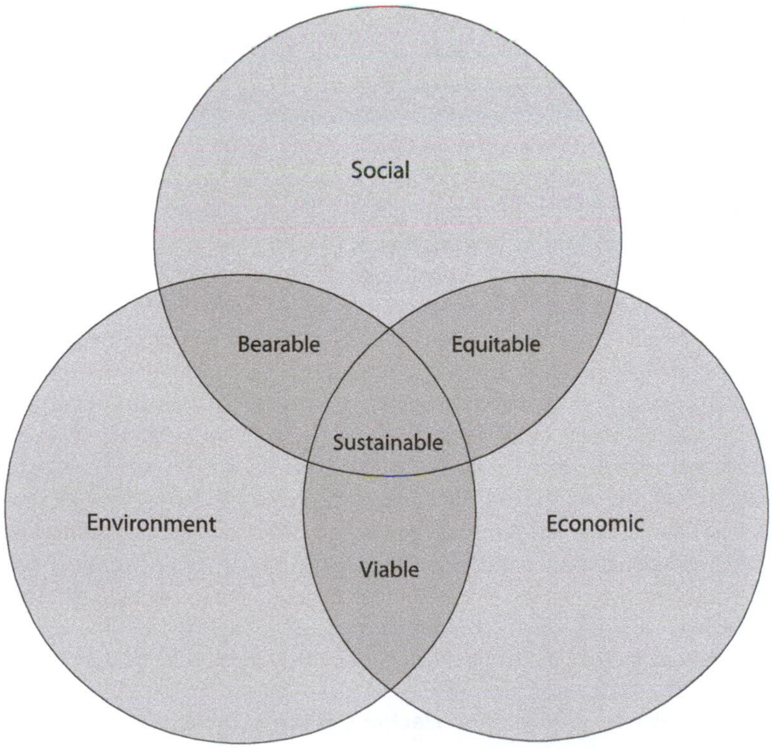

Figure 1.1 The 'triple bottom line' represented as three overlapping sectors

ideas associated with the overarching concept of sustainability articulated in the Brundtland Report are very human-centred, there is little doubt that they have put environmental issues onto other policy and practice agendas and they have also encouraged environmentalists to think more deeply about the nexus between human needs and environmental protection. As a representation of key ideas in the Brundland Report, Elkington's triple bottom line model highlights the need to balance often competing policy and practice agendas in the present. Even more challenging, however, is the call to stretch our thinking way beyond short-term political or policy cycles, or even lifetimes, in order to contemplate the legacy we are creating for the young and those yet to be born. 'Intergenerational equity' is, perhaps, a rather bland name for such a radical idea but it is an idea which is hard to ignore, whether you are a policy-maker of simply a parent.

WORKING BETWEEN THE GLOBAL AND THE LOCAL

Rio Earth Summit (1992) was a gathering initiated by the United Nations Commission on Environment and Development for heads of state, other representatives of national governments and representatives of a wide range of international and national organisations. It attracted around 17,000 delegates.

Copenhagen and Paris Climate Change summits (2009 and 2015) were part of a series of UN-sponsored global gatherings aimed at negotiating international agreements to reduce emissions of greenhouse gases. The first conference in the series was held in Kyoto in 1997.

Rio+20 was held in Rio 20 years later with more delegates but fewer heads of state in attendance.

The Brundtland Report reflected the growth of global awareness which may have triggered plans for the impressive '**Earth Summit**' held in Rio de Janeiro in 1992 and this probably represents the high point of global optimism about our capacity to successfully meet the challenges of global sustainability while the 2009 **Copenhagen summit on climate change** may represent a low point, before world leaders decided to act with much more resolution at the follow-up climate change **summit held in Paris** at the end of 2015. Of course, we should avoid reading too much into individual events or global developments because action needs to be both ambitious and sustained to address trends such as those reviewed in Chapters 3–5. However, there can be little doubt that the complexities associated with global climate change have undermined confidence in humanity's ability to act globally. According to the communiqué that emerged from the **Rio+20** gathering held in 2012, global humanity knows what needs to be done but lacks the 'political will' to do what is needed.

This book will confirm that global climate change is indeed a 'wicked problem' that cannot be resolved with particular, short-term, responses. Similarly, it will argue that global poverty cannot be easily 'ended' and that our growing global dependency on oil and other 'fossil fuels' is making human societies much more vulnerable to forms of collapse than we dare to imagine. It is easy for most people in the world to think that problems of this magnitude are matters for heads of state and international agencies and that there is little that individuals can do. This book will argue that this response is a form of denial because there is much that individuals can, and should, do. However, we do not encounter and interact with global systems and global change at a global level but rather at the level of daily living within localised environments. We encounter local weather rather than the global climate; we make daily decisions about our use of energy; and we interact with the global economy – and its global social consequences – in local shops and markets.

The US-based science writer **Rachel Carson** is widely acknowledged as being the mother of the modern environmental movement which began in the USA before achieving global reach and significance in the 1970s. Carson died in 1964 before witnessing the growth of the movement that she simulated but it was her cry-from-the-heart book of 1962 – *Silent Spring* – that made people realise that synthetic chemicals sprayed on crops in the USA were capable of killing fish and birds in remote locations, even outside the borders of the nation. We live in a world in which global communication technologies have largely dissolved old boundaries imposed by space and time; we can be in real-time contact with people anywhere on the planet. However, we live within local ecosystems where our environmental impacts begin before spreading through the kinds of **ecological flows** that were depicted by Carson. We need to understand both the globalisation of social systems – including the economy – and the ways in which ecological flows link local ecosystems into the **biosphere**. This book will argue that we need greater social *and* ecological literacy in order to understand the dynamic interrelationships between the local and the global.

Rachel Carson (1907–64) trained as a zoologist before becoming editor-in-chief of US Fish and Wildlife Service publications and a newspaper columnist. Before the publication of *Silent Spring* in 1962 her main publication was *The Sea Around Us* (1952).

ecological flows is a term used in this book to highlight the ways in which materials and energy flow through ecosystems at all levels for the local to the global.

biosphere is the term used to refer to the zone surrounding the planet in which living organisms can thrive. It extends from just below the surface of the planet to the part of the atmosphere which contains sufficient oxygen to sustain life.

BRINGING IN THE PERSONAL

As mentioned above, the 'triple bottom line' model introduced by John Elkington is often represented as a 'three-sector' diagram and this representation has been very influential. However, as we will see in Chapters 6 and 9, many scholars have questioned the suggestion that economic policy and practice can serve needs which are somehow outside the domain of social wellbeing and this has prompted a move to place economic thinking inside the social sphere. This line of thinking prompted the development of a 'Social Ecology' model of sustainability – used in an innovative Social Ecology teaching programme at the University of Western Sydney – which shifts economic thinking into the social sphere in order to make way for naming the 'personal' as a major sphere for acting on sustainability challenges (see Figure 1.2).

There is no need to counterpose the Social Ecology model with the triple bottom line model because the latter continues to challenge existing areas of

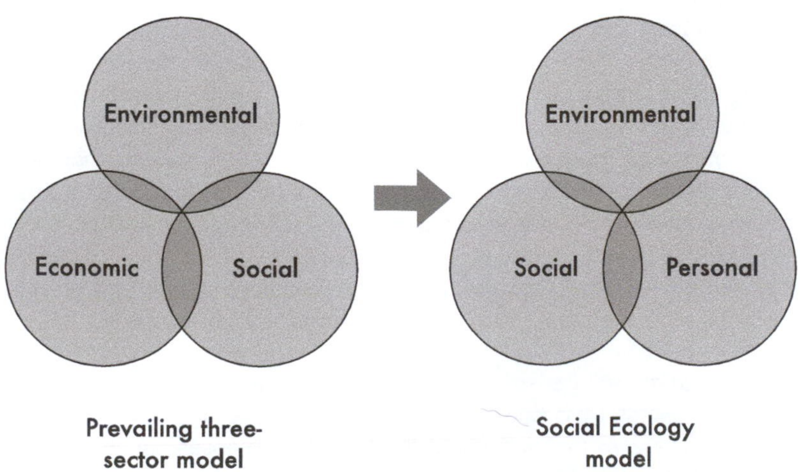

Figure 1.2 From the prevailing model to the Social Ecology model

policy and practice, as they are currently conceived. However, the Social Ecology model helps to bring the personal into view and this has strong pedagogical merit. The Social Ecology model underpins the way the introduction to sustainability course is taught at RMIT University and it has a major influence on the way this book is structured. Use of the Social Ecology model has enabled the teaching team at RMIT to focus on both the professional and personal dimensions of sustainability work. This helps to counter the assumption that sustainability is a matter for designated experts. Bringing sustainability back to the personal scale can also help to counter some of the despair we may feel when we contemplate global trends and challenges. There is always something we can do at a personal level, and personal action can lead us into broader forms of social action. At the same time, personal action can only ever be an entry point into the challenges that stretch across scales from the local to the global. Rather than enabling us to keep despair at bay, personal action takes us into the enduring battle between hope and despair, which will be further discussed in Chapters 9 and 10.

BUZZWORDS AND KEYWORDS

The concept of 'environmentally sustainable development' tends to suggest that we can have our cake and eat it too. This has prompted many reviewers – such as Hayden Washington (2015) – to argue that it has become imperative to distinguish between 'weak' and 'strong' interpretations of what 'sustainability' means. There is a danger, such scholars note, that weak interpretations of the concept can turn it into nothing more than benign policy rhetoric. In Chapters 2 and 7 we will discuss the suggestion that the concept of 'resilience' may have gained more urgency than the concept of 'sustainability'. There are plenty of commentators who feel that sustainability has lost its radical, transformational, appeal.

keywords is a term introduced by cultural theorist Raymond Williams in 1976 to refer to words in the English language which have particular significance and enduring appeal.

However, this book takes a lead from the suggestion made by pioneering cultural theorist Raymond Williams (1976) that particular words become '**keywords**' in any language partly because they are open to competing interpretations. Language can only ever provide entry points into complex human experiences, Williams argued, and 'keywords' are those which endure because they signify something of enduring importance. The author has noted that Williams picked 'community' as a keyword in English even though it can have almost opposite meanings to different people because the desire to experience community is a deep human need. This book accepts that 'sustainability' and 'resilience' have also become keywords – not buzzwords – in English even though they defy simple or one-sided definitions. Because they touch on deep and complex human experiences 'keywords' – extended to included phrases – tend to be either used uncritically or contested rather fiercely and this applies to a number of words and phrases associated with debates and discourses on 'sustainability'. For example:

- *Limits to growth* is a term that is gaining rather reluctant support although the two words 'limits' and 'growth' can both be misleading if they are used simplistically. At the global level the biosphere imposes certain limits to economic growth; limits that are being exceeded in relation to the emission of greenhouse gases. Economic growth and development are often necessary for social wellbeing and even for environmental protection and limits are always context dependent. However, the **discourse** on limits has called into question the cherished notion that endless growth is the only thing that makes economies function.

discourse is a term used to refer to ongoing debates and dialogues on a particular topic. Contributions to a discourse can take many forms; from academic papers to public commentary and policy formulations.

- *Diversity* is a term that is used uncritically in the sense that it is generally assumed to be a good thing without questioning why. Ecologists have long understood that 'functional diversity' is needed to make particular ecosystems dynamic and adaptable but this is not diversity for its own sake but rather *enough* diversity to enhance adaptability. In this sense diversity has functional value, not just normative value and the same applies to social and cultural diversity. Taken to its extreme, diversity – as in the multiplication of difference – could undermine interdependence and community.
- *Community* is a term that is also used uncritically in the sense that it is assumed to be universal good. However, a community excludes as much as it includes and the functional value of community formation needs to be understood in particular contexts or settings. This book will argue that a sense of belonging to community is no longer a given within contemporary human societies; rather, it needs to be consciously constructed and this, in turn, poses many questions about who is included in, or excluded from, any particular community.
- *Resilience* is a term that is gaining popularity because it is widely assumed that it has more substance than the concept of 'adaptability'. Resilience – generally understood as a capacity to 'bounce back' after some kind of disturbance – implies strength as well as adaptability. However, this book will argue that prevailing discourses on 'risk management' tend to legitimise risk aversion even though a capacity to cope with risk and uncertainty are key requirements for resilient individuals and resilient systems.

RMIT SUSTAINABILITY PRINCIPLES

Even though many attempts have been made to support the broad notion of sustainability with a set of guiding principles, Chapters 2 and 6 will make it clear that there is no consensus on this matter in the relevant literature. The Brundtland Report introduced a number of terms and concepts that can be turned into principles and chief among them are the principles of intragenerational and intergenerational equity. The problem in posing a set of 'guiding principles' for sustainability is that they might be treated as a rather banal 'tick-box' exercise, yet the principles of intragenerational and intergenerational equity defy such banal consideration and they lay the foundation for a more challenging set of guiding principles. In teaching an introduction to sustainability course at RMIT University, the author has found it pedagogically useful to build a set of nine guiding principles around the foundations of intragenerational and intergenerational equity in order to mitigate against any banal interpretation of what is implied. Like 'keywords' such 'guiding principles' can have enduring significance precisely because they defy simple interpretation. They can serve as enduring guiding principles for personal or professional action *because* their provocations can never be extinguished

RMIT Sustainability Principles

1. Acknowledge interconnections at all levels within the biosphere.
2. Acknowledge that there are limits to growth.
3. Remember that prevention is better than cure.
4. Work to improve intragenerational equity.
5. Face up to the challenges of intergenerational equity.
6. Respect requisite diversity in both nature and culture.
7. Work for relocalisation with global connectedness.
8. Move from consumerism to quality-of-life goals.
9. Learn how to travel hopefully in a world of uncertainty.

THE STRUCTURE OF THE BOOK

Social Ecology model of sustainability reworks the 'triple bottom line/three sectors' model in order to bring the 'personal' into view. It was introduced into a Social Ecology teaching programme at the University of Western Sydney by Professor Stuart Hill in the late 1990s.

Part I of this book reflects the way in which the introduction to sustainability course at RMIT University is run over a period of 12 teaching weeks. Chapters 8–10 reflect the use of the **Social Ecology model of sustainability** as a teaching heuristic. However, there is no simple or obvious way to break the very big topic of sustainability into a set of smaller topics for separate book chapters and other authors would have used different headings and a different sequence for the way the material is covered. Chapters 11–16 have been added in response to requests made, and feedback offered, by academics running sustainability courses in a wide range of universities in a wide range of countries. However, all the chapters aim to be relatively independent so that they can be used selectively and in different sequences. There may well be enough material in the book to support more than one course, especially if the book is used in conjunction with the companion website.

While the book relies on contributions made by a number of chapter co-authors, the selection of topics and the book structure as a whole reflect the author's personal preferences and preoccupations. This includes the decision to start with the notion of travelling hopefully – as the students begin their shared journey – and end the first sequence of chapters – i.e. Chapter 10 – with a presentation of 'arguments for hope'. This is not a shallow gesture, because the opportunity to join a global movement for sustainable living is an enticing one. It is often said that humans have a demonstrated capacity to cope well in crisis situations and rise to meet big or unexpected challenges. This will be put to the test in the challenging times that lie ahead but we might learn to focus as much on the journey – and all its emergent possibilities – as much as the destination we hope to reach.

NOTE

1 See www.youtube.com/watch?v=ZNTw3kyQkyk

REFERENCES

Mulligan, Martin (2008) 'To Travel Hopefully', *Arena Magazine*, no 97, Melbourne, 19–22.

Washington, Haydn (2015) *Demystifying Sustainability: Towards Real Solutions*, Abingdon: Earthscan/Routledge.

PART I

History, key concepts and operating principles

CHAPTER 2

Biography of a concept

> **Key concepts and concerns**
>
> - emergence of global environmental concerns in the 1970s
> - significance of Rachel Carson's 1962 book *Silent Spring*
> - Brundtland Report (1987) defines sustainability
> - Brundtland Report links the environmental and social dimensions
> - intragenerational and intergenerational equity
> - outcomes of Rio Earth Summit of 1992
> - strengths and weaknesses of global summits
> - building global political will
> - RMIT Principles of Sustainability

INTRODUCTION

The 1987 publication of the report by the United Nations Commission headed by three-times Norwegian Prime Minister **Gro Harlem Brundtland** proved to be a turning point in giving the word sustainability the meaning it now carries globally. **The Brundtland Report** did not coin the term 'sustainability' and nor was it the first publication to warn that human impacts were imposing unsustainable pressures on planetary ecosystems. However, it presented a concise and compelling overview of disturbing global trends and it firmly established the principle that the challenge to achieve sustainability involves an interplay between environmental and social factors. It coined the term 'environmentally sustainable development' (ESD) and defined this as development which 'meets the needs of the present without compromising the ability of future generations to meet their needs'.[1] For people with a strong concern for protection of the world's natural environment this seems like a rather human-centred definition of sustainability, however the report introduced the innovative 'intergenerational equity' principle in order to encourage people to think more deeply about the possible future consequences of what they do in the present.

The publication of the Brundtland Report reflected the fact that the UN had taken the lead in contemplating the global dimensions of the sustainability challenge ever since it held a landmark conference in Stockholm in 1972 on the

Gro Harlem Brundtland served three separate terms as Norwegian prime minister between 1981 and 1996. She was in her first term when she was asked by UNCED to oversee the production of the landmark report which was published by Oxford University Press in 1987 under the title *Our Common Future*.

The Brundtland Report is the short name used for a report that emerged from the work of the World Commission on Environment and Development that was established by the United Nations in 1983.

'human environment' which produced a statement with 26 principles for ensuring wise use of the world's 'natural resources'. The convening of Stockholm conference, in turn, reflected the steady growth of global awareness about global 'limits' which is often attributed to the fact that people living in the 1960s saw, for the first time, images of our rather lonely looking blue planet taken from circling spaceships. In 1970 an estimated 20 million people had turned out for 'Earth Day' rallies in the USA and the global environmental organisations Friends of the Earth and Greenpeace were formed in 1971 and 1972 respectively. A number of organisations began to use the word 'sustainability' during the 1970s; however the Brundtland Report deserves credit for articulating the concept as we know it today.

The Brundtland Report shone a spotlight on the intractable problem of global poverty because it stressed that poor people and poor communities are often most vulnerable to environmental hazards and, at the same time, they lack the resources to implement nature conservation strategies. It is hard to think about environmental wellbeing if you are desperate to access clean water, reliable supplies of food and adequate shelter. Furthermore, long-running regional and civil conflicts – often triggered by competition for resources – make it even harder. While poverty is worst in particular parts of the world, there are pockets of poverty and disadvantage in every country, and a strength of the Brundtland Report was that demonstrated that global environmental sustainability is bound up with the need to radically reduce poverty and disadvantage. The Brundtland Report set in train plans for a series of global gatherings discussed in this chapter and its concept of 'environmentally sustainable development' was fleshed out in the influential '**triple bottom line**' model developed by UK planner and consultant **John Elkington** in 1994. While the report was the culmination of a lot of earlier work, the decision by the drafting commission to pull no punches ensured that its publication was a turning point in the evolution of a concept (see Figure 2.1)

triple bottom line is a way of teasing out the key principles articulated in the Brundtland Report in order to highlight the need to counterbalance economic policies and practices with equal concern for environmental and social needs.

John Elkington (b. 1949) is a UK planner and psychologist turned consultant who introduced the triple bottom line concept in 1994.

In the history of human thought the concept of sustainability, as we know it today, emerged and spread quickly and it is important to keep that in mind whenever we worry about the apparent lack of progress in enacting its principles. This chapter will briefly review the history of that emergence before turning to efforts that have been made since 1987 to turn the emerging consciousness into global agreements for action. The chapter will focus on:

- achievements and limitations of global action;
- the prospects for building a new global movement for sustainability; and
- efforts to build on principles articulated in the 1987 Brundtland Report in order to develop a more comprehensive set of sustainability principles.

EARLY INFLUENCES: SPACESHIP EARTH AND 'LIMITS TO GROWTH'

The startling colour images of Planet Earth that were sent back from early spaceships showed that our planet is unlike any other in our solar system and gave people a new sense of the vulnerability of the conditions that have made life

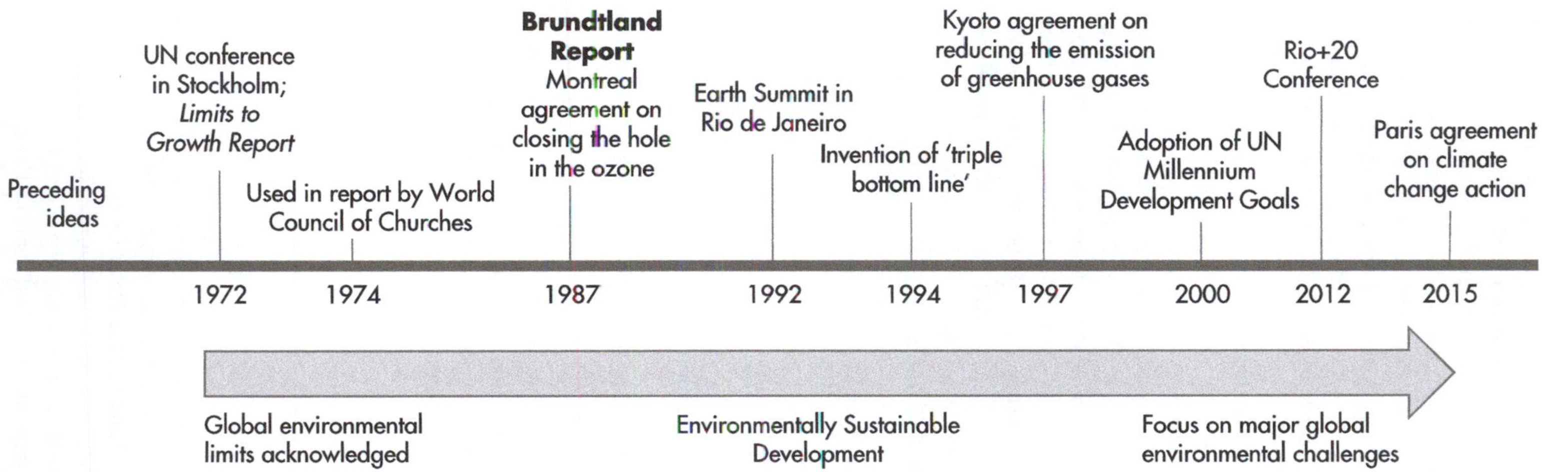

Figure 2.1 A timeline of key events in the evolution of sustainability thinking

Spaceship Earth was probably coined by US Ambassador to the UN, Adlai Stephenson, in a speech given at the UN in 1965, shortly before he died. It was made famous by Kenneth Boulding in 1966.

Kenneth Boulding (1910–93) was born in England and educated at Oxford University before taking up US citizenship in 1948 to work as an economist at the University of Michigan. As well as being a renowned economist he was a peace activist and a devout Quaker.

Gilbert White (1720–93) was a rather obscure parson in an unrermarkable English village before the publication of his lovingly written *Natural History and Antiquities of Selborne* in 1789. He is widely seen as the father of the 'natural history' movement in England and his work inspired many people, including a young Charles Darwin.

Henry David Thoreau (1817–62) was a US-based writer and philosopher who was influenced by the European Romantics and by the 'transcendentalist' school of philosopher established by his mentor Ralph Waldo Emerson. A skilled writer and public speaker, Thoreau

possible on our particular floating planet. Richard Buckminster Fuller may have coined the term '**Spaceship Earth**' when he published a book titled *Operating Manual for Spaceship Earth* in 1968 although Sharon Beder (2006) also credits US Ambassador to the UN, Adlai Stephenson, for popularising the idea that our blue planet can be seen as a kind of isolated spaceship with its inbuilt life support systems, floating in the vastnesss of space and 'saved from annihilation only … by care and work'.[2] The term was subsequently picked up by economist **Kenneth Boulding** in his pioneering work on the economics of sustainability published in 1966.

The prominent historian of western environmental awareness, Donald Worster (1994), argues that the seemingly obscure English rural parson and nature lover **Gilbert White** (1720–93) was responsible for triggering a 'natural history' movement in England and beyond which aimed to increase public concern for the protection of nature. He goes on to suggest that a western 'Arcadian' school of thinking about the need to respect nature can be depicted in the work of writers and scholars ranging from William Wordsworth in England to Johann Goethe in Germany to **Henry David Thoreau** in the USA. Worster also stresses that Charles Darwin's epic work gave birth to modern western understanding of ecology which serves to remind humans that our own wellbeing is dependent on the wellbeing of many non-human species and ecological systems. So post-European Enlightenment thinking about human 'mastery over' nature has long been contested by significant schools of environmental thought. However, it is widely believed that the 1962 publication of a book by US science writer Rachel Carson – entitled *Silent Spring* – sparked an upsurge in ecological awareness; thereby giving birth to the 'modern' environmental movement (see Photo 2.1 and the box on Rachel Carson).

Emergence of global environmentalism

1. 1962: Publication of *Silent Spring* by Rachel Carson
2. 1966: Publication of *Spaceship Earth* by Kenneth Gouding
3. 1969: Friends of the Earth formed in USA
4. 1970: 20 million people turn out for Earth Day in the USA in 1970
5. 1971: International Friends of the Earth established
6. 1972: Greenpeace formed
7. 1972: UN Conference held in Stockholm, Sweden
8. 1972: Club of Rome *Limits to Growth* report published

In 1968 an international think-tank established by Italian businessman Aurelio Peccei – the Club of Rome – commissioned a study on the implications of recognising that we live on a finite and ultimately vulnerable planet. This study was undertaken by a team of scientists at the Massachusetts Institute of Technology headed by **Donella Meadows**. Using modelling techniques available to them at the time, they put forward the argument that the planet's finite resources ultimately impose 'limits to growth' and their report to the Club of Rome was ultimately published as a book with that name in 1972.

The computer modelling programs and techniques available to Meadows and her team were rudimentary and this subsequently allowed critics to say that the predictions were astray and too alarmist. As Beder notes,[3] a key criticism was that the discovery of new resources and new ways of using resources efficiently were not factored into a model which assumed an absolute limit on resources needed to meet human needs. The approach taken by Meadows *et al.* has been dismissed as being '**neo-Mathusian**' in reference to similar predictions about human needs outstripping available resources made by English political economist and demographer **Thomas Malthus** in 1798, which proved to be unnecessarily gloomy. However, Meadows *et al.* responded to the criticisms in a book published to mark the 30th anniversary of *Limits to Growth* (see Meadows *et al.* 1972) by saying that the difficulties involved in trying to predict the future should not detract from the underlying argument that population growth and increasing global consumption will, at some point, outstrip our capacity to find enough resources on of Planet Earth. Furthermore, they argued that the onset of global climate change suggests that humanity is already exceeding global limits to growth in ways they could not predict in 1972.

Rachel Carson

Photo 2.1 Scientist Rachel Carson (1907–64), appearing before a Senate Government Operations subcommittee studying pesticides (4 January 1963). Author of *Silent Spring*, which established the harm caused to wild animals by the chemical DDT
© Everett Collection Historical/Alamy

Rachel Carson would not have expected the response that her book *Silent Spring* received after it was published in 1962 – and sadly she died, in 1964, before its full impact could have been known. Written in an

created an enduring body of work on the joys of reconnecting with nature.

Donella Meadows (1941–2001) was a pioneering US environmental scientist who gained her Ph.D. in biophysics from Harvard University in 1968. She is best known as the lead author of the report entitled *Limits to Growth* which analysed global trends in resource use modelled at MIT University in Boston. She later became a leading scholar in systems thinking.

neo-Malthusian When Malthus's dire predictions of escalating crises did not materialise, he was widely dismissed as an alarmist and the term 'neo-Malthusian' was used to dismiss environmental writers of the 1960s and 1970s who raised new concerns about the sustainability of uncurtailed global population growth.

Thomas Malthus (1766–1834) was a prize-winning classics scholar at Cambridge University before taking his orders as an Anglican priest. He ended his career as a professor of political economy but it was his 1798 essay *An Essay on the Principles of Population* that has given him enduring fame. The essay – published six times between 1798 and 1826 – predicted that uncurtailed growth in human population worldwide would result in widespread famine, disease and conflict.

DDT (Dichlorodiphenyltrichloroethane) is a synthetic compound first produced by Swiss chemist Paul Muller in 1939. It was initially used to kill mosquitos carrying malaria and parasites responsible for the spread of typhus during the Second World War, before being released commercially after the war for use in controlling pests in US agriculture.

authoritative scientific voice but with evocative and accessible style, the book showed that the use of inorganic pesticides on crops in the USA was having deleterious effects on birdlife, fish in nearby streams and even for marine life in areas where the persistent toxins were entering the oceans. Readers of *Silent Spring* were startled to learn that the most commonly and widely used pesticide in US agriculture – **DDT** – was turning up in the fatty tissue of penguins in the Antarctic and in the breast milk of lactating US mothers. In her masterful book, Carson had revealed that human action always has unforeseen ecological consequences and she demonstrated that inorganic compounds can enter a system of 'ecological flows' that begin locally before spreading vast distances. Public concern triggered by Carson's book is said to have led to the formation of the US Environmental Protection Agency in 1970 – the first of its kind in the world – and in the same year huge crowds turned out for the celebration of Earth Day in April.

No one could predict that Carson would become a significant national figure when she was born in Pennsylvania in 1907. She graduated from the Pennsylvania College for Women in 1922 and in a rare achievement for women of her time she gained a Master's in Zoology in 1932 and began a long career working as a federal service scientist in 1936. Fortunately, her supervisors in the US Bureau of Fisheries recognised her writing talent and after beginning her writing-for-the-public career by writing radio scripts she subsequently rose to become editor-in-chief of all US Fish and Wildlife Service publications. She retired from government service in 1952 to become a full-time writer and her first significant book was *The Sea Around Us* published in that year. Carson also wrote feature articles for the *Baltimore Sun* and a range of pamphlets and books aimed at children and their parents. *Silent Spring* captured attention with the shock suggestion that we might be facing future spring mornings without the reassuring sound of bird song. Her manifest passion for the wellbeing of non-human life and her evocative writing style gave her an important place in the history of environmental thought.

Carson's warning that inorganic compounds that humans put into the environment can travel far and wide as a result of 'ecological flows' is now reverberating in the ways in which plastic waste is accumulating in 'garbage patches' in the Pacific Ocean and showing up in the stomachs of seabirds and marine animals far from human settlements. Even more worrying, perhaps, is the way in which plastic waste is breaking down into 'microplastic' particles which are accumulating in global marine environments (www.unep.org/story/plastics-and-microplsatics-in-our-oceans).

GLOBAL GATHERINGS FOR GLOBAL ACTION

The 1972 UN conference in Stockholm not only set in chain the process that led to the establishment of the Brundtland Commission and its influential report of 1987, it also set in chain plans for follow-up global gatherings. The most significant of these was the 1992 'Earth Summit' held in Brazil's Rio de Janeiro. The build-up to the **Rio Earth Summit** was a very public affair and it became the biggest UN gathering ever held outside New York, with 172 governments represented and 108 heads of state in attendance. A total of 17,000 delegates participated in the conference sessions. Many feared that expectations of what could be achieved by this global gathering were unrealistic and there was considerable criticism about choosing to hold it in a city with some of the worst urban slums in the world and in a country that was responsible for alarming rates of deforestation in the globally important Amazon rainforests. However, the Summit did produce some important outcomes (see box) and most delegates would have left with a heightened sense of responsibility and increased optimism about the possibility for global agreements and global action.

Rio Earth Summit (1992) was a UN-sponsored Summit held, rather controversially, in the Brazilian city of Rio de Janeiro with 108 heads of government present to discuss the implications of the Brundtland Report.

Achievements of the 1992 Earth Summit

- Development of a 308-page action plan for environmental sustainable development which bore the name *Agenda 21*. Although this was a non-binding summit outcome, it was soon endorsed by 178 nations and that number eventually reached 197.
- Development of a supplement to *Agenda 21* – entitled *Local Agenda 21* – aimed at devolving responsibilities for ESD to sub-national levels of government, putting this matter on the agenda for local government for the first time.
- Adoption of a Climate Change Convention which set in train plans for a binding protocol on reducing greenhouse gas emissions which was brought to a special-purpose conference held in Kyoto in 1997.
- Development of a UN Convention of Biological Diversity which became a binding international treaty signed by 193 nations in December 1993.
- Establishment of a Global Environment Facility (GEF) funded by 'developed nations' to support ESD initiatives in 'developing nations'.

Local residents of Rio were excluded from many parts of the city to make way for the influx of international visitors and it is rather poignant to think that people living in the city's massive slums – known in Brazil as *favelas* – watched on as tens of thousands of conference attendees held their meetings (see Photo 2.2). This symbolises the fact that the poor of the world have little choice but to watch and wait for meaningful global action on the related problems of environmental degradation and entrenched poverty.

The relative success of the Earth Summit created a strong appetite for further global gatherings hosted by the UN and many were held – with limited success – in the period leading up to a return to Rio for an event known as **Rio+20** in 2012. Rio+20 had even more participants than the original Earth Summit; with an estimated 45,000 conference-goers. However, it did not set in train any new global initiatives and an earlier promise to set up a new global fund of $US30 billion to

Rio+20 (2012) was a UN-sponsored Summit held to mark the 20th anniversary of the 1992 Earth Summit. It had more government representatives but fewer heads of government present than the 1992 Summit and released a call to arms titled *The Future We Want*.

Photo 2.2 The poor are watching! Some of the biggest slums in the world surround the CBD in Rio De Janeiro, where leaders gathered for 1992 Earth Summit
Photo by Alicia Nijdam (Wikimedia Commons)

help developing nations reduce their greenhouse gas emissions was dropped, essentially because key European governments argued that the combined effects of the Global Financial Crisis of 2008–9 and ongoing economic woes within the European Union had undermined their capacity to contribute to such a fund. Furthermore, while there may have been more people at the 2012 summit than for 1992 and even more governments represented (192), only 57 heads of state were in attendance (compared to 108). Key western leaders – including the US president, German chancellor and the British prime minister – were absent. The summit produced a call to action – under the title *The Future We Want* – with a total of 283 'commitments' to be considered. Like *Agenda 21*, this is a non-binding summit outcome, yet the critics suggested it did not contain anything new or innovative.

However, the failings of Rio+20 were at least partially offset by the fact that host nation Brazil – with a more 'progressive' government than it had in 1992 – was able to play a big role in ensuring that *The Future We Want* contains some fairly sharp criticisms of the lack of progress made since the 1992 Earth Summit. Other rapidly developing nations, such as China and India, also played a more significant role in this summit; perhaps confirming a shift in global leadership on the question of sustainability. Summit documents like *The Future We Want* have to use cautious language to attract wide endorsement. Yet it suggested that there had been 'areas of insufficient progress or setbacks' since 1992 and that the time had come to 'reinvigorate political will' for acting on international agreements and action plans. Arguably, the relative success of the 1992 Earth Summit set unrealistic expectations for what might come out of big global gatherings because little can be achieved without a quantum shift in political will to take on big and seemingly intractable challenges.

SUCCESSES AND FAILURES AT A GLOBAL LEVEL

The optimism that infused the 1992 Earth Summit and its outcomes can be at least partially attributed to the fact that global political leaders managed to negotiate a fairly successful 'protocol' for phasing out the use of 'aerosol' gases that were blamed for thinning the atmosphere's 'ozone layer', which screens out harmful ultraviolet rays from the sun. Concerns about **ozone** thinning were sparked by a scientific study published in 1985 which suggested that an annual 'hole' in the ozone layer over Antarctica was getting bigger and that periodic holes were also appearing over the North Pole. The study suggested that chlorofluorocarbons (CFCs) gases being used commonly in aerosol sprays were contributing to ozone thinning because they break down under UV radiation to produce 'free radical' chorine molecules that attack the ozone layer. Alarm at the possibility of rapid increases in cancer-causing UV radiation reaching the surface of the planet sparked unprecedented global action with an international conference being called in Montreal in 1987 to examine ways to rapidly phase use of CFC gases. The negotiated agreement – known as the Montreal Protocol – was immediately endorsed by 197 governments and a $US2.5 billion fund was established to help developing nations introduce the substitute technologies. While scientific debate continues on the dangers of ozone depletion and the possible dangers posed by the use of alternative gases in aerosols, evidence suggests that ozone depletion has been significantly contained and fears about ozone depletion have diminished.

The relative success of the Montreal Protocol shows that effective global action can be taken when there is sufficient political will. However, it needs to be remembered that the thinning of the ozone layer had a clearly identified cause and that substitutes had already been identified for ozone-depleting gases. Other global environmental concerns – notably the onset of human-induced global climate change – have more complex and diffuse origins and technological 'solutions' are much harder to find. It is far more difficult, for example, to radically reduce global dependence on the use of carbon-emitting 'fossil fuels' than to switch to alternative aerosol sprays. The relative success of the Montreal Protocol probably created unrealistic expectations about what might come out of the global conference on **human-induced climate change** held in the Japanese city of **Kyoto** in 1997. However, the enormous economic and political ramification involved in reducing emissions of greenhouse gases undermined political will to act in many countries and the governments of leading greenhouse gas emitting countries – including the USA and Australia – boycotted the gathering.

The 1997 Kyoto Protocol on setting targets for a steady reduction in the emission of greenhouse gases succeeded in sharpening political debate globally about what needs to be done and in the period since almost all national governments around the world have felt obliged to adopt greenhouse gas reduction strategies. As more of the 'developed' nations endorsed the Kyoto Protocol,

ozone hole refers to the annual thinning of the ozone layer over Antarctica was first reported in a scientific paper in the journal *Nature* in May 1985 and concern quickly arose that the 'hole' was getting incrementally larger each year. Chlorofluorocarbons (CFCs) stay in the upper atmosphere for a long time so it is hard to monitor the effectiveness of the CFC ban. However, reports published in 2013 suggested that the hole had been contained, with the 2012 manifestation being the smallest in ten years.

human-induced climate change concern about the global warming effects of increasing emissions of CO_2 caused by human use of 'fossil fuels' have been expressed since 1824. Regular reports produced by International Panel on Climate Change (IPCC) since 1990 have increased concerns about human-induced global climate change.

Kyoto climate summit was a UN-sponsored gathering of government representatives held in the beautiful Japanese city of Kyoto in December 1997 aimed at reaching agreement on implementing the 1992 UN Framework Convention on Climate Change. Although the summit was boycotted by significant national governments – most notably that of the USA – it did agree on the Kyoto Protocol which had an initial commitment period from 2008 to 2012.

Paris climate summit (COP21) 2015, was the 21st meeting of the Conference of Parties to the UN Framework Convention on Climate Change and the 11th meeting of parties to the Kyoto Protocol. In contrast to the Kyoto summit of 1997, the USA and China were very active participants in the Paris summit.

expectations rose for the outcomes of a global summit on tackling the causes of global climate change to be held in Copenhagen in 2009. Whereas the Kyoto gathering had essentially been a meeting of representatives of the world's 'developed nations', the Copenhagen summit included representatives from nations with rapidly expanding economies and, consequently, rapidly expanding greenhouse gas emissions; most notably China. The Copenhagen Summit failed to live up to expectations – issuing a rather weak final agreement. While it did lay the foundations for bilateral negotiations between the world's largest greenhouse gas-emitting nations – the USA and China – most observers considered it to be a lost opportunity. However, the relative failure of Copenhagen sparked a bigger effort behind the scenes to ensure that the next summit, the **Paris climate summit (COP21)** – held in Paris in December 2015 – would make more progress. It was decided that more consensus would be built by allowing each nation to set its own emission reduction targets but it was agreed that the targets and implementation plans would be subjected to open review in 2018 and 2023. Wealthier nations agreed to contribute to a $US100 billion fund to facilitate international action and delegates were pleasantly surprised when the final agreement included the very ambitious target of keeping global warming below 1.5 degrees. Television cameras captured scenes of overt euphoria on the floor of the conference when the details of the final agreement were announced.

Significant global gatherings

1972: UN Conference on the 'human environment', Stockholm
1987: International Conference on reducing the use of ozone-depleting aerosols, Montreal
1992: UN Earth Summit, Rio de Janeiro
1997: Global gathering on reducing greenhouse gas emissions, Kyoto
2000: UN Millennium Summit in New York adopts eight Millennium Development Goals (MDGs)
2009: Copenhagen Summit on reducing greenhouse gas emissions
2012: Rio+20 UN Earth Summit, Rio de Janeiro
2015 (September): UN Summit turns MDGs into 17 Sustainable Development Goals
2015 (December): Paris Summit on reducing greenhouse gas emissions

Before and after the Paris summit, China and the USA pushed each other to set more ambitious greenhouse gas emission targets. While China had surpassed the USA as the world's biggest emitter, and it continued to build new coal-fired power stations, it also surpassed the USA in its reduction targets. By 2010, China had become the world's biggest producer of both wind turbines and solar panels. Global gatherings held since the Rio Earth Summit in 1992 have undoubtedly put pressure on nation states to take global challenges more seriously. While narrow or short-sighted perceptions of 'national interest' have often undermined the strength of global agreements, the Paris agreement suggests that nations and sub-national entities – such as cities – need some 'wriggle room' to set targets and development implementation strategies. At the same time, they need to come under sustained scrutiny and pressure from global organisations and informed citizenry to make sure they set ambitious targets and take them seriously.

The arrival of the new millennium prompted the United Nations to hold its biggest gathering of world leaders yet and this summit – held in New York in 2000 – adopted eight **Millennium Development Goals** (MDGs) which were mainly focused on the 'eradication' of extreme poverty, hunger and preventable diseases. The decision to set 2015 as the deadline for achieving the MDGs proved to be wildly ambitious; however the follow-up UN summit – held in September 2015 – resulted in an agreement to extend the eight MDGs into 17 **Sustainable Development Goals** (SDGs) to be achieved by 2030. Even though it is impossible to achieve such ambitious goals in such short time frames, the 2015 summit felt the MDGs had set important challenges for participating nations and it is interesting to note that the SGDs include goals that are more explicitly focused on environmental impacts. This includes the need to act more resolutely to address global climate change. In effect, the SDGs are infused with the principles first articulated in the Brundtland Report.

Millennium Development Goals (MDGs) are eight goals that were adopted at a special UN Millennium Summit held in New York in May 2000.

Sustainable Development Goals (SDGs) are a 2015 extension of the UN's 2000 MDGs that are largely aimed to eradicate extreme poverty and disadvantage by 2015. Eight MDGs were expanded into 17 SDGs and they strongly reflect the principles outlined in the 1987 Brundtland Report.

BUILDING GLOBAL POLITICAL WILL

The international environmental movement that emerged in the late 1960s and early 1970s often focused on issues that extended beyond the domains of particular national governments, such as nuclear proliferation, whaling, the steady loss of forests (especially rainforests). However, they largely focused on getting national governments to take action and used established forms of political action, such as protest events and marches and political lobbying. The onset of human-induced global climate change serves to highlight the fact that many of the big sustainability challenges have become more globally integrated and complex; posing the need for more international or global action rather than action by national or sub-national governments and government agencies. Economic **globalisation** – manifested most clearly in the rising dominance of multinational corporations – also poses the need for global, rather than national or sub-national, action.

At present we live in a world where global forms of governance are still relatively weak in relation to the political power of nation states. While new communication technologies have greatly enhance our ability to be in real-time conversations with people anywhere on the planet, we are still learning how to use such technologies to build enduring movements for social and political change. Furthermore, Rachel Carson's influential book on the ecological impacts of inorganic pesticides made it clear that human impacts on natural ecosystems tend to begin at local points of contact before spreading more widely through processes of what we are calling 'ecological flows'. Environmental sustainability will commonly begin with a consideration of local impacts before considering wider – sometimes global – implications. This suggests a need to develop new ways to link local and global action for change.

globalisation is often used to refer to the rise of an increasingly integrated global economy that has been taking shape since the 1980s. However, the term was probably coined by University of Aberdeen sociologist Roland Robertson in 1992, and he intended it to have a much wider meaning as the intensification of consciousness of the world as a whole.

Paul Hawken was born in 1946 and as a teenager he followed in the footsteps of the famous US conservationist John Muir by roaming in the high Sierra Nevada range. Famous for suggesting that environmental awareness can bring about a deep and positive change in how we conceive and practice economic activity. Hawken's book *Blessed Unrest* (2007) was popularised by a series of public talks focusing on 'the great transformation'.

The influential US environmentalist **Paul Hawken** has argued that a global movement for sustainable living is already gathering momentum without attracting the attention that earlier social and political movements might have attracted.[4] In Hawken's analysis, this large and diffuse movement is sneaking up on us because while it contains organisations that are campaigning for particular forms of political change it is not dominated by them. Hawken describes a loosely networked array of organisations that are mostly community-based in origin and which have sprung up in almost every part of the world. While such community-based organisations are not new, the new communication technologies enable them to have a sense of being globally connected and hence part of a 'movement'. How new is the movement that Hawken described and how effective can it be in mobilising the global political will to act more resolutely on the big global sustainability challenges? It is too early to answer such questions but Hawken offers the enticing suggestion that it is much easier than most people think to become part of the movement for global change which will eventually transform our ways of living everywhere. Political action, he suggests, starts with the decision to join local and connected movements for sustainable living.

While we continue to work for a shift in the global political will needed to take more resolute action on the big sustainability challenges we can take heart from the fact that the global discourse on sustainability has achieved a lot since the publication of the Brundtland Report in 1987. For example, a report released by the Organisation for Economic Co-operation and Development in 2011[5] claimed that substantial progress had been made in developing the policy framework for sustainable development at a national level in the 34 member countries. The report noted that old ways of measuring economic progress – primarily gross domestic product (GDP) – do not generate the data we need to assess progress on making national economies more sustainable and so the OECD has joined a range of other international agencies to develop new indicators of progress in order to collect more diverse forms of data. We need new tools to know if economic development is improving the 'bottom line' in relation to environmental and social wellbeing as well (see Chapter 9).

Corporate social responsibility and 'greenwashing'

While many sustainability advocates express alarm at the growing economic and political power of large multinational corporations, others take heart from the fact that many such corporations have adopted the rhetoric of sustainability. Business leaders often argue that it is good for the long-term viability of any business to take sustainability challenges seriously; adding that business leaders are also citizens of Planet Earth who may be as concerned as anyone else about the future for their children or grandchildren. The term 'corporate social responsibility' (CSR) is widely used to identify efforts made by corporations to seriously address the social and environmental consequences of their business activities. Many informed commentators – notably Sharon Beder (2000) – have suggested that major corporations have adopted the rhetoric of sustainability only to undermine the political influence of the environmental movement. Others may cynically use the rhetoric of environmental responsibility to increase their 'market share' among ethical consumers, in the phenomenon known as '**greenwashing**'. Meaningful corporate responsibility and greenwashing are both real and it is up to consumers and government agencies to know how to distinguish them from each other.

greenwashing is an adaptation of the term 'whitewashing' and it is used to refer to deceptive efforts made by producers of goods and services to convince consumers that their products have good or benign environmental impacts.

ARTICULATING UNDERLYING PRINCIPLES OF SUSTAINABILITY

Many authors have considered how to extend the ideas outlined in the Brundtland Report in order to pinpoint a number of underlying principles that might serve as reference points for the development of policies or action plans. It is widely agreed that the report emphasised the importance of 'intragenerational equity' by highlighting the importance of reducing the gap between the world's rich and poor, while it added the innovative principle of 'intergenerational equity' to encourage greater consideration of the needs of people living in the future. Several authors – such as Beder (2006) – have suggested adding the pre-existing 'precautionary principle' – which urges caution in doing anything that may have unexpected environmental consequences – to the principles discussed in the report. Beder went on to suggest the addition of a 'polluter pays principle' but in a rather curious move she suggested that this sits alongside a 'sustainability principle'. A book by Simon Dresner (2008) probably includes the best overview of thinking about the 'principles of sustainability' and he gives prominence to a set of principles outlined by the radical environmental economist **Herman Daly** (see box).[6]

Herman Daly was born in 1938 and as an academic economist he published a collection of writings under the title *Toward a Steady-State Economy* in 1973. He worked in the World Bank (1988–94) before returning to academia. Between 1992 and 2008 he was honoured with a string of international awards for his lifetime of work on 'ecological economics'.

Herman Daly's sustainability principles

1. Limit the human scale to that which is within the Earth's capacity.
2. Ensure that technological progress is efficiency increasing rather than throughput increasing.
3. For renewable resources, harvesting rates should not exceed regeneration rates and waste emissions should not exceed the assimilative capacities of receiving environments.
4. Non-renewable resources should be explored no faster than the rate of creation of renewable resources.

Daly's principles imply radical change at the level of macro-economic policy and planning but, unlike the concepts of 'intragenerational' and 'intergenerational' equity, they are not very useful for guiding action that might be taken by individuals, households, communities or small organisations. A similar problem arises in adopting the UN Sustainable Development Goals (SDGs) as the underlying principles of sustainability, even though some of them are easier to apply to individual action than Daly's principles. The SDGs imply the need for more resolute action at the level of nation states and international agencies, making it easy for readers to assume that this has little to do with them personally.

As mentioned in Chapter 1, the author uses a model of sustainability – the Social Ecology model – which explicitly aims to bring the personal into view – when teaching the introduction to sustainability course at RMIT University in Melbourne. However, for teaching purposes this rather abstract model needs to be underpinned by a set of 'operating' principles. The principles included in the set of nine used to underpin the way the concept of sustainability is taught at RMIT (see box) are drawn from a range of sources, however they share the ability to be relevant for individual people as much as organisations or government agencies. The principles are deliberately designed to be aspirational, rather than easily achieved, in order to avoid any tendency to treat principles as a kind of 'tick-box' exercise. The challenges we face are complex and enduring and the work we need to do to live sustainability is never over. The RMIT Sustainability Principles are a valuable teaching heuristic and they contain ideas that will be discussed in Chapters 3–12 of this book.

RMIT Sustainability Principles

1. Acknowledge interconnections at all levels within the biosphere.
2. Acknowledge that there are limits to growth.
3. Remember that prevention is better than cure.
4. Work to improve intragenerational equity.
5. Face up to the challenges of intergenerational equity.
6. Respect requisite diversity in both nature and culture.
7. Work for relocalisation with global connectedness.
8. Move from consumerism to quality of life goals.
9. Learn how to travel hopefully in a world of uncertainty.

Discussion questions

1. What are some of the events and developments that led to publication of the Brundtland Report in 1987?
2. Why did the Brundtland Report argue that there is a causal link between poverty and environmental degradation? Is the idea of linking social and environmental sustainability still relevant? If so, why?
3. What are some of the things that have been achieved by global sustainability gatherings between 1972 and 2015, and why are there some limits on what can be achieved by such global summits?
4. What is our best hope for achieving sustainability: global agreements, action by separate national governments, social change from below, or a combination of these approaches?
5. What do you think it will take to increase the political will to act at a global level and do you feel optimistic that this will happen? If so, why?
6. Why has the idea of 'limits to growth' been so controversial? Do you think there are limits to growth and, if so, what are they?

KEY READINGS

Beder, Sharon (2006) *Environmental Principles and Policies: An Interdisciplinary Approach*, Sydney: UNSW Press.

Blewitt, John (2015), 2nd edn, *Understanding Sustainable Development*, London: Earthscan.

Dresner, Simon (2008), 2nd edn, *The Principles of Sustainability*, London: Earthscan.

Robertson, Margaret (2014) *Sustainability: Principles and Practice*, Abingdon: Earthscan/Routledge.

Shiva, Vandana (2005) *Earth Democracy: Justice, Sustainability and Peace*, Cambridge, MA: Southend Press.

Washington, Haydn (2015) *Demystifying Sustainability: Towards Real Solutions*, Abingdon: Earthscan/Routledge.

Are there limits to growth?

thematic essay

When Thomas Malthus first published his *Essay on the Principles of Population Growth* in 1798 most people in Europe and North America were probably feeling optimistic about the future. The noble aspects of the French Revolution had been dulled by the reign of terror but not yet by the Napoleonic Wars, the Industrial Revolution was in full swing in Britain and although America had won its independence from Britain the European empires still seemed great and powerful, with unprecedented global reach. American society was still celebrating its success in the costly war of independence, with civil war some distance away. This was probably not an auspicious time for a learned demographer to suggest that rising population pressure would soon outstrip the world's capacity to provide everyone with a reasonable standard of living and that the lessons of history suggested that a growing gap between population and resources would eventually result in epidemics, war and a 'gigantic inevitable famine'. Malthus had studied at the University of Cambridge where he first excelled in the classics before undertaking further study in mathematics. He became an Anglican curate in the same year that his famous *Essay* was first published and this probably influenced the moral tone of the essay. However, timing aside, Malthus's mistake may have been to apply a rather simplistic mathematical logic in his suggestion that the exponential growth curve of population must inevitably cross over the linear growth in available resources.

It is not surprising that Donella Meadows and her colleagues at MIT were accused of being 'neo-Malthusian' when they also used rather simplistic mathematical modelling to suggest that humanity is fast approaching global 'limits to growth' in their 1972 book of that name. Even with subsequent advances in computer technologies it is dangerous to base an argument on a capacity to predict what will happen in the future, especially when increasing numbers of variables seem to be coming into play. This has played out again in polarising debates about the reliability of climate change predictions even though climate scientists have been constantly adding the caveat that climate systems subjected to global warming are becoming more volatile. We seem reluctant to pull back from our desire to know in advance what the future holds for us. Yet anyone predicting the future can be made to look foolish by the way that things unfold. Nevertheless, the onset of human-induced global climate change suggests that there are 'planetary limits' to growth in human exploitation of the planet's resources even if growth and decline trajectories can play out differently at lower scales.

In 1977 the economist Herman Daly detached the limits-to-growth argument from predictions about the future by invoking the precautionary principle to argue for an immediate shift from growth-driven economics to what he called 'steady state economics'. Daly's bold suggestion for reframing the parameters of economic theory and policy was so appealing that the World Bank invited him to join the organisation in 1988. It was difficult for Daly's voice to be heard in an institution dominated by economists who had been schooled to think that economic 'growth' is a kind of holy grail and at a time when Milton Friedman's 'free market' economic ideology had been adopted enthusiastically by the US President Ronald Reagan and the UK Prime Minister Margaret Thatcher. Indeed, it is probably surprising that Daly was able to continue working within the World Bank for six years; however, he did eventually decide that he could have more impact by returning to academia and by writing books aimed at a wide reading audience. Across his career, Daly has followed in the footsteps of Karl Polanyi in the 1940s, Kenneth Boulding in the 1960s and his own mentor Nicholas Georgescu-Roegen in the 1970s in rethinking the relationship between economics and ecology. When a new branch of 'environmental economics' emerged in the 1980s to consider ways of attributing economic value to environmental 'resources' and 'services' that not previously been costed, Daly was among those who suggested that this did not go far enough in trying to ensure that economic theory and practice is subservient to ecological processes, rather than the reverse.

The 'free market', neoliberal economic theory that was popularised by Reagan and Thatcher in the early 1980s has held sway ever since, although it came under renewed criticism with the onset of the Global Financial Crisis (GFC) in 2008–9. Globally the environmental and social costs of 'free market' economics continue to mount and previously marginalised economists – such as Polanyi and John Maynard Keynes – have been reconsidered. Although shaken by events such as the GFC, mainstream economists are reluctant to jettison the formative idea that growth is the essential driver of economic wellbeing. At the tail end of the GFC, economist Tim Jackson wrote a report for the UK Sustainable Development Commission which proved so popular that it was published as a book in 2009.[7] Jackson argued that the persistence of global poverty and the onset of global climate change should make it clear that a return to strong growth is not the answer to recessions and economic fragilities. He suggested that economic policies and practices need to consider what it takes to deliver 'prosperity' – or human flourishing – without increasing strains on our 'finite planet'.

Of course, 'growth' can be understood as a growth in capacity as much as an expansion in the volume of economic output. However, unexamined attachment to the idea of 'growth' encourages economists to disparage all notions of 'limits to growth'. Economists should not be held solely responsible for the emergence of a widespread 'growth fetish'[8] because belief in the possibility of unlimited growth probably reflects the lingering legacy of the European Enlightenment of the seventeenth and eighteenth centuries when confidence in scientific and rational thinking became a kind of secular religion. The Enlightenment is rightly seen as the time in European history when reason began to triumph over dogmatism and the capacity to think for oneself began to take precedence over duty and subservience. This, in turn, unlocked unprecedented enthusiasm for the capacity of humans to become the masters of their own destiny and one of the great thinkers of the Enlightenment, Francis Bacon, was moved to suggest that 'men of science' should aim to ensure that 'nature takes orders from man and works under his authority'. There is always a danger in taking such sentiments out of their historic context and yet we can see in this the potential for treating non-human nature with arrogant disdain.

Putting aside any consideration of how long it might take for humanity to cross a threshold in sustainable use of the planet's resources, use of the word 'limits' may suggest that such thresholds are fixed and that any return from crossing them may be impossible. We know that natural systems are more resilient than we often imagine and that we can take action to help degraded systems recover. At the same time, it has now become clear that global humanity will pay an increasing cost for putting intolerable pressures on the global ecosystems that sustain us and unexamined belief in unlimited growth is a luxury we can no longer afford. Although it was rooted in the emergence of 'rational' science, belief in unlimited growth has become deeply irrational.

NOTES

1 See *Our Common Future* (1987: 8).

2 Beder (2006: 12).

3 Ibid.: 15.

4 Paul Hawken, *Blessed Unrest* (2007).

5 See www.oecd.org/greengrowth

6 See Dresner (2006: 89).

7 Tim Jackson (2009) *Prosperity Without Growth: Economics for a Finite Planet*, Abingdon: Earthscan/Routledge.

8 A term used by Australian environmental economist Clive Hamilton.

CHAPTER 3

Consumption and consumerism

Key concepts and concerns

- the rise of hyperconsumption
- individualism and cocooning
- planned obsolescence and the generation of desire
- illusions of choice
- addictive consumption
- ethical consumption and voluntary simplicity
- collaborative consumption
- the search for the good life

INTRODUCTION

The combination of a growing global population and the spread of mass consumption into rapidly 'developing' nations such as China and India is taking us ever deeper into a crisis of unsustainable consumption. According to **Worldwatch Institute**, global private consumption spending increased fourfold between 1960 and 2000 to reach a staggering $US 20 trillion and by 2014 the global 'consumer class' had grown to 1.7 billion members. Global meat production quadrupled over a period of 50 years, reaching a record 308 million tons in 2013, while global production of plastic materials had reached 299 million tons by the same year. According to publications of the global motor vehicle industry the number of operating vehicles had passed one billion in 2010 with over 16 million new vehicles sold in 2013 (over 25 per cent of these in China). Increases in production and consumption are driven by the increasing use of energy and the **International Energy Agency** has reported that energy extracted from multiple fuel sources doubled between 1971 and 2005.

Worldwatch Institute is an environmental research organisation in Washington, DC, founded by Lester Brown in 1974 and famous for producing an annual *State of the World* report since 1984.

International Energy Agency is a Paris-based intergovernmental agency set up by the Organisation for Economic Co-operation and Development in 1974, following the global 'oil shock' of 1973.

The **Global Footprint Network** has rather famously suggested that on current population and consumption trends, we would need the equivalent of three planets to sustain current consumption levels for an anticipated population of 9 billion by 2050.[1] The footprint calculator suggests that we have already passed the capacity of the planet to sustain our consumption of energy and raw materials, taking into account the need to dispose of 'waste' materials. Ecological footprint

Global Footprint Network is a US-based non-profit organisation established in 2003 to promote the use of ecological footprint calculators to promote environmental awareness.

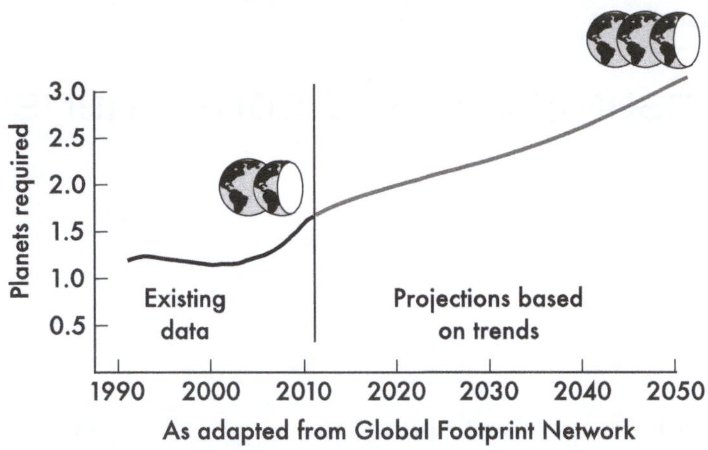

Figure 3.1 Global Footprint Calculator: resources required and waste disposal impacts
Source: derived from use of the Global Footprint Calculator (www.footprintnetwork.org)

calculators lack the sophistication to anticipate changing patterns of consumption. However, the raw figures serve to remind us that a crisis of overconsumption is already upon us.

Startling statistics

- By 2008, China was responsible for half of the world's coal use to fuel its rapid economic development. At this time the USA was still responsible for around 25 per cent of global fossil fuel use with only five per cent of the world's population.
- Between 1960 and 2010, global motor vehicle registrations rose from 127 million to over one billion. In 2013 alone, over 16 million new motor vehicles were sold, with over 25 per cent of these sold in China alone.
- Global meat production quadrupled in the space of 50 years to reach a record 308 million tons in 2013.
- Global production of plastic materials has increased every year for the last 50 years with more than 299 million tons produced in 2013 alone.

addictive consumption is a widely used term that was given particular meaning by one-time chemical engineer John Ehrenfeld, who retired from academic life in 2000 and went on to become the executive Director of the International Society for Industrial Ecology.

Overconsumption has obvious negative implications for the depletion of the planet's 'natural resources' and consequent reductions in biodiversity. It is generating ever-expanding 'waste streams' which can have negative environmental and human health impacts as well as being costly to manage (see Chapter 16). While much attention has focused on the negative environmental costs of overconsumption, '**addictive consumption**' can have also negative health impacts for the consumers – with one survey revealing that 65 per cent of Americans are either overweight or obese. Addictive consumption has also contributed to the rise of what many commentators have called the 'cult of the individual' with a consequent decline in social participation or community-building activities. Overconsumption is unsustainable for environmental, social and personal reasons.

The key learning objectives in this chapter are:

- understanding the global rise of 'hyperconsumption';
- understanding the associated rise in individualism, which is partly fuelled by the 'generation of desires';
- understanding how overconsumption becomes a form of addiction that is dissociated from real needs;
- detecting some encouraging trends in regard to 'ethical consumption', 'voluntary simplicity', 'collaborative consumption' and 'relocalisation';
- introducing a particular model for removing social and cultural drivers of high consumption.

THE EMERGENCE OF 'HYPERCONSUMPTION'

According to French philosopher **Gilles Lipovetsky** (2011) we live in a global era of '**hyperconsumption**' because 'all previous geographical and time constraints on consumerism are dissolving'.[2] In western societies, Lipovetsky notes, Sundays are no longer a day of rest and religious observance because we can now engage in consumerism 'at all hours and in all places'; from the supermarket to the museum or religious festival. 'The empire of brand names and market share extends everywhere', Lipovetsky exclaims.[3]

According to Lipovetsky, 'hyperconsumption' is the third phase in the development of 'consumer capitalism'; with the first phase focusing on the proliferation of standardised goods sold at low prices starting around 1880 and continuing to the Second World War; the second phase focusing on a rapid global increase in the availability of consumer goods lasting only about 20 years; and the phase of 'hyperconsumption' focusing on a rapid expansion in the quantity of consumer goods 'required' by individuals and households to operate effectively beginning in the late 1970s. Modern homes, Lipovetsky suggests, have been 'technologized' and 'multi-equipped' with an upsurge in the number of homes with more than one car, television, phone connection and internet device. Ever-increasing opportunities to consume more and more consumer goods means that consumption has become a 'self-animating force'[4] and increasing numbers of people are working in order to consume. The growing emphasis on individual consumption is causing a 'veritable explosion of individualism', Lipovetsky contends,[5] and he uses terms such as 'emotional consumerism' and 'hedonistic consumerism' to suggest that hyperconsumption can easily become a way of life.

In part, this is driven by an anxiety about not succeeding in life but Lipovetsky also contends that more and more people believe they can consume their way to a better life by using products that claim to improve personal health and emotional wellbeing. Increasing numbers of home and garden magazine convince us that we can buy or create the 'dream home'; food and health magazines convince us that we can eat our way to health and wellbeing, with the aid of various pharmaceutical products; and travel magazines hold out the promise of the 'perfect' holiday

Gilles Lipovetsky (b. 1944) participated in the student-led protests of 1968 in Paris and he moved from being an orthodox Marxist to a postmodernist before focusing on the pervasive influences of 'hypermodernity'. He is a professor of philosophy and sociology at the University of Grenoble.

hyperconsumption is a term used to refer to excessive or non-functional consumption, which has been given particular meaning by French philosopher Gilles Lipovetsky in relation to historic trends in mass consumption.

Tim Jackson (b. 1957) spent five years at the Stockholm Environment Institute in the early 1990s before joining the University of Surrey where he became Professor of Sustainable Development in 2000. He served as the Economics Commissioner on the UK's Sustainable Development Commission from 2004 to 2009, where he undertook the work which led to the publication his influential book on 'prosperity' in 2009.

destination. British ecological economist **Tim Jackson** (2009) has noted that rampant consumerism rewards self-seeking behaviour while psychologists have pointed out that humans are also inclined towards 'other-seeking' behaviour. Jackson also argues that prevailing economic policies and practices fail to acknowledge human interest in novelty and creativity and hence they only motivate about a quarter of the 'human soul'.

Hidden costs of hyperconsumption

Increasing production and consumption of goods that either have plastic components or which are wrapped in plastic has seen global production of plastic materials reach 300 million tons by 2013. Plastic waste that is not buried in landfill often ends up in waterways and, eventually, in the world's oceans. The problem is partly visible when ocean currents create large 'garbage patches' in the Pacific Ocean and when plastic bits and pieces are found in the stomach contents of dead seabirds or marine animals very far from the nearest human settlements (see Photo 3.1). What is worrying marine biologists even more, however, is that much of the plastic waste enters the oceans as invisible microplastic particles which then accumulate in the bodies of marine creatures. While we can see growing mountains of trash piling up in city streets, in landfill sites or in polluted waterways we cannot see much of the waste that enters the food chain of other animals.

Photo 3.1 The stomach contents of a dead albatross on Midway Atoll in the Pacific Ocean show how far plastic waste is spreading through the world's oceans

Photo by Chris Jordan, US Fish and Wildlife Service (Wikimedia Commons)

Hyperconsumption not evenly spread

Although hyperconsumption is being globalised with the growth of the 'consumer class' in countries such as China and India, the problem began in western societies and there is still a massive difference in *per capita* consumption between the world's rich and poor nations. Per capita energy consumption is a good overall indicator of consumption levels and to make comparisons between nations the World Bank uses the measure of kilograms of oil equivalent used. This does not represent the true consumption practices for some of the oil-producing nations, with Qatar and Trinidad and Tobago topping the list for 2013. However, the following comparisons are revealing:

Canada: 7,202
USA: 6,916
Australia: 5,586
Germany: 3,868
France: 3,840
UK: 2,978
China: 2,226
India: 606
Bangladesh: 216
South Sudan: 59

In other words, people living in North America use around 35–120 times as much energy as people living in Bangladesh or South Sudan.

INDIVIDUALISM AND COCOONING

A wide range of leading sociologists have noted the trend towards 'individualism' and the consequent demise of old 'institutions' that once helped individuals to find a sense of belonging and purpose; including churches, stable local communities, clubs and organisations with long-running traditions.[6] This will be discussed further in Chapter 9, however Lipovestsky's emphasis on the hyperconsuming household has particular significance for understanding both the environmental and social costs of this kind of consumerism.

Increasing numbers of people are going to the outer margins of growing cities to find their 'dream home', often in a newly constructed housing estate. This means that they have to spend more time travelling – mostly by car – to work, shops or to visit friends or relatives. Increasing use of cars increases levels of carbon emissions, while congested roads add to personal and social frustrations. In such circumstances, people are less likely to have meaningful connections with others who share the same neighbourhood and the need to spend more time travelling to get to work, shops or family means that they have less time or opportunity to get to know their neighbours and the local community. This leads

cocooning is a term that was probably coined by prominent New York-based futurist Faith Popcorn (born Faith Plotkin) in the 1990s. It refers to a tendency for people to spend more time inside their homes.

to the phenomenon that has been called '**cocooning**', in which people spend most of their non-work time inside their own homes, keeping in touch with family, friends or the world at large by using the growing number of electronic devices that vastly increase our ability to communicate across distance.

People who tend to stay within their own home and garden rather than venture into the neighbourhood can lose sight of where they are located in the world. It is easy to ignore, for example, the question of where water comes from when you turn on a tap, or where waste products go when you flush them away or put your garbage out for collection. Maria Kaika (2005) has expanded the notion of 'cocooning' by suggesting that people living in western societies have come to view their private home as a kind of safe haven – even utopia – from which they can screen out unwanted environmental or social intrusions. We allow in the things we need – e.g. clean water, food, family and friends – while we exclude or expel other things – e.g. strangers, waste water and other waste. We want to be surrounded by non-threatening – e.g. planned or manicured – landscapes; hence the popularity of newly constructed housing estates. In such circumstances people are screened from 'natural' landscapes and ecosystems and this makes it harder for them to be conscious of their environmental impacts.

social and ecological flows in this book 'social flows' is used to refer to the global movement of people, goods, information and ideas and 'ecological flows' is used to refer to the flow of water, energy and nutrients through local, regional and global ecosystems.

Kaika suggests that Athens became the first 'great' western city precisely because it was the first to be able to manage the supply of safe drinking water and the removal of 'bad' water. However, city-dwellers, she argues, can lose sight of the ecological flows – of water, food, energy – as they pass through our bodies, households and communities. At the same time, she suggests, city-dwellers may be more likely to retreat to the private home to feel safe from perceived social threats or a sense of not belonging. High density urban living creates possibilities for efficiencies in the provision of energy, food and water and the management of waste. However, Kaika reminds us that cities stand at the intersection of both **social and ecological flows** which can undermine a secure sense of belonging as well as an awareness of environmental impacts.

Environmental, social and personal costs of hyperconsumption

- unsustainable use of natural resources and environmental pollution;
- loss of global biodiversity and habitats for non-human species;
- increasing emissions of greenhouse gases that are leading to global warming (see Chapter 4);
- rising economic costs related to increasing production and transport of goods and the disposal of increasing volumes of waste;
- a loss of social connectedness and a sense of belonging to a community;
- stresses associated with working hard to sustain high levels of consumption, including the problem of being 'time poor'; and
- a relentless feeling of being on a 'treadmill' of never-ending consumption.

PLANNED OBSOLESCENCE AND THE GENERATION OF DESIRE

Economies that are driven by a growth imperative are always looking for ways to increase the volume and speed of production and consumption. This can involve conscious efforts to reduce the 'lifespan' of a product – otherwise known as 'planned obsolescence' – so that they need to be replaced. Whereas a light bulb first installed in a California fire station in 1901 is still operating and the earliest motor cars were designed to last for many decades, 'modern' consumer goods are designed to wear out or break down. The lifespan of most motor vehicles has been reduced and repairs have become more costly; it has become easier and often cheaper to replace rather than repair clothing and footwear. 'New generation' electronic devices are rendered 'obsolete' by even newer versions and the generational lifespan of such devices has been reduced. The term 'new generation' is being used to refer to objects ranging from computers to toothbrushes.

Consumers are led to believe that their life is incomplete without the latest and 'best' consumer goods. Lipovetsky (2011) suggests that the growth of mass consumption means that social status is no longer associated with 'conspicuous consumption'.[7] Yet the advertising industry is clearly and unapologetically driven by its need to generate desire for new products or services even if there is little evidence to suggest that they meet any real needs. The growing wealth and power of multinational corporations has given new force to advertising and Lipovetsky argues that we have witnessed a 'tidal wave' of globally recognised brand names. Consumers can adopt a cosmopolitan posture in their desire for products with globally famous names and clever advertising can create 'brand loyalty' even if rival brands aim to disrupt this by setting out to change tastes and

Photo 3.2 Major sporting and cultural facilities are being rebranded with corporate names: Arsenal's home ground in London
© Roberto Herrett/Loop Images/Corbis

'fashions'. The promotion of brand has become more pervasive than ever with lucrative sponsorships giving corporations 'naming rights' in the promotion of major sporting or cultural events. Brand names have commonly replaced place names in the title given to major sporting arenas.

Illusions of choice

Underpinning hyperconsumption is the cherished notion of freedom of choice. However, the choice we think we have when we go into a supermarket full of rival products is often an illusion because underneath the packaging the products often have very little difference. Even different brands of motor cars may have identical engines and many shared body parts. Our choices are often influenced more than we realise by advertising, 'brand loyalty' and the generation of desire (discussed above).

Furthermore, western consumers often have choice because people working in factories in countries ranging from Bangladesh to El Salvador have very little choice about where they work or the conditions in which they work. People making 'top brand' shoes may not be able to afford shoes at all and many of them will struggle to get enough to eat rather than fuss about which brand of food they might purchase.

brand power is the effective promotion of a product or service by focusing on its brand name; this has achieved 'global reach' in recent decades.

While advertisers try to establish a link between brand name, quality and aesthetics, global **brand power** disrupts this link as corporations seek to produce their goods at the lowest cost, often in places where quality control or controls on environmental impacts or the exploitation of workers are not enforced. While brands have become ubiquitous they have become a less reliable guide for consumers in relation to the link between quality and price. The very same engine make, for example, might be used to drive a Ford or Mazda motor car and there may be little overall difference, yet one may be more fashionable than the other. Consumer choice is often an illusion and the unwitting consumer can feel overwhelmed by the variety of branded products that are essentially the same thing. It can be difficult to look beyond the brand to learn something about the product; including its quality and information about where and how it was produced.

ADDICTIVE CONSUMPTION

commodification is the processes which turn goods and services into 'commodities' for exchange within a market economy.

In discussing growing levels of consumption in western societies John Ehrenfeld (2008) has drawn a distinction between 'commodified consumption' and consumption that meets 'authentic' needs. A search for authenticity is deeply embedded in what it means to be human, Ehrenfeld contends, yet it can be very difficult to distinguish between authentic needs and perceived needs when participating in a market economy. When goods and services become tradable items within a market economy they are better understood as '**commodities**' that circulate within endless cycles of production and consumption; a process which blurs distinctions between the 'use value' and 'exchange value' of each commodity. Hence, Ehrenfeld uses the term 'commodified consumption' to refer to the cycles of purchase and consumption of products which seem to address our perceived needs and yet we find that the cycles never end and our needs never seem to be met.

Commodified consumption does not always produce addiction, Erhenfeld notes, because we frequently purchase commodities that do satisfy authentic needs. However, endless cycles of purchase and consumption can seduce us into thinking that new and more products and services will meet our needs even better and this can take us into endless cycles of addictive consumption. Ehrenfeld draws on systems modelling to suggest that we need to add a feedback loop to the cycle of consumption so that we take time to reflect on the extent to which our consumption is giving us an 'authentic mode of satisfaction'.[8] Put more simply, we need to take time to think more deeply about the difference between needs and wants and consider the personal costs of being trapped within endless cycles of addictive consumption. Ehrenfeld credits British psychologist Oliver James with the observation that 'we have become addicted to having rather than being'[9] (p. 36) and we need to take the time to contemplate other ways to achieve life satisfaction. It is useful here to return to the famous work by American psychologist **Abraham Maslow** in the 1960s on what he called a 'hierarchy' of human needs ranging from physiological to 'self-actualisation' (see Figure 3.2 and box).

Abraham Maslow (1908–70) was born in Boston as the oldest child of immigrant parents, Maslow was deemed to be 'psychologically unstable' as a child. He studied both psychology and law and became famous for his 'hierarchy' of human needs in the 1960s.

Maslow's pyramid of needs

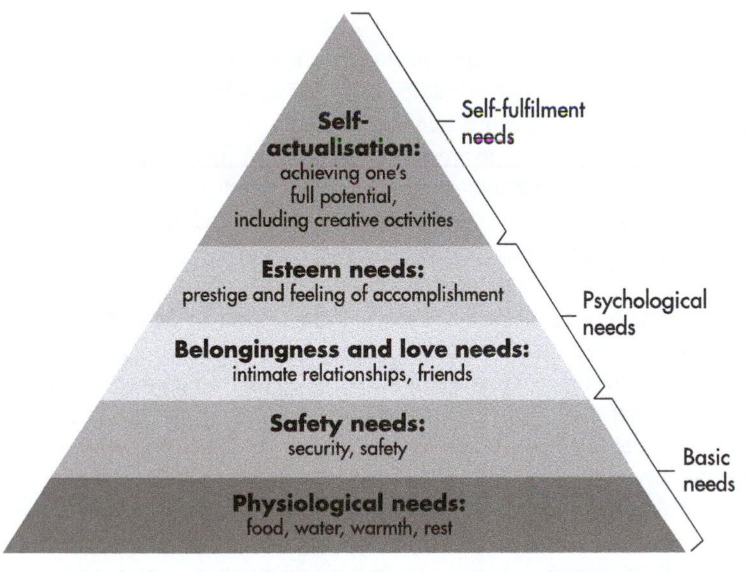

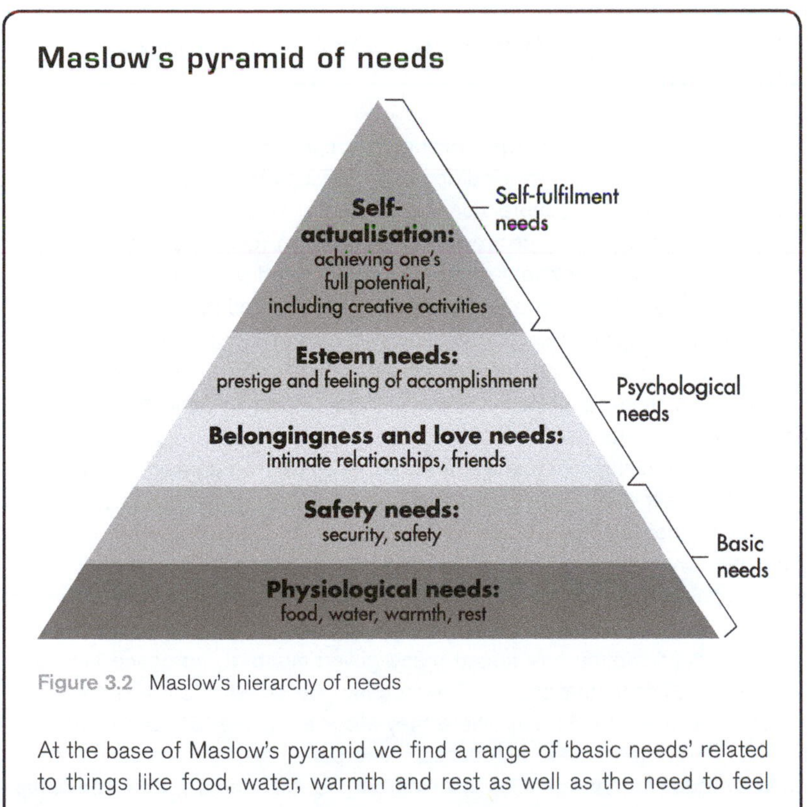

Figure 3.2 Maslow's hierarchy of needs

At the base of Maslow's pyramid we find a range of 'basic needs' related to things like food, water, warmth and rest as well as the need to feel reasonably safe and secure. Higher up the scale we find the need to have a sense of belonging within networks of personal relationships, including family and friends, along with a desire for self-esteem which might be measured by 'prestige' or 'feelings of accomplishment'. At the peak of Maslow's hierarchy is the notion of 'self-actualisation', by which he meant the extent to which any of us might feel that we are able to achieve our 'full potential', partly by having the opportunity to participate in creative activities. This hierarchical way of representing human needs cannot do justice to the complex interplay of needs and aspirations or to ways in which we might achieve satisfaction and fulfilment by finding creative and sustainable ways to meet 'basic needs' for ourselves and others. For example, the provision of food and shelter can be turned into an exercise in creating a sense of belonging to community and creative producers of food and shelter can achieve self-fulfilment from the skilful ways in which they might exercise their craft. However, the notion of 'self-actualization' overlaps with Ehrenfeld's search for 'authenticity' and it suggests that the deepest ways to achieve a sense of fulfilment may have little or nothing to do with the consumption of goods and services produced by others.

ethical consumption refers to a values-based approach to purchase and consumption which puts the onus on the consumer to exercise his or her choice wisely.

ETHICAL CONSUMPTION AND VOLUNTARY SIMPLICITY

In his penetrating critique of hyperconsumption, Lipovetsky is surprisingly positive about the long-term benefits of individualised consumption because it can enable consumers to exercise more conscious control over what they consume. Hyperconsumption 'has not destroyed morals, altruism, resentment or the value of love', he writes,[10] and we might see the rise of values-driven consumption within a globalised market. The term that is most commonly used to refer to a desire to consume carefully and wisely is 'ethical consumption' and many commentators have suggested that it is on the rise globally; partly because consumers can use globalised communication technologies and participate in ethical consumption networks. Concerns about negative human impacts on the world's natural environment probably triggered an upsurge in ethical consumption in the 1980s and 1990s, especially in western nations. However, ethical consumers are increasingly motivated by a desire to avoid consumer goods that are produced in conditions where the producers are treated badly and trapped in endless poverty. Ethical consumption for environmental and social sustainability overlaps with a growth in individual concern about healthy living (mentioned above) and the rise in ethical consumption has forced many governments to introduce laws and regulations to ensure that products are properly labelled, with detailed information about what they contain and where they were produced. Some national and regional governments have introduced rating systems so that products can be rated by independent agencies in relation to set standards for environmental impacts, in particular. Most commonly this means that certain products get a tick of approval from the rating agency while others do not. However, efforts are being made to introduce more nuanced ratings systems (see box).

Star ratings

Australian energy efficiency advocate, consultant and academic Alan Pears was considering his options for taking in a movie one night when it suddenly struck him that the star-rating system used by film critics could also be applied to consumer goods. He was able to use his extensive networks to convince the state government in Victoria to introduce a star-rating system for household appliances – such as refrigerators, televisions and washing machines – in which each produce would be given a star rating from 0 to 5 for both energy and water efficiency. Although first used by film critics in the 1920s, star ratings are now used widely for rating hotels, restaurants and a wide range of services. The star system for rating the energy and water efficiency of household appliances is spreading globally.

While ethical consumption often focuses on the choices that individual consumers might make – especially those living in the richer nations of the world – it has also sparked the growth of global networks and projects. For example, the contemporary global Fair Trade movement has many precedents going back 50 years or more, however it has grown strongly in recent decades and Fairtrade International claimed that it had 1.2 million registered producers in 63 countries by 2011, with total sales increasing by 24 per cent since 2008. Fair Trade often overlaps with the global movement to promote 'organic' production of food and other commodities in order to reduce the use of environmentally damaging synthetic chemicals in farming and products that are clearly labelled as 'organic' are also increasing their market share. Fair Trade products are often also labelled as being organic.

As well as being more thoughtful about our modes of consumption we might also aim to consume less and Amitai Etzioni (2006) suggests that a '**voluntary simplicity**' movement, first associated with the 'counter-culture' of the 1970s, has gathered force recently in a wide range of western societies. Etzioni identifies three different levels of intensity among those who have opted for voluntary simplicity in the USA: 'downshifters'; 'strong simplifiers'; and those who participate in a 'simple living movement'. Etzioni is not convinced that many of the high income people who may decide to 'dress down' or choose an inexpensive car are likely to sustain a low-consumption lifestyle. That is why he distinguishes the 'strong simplifiers' who make more radical decisions, such as giving up well-paid jobs or moving into more modest housing where they can also access public transport. Those who consciously participate in the international 'simple living movement' are likely to become strong advocates of the benefits of relatively frugal lifestyles and Etzioni notes that it is easier to sustain low-consumption lifestyles if you feel you are part of a global movement.

voluntary simplicity refers to efforts to live with less as a result of a conscious decision to avoid waste or complexity in life.

relocalisation refers to the suggestion that globalisation has gone too far and that people should seek to satisfy their needs and aspirations by turning more to the local context.

RELOCALISATION

A desire to consume food that has not been produced in large-scale 'factory farms' – most commonly situated a long way from where the consumer lives – has led to the proliferation of a number of global movements promoting localised food production. These include the International Slow Food movement and the proliferation of farmers' markets and both these movements will be discussed below and in Chapter 14. Local production of food and other goods will not always deliver the best social and environmental outcomes. On the one hand, reductions in the global trade of goods could undermine employment in many 'developing' nations and, on the other hand, localised production may not suit local ecological realities conditions. For example, it defies ecological logic to be producing rice in arid Australian landscapes when it can be imported from the wet tropics of nearby Asia. However, the concept of 'relocalisation' points to a need to rethink the balance between local and globalised production and we will return to this in Chapter 9. However, relocalisation is not restricted to the production and consumption of food as we can see a proliferation of community festivals, neighbourhood-level recycling, and even the use of local currencies such as the 'Bristol Pound'.

While noting that globalised consumption is here to stay, Richard Wilk (2011) has suggested that it has not rendered the local irrelevant. Citing some survey evidence, Wilk suggests that those who may have most to gain by having access to global culture – i.e. teenagers – continue to put family and country first in their preferences and he suggests that parochialism may even be on the rise globally. 'Real people are caught somewhere between the extremes of the local and the global', Wilk writes,[11] and this means that consumer culture is 'messy, accidental, and contingent, in a constant state of improvisation, collapse and renewal'. The

Photo 3.3 A farmers' market in Portland, Oregon: the global proliferation of farmers' markets is a trend towards relocalisation
Wikimedia Commons

complex consumption choices that 'real people' make lie at the heart of the global movement for environmental and social sustainability.

THE RISE OF COLLABORATIVE CONSUMPTION

A 2010 book by Rachel Botsman and Roo Rogers suggesting a global movement towards collaborative forms of consumption has triggered considerable debate and controversy. Botsman and Rogers begin their book by telling the story of two young men in San Francisco who started a global enterprise for matching accommodation requests to hosting offers after finding that this was the best way to solve accommodation problems for people wanting to attend an industrial design conference that they were helping to organise. The young men in question were Brian Chesky and Joe Gebba and their enterprise – first called Air Bed and Breakfast and now simply Airbnb – has probably exceeded the expectations of Botsman and Rogers. The example certainly demonstrates that collaboration sometimes works better than competition in ensuring maximum use of limited resources. Botsman and Rogers went on to note a global rise in the number of websites aimed at facilitating the swapping of goods and services and others aimed at ensuring that unwanted goods can be delivered to people in need. The term 'collaborative consumption' also refers to the emergence of cooperatives aimed at collective purchasing of housing, food, motor vehicles, bicycles and more. Botsman and Rogers note the rise of very flexible car hiring or car-share schemes that enable some city-dwellers to go without a car of their own. Many versions of co-housing are emerging in cities where private housing options have become expensive.

Collaborative consumption is primarily aimed at reducing costs and wastage but many advocates also highlight the social benefits in doing more things with other people, rather than alone. An interesting example of this is the Men's Shed movement that originated in Australia to provide places where isolated men could go to undertake craft work in the company of other men. Advocates of collaborative craft-making projects argue that they highlight the benefits of making, rather than purchasing, things and collaborative consumption overlaps, to an extent, with the call to revalue 'craftsmanship' made by Richard Sennett, among others.

collaborative consumption refers to efforts to increase collaboration or cooperation in the purchase and consumption of goods and services; most commonly driven by the view that individual consumption is often wasteful and environmentally damaging.

Botsman and Rogers have been accused of exaggerating the strength and influence of collaborative consumption and some have noted that informal ways of sharing goods with other people are far from new. However, Botsman and Rogers make an important point in arguing that new communication technologies have given collaborative consumption schemes a greater chance of success.

PROMOTING BEHAVIOUR CHANGE

While ethical consumption, voluntary simplicity and collaborative consumption all focus on enabling people to exercise their personal consumer power to achieve better personal, social and environmental outcomes, Tim Jackson (2006) has focused on what government agencies can do to facilitate a wider public shift towards reduced consumption. Governments need to create a policy framework that both encourages people to break their existing consumption habits and penalises wasteful consumption, Jackson argues. Jackson favours an approach to policy formation that was advocated by the UK Department for Environment, Food and Rural Affairs (DEFRA) in 2005 that might be called the four Es model because it involves:

- **E**nsuring that incentive structures and institutional rules favour more sustainable behaviours;
- **E**nabling access to pro-environmental (and pro-social) lifestyle choices;
- **E**ngaging people in initiatives to help themselves; and
- **E**xemplifying the desired changes within government's own policies and practices.

Discussion questions

1 Why should we be concerned about the global spread of mass consumption?
2 According to Lipovetsky, what factors brought about the global shift from mass consumption to 'hyperconsumption' from the late 1970s onwards?
3 What are some of the personal, social and environmental costs of hyperconsumption?
4 What is meant by the term 'cocooning' and what are some of its environmental or social consequences?
5 Should we be concerned about global 'brand power' and, if so, why?
6 In John Ehrenfeld's analysis, what creates cycles of addictive consumption and why are they so hard to break?
7 How important are ethical consumption, voluntary simplicity and collaborative consumption for achieving social and environmental sustainability? What are their strengths and weaknesses?
8 What would help you to achieve the 'good life'?

KEY READINGS

Ehrenfeld, John R. (2008) 'Consumption: A Symptom of Addiction', in John Ehrenfeld (ed.), *Sustainability by Design: A Subversive Strategy for Transforming Our Consumer Culture*, New Haven, CT: Yale University Press, pp. 35–47.

Etzioni, Amitai (2006) 'Voluntary Simplicity: Characterization, Select Psychological Implications and Societal Consequences', in Tim Jackson (ed.), *The Earthscan Reader in Sustainable Consumption*, London: Earthscan, pp. 158–77.

Jackson, Tim (2006) 'Challenges for Sustainable Consumption Policy', in Tim Jackson (ed.), *The Earthscan Reader in Sustainable Consumption*, London: Earthscan, pp. 109–26.

Jackson, Tim (2016) 2nd edn, *Prosperity Without Growth: Foundations for the Economy of Tomorrow*, London: Routledge.

Lipovetsky, Gilles (2011) *Hypermodern Times*, Cambridge: Polity.

Lipovetsky, Gilles (2011) 'The Hyperconsumption Society', in Karin Ekstrom and Kay Glans (eds), *Beyond the Consumption Bubble*, New York: Routledge, pp. 25–36.

Wilk, Richard (2011) 'Consumption in an Age of Globalization and Localization', in Karin Ekstrom and Kay Glans (eds), *Beyond the Consumption Bubble*, New York: Routledge, pp. 37–51.

thematic essay

Seeking the 'good life'

The suggestion that consumption can ultimately *reduce* personal satisfaction is not new. Greek philosopher **Epicurus** made this argument around 2,300 years ago with statements like 'If you want to make a man rich, be not adding to his money but subtracting from his desires' and 'If you live according to nature, you will never be poor; if you live according to opinions you will never be rich.' To be an 'epicurean' in the world today is to be rather self-indulgent, especially in regard to food and drink. However, that is not fair to the philosopher who gave his name to the movement, for he was interested in the search for tranquillity – *atoraxia* – rather than the mindless pursuit of pleasure. For Epicurus freedom from fear comes from eschewing status in order to enjoy the pleasure that can come from simple things like the enjoyment of good food, especially when it is shared with other people.

Epicurus (341BC–270BC) was a Greek philosopher who was born in Samos, Greece. His philosophical writing focused on the pursuit of a tranquil life and he founded the Epicurean school of thought.

Swiss-born, London-based writer Alain de Botton is among those who have tried to retrieve Epicurus' reputation, finding echoes of his ideas in the work of other thinkers, from Socrates up to nineteenth-century German philosophers Arthur Schopenhauer and Friedrich Nietzsche (de Botton 2000). Echoes of Epicurus can also be found in the international Slow Food movement which grew out of a 1986 campaign in Rome to stop a proposal to open an outlet of the McDonald's food chain near the city's famous Spanish Steps. The leader of that campaign, Carlo Petrini, was keen to use the campaign impetus to educate people more widely on the dangers posed to human health and the natural environment from the growing addictions to fast food and in 1989 delegates from 15 different countries gathered in Paris to sign the founding manifesto of the international Slow Food movement. This manifesto not only called on adherents to highlight the dangers of fast food but to campaign against the use of pesticides and genetic engineering in the production of food. It called on people to support 'local' and 'traditional' food and 'small-scale processing' in order to end the dominance of 'commercial agribusiness' and 'factory farms'. It suggested that people would change their food consumption habits when they rediscovered the importance of taste over convenience and Slow Food places an emphasis on teaching gardening skills to young people. The Slow Food movement associates itself with 'ethical consumption' but it echoes Epicurus in highlighting the simple pleasure that comes from sharing good food with other people.

Resistance to the growing dominance of large corporations in the global food industry has also come in the form of a global surge in the popularity of 'farmers' markets'. A farmers' market is defined as a market in which food producers sell their produce directly to consumers, without the mediation of food wholesale and retail businesses. Of course, farmers' markets have ancient origins and many towns and communities right across the world have long-standing produce markets which function in this way. Many big cities also have long-standing produce markets, although these are sometimes targeted at food retailers rather than consumers. It is a little surprising to find that Los Angeles has managed to maintain an active farmers' market since 1934, despite the rise of the car culture in that city. What is even more remarkable, however, is that farmers' markets have now become popular in a wide range of US and European cities, with more than 100 operating in New York alone. The US food activist and writer Mark Winne claims that between 1994 and 2010 there was a tenfold increase in the number of farmers' markets in the USA, from around 1,700 to around 17,000 (Winne 2010).

The suggestion that a preference for local food will ultimately be more environmentally and socially sustainable is also reflected in the popularity of the concept of 'food miles', which urges consumers to consider the negative consequences of transporting food long distances from where it is produced to where it is consumed. The term was coined by London academic Professor Tim Lang when he was associated with the Sustainable Agriculture Food and Environment (SAFE) Alliance in the early 1990s. In particular, it seeks to highlight the negative environmental impacts of food transport when most modes of transport use fossil fuels; however it also suggests that processing to make food ready for long-distance transport reduces the nutritional standards of most produce. As mentioned earlier, it is rather misleading to suggest that food produced closer to where it might be consumed will always be better for the environment and a simple focus on distance travelled is too simplistic. Many factors need to be taken into account in determining whether or not food is being produced sustainably in any particular location. However, the concept of food miles can still be a good starting point for thinking more carefully about the food we consume. It is clear that Lang did not intend it to be taken as the sole determinant of sustainable food production and consumption.

There is no simple way to switch from unsustainable to sustainable modes of consumption and the production and consumption of food is only one aspect of a much broader problem. Gilles Lipovetsky extended his argument about the era of 'hyperconsumption' to argue that 'hypermodern' people are addicted to pleasure and hedonism yet wracked with anxiety about the loss of traditions in an uncertain world (2011). However, in his very influential critique of 'growth economics', British economist Tim Jackson (2009) argued that humans are not solely motivated by self-seeking behaviours because we value our relationships with a wide range of other people and have an endless fascination with novelty and creativity. Noting that the word 'prosperity' is based on the Latin for hope (*sperare*), he suggested that the pursuit of 'prosperity without growth' is the kind of creative challenge that can motivate the 'human soul' far more that the mindless pursuit of economic growth. As did Epicurus long before him, Jackson argued that sharing simple pleasures with other people can trigger a more mindful pursuit of the good life.

NOTES

1 www.footprintnetwork.org
2 Lipovetsky (2011: 25).
3 Ibid.
4 Lipovetsky (2011: 29).
5 Ibid.: 27.
6 Notable here are works by Anthony Giddens, Ulrich Beck, Richard Sennett and Zygmunt Bauman.
7 Lipovesky (2011: 29).
8 Ehrenfeld (2008: 37).
9 Ibid.: 36.
10 Lipovetsky (2011: 35).
11 Wilk (2011: 45).

CHAPTER 4

Global challenges as wicked problems

Key concepts and concerns

- the concept of 'wicked problems'
- climate change mitigation and adaptation
- threats and opportunities posed by climate change
- inadequacy of 'poverty line' estimates of global poverty
- a community development approach to poverty reduction
- focusing on 'adaptive capacity'

INTRODUCTION

In a book aimed at shifting the way we think about the biggest environmental challenge facing global humanity, Mike Hulme (2009) made the rather surprising suggestion that it is useful to think of climate change as a 'wicked problem' of unprecedented scope and likely duration. This is because it helps us move from thinking of climate change as a 'problem to be solved' in order to see it as a 'condition in which we are enmeshed', Hulme wrote.[1] The identification of '**wicked problems**' as ones which defy any 'true-or-false' solutions, partly because they are commonly symptoms of other problems, was first advocated by planning theorists Horst Rittel and Melvin Webber (1973). Rittel and Webber noted that planners have to grapple

wicked problems is a term first coined by design theorist Horst Rittel at the University of California Berkeley (UCB) in the 1960s. Rittel collaborated with UCB urban planner Melvin Webber to develop the concept of wicked problems in regard to urban planning in a book published in 1973. The term is used to refer to complex problems that have no single, complete or trial-and-error solutions; problems which may emerge as symptoms of other complex problems.

Key characteristics of 'wicked problems'

1. There can be no definitive definition of the problem.
2. There are no true or false solutions, only relatively good or bad responses.
3. They can all be seen as symptoms of other interacting problems.
4. They are unique so there can be no template to follow in responding.
5. Responses are 'one-shot' efforts that cannot be replicated.
6. Responses include many 'stakeholders' with a wide range of values and priorities.

with unpredictable human behaviour in trying to meet sometimes competing social needs and there is a touch of humour in their use of a term which suggests that some problems are too devious for us to tame. Horst and Rittel articulated ten characteristics of 'wicked problems', however they can be boiled down to six.

We will return to Hulme's interesting perspectives on living with climate change later in this chapter, however, we will begin by focusing a little on how we got enmeshed in the climate change condition. This chapter suggests that it is useful to think of three global challenges to sustainability as wicked problems and these are:

1 the emergence of human-induced global climate change;
2 the growing dangers of oil dependency; and
3 the intransigence of global poverty.

Debate continues to simmer globally about the contribution that humans have made to the global warming phenomenon that is changing the planet's climate. However, the **Intergovernmental Panel on Climate Change** (IPPC) released its fifth global assessment report in 2013 and the assessment reports that have had contributions from thousands of the world's leading scientists since 1990 point inexorably to a human contribution. The suggestion that the world is rapidly approaching a point of peak in the extraction and processing of oil was first made by US geophysicist **M. King Hubbert** soon after the first big global oil supply crisis in 1973. Hubbert's dire prediction has been widely dismissed as being excessively 'alarmist' in the years since that oil shock and yet Chapter 5 will show that supplies of easily accessible oil are declining and that oil companies are having to go to remote locations and extract oil from 'difficult' sources in order to sustain supply. The world depends very heavily on oil and other 'fossil fuels' for its systems of transport, manufacture and agriculture and products emanating from the petrochemical industry – including the vast array of plastics – are found in almost everything we use on a daily basis. Ultimately, fossil fuels are in finite supply and their burning turns stored carbon into the gas – CO_2 – which is making the biggest contribution to human-induced climate change. There are many reasons to act now rather than wait for future global oil shocks but tackling oil dependency is truly a 'wicked problem', as will be shown in Chapter 5.

Global poverty is the third 'wicked problem' featured in this book because it was a key barrier to sustainability identified in the 1987 Brundtland Report. Since 1987 numerous efforts have been made at a global level to tackle the entrenched problem of global poverty by lifting all people above the **World Bank's income 'poverty line'** of $US1.25 per day. The elimination of global poverty was enshrined in the Millennium Development Goals adopted by the United Nations in 2000 and, as we will see later, the World Bank has claimed that the global effort is having some success. However, income is a very inadequate poverty indicator and the workings of the globalised market-driven economy appear to be making poverty even worse in parts of Africa, Asia and Latin America. Despite the growth of the 'middle class' in countries such as India, China and Brazil, the overall gap between the world rich and poor seems to be actually increasing and this is at least partly responsible for many of the wars and conflicts that rage across Africa and Central Asia, in particular.

Intergovernmental Panel on Climate Change was formed in 1988 by two UN organisations – the World Meteorological Organisation and the United Nations Environment Programme – to collate information from scientific studies of human-induced climate change. Its first report was published in 1990.

M. King Hubbert (1903–89) trained in geology, physics and mathematics at the University of Chicago where he received his Ph.D. in 1937. He worked for Shell Oil Company from 1943 to his retirement in 1964 and it was in 1956 that he made his prediction that oil production in the US would reach a peak around 1970.

World Bank poverty line the concept of a poverty line has been in use since the early twentieth century; in recent decades it has become popular to say that extreme poverty means that people exist on less than $US1 a day. In 2006 the World Bank set the line for extreme poverty at $US1.25 a day on the estimate that this was equivalent in spending power to $US1 a day in 1996. While the World Bank draws a distinction between 'absolute' and 'relative' poverty the arbitrary poverty line adopted in 2006 has been a focus of attention.

Startling statistics

- Scientists predict that if post-industrial increases in surface temperatures exceed 2°C the world's coral reefs are all doomed and the massive Greenland ice shelf is likely to collapse.
- We are already halfway to the 'dangerous threshold' of 2°C increase in atmospheric temperatures.
- We are witnessing increased frequency and intensity of extreme weather events, including floods, fires, droughts, cyclones and storm surges.
- An estimated 70,000 people died in the record European heatwave of 2003.
- 43 per cent of people in the world earn less than $US2 per day.
- 12 per cent of the world's population is responsible for 60 per cent of private consumption.

Of course, there are many other global sustainability challenges beyond the 'big three' mentioned above. They include **deforestation** and **desertification**, declining soil fertility and declines in global fish stocks, **transborder pollution**, unresolved wars and conflicts and increasing flows of refugees and asylum seekers, and continuing dangers posed by the use of nuclear power. All of these are 'global problems', because the capacity to address them effectively at local or even national levels is limited, even if global action must be driven from below. However, many of these big problems are now framed by the need to tackle the 'big three' sustainability challenges and any successes in managing climate change, reducing oil dependency and reducing global poverty will have help us tackle all the other problems.

deforestation refers to the clearing of a forest or stand of trees where the land is subsequently converted for non-forest use.

desertification refers to a form of land degradation in which an area loses its natural reserves of water and existing forms of vegetation and wildlife.

transborder pollution refers to any form of pollution that cannot be contained within national borders, or waste materials that are deliberately transported beyond the borders of the country in which they were generated.

This chapter will focus on:

- Understanding the key causes of human-induced global climate change and some of its emerging consequences.
- Broadening our understanding of how we can mitigate climate change impacts while also learning how to adapt to changing climates.
- Considering how we can use the onset of human-induced climate change to rethink unsustainable assumptions, values and practices.
- Deepening our understanding of what it means to live in entrenched poverty and examine why global poverty elimination strategies have had limited success.
- The need to extend our empathy and responsibility for the wellbeing of all humans and non-human forms of life living on our planet now and in the future.

UNDERSTANDING HUMAN-INDUCED GLOBAL CLIMATE CHANGE

The idea that humans are either causing or accelerating global climate change has only become a matter of broad public concern since around 2006. It has, of course, concerned climate scientists for much longer and it has become the stuff of legend that **climatologist James Hansen** took his concerns to the US Congress in 1988 to seek government action on his proposal to cut greenhouse gas emissions in order to prevent a slide into dangerous levels of climate volatility. Hansen was responsible for setting widely accepted targets of climate change **mitigation**, aiming to keep the increase in surface temperatures below 2°C and the concentration of **greenhouse gases** in the upper atmosphere below 350 parts per million. Hansen's core argument was that if human activity has increased greenhouse gas emissions to dangerous levels, then we can also take action to reduce those emissions and stabilise atmospheric warming.

climatology is a subset of atmospheric science and physical geography devoted to understanding the functioning of the Earth's climate systems.

James Hansen was born in Iowa in 1941 and he gained his Ph.D. in physics from the University of Iowa in 1967. He was Head of the NASA Goddard Institute for Space Studies located in New York City (1981–2013).

mitigation refers to attempts to reduce emissions of greenhouse gases, while climate change *adaptation* refers to action taken to adapt to the impacts of climate change.

greenhouse gases refers to a group of gases that have the ability to absorb and re-radiate solar energy. They include water vapour, ozone, carbon dioxide, methane and nitrous oxide, with the latter three increasing in the upper atmosphere concentrations as a result of human activity.

Joseph (Jean-Baptiste) Fourier (1768–1830) was the son of a tailor who became an orphan at the age of nine. He was active in the French Revolution, jailed in

Of course, global climate change in itself is not a new phenomenon and we have long known that there have been extended periods in the history of the planet when ice has covered much more of the Earth's surface that it does today. What concerned James Hansen, however, was the mounting evidence that human industrial and farming activity is contributing to an observable rise in global atmospheric and surface temperatures by pumping 'greenhouse gases' into the upper atmosphere. It also needs to be noted that Hansen was far from being the first scientist to detect the human contribution to global warming. Indeed the possibility that certain gases accumulating in the upper atmosphere could contribute to global warming by trapping solar radiation within the atmosphere – i.e. create a 'greenhouse effect' – was first mooted by the French scientist **Joseph Fourier** in 1824 and demonstrated empirically by the English physicist John Tyndall in 1859. It became evident that human activity is increasing concentrations of a number of greenhouse gases in the upper atmosphere and in 1917 the eminent Scottish scientist and inventor Alexander Bell urged the fastest possible transition from the use of carbon-based fuels to the use of solar energy.

Hansen's appearance before the US Congress in 1988 undoubtedly helped to put the science of climate change on the political agenda and the United Nations established the IPCC in the same year and it collated input from hundreds of scientists to release its first 'assessment report' in 1990. Its fifth assessment report – an overview of a series of separate reports – was released in September 2013 and it included the assessment that it is 95 per cent certain that humans are contributing to an observable increase in global temperatures. It is not really surprising that there are some scientists who dissent from the assessments contained in IPCC assessment reports because it is the nature of scientific inquiry to contest interpretations of data. The surprising, and alarming, thing is that thousands of scientists – operating in a wide range of fields – have reached the levels of consensus reported in the fifth IPCC report. Dissenters – many of them having little or no scientific credibility – have received a disproportionate share of media attention.

Climate change sceptics focus on the fact that average surface temperatures can fluctuate from one year to the next or from one decade to the next. However, it is becoming increasingly obvious from one IPCC assessment report to the next that the long view – which looks beyond short-term variability – shows that average surface temperatures have turned upward quite dramatically alongside the growth in human industrial activity over the last 100 years or so and the 2013 assessment report included a set of graphs showing 'multiple observed indicators of a changing climate' (see Figures 4.1 and 4.2). Graphs of long-term indicators

the reign of terror and served in Napoleon's army before gaining distinction as a mathematician and physicist. He became famous for his work on heat transfers and he theorised the 'greenhouse effect' for Planet Earth in a paper published in 1824.

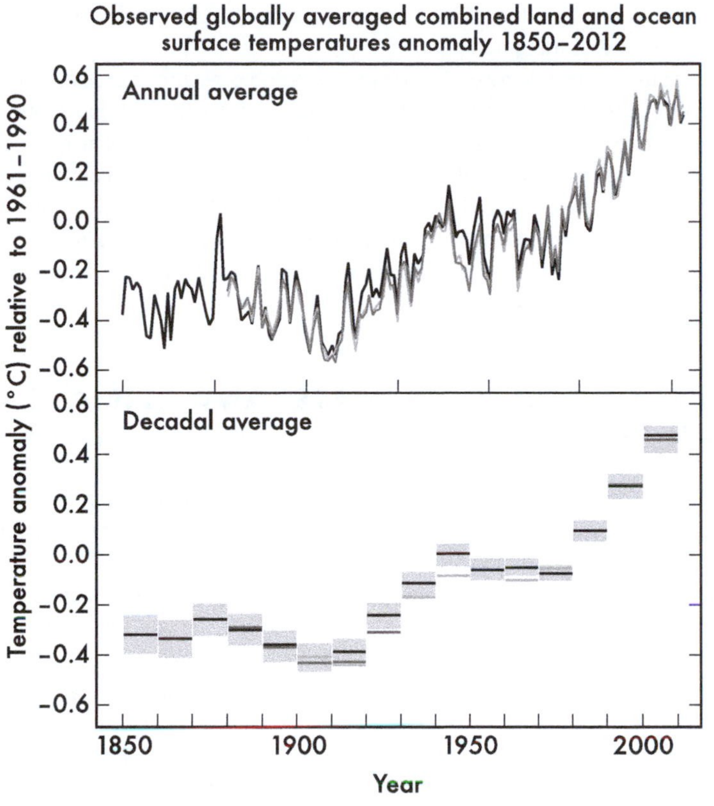

Figure 4.1 Observed globally averaged combined land and ocean surface temperature changes 1850–2012
Source: Figure SPM:1 in IPCC Working Party 1 Report, 2013 (www.climatechange2013.org/report/reports-graphic/report-graphics)

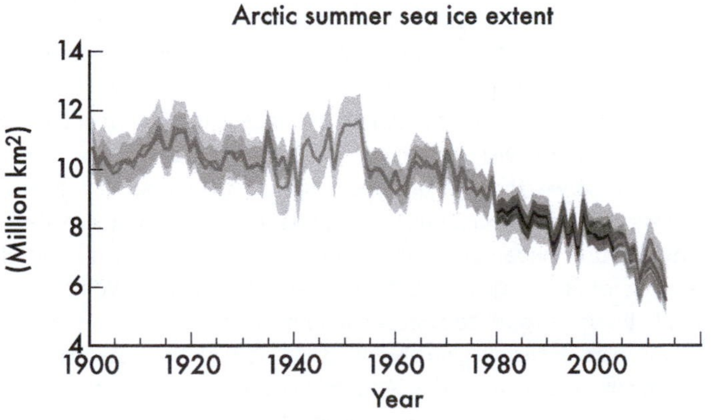

Figure 4.2 Arctic summer sea ice extent
Source: Figure SPM:3 in IPCC Working Party 1 Report, 2013

of global warming tend to show a 'hockey stick effect' in that they turn up sharply towards the end of the graph period.

Climate scientists are coming under increasing pressure to provide accurate predictions about the consequences of rising surface temperatures but their modelling reveals that increasing heat creates greater climate volatility, meaning that future predictions are likely to be less reliable. However, the signs of change are accumulating with record low levels of Arctic ice, increasingly intense and frequent floods, droughts and 'extreme weather events'. It is hard to imagine what more the scientists can do to prepare us for what lies ahead and to encourage governments to take more resolute mitigation action.

UNDERSTANDING 'CLIMATE' AND CLIMATE SYSTEMS

Having been exposed to the well-publicised views of climate change sceptics, people without scientific training could be excused for thinking that unseasonably cold weather puts in doubt the predictions about global warming or that fluctuations between heatwaves and flooding rains put any underlying trend in doubt. The first thing that needs to be understood is that 'weather' and 'climate' are not the same and that incremental shifts in climate can actually increase the variability of the weather patterns we might experience. A warmer atmosphere means warmer surface temperatures and warmer seas and we know that changes in weather result from temperature differences between land, sea and atmosphere, with storm systems often forming in the interplay between **ocean currents** and the movement of water molecules in the atmosphere. A warming of climate systems makes such interplays even more dynamic and less predictable and this is why climate scientists prefer to talk about 'climate change' rather than 'global warming'. The global climate system is a single system but the addition of more heat is making it behave more unpredictably. Ocean currents have an enormous influence on weather systems and many models have been released to show how these currents act as a 'global conveyor belt' which can distribute weather disturbances globally (see Figure 4.3). We can only really understand global climate change if we know something about global – rather than local – climate systems.

ocean currents can be caused by wind or by movement arising from density differences in water caused by differences in temperature or salinity.

A common misconception about climate change is that incremental increases in surface temperatures will result in incremental increases in sea water levels and in the kind of weather we might experience from one year to the next. Climatologists can now predict periods of prolonged wet and dry related to the global movement of ocean currents but the consequences of climate change for these kinds of global climate fluctuations is not yet known. What is known is that it is only the melting of ice sheets sitting on land masses – rather than 'sea ice' – that will raise sea levels globally and scientists fear that a steady weakening of ice sheets covering Greenland or Antarctica could eventually result in a rather dramatic collapse and a surge in ocean levels. Natural systems rarely change in a linear way and ecologists have long known that a seemingly stable ecosystem can suddenly experience a devastating 'tipping point'. We need to be prepared for the unexpected, but that runs counter to our cherished belief that scientific knowledge can gives us ever-greater certainty about how our world operates.

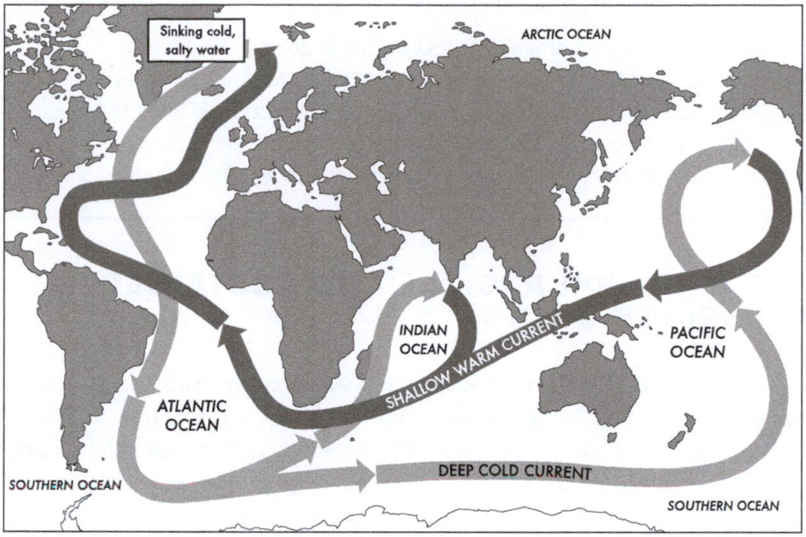

Figure 4.3 Image of ocean conveyer belt

Confidence in science is deeply embedded in western culture, even if it sometimes points to an 'inconvenient truth'.[2]

In his aforementioned book, Mike Hulme (2009) stresses that the word 'climate' is used rather loosely. We tend to think of ourselves as living in places with a particular kind of climate – be it wet, dry, humid or variable – and the perceptions, as well as the reality, influence our ways of living. Human societies have adapted to very different prevailing climates and their cultural practices, Hulme points out, are strongly influenced by those kinds of adaptations. In other words, our relationship with climate is framed by culture as much as the scientific meaning of climate and communities of people find remarkable ways to adapt to the extremes of climate that they expect to experience; whether that involves sheltering from extreme heat or extreme cold. Talking about the weather can open up communication channels and create a sense of solidarity, especially when the weather is challenging.

Tipping point: collapse of the North Atlantic cod fisheries

Ecologists have long understood that incremental changes to a self-regulating ecosystem can eventually overwhelm its capacity to adapt to the changes; it reaches a 'tipping point' at which the functioning of the system undergoes rapid change. A famous example of this occurred in the northern summer of 1992 when the Newfoundland fishing fleet caught less than 1 per cent (by biomass) of North Atlantic cod compared to previous seasons. Harvests had been falling due to overfishing of the cod during the 1960s and 1970s but no one had imagined such a dramatic collapse in fish numbers. This was a devastating blow to the centuries-old Newfoundland fishing industry with around 35,000 people in coastal communities losing their livelihoods and many people being forced to leave the province. A moratorium was imposed on catching the remaining cod and there has been a very slow recovery in numbers since. However, the collapse serves as a reminder that incremental changes can eventually lead to a rapid change.

THE CASE FOR RADICAL AND SUSTAINED EMISSIONS CUTS

While it is impossible to predict accurately how global warming affects climate systems, some trends are already clear, and broad predictions made by climate scientists are being confirmed. There is not enough space here to cover all the trends and predictions but the following suggest the need to take radical and sustained action to reduce greenhouse gas emissions.

Accumulating impacts

- Unprecedented extreme weather events, such as 'Superstorm Sandy' slamming into New York and parts of New Jersey in 2012 and regular cyclones and typhoons in the Pacific region from 2013 to 2016.
- More frequent and intense flooding events, such as those occurring in the UK in February 2014 and even more devastating flooding in Pakistan in 2010.
- More frequent and intense heatwaves, with the 2003 heatwave in Europe being responsible for an estimated 70,000 deaths.
- Increasing acidification of the oceans causing increased coral bleaching.
- Record low summer levels of sea ice in the Arctic and noticeable thinning of the massive Greenland ice shelf.

If trends continue unabated ...

- Sea level rises of ten metres or more causing extensive inundation of coastal cities and towns, including megacities such as Shanghai, Mumbai and New York.
- Inundation and **salinisation** of major food producing areas in the deltas of rivers such as the Nile in Africa and the Mekong in Asia.
- Increasing droughts threating supplies of food and freshwater, especially in Africa.
- Likely loss of all the planet's coral reefs with devastating consequences for marine biodiversity.
- Increasing extinctions for species that lose required habitat.
- Major problems for humans posed by more frequent and intense heatwaves, floods and by reduced supplies of freshwater.

salinisation refers to increasing concentrations of water soluble salts in soil which can impede plant growth.

GROUNDS FOR FRUSTRATION AND HOPE

Scientists contributing to IPCC Assessment Reports are not the only ones to feel frustrated about the slow and spasmodic policy responses to the growing risks associated with climate change. As discussed in Chapter 2, considerable expectations were invested in the outcomes of the 2009 Copenhagen Summit on climate change and the outcomes were seen as being disappointing. However, the real achievement of the Copenhagen Summit – often overlooked in the commentary – was that delegates included representatives of the rapidly developing nations – such as China and India – and also many of the small nations that are most vulnerable to climate change impacts – including small island nations in the Pacific Ocean. While China is continuing to increase its use of coal for the generation of electricity, it has also set relatively ambitious targets for reducing its greenhouse gas emissions and by 2012 it had become the largest producer of solar panels and wind turbines in the world. As also discussed in Chapter 2, the failings of Copenhagen in 2009 stimulated intense behind-the-scenes negotiations to ensure a better outcome at the next summit held in Paris in December 2015. With the biggest greenhouse gas emitters, China and the USA, agreeing to take more resolute action before the Paris meeting convened, momentum had shifted and the Paris summit set rather ambitions climate change mitigations target for participating nations, to the obvious delight of all present when the final announcements were made.

While they continue to get disproportionate media attention, climate change deniers and sceptics are rapidly losing their influence and all national governments now agree that action must be taken to reduce emissions and prepare for accumulating impacts. Yet the key indicators are all still heading in the wrong direction and national policies and political rhetoric largely lack the required ambition and urgency. Weaning ourselves off fossil fuel dependency is the biggest change humanity has been obliged to make and even when emissions begin to fall, global climate systems will be slow to respond; a prolonged period of climate volatility is already locked in. However, just as incremental accumulations can trigger 'tipping points' in the behaviour of natural systems, global action on climate change will gather momentum and our ability to act resolutely in times of crisis will come to the fore. As was shown with the international campaign to end human slavery, action can grow rapidly when inaction becomes morally repugnant.

Expect the unexpected!

When Hurricane Katrina struck New Orleans in August 2005, it overwhelmed the city's defences with over 50 breaches of the hurricane defence levees. Around 80 per cent of the city was flooded and over 80 per cent of residents were evacuated. The final death toll was put at 1,464. Hurricanes are certainly not unexpected in New Orleans because the records show that 49 hurricanes have hit the coast of Louisiana between 1851 and 2004. However, the intensity of the storm surge that came with Katrina took authorities and residents by surprise and preparations for such an event proved to be woefully inadequate. The authorities and residents of New York, by contrast, had not even imagined that they could be in the path of a major hurricane, so the shock was even greater when 'Superstorm Sandy' slammed into the city and nearby areas in October 2012 destroying homes and businesses and flooding parts of the New York subway and most of the city's road tunnels. The massive storm surge caused an estimated $US68 billion in damage and the final death toll was 44. Sandy emerged out of the largest Atlantic hurricane on record yet technically it became a 'superstorm' rather than a 'hurricane' when the core cooled before making landfall. Nobody expects hurricanes in New York and the definition of what it was only added to the surprise and confusion. IPCC Assessment Reports have repeatedly warned that 'extreme weather events' will become more common and more intense and, as Sandy demonstrated, they may hit where they have rarely hit before.

RETHINKING CLIMATE CHANGE RESPONSES

James Hansen's 1988 call to contain the concentration of greenhouse gases in the upper atmosphere to less than 350 ppm focused attention squarely on strategies for reducing greenhouse gas emissions and the need to significantly reduce our reliance on 'fossil fuels', either by using them much more efficiently and frugally or by finding alternative sources of energy. This inevitably puts the focus on new or alternative technologies and it became popular to talk about the creation of 'carbon neutral' households, neighbourhoods, towns, cities and farms. This kind of work and effort is clearly very important, both to reduce greenhouse gas emissions and move away from a dangerous dependence on fossil fuels. Furthermore, the targets set by Hansen have provided a valuable focus for what needs to be done, even if we have already passed 350 ppm and it seems increasingly difficult to contain the temperature rise to less than 2°C. Scientists warn that the impacts of rising temperatures are not linear and the impacts would be much less if the rise is kept to around 1.5°C or 1.6°C rather than 2°C and significant declines in emissions can still reduce the concentrations below 350 ppm. However, the focus on Hansen's targets keeps discussion on mitigation focused on avoiding 'dangerous' climate change to come rather than dealing with changes already under way. The overwhelming focus on mitigation has overshadowed the need to also consider what climate change adaptation requires. It has also taken attention away from the discussions we need to have the beliefs and assumptions that have enabled us to ignore warnings about our global environmental impacts for so long. A focus on technological innovation encourages the belief that the responsibility lies with 'experts' or policy-makers rather than with the public at large.

Mike Hulme's thought-provoking book (2009) argues that climate change is no longer a problem for scientists or experts because the barriers to effective action are largely cultural. At the same time, he argues that climate change can also be seen as a kind of opportunity to open up meaningful dialogues about problematic cultural beliefs and practices and the need to make radical changes to the ways in which we live (see the essay at the end of this chapter). The onset of global climate change can also serve to underline the work of the German sociologist Ulrich Beck on the globalisation of risk and the emergence of what he called the 'risk society' (1992). Having witnessed the secretive and patronising regime in post-Second World War East Germany, Beck was well placed to warn of the dangers of risk denial and he used the example of the 1986 Chernobyl nuclear plant accident in Ukraine and an overlapping outbreak of foot-and-mouth disease in sheep and cattle to point out that risk can no longer be contained within regional or national boundaries. We need to learn how to live with, rather than try to avoid, increased levels of risk and that will be the subject of Chapter 7.

THE WICKED PROBLEM OF GLOBAL POVERTY

In highlighting links between entrenched poverty and environmental degradation, the 1987 Brundtland Report provided extra incentives to reduce global poverty and this has been a recurring topic of conversation ever since. It featured in the outcomes of the 1992 Rio Earth Summit, it was adopted as one of the UN Millennium Development Goals (MDGs) in 2000 and it became the focus on the global 'Make Poverty History' campaign which reached its peak in 2005. Indeed the first MDG to 'eradicate extreme poverty' morphed into a more ambitious Sustainable Development Goal (SDG) in 2015; to 'end poverty in all its forms everywhere'. A convenient focus for global efforts to 'eradicate extreme poverty' between 2000 and 2015 has been the World Bank's international 'poverty line' which was for many years set at an income of less than $US1 per day before that figure was adjusted to $US1.25 per day in 2005. As we will see below, the World Bank has recently claimed that the world is on track to achieve the goal of

Photo 4.1 Poverty is rife and highly visible in countries such as India, as seen here in Kolkata
Photo by Arne Huckelheim (Wikimedia Commons)

eradicating extreme poverty – even if the 2015 target proved to be too ambitious – because of the clear decline in the number of people living below the income-related poverty line. However, the very idea of an international 'poverty line' has many critics, both because the income level has been set so low and because monetary income does not reflect numerous causes of poverty and disadvantage, such as access to adequate food and clean water supplies, access to adequate health care, safety from violence and access to education. While it is true that there has been a welcome drop globally in the number of people earning less than $US2 per day and a **Global Hunger Index** suggests a 27 per cent reduction between 2000 and 2015 in the number of people living with chronic hunger, the global spread of poverty has changed very little and the gap between extreme wealth and extreme poverty has grown. Millions of people have died in entrenched civil and transnational wars in Africa and the Middle East in recent decades and there are more refugees and 'forced migrants' on the move around the world than at any time since the Second World War. Entrenched poverty is spread very unevenly across the world and there is a lot of data suggesting that in parts of Africa and Asia, in particular, things are getting worse rather than better.

Global Hunger Index is published annually by the Washington-based International Food Policy Research Institute. It combines data on undernourishment, child mortality, child 'wasting' and child 'stunting' due to malnutrition.

The single word 'poverty' masks a complexity of forms and causes of environmental, economic and social disadvantage and some economic development strategies aimed at reducing poverty can make things worse; for example, by relocating people out of established 'illegal' slum communities with strong social networks or by actually drawing more people from rural settlements into urban 'slums' as they seek paid employment in newly established industries. Multinational corporations frequently take advantage of the fact that wages are very low and working conditions are unregulated in many 'underdeveloped' nations while 'deindustrialisation' and rising living costs are resulting in entrenched

Photo 4.2 Poverty is rife but less visible in countries such as the USA, as seen here in New York
Photo by Robert Scifo (Wikimedia Commons)

pockets of poverty and rising numbers of 'working poor' in a range of 'developed' nations, such as the USA, Greece and Spain. The fact that many more people in countries such as India and China are entering the 'consumer class' is also frequently touted as a sign that global poverty is in decline. However, as we noted in Chapter 3, increasing consumption is generating a host of new environmental and social problems.

There can be no single strategy to reduce – let alone eradicate – global poverty and the fact that economic 'development' can inadvertently increase the gap between the rich and the poor means that global poverty should be seen as a 'wicked problem' rather than one which can be 'resolved'. We also need to note here that the wicked problems of global climate change and the rising cost of oil dependency interact to make things even more difficult for poor people and communities because they are likely to be most vulnerable to things such as extreme weather events and rising food prices (caused by the rising cost of oil). Studies of homelessness in countries such as Australia, the USA and the UK reveal how easy it is for individuals, families or whole communities to fall into very difficult and challenging circumstances and this reminds us that poverty will be ever present in human societies. The hallmark of a caring and inclusive society will not be that it has succeeded in 'eradicating' poverty but that it pays constant attention to emergence and/or continuation of poverty 'traps'. At all levels from the local to the global, poverty is a perennial threat that calls for unlimited compassion and endless vigilance.

EXAMINING CLAIMS OF PROGRESS ON POVERTY REDUCTION

In March 2012, the World Bank released a report on global poverty which carried the good news that in the period from 2005 to 2008 the number of people living below the poverty line of $US1.25 per day had decreased from 1.38 billion to 1.27 billion. This news was widely welcomed in global news media with *The Economist* reporting that the world is on track to achieve UN poverty reduction targets underpinning the MDG of poverty 'eradication'. While any progress in reducing global poverty is indeed welcome, the trends reported by the World Bank are much less impressive when subjected to close scrutiny. Much of the improvement in the headline global statistic can be attributed to rapid economic growth in China alone. Furthermore, the choice of a particular income-based benchmark for poverty is rather arbitrary and the Worldwatch Institute reported in 2012 that if you lift the nominal poverty line to just $US2 per day an alarming 43 per cent of the world's people are still below this line and 70 per cent of people living in South Asia and **sub-Saharan Africa** are in that category.[3] Echoing the World Bank report on poverty reduction, the Global Hunger Index compiled by the International Food Policy Research Institute indicated that between 2000 and 2015 there had been a welcome decline of 27 per cent in the number of people living with chronic hunger. Yet this still leaves 795 million people living in hunger and recent reports from UNICEF suggest that an alarming 25 per cent of children in 'developing' nations are stunted by malnutrition and it still accounts for around 45 per cent for the deaths of children under five. While the **Sustainable Development Goals**

sub-Saharan Africa refers to a band of countries – from Mauritania to Somalia – that are located south of the Saharan desert and north of sub-tropical forests and savannahs.

Sustainable Development Goals (SDGs) are a 2015 extension of the UN's 2000 Millennium Development Goals (MDGs) which largely aimed to eradicate extreme poverty and disadvantage by 2015. Eight MDGs were expanded into 17 SDGs and they strongly reflect the principles outlined in the 1987 Brundtland Report.

(SDGs) continue with the 'no poverty' and 'zero hunger' rhetoric of the MDGs it is clear that the rhetoric is far from the reality, especially when the gap between the rich and the poor continues to grow. The Worldwatch Institute report from 2012[4] indicated that 12 per cent of global population – living mainly in North America and Western Europe – account for 60 per cent of private consumption, while a third of the world's people – living mainly in South Asia and sub-Saharan Africa – account for just 3.2 per cent of global consumption.

Of course, any successes in lifting people and communities out of poverty are welcome and there is some good news within the reports of progress emanating from the World Bank and other global agencies. The simplistic and misleading 'poverty line' indicator has been challenged by much wider indicators, such as the UN **Human Development Index**, which includes data on malnutrition, infant mortality and education levels alongside per capita income estimates. This broadening of the indicators of poverty and disadvantage is also reflected in the way in which eight MDGs became 17 SDGs 15 years later. However, indicators do not identify causes, and poverty reduction strategies continue to be underpinned by the mantra of economic growth. Access to paid employment is certainly an important factor, however for some communities, access to safe drinking water and adequate supplies of food may be even more pressing. In many parts of the world – particularly in parts of Africa, the Middle East and the Central Asia – an end to war and violent conflict is an essential precondition for doing anything about rising poverty. People need to have a reasonable level of physical security before they can even think about their employment prospects. The growing refugee crisis means that international humanitarian relief agencies are now obliged to focus more of their attention and resources on people living in refugee camps while their wider focus is shifting to priorities such as water security rather than paid employment. Perhaps the best critique of the narrow approaches adopted by the World Bank and other international agencies on poverty reduction has emerged from the **Wuppertal Institute** in Germany, where they take the link between the social and environmental dimensions of the problem as their starting point (see Sachs and Santarius 2007).

Human Development Index was first proposed by Pakistani economist Mahbud ul Haq in 1990 as a way to add indicators related to health and education opportunities to the single index for per capita income. It was adopted by the United Nations in the early 1990s and uses date on life expectancy, education achievements and per capita income.

Wuppertal Institute for Climate, Environment and Energy is an independent research centre that works with a number of German universities. Wuppertal is located in the Wupper Valley not far from the large city of Dusseldorf; the institute was set up in 1991.

Even when attention turns to income generation for poor people and communities, the definition of income is often too narrow because household 'livelihoods' can depend on non-cash components, such as food or other forms of exchange. While the World Bank and other international agencies focus on incomes, most humanitarian agencies work with a much broader definition of 'livelihoods'. The author was a lead researcher on a research project focusing on social recovery from the 2004 tsunami disaster in Sri Lanka and southern India (see Mulligan and Nadarajah 2012) and this highlighted the fact that people living in poor communities are commonly obliged to find a range of strategies to sustain their households. This might include growing and swapping food and other 'informal' trade in non-monetised goods and services. In many cases monetised income only accounted for a relatively small proportion of the household 'income'. The study noted that the informal economy relies on the development and maintenance of good social networks, yet these were often disrupted when well-meaning agencies decided that the disaster victims needed to be relocated into 'more secure' new settlements.

POVERTY IN THE 'DEVELOPED' WORLD

The term 'global poverty' evokes images of starving people in Africa or slum-dwellers in countries ranging from India to Brazil. Poverty in the 'developed' world is less visible but in many cases it is no less entrenched. The Organisation for Economic Co-operation and Development (OECD), which aims to represent the interests of many of the nations with the most developed economies – excluding China, Brazil, South Korea, South Africa and India – published a report in 2009[5] indicating that in 75 per cent of 32 member countries, the gap between rich and poor had increased in the period from 2005 to 2008. The nation with the biggest economy at the time – the USA – rated third worst for the length of time that people remain trapped in poverty; rating above only Mexico and Turkey. It was no great surprise to find that Mexico had the most entrenched pockets of poverty, even though it was home to the world's richest man of the time, Carlos Sim. It was more surprising, perhaps, to find that poverty had become more entrenched in the USA, even before the onset of the Global Financial Crisis of 2008–9. Among the wealthy nations of the world, the USA has a notoriously weak social welfare system. This reflects its historic confidence in the 'trickle down' benefits of 'free market' economic development; however, the OECD report suggests that this confidence is misplaced when it comes to poverty reduction.

People and families in developed nations can fall into poverty when things go wrong, but some manage to haul themselves out of the poverty trap. However, poverty is often intergenerational because the children of poor people tend to have less access to education or to secure employment. A 2016 report, from the Australian humanitarian agency Jesuit Social Services, noted that in the state of New South Wales, nearly 50 per cent of those experiencing chronic disadvantage – on a broad range of indicators – live in just 6 per cent of the state's 'postcode' areas, indicating the existence of 'postcode poverty'. The report confirmed that whole communities could be disadvantaged by having limited access to sources of employment, education facilities, community facilities or even spaces for recreation. Affordable housing is often found in areas with poor public transport and people without motor cars often have poor access to shops and services. Different forms of disadvantage compound each other and exit routes are hard to find.

social inclusion became a policy orientation of the Blair Labour government in the UK after leader Tony Blair gave a famous speech titled 'Bringing Britain Together' in London in 1997. The government established a special Social Inclusion Unit. The government's ability to build a more inclusive society did not live up to Blair's rhetoric but the 'social inclusion agenda' had a significant influence on public policy in many other countries.

POVERTY REDUCTION STRATEGIES

Welfare payments and charity may enable people to survive but they do not offer pathways out of poverty. When he became British prime minister in 1997, Tony Blair argued for a shift in emphasis away from identifying and defining poverty to identifying barriers for stronger '**social inclusion**'. By focusing initially on factors that seem to exclude certain people and communities from opportunities available to other people and communities it may then become possible to focus on strategies for inclusion, or pathways towards greater participation. The Blair government's strategy for social inclusion focused almost entirely on removing barriers for participation in paid employment when a broader understanding of social exclusion and inclusion might have benefited many more people, families and communities. Furthermore, the government's initial enthusiasm for its social inclusion agenda slowly subsided as Blair and his senior ministers became preoccupied with other national and international challenges. However, the innovative shift in public policy showed enough potential to encourage a strategic shift of emphasis for all agencies concerned with poverty reduction.

It should also be noted that people living within poor communities are likely to have the best understanding of the various barriers to greater social inclusion. People with a detailed knowledge of a particular community will know about the community's existing coping strategies and they are best placed to determine the community's most promising 'assets'. A community development approach to poverty reduction aims to use such insider knowledge to ensure that any injection of new resources is well targeted and is likely to benefit those who can turn assets into community-based enterprises. Community development workers – whether they be insiders or empathetic outsiders – can ensure that short-term assistance can have some long term benefits. A community development approach aimed at strengthening social inclusion has more chance of success than either charity or a belief in the 'trickle down' benefits of wealth accumulation. A community development approach to poverty reduction is relevant for 'developed' and 'underdeveloped' nations alike.

'Developed nations' have often accumulated wealth by exploiting the natural and human resources of nations that were once colonised by European powers. The terms 'developed' and 'underdeveloped' tell us nothing about how this distinction emerged historically and it is better to think of 'underdeveloped' nations as those in which the citizens have benefited little from the exploitation of the country's natural resources or from its wealth-generating enterprises. Rather than being seen as charity for the less fortunate, most forms of international aid should be seen as partial compensation for past and continuing exploitation and meaningful poverty reduction work should be seen as an obligation for the 'developed world'. Much more should be done at a global level to 'lift all boats' in terms of minimum pay and working conditions. Globally integrated taxation arrangements could ensure that multinational corporations are obliged to reinvest in the nations from which they have been able to generate their wealth.

As mentioned above, climate change and the rising cost of oil will impact most heavily on poor communities and on frail people. Poor people – often living in rather flimsy housing in crowded settlements – tend to be most highly exposed to floods, droughts and extreme weather events while the elderly and frail suffer the most from heatwaves and floods. The poor are obviously most vulnerable to the impacts of rising prices and poor nations lack the resources to reduce oil dependency and adopt low-carbon technologies. Growth industries of the future include international aid and disaster management and this work needs to be done well to prevent a growth in social and economic exclusion and consequent increases in tension and conflict.

SHIFTING THE EMPHASIS TO ADAPTIVE CAPACITY

Big global challenges – such as climate change and global poverty – remind us all that we live in a risky and uncertain world and the risks are increasing. Climate scientists have argued that we are entering a new phase in the history of life on Earth and that history is becoming an unreliable guide for what may lie ahead. We need to be prepared for the unexpected and this implies that we need to be more adaptable and resilient, both individually and collectively. If the future is becoming less predictable, then adaptation becomes a matter of being able to cope with the unexpected and the term 'adaptive capacity' is being used more widely.

As we will see in Chapter 7, adaptive capacity lies at the heart of the concept of 'resilience', which is also being applied more frequently and liberally. We can contemplate what makes some people more adaptable or resilient than others, but it is becoming increasing important to consider what can make some communities of people more resilient and this is the core concern of a community development approach to poverty reduction. In this book we are using the term 'wicked problems' to avoid the trap of thinking that the big global challenges can ever be 'resolved' or designed out of existence and we have noted that seemingly separate wicked problems – such as climate change and global poverty – interact in some dangerous ways. The concept of adaptive capacity makes the link between environmental challenges, such as climate change, and social problems, such as entrenched poverty.

Discussion questions

1. What benefits can come from thinking of big global challenges as 'wicked problems' rather than as problems to be resolved?
2. Why has the world been slow to respond to consistent messages emerging across the series of IPCC Assessment Reports since 1990?
3. Why do many climate scientists argue that history is becoming an unreliable guide for what lies ahead and what is creating greater uncertainty?
4. What do you think of Mike Hulme's suggestion that climate change presents major opportunities as well as threats for humanity?
5. What is wrong with prevailing thinking about how to measure and reduce global poverty?
6. What is meant by a 'community development' approach to poverty reduction?
7. What is meant by the term 'adaptive capacity'?
8. Is it defeatist or useful to focus on adaptive capacity?

KEY READINGS

Hopkins, Rob (2008) *The Transition Handbook: Creating Local Sustainable Communities beyond Oil Dependency*, Sydney: Finch Publishing.

Hulme, Mike (2009) *Why We Disagree About Climate Change: Understanding Controversy, Inaction and Opportunity*, Cambridge: Cambridge University Press.

IPCC (2013) *Fifth Assessment Report* (www.ipcc.ch/report/ar5/).

Sachs, Wolfgang and Tilman Santarius (eds) (2007) *Fair Future: Limited Resources, Conflicts, Security and Global Justice*, London: Zed Books.

Whitehead, Mark (2014) *Environmental Transformations: A Geography of the Anthropocene*, London: Routledge.

thematic essay

Embracing uncertainty

Professor Mike Hulme was browsing in a bookshop when he decided to write a book urging the world to let go of the desire for agreement on what to do about global climate change. He had been trying to convince the world to take more notice of climate change warnings – first as a long-standing member of East Anglia University's Climate Research Unit and then as the founding director of the highly regarded Tyndall Centre for Climate Change Research. By 2008, however, he was beginning to despair about public debates that were focusing on the accuracy, or otherwise, of climate science. Science, he noted in his book, is all about performance and contestation. It is very unusual to find the levels of consensus among scientists that have been reflected in the climate change reports emanating from the IPCC, Hulme noted, so we have to assume that human activity has changed the conditions in which we must live. However, across the course of our long history on Planet Earth, human societies have adapted to a wide array of climatic conditions and, indeed, climates have played a big role in shaping the societies and cultures that have evolved. In this sense, Hulme suggested, we need to think of climate as 'not merely a physical boundary for human action … [but a] more fluid, imaginative condition for human existence' (2009: 359).

Learning to live with more volatile climates will make us think more deeply about what we value, Hulme stressed, and we can become more conscious of our interactions with climate systems and with other forms of life on Earth. Describing himself as a person with 'orthodox Christian beliefs' and 'democratic socialist political preferences' (ibid.: xxxiv), Hulme called for more open conversations about climate change which would enable us all to rethink our core values and beliefs in a spirit of renewed tolerance. We have more capacity to adapt to change than we tend to believe, Hulme argued, and for this reason climate change could become as 'an imaginative resource which can be made to work for us' (ibid.: 359). However, we have to get beyond thinking of it as a scientific or technical problem to be solved; rather we have to 'harness the full array of human sciences, artistic and spiritual endeavours … civic and political pursuits' (ibid.: 362).

Geographers, psychologists and political scientists have turned their attention to the social, cultural and political challenges posed by the growing realities of climate change (see Moser and Dilling 2007; Lever-Tracy 2010; Urry 2011; Whitmarsh *et al.* 2011). Mostly they have been focusing on ways of moving from fear to action and on ways of talking about the challenges that might engage the public more fully. Sociologist John Urry (2011) has suggested that social scientists have been slow to grapple with the problems of fossil fuel dependency, imaging that this was not within their domain. We now have to use our imagination to contemplate the possibilities of various kinds of catastrophes, on the one hand, but also the possibilities of 'post-carbon' societies, on the other. To move in the latter direction, Urry argued, we need to work out how to 'embed' low carbon systems within a wide array of social contexts (ibid.: 160).

Imagination will play a big role in enabling us to deal with climate change impacts and put in place new low-carbon systems. In this regard we might take our lead from people who have particular skills in imagining what it might be like to face up to previously unimagined challenges; people such as creative writers, visual artists, film-makers. The Nobel Prize-winning writer J. M. Coetzee has said that fiction writers commonly imagine how humans might manage to deal with deep physical or moral challenges and he suggested that this is achieved through 'pure writerly attentiveness, pure submission to the experiences of a world which, through being submitted to in a state close to spiritual absorption, becomes transfixed, real' (cited in Lamb 2010: 177). Those of us living in relatively comfortable western societies can learn a lot about adaptability and resilience from the experiences of people living within poor communities. For example, living poor in the Indian city of Mumbai must be one of the biggest challenges of all and the beautifully written novels of Rohinton Mistry (*Such a Long Journey*, 1991; *A Fine Balance*, 1995; *Family Matters*, 2002) take the reader on an emotional roller-coaster ride through the depths of despair and the triumphs of the human spirit. Ultimately there is something wonderful about the capacity of some humans to cope with adversity in all its guises.

NOTES

1 Hulme (2009: 364).
2 The term used for the title of an influential 2006 film about climate change narrated by former US Vice President Al Gore.
3 See www.worldwatch.org/node/81
4 Ibid.
5 The OECD report was entitled *Growing Unequal* (www.oecd.org/els/soc/41527936.pdf).

CHAPTER 5

Energy and society

Anthony Richardson and Martin Mulligan

Key concepts and concerns

- Peak Oil
- energy-driven complexity
- environmental and social costs of high energy consumption
- energy investment for food production
- pathways out of oil dependency
- relocalisation

INTRODUCTION

Ready access to sources of energy is obviously of critical importance to all living things and the ultimate source of energy for life on Planet Earth is our sun. Animals rely on the capacity of plants to trap solar energy in order to produce complex compounds made of carbon, hydrogen and oxygen atoms which then serve as the fuel for animal bodily functions through the processes of digestion. At the same time, systems theory recognises that energy is a fundamental component of all complex systems, including those designed and maintained by humans. We have learnt how to burn plant material to produce heat energy and this has extended to using fossilised plant material – in the form of coal, oil and associated gases – to produce the heat that can be turned into electricity or used to drive motor vehicles. Just as animal digestion and metabolism produces unused heat and waste materials, the burning of **fossil fuels** gives off 'excess' heat and the gas emissions known to produce the global greenhouse effect. In other words, there are always 'by-products' arising from the generation of energy and some of them can be hazardous to life. The discovery of the greenhouse effect, discussed in Chapter 4, has stimulated the effort to find less polluting sources of energy for human consumption, including solar energy, 'geothermal' heat and wind power. This search is also driven by the knowledge that the planet's stocks of 'fossil fuels' is ultimately finite while solar energy and wind power, in particular, are in unlimited supply and hence constantly 'renewable'. There is some controversy over what really constitutes 'renewable' energy – given that all **energy generation**

fossil fuels are fossilised plant material (hydrocarbons) that take the form of coal, oil and natural gas.

energy generation refers to the creation or renewal of the ability to produce action.

produces forms of waste – and there is little prospect that humans will accomplish a wholesale shift to the use of non-polluting energy sources any time soon. However, the dangers associated with the use of fossil fuels – including the devastating impacts that oil spills can have on marine and coastal ecosystems – are forcing us to think more deeply about how to meet our energy needs in environmentally sustainable ways.

The 'spectre' of Peak Oil was listed in Chapter 4 as being one of the growing 'wicked problems' of global sustainability. So much of what we do is driven by the burning of fossil fuels – from our modes of transport to modern methods for producing food – and so many of the plastic products that we use every day are 'by-products' of the petrochemical industry that it is very hard indeed to imagine how we might be able to wean ourselves off our oil dependency. This is undoubtedly why the notion of Peak Oil, that was first articulated by US geophysicist M. King Hubbert in the late 1950s, has been widely dismissed as being unnecessarily alarmist. However, it is important to remember that Hubbert's warning was not based on the assumption that oil supplies are about to dry up, but rather that the cost of accessing enough oil to satisfy the growing demand for it would lead to oil shortages and big increases in oil prices. The Peak Oil warning refers to the availability of 'cheap oil' and this chapter will make it clear that the prediction Hubbert made for the production and consumption of oil in the USA is now playing out on a global scale.

Hubbert's Peak Oil prediction

Marion King Hubbert (1903–89) was a geoscientist who worked for Shell Oil at its research lab in Houston, Texas. He is most famous for his theory that the amount of petroleum produced – whether from an individual oil field, a country or the planet as a whole – will, over time, resemble a bell curve. That is, it will increase at first, level off when approximately half the oil has been extracted, and then decline.

In 1956 he presented a famous paper to a meeting of the American Petroleum Institute which brought the concept of Peak Oil to a wide audience. In this paper he predicted that overall petroleum production in the USA would peak some time between the late 1960s and the early 1970s. While at first he was ridiculed for this prediction he became famous when it was in fact proved correct in 1970; the year oil production in the USA peaked and started the decline which has continued to this day. The Peak Oil bell curve that Hubbert drew in 1956 has become rather iconic (see Figure 5.1).

Source: https://www.princeton.edu/hubbert/the-peak.html

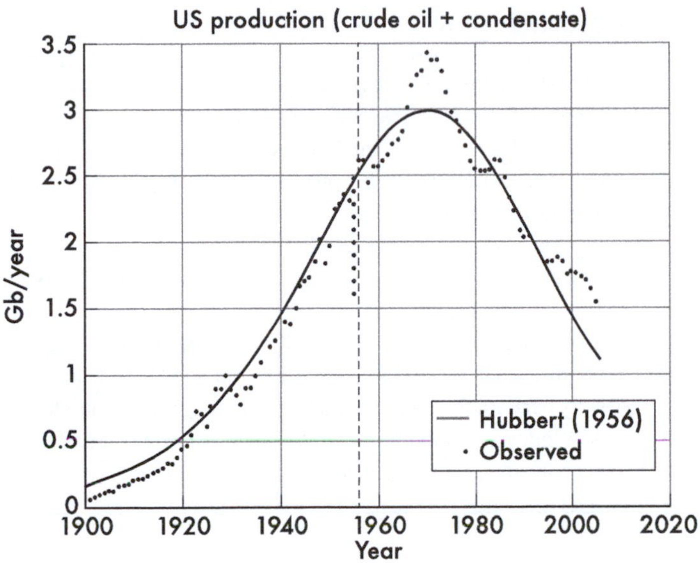

Figure 5.1 Hubbert's prediction compared to observed US oil production

While Hubbert's core prediction has been vindicated, he could not have anticipated the growth in global demand for oil and oil-based products driven by developments such the rapid growth of 'emerging economies' in countries such as China and India and the global explosion in the use of electronic devices that use a host of oil-based components. Nor could Hubbert have predicted the rapid expansion of 'industrial agriculture' which has increased global food production but at the cost of accelerating energy use. Tainter and Patzek (2012) have pointed out that the growing complexity of our systems is designed to satisfy the needs and demands of human consumption, but it is resulting in an ever-diminishing return on energy invested. This dynamic will be explained later in this chapter. The **Energy Return on Investment (EROI)** on all our energy consumption is declining.

Energy Return on Investment (EROI) is a measure of the inputs of energy required to generate energy, expressed as a ratio.

Declining efficiency in the use of energy makes the problem of oil dependency even greater, but it also raises serious questions about the benefits of being locked into a spiral of increasing energy use. If the growing complexity in the ways in which we meet the demands of consumption is reducing our energy efficiency then it might be time to simplify some of those systems again. We will explore this possibility by focusing on the topic of food production and consumption which was raised in Chapter 2 and which will be discussed further in Chapter 14. If it is not only a matter of switching from our current dependency on oil and other fossil fuels to the use of 'renewable' energy sources but also a matter of working out how to reduce our total energy consumption and use it much more efficiently, then we are obliged to rethink many of our assumptions and practices in areas such as transport and food production. A focus on energy brings us back to the notion of 'relocalisation' that was raised in Chapter 2 and will be discussed further in Chapter 9.

Startling statistics

1. Google's 'data centres' use an average of 260 million watts each; enough to power a city of 100,000–200,000 people.
2. A gallon of petrol is the energy equivalent of a person working 400 hours, while a bottle of petrol provides energy equivalent to about 50 people pushing a small modern car for two hours.
3. Gathering roots for food produces 30–40 units of food energy for every unit of energy invested, while industrial agriculture produces one unit of food energy for every ten invested.
4. In modern industrialised agriculture only one-fifth of the energy cost is actually involved in agriculture, with the rest going towards transport, processing, packaging, marketing, and food preparation and storage.
5. In the USA today, less than 5 per cent of food is locally produced and it travels an average of 1,500 miles before being consumed.

ENERGY AND 'PROGRESS'

We have to begin with the inescapable fact that energy is the crucial component of our complex, highly urbanised and industrial (or 'post-industrial') societies. Research by Brown *et al.* (2011) shows that there are direct connections between energy use and indicators of social development, including life expectancy, infant mortality, doctors per 100,000 people, Nobel prizes per head of population, and even levels of meat consumption. Without easy access to dependable and ever-increasing supplies of energy we could not lead the lives that we do.

This is not a recent development because energy has always been the bedrock on which social developments have been based. Ancient societies were built on the use of solar energy – i.e. photosynthesis for crops and wood for construction and fire – yet by the mediaeval era developments in metallurgy required huge amounts of charcoal to produce machinery, weaponry and other technological artefacts. This appetite for charcoal accelerated the deforestation of Europe, which had been continuing since the classical Greek period. A solution to this 'Peak Wood' situation was only provided by the switch to a new, and much more concentrated, form of hydrocarbon energy: coal.

Accessible and plentiful coal supplies and the development and widespread use of steam-powered machinery – including steam-powered water pumps that enabled coal mines to be dug deeper than before – ushered in the Industrial Revolution and the start of our modern lifestyles. The use of Thomas Newcomen's steam-powered water pump in coal mines illustrates the interplay between the use of energy and the development of new technologies.[1] This interplay is also seen in the invention and use of the internal combustion engine because while early models of the engine were invented as early as the seventeenth century it was not until oil became widely available that the use of the internal combustion engines became widespread. From the first 'horseless carriages' to the modern car, oil-driven ships and powered flight, the internal combustion engine has transformed our lives and our settlement patterns.

Photo 5.1 The age of oil has resulted in an explosion of motor vehicle use and widespread traffic congestion in major cities, such as Mexico City
© Eye Ubiquitous/Alamy

ENERGY AND ECONOMIC GROWTH

Connected to the cherished idea of progress is the largely unchallenged belief in unlimited economic growth, conventionally measured as GDP growth. Yet economic growth is absolutely dependent on energy and so belief in economic growth implies an ability to *increase* the supply and use of energy. Figure 5.2 shows the connection between energy and GDP.

While it is impossible to attribute fluctuations in global financial markets to specific causes, Tverberg (2012) has noted that the Global Financial Crisis of

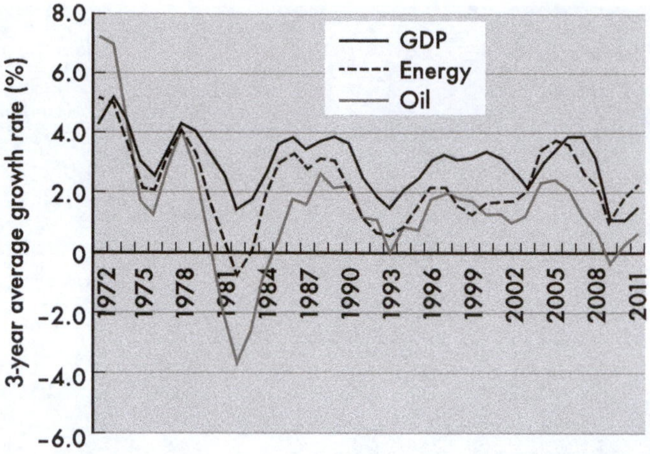

Figure 5.2 World growth in GDP, energy and oil

2008–9 followed the 2007–8 surge in global oil prices. Given the centrality of oil for all forms of production and transport, rising oil prices increase inflation and this, in turn, deflates public spending. Like wood in mediaeval Europe, oil has become the critical energy source for all forms of manufacture and without cheap oil our economies would grind to a halt. While public debate has focused on the need to reduce global reliance on coal for generating electricity and petroleum products for powering motor vehicles, very few people have seriously contemplated the phasing out of plastic chairs, CDs and DVDs, foam mattresses, synthetic carpets, computers, mobile/cell phones, credit cards and most cosmetics. The production and consumption of many of these products has stimulated global economic growth and many of them influence the ways in which we think about ourselves and our interactions with other people. Weaning ourselves off oil dependency has many implications for our economies and for our prevailing cultural beliefs and practices.

CULTURAL IDEAS OF 'PROGRESS'

The link between hyperconsumption and our sense of personal wellbeing – which was discussed in Chapter 2 – helps to explain the cultural challenges posed by the need to reduce oil dependency. However, the link between energy consumption and 'progress' has even deeper historical roots in western societies. For example, our love affair with the motor car and what it represents – e.g. freedom, speed, convenience and 'modernity' – is a prime example of how energy use by industrialised human societies is also driven by sociocultural factors and the underlying idea of 'progress'. Rising to prominence during the European Enlightenment and the associated Industrial Revolution, the idea of progress has had a powerful grip on our imagination. 'You can't stop progress' has become the familiar refrain of modern societies, with the underlying assumption that progress implies an increasing complexity of social interactions and an associated increase in energy use. In other words, **energy-driven complexity** is seen as an indicator of human improvement.

energy-driven complexity refers to the consumption of increasing amounts of energy to drive increasingly complex systems, such as modern food production systems.

However the importance of energy within the equation 'complexity = progress' is implied rather than openly considered. Access to energy has not been seen as a constraint on 'progress' until the notion of Peak Oil raised its ugly head and the very idea that progress might founder on such a constraint led to an upsurge in technological optimism about our human capacity to solve problems of resource shortages. The widespread assumption that human ingenuity has always got us through crises of the past underpins the difficult-to-justify belief that we will be able to find ways to satisfy increasing global hunger for oil and oil-based products. It underpins the even more surprising belief that we will find a way to continue accessing 'cheap' hydrocarbons. For many people, the extent of change required to radically reduce oil dependency seems to be beyond comprehension and denial is the easier pathway. This suggests that the challenge now is to make the alternatives to oil dependency less scary and therefore more culturally acceptable.

FOCUSING ON FOOD

Historically, food production and energy use have been closely connected with each other and this link has, in turn, played a big role in determining forms of social organisation. At the time of the Roman Empire, for example, the estimated 60 million people living under Roman rule were fed by farms that relied on human or animal power. This continued to be the case right up until Europe's Industrial Revolution when first steam power and then the use of internal combustion engines made possible a surge in agricultural production and this, in turn, made it possible for many more people to live in cities. A steady reduction in demand for human labour in agriculture – as represented in Figure 5.3 – coincided with the increasing demand for labour in industrial manufacture and this sparked the process of urbanisation which now means that more people globally live in cities than in rural areas (see Chapter 15).

The effects of changing relationships between industry and agriculture on social, class and family structures have been immense. For example, in 1911 the

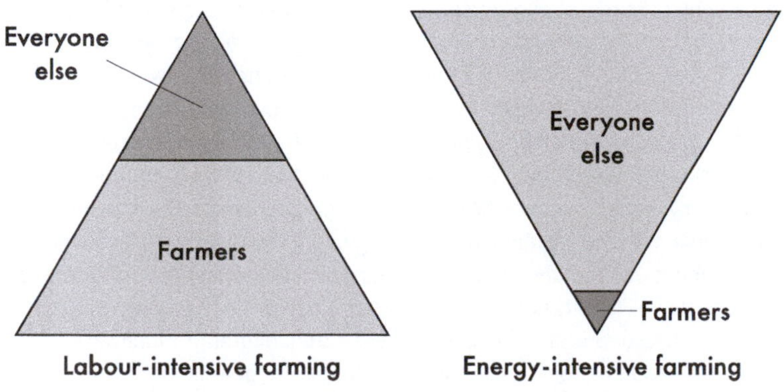

Figure 5.3 Participation in labour-intensive and energy-intensive farming
Source: Schnepf, R. (2004) Energy Use in Agriculture: Background and Issues, CRS Report for Congress, Congressional Research Service, The Library of Congress

three largest occupations in England and Wales – in terms of numbers of employees – were domestic service, agriculture and coal mining, while in 2008 the largest categories had become sales personnel, middle managers and teachers.[2] In other words, the switch in sources of energy – from **human labour** to the use of mechanical engines – not only changed where most people live but also what they do on a daily basis.

human labour replacement the age of oil led to the increasing use of machines to replace human labour in the production of food and other goods. Dependency on external sources of energy consequently grew.

industrial farming refers to farming that relies on the intense use of machines and large-scale production processes.

The system of modern **industrial farming**, which has also grown out of the changes in energy use, is highly successful at producing more food from the same amount of agricultural land, and this has reduced the spectre of famine and undernourishment in many parts of the world (see Chapter 14). Indeed many countries have moved from conditions of food scarcity to an overabundance of food and calorie-rich diets are now causing a global epidemic in diet-related diseases such as obesity and diabetes. Hydrocarbons have replaced hard-working humans and animals and the modern farmer can do the work of many from his seat on his tractor and by using oil-based fertilisers and pesticides. By the end of the twentieth century, US farms, for example, had reached the point where 80–100 per cent of energy use came from hydrocarbons.

All this means that modern farms can produce more food per hectare of land but they use about 20 times as much energy to produce a certain quantity of food energy – i.e. calories – compared to the 'traditional', or pre-modern, farm.[3] By some calculations,[4] the US agricultural industry uses ten units of energy for every one unit of food energy it produces. This is a clear example of falling returns on energy investment: from 30 units of energy for every one unit invested, to one-tenth of a unit of energy for every unit invested. Another way to put this is that modern farming has intensified food production but in doing so it has increased its rather dangerous dependence on hydrocarbon energy.

ENVIRONMENTAL AND SOCIAL COSTS OF COMPLEX FOOD PRODUCTION SYSTEMS

Just as the *production* of food has become more intense, complex and dependent on a particular source of energy, so too has the global *distribution* of food. While modern food distribution systems have become highly efficient they have become incredibly expensive in terms of energy use. According to Brown (2008),[5] only 20 per cent of the energy used to put our food on our plate is actually used for production because the other 80 per cent is used for transport, processing, packaging, marketing, preparation and storage. Industrial farming and modern food distribution systems achieve efficiencies through economies of scale and speed. However, this has also resulted in increasing use of fertilisers and pesticides and the tendency towards monocultural farming, which has disastrous long-term consequences for soil fertility and biodiversity (see Chapter 14). More recently, genetic engineering has been introduced to increase agricultural productivity but there can be unforeseen dangers in tampering with natural genetic diversity.

Industrial food production and distribution systems have been modelled on other globalised forms of production and distribution in that they have become both energy-intensive and highly efficient. Efficiency depends on speed and the implementation of 'just in time' principles for responding to market needs. However, all this is predicated on the assumption that energy derived from fossil fuels will continue to be cheap and readily available. Surges in global oil prices – like the one that occurred in 2007–8 – quickly flow through to price increases for food and this has particularly serious consequences for poor people and poor communities. The underlying global oil price has climbed steadily in recent decades – despite a drop during the Global Financial Crisis of 2008–9 – and this is increasing food vulnerability for many.

Globally integrated food production systems have reduced some of the localised food shortages of the past. However, the tendency to reduce genetic diversity in search of production efficiency and the heavy reliance on cheap sources of energy make these systems more vulnerable than most people realise. Cuba was one country which experienced this vulnerability in a sharp way when the collapse of the Soviet Union in the late 1980s deprived Cuba of its access to cheap oil (see box). The problem is not entirely new because a recent study by Northrop and Connor[6] has argued that monocrop production and a reduction in genetic diversity was responsible for the disastrous Irish Potato Famine of 1845. When Irish potato crops were devastated by an infestation of a particular strain of potato blight, the authors point out, nearly all of the potatoes were of one type only – known as the Irish Lumper – and about one-third of the people in Ireland were dependent on this one species for their sustenance. Around one million people died of starvation when their dangerous dependence on a single food source failed them and another million people emigrated to other parts of the world. Food vulnerability today is less likely to be caused by heavy reliance on a particular local food source. However, the risk of crop failures persists and the heavy reliance on cheap hydrocarbons for food transport has introduced a new kind of spatially dispersed vulnerability.

BACK TO HUBBERT'S PREDICTION

Hubbert's famous 1956 bell curve of oil production and demand was based on the assumption that production always lags behind the discovery of new sources and that for any particular oil field or area the peak of production is reached when the volume used has reached the halfway point. The peak of the curve is thus the point at which demand for oil outstrips the ability to produce it at reasonable cost and *not* the point at which supplies begin to dry up. A study of long-term trends shows that US oil production did indeed peak around 1970 with the amount of oil produced in the US declining every year since. Of course, the difference can be made up by importing oil from elsewhere in the world but the same dynamic applies on a global scale and the problem is exacerbated by the fact that increasing global demand is forcing producers to tap into smaller, more remote and lower-quality supplies. Production declines have been recorded across nearly all the oil producing nations and Hubbert's prediction now has a global dimension.

While Hubbert's concept of Peak Oil has been ridiculed by many in the oil industry, it has been taken seriously by organisations ranging from particular oil companies to the Pentagon. Steady increases in the global price of oil confirm that the **age of cheap oil** is coming to an end and debate has largely shifted to when, rather than if, the world will begin to experience a steady decline in oil

the age of oil, first coal and then oil have become the dominant source of energy for human systems since the Industrial Revolution in Europe. For two centuries, oil proved to be a readily available and cheap source of energy. However, the cost of accessing oil is steadily growing.

production and a consequent surge in prices. Oil industry advocates insist that supplies are still keeping pace with growing global demand but what they forget to add is that extraction costs are trending upwards.

Trends in oil production do not follow the smooth curve of prediction. Many factors other than supply affect demand for oil and prices fluctuate with the ups and downs of demand. The 2008–9 Global Financial Crisis, for example, led to a fall in both oil use and demand and a consequent reduction in oil prices.[7] However, this led to job losses in the oil industry and a loss of investment and falls in production as many potential sources of oil were not viable at the lower price.[8] The resulting lower production, along with the end of the Global Financial Crisis and increasing global demand driven by rapid industrialisation in countries such as China, India and, to a lesser extent, Brazil and Indonesia, has meant that the prices have resumed their upward trend. Wars have already been fought over access to oil in the Persian Gulf region and competition for supplies is creating conflict zones in Nigeria, South Sudan and in the Caucasus.

Cuba experiences Peak Oil

Cuba provides a well-known example of just how dependent modern farming is on inputs of hydrocarbon energy. When the Soviet Union collapsed in the late 1980s, Cuba no longer had access to cheap subsidised oil from the USSR and agricultural production more than halved. Studies by Borowy (2013) and Cruz and Medina (2003) have shown that calorie intakes fell to dangerous levels – especially for the frail – and the threat of widespread famine forced a rapid and radical change in Cuban agriculture. Without cheap oil the production of sugar for export became economically unviable and this coincided with the need to expand the production of food for local communities. This created new opportunities for family-owned or small communal farms and a big effort went into opening up a new sector of urban farming. Without access to cheap fertilisers and pesticides the emphasis also shifted to organic farming and urban permaculture. Premat (2005: 171) has estimated that as much as 60 per cent of the vegetables consumed in Havana were being grown within the boundaries of the city. While the overall level of calories consumed by Cubans remains lower than in the 'developed' world – and the diet has become much less varied – Cruz and Medina show that calorie intakes have stabilised at a higher levels than at the height of the oil crisis. Borowy adds that there have also been reductions in rates of obesity, heart disease and diabetes. Of course, Cuba did not choose to reduce its dependence on access to cheap oil but its ability to survive the crisis fairly well offers some hope for a world facing the spectre of Peak Oil.

Photo 5.2 A man works in an urban garden in Havana, October 2008. Cuba's urban agriculture movement, developed in the 1990s as a response to the food crisis after the collapse of its former benefactor the Soviet Union, provides over 50 per cent of the vegetables that Cubans eat © Enrique De La Osa/Reuters

ENERGY RETURN ON INVESTMENT

At its most simple level the idea of Peak Oil relates to the human tendency to exhaust supplies of resources that are easiest to reach. This tendency plays out when children set out on an Easter egg hunt or when adults rush into a store to take advantage of a bargain sale. An even better analogy is when a camping site becomes

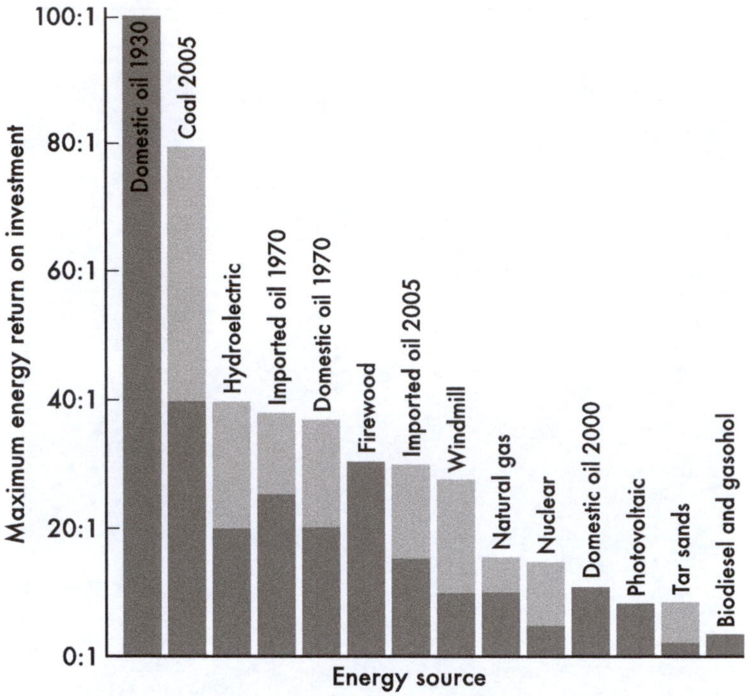

Figure 5.4 Energy return on investment
Source: adapted from C. Hall and J. Day (2009) 'Revisiting the Limits to Growth after Peak Oil', *American Scientist* 97: 230–7

popular and campers have to go further and further to fetch firewood. In this case, the absolute supply is not exhausted but more effort, energy and money must be expended to access more remote, and often more technically difficult, supplies.

This rather basic principle has led to work on what is known as energy return on [energy] invested, or EROI. This involves the calculation of how much energy it costs to utilise a particular energy source and the results are revealing. For example, Figure 5.4 suggests that at the beginning of the era of cheap oil the USA was able to obtain 100 barrels of oil for every barrel of oil required to access and process that oil; producing an EROI of 100:1. By 1970 the EROI on domestic oil in the USA had fallen to less than 40:1 and by the end of the twentieth century it had fall further to 15:1. This trend reflects an increasing reliance on offshore and deep water oil drilling because it is more difficult and expensive to operate offshore and the operations are more exposed to disruption caused by bad weather.

EROI ratings for energy sources other than hydrocarbons commonly show, perhaps counter-intuitively, that the return on investment tends to be higher even if the total energy output is not as high. Coal, for example, scores a relatively high EROI rating because the cost involved in digging up coal reserves is fairly low. This probably explains the ongoing attraction of coal even though the burning of coal for electricity is seen as being a major contributor to the generation of greenhouse gases.

EROI ratings have their limitations; for example, controversy has raged over whether or not the expensive storage of nuclear waste should be taken into account in calculating the EROI of nuclear power sources. However, they do give new urgency to the concept of Peak Oil and highlight the need to radically reduce oil dependency.

EXTENDING THE CHASE FOR HYDROCARBONS

The growing problem of dwindling oil supplies has resulted in a rather desperate effort to find and exploit 'untapped' supplies and to make the oil go further by adding supplements. The effort involves drilling into ever deeper seas, squeezing oil out of low-grade sources such as **tar sands** or shale, '**fracking**' and extracting gas from extensive coal seams, and using biofuels such as **ethanol** as a supplement. Some of these extraction methods are not as new as advocates might suggest. For example, extraction of oil from shale has been around for a very long time and it experienced an upsurge at the time of the First World War. For a long time **shale oil** extraction was not worth the investment but growing global demand for oil has brought similar operations back online and this extends to renewed efforts to extract natural gas from shale rock. However, 'fracking' – i.e. extraction of natural gas from deep layers of shale rock by injecting water under very high pressure to create fissures that allow the gas to escape – is a very disruptive practice and the hunt for **coal seam gas** is an extensive process for tapping small deposits which is competing with agricultural land use in many areas. A massive tar sands operation in Alberta, Canada, has led to extensive clear-felling of native forests and the pollution of waterways.[9] The EROI rating for tar sand oil extraction is very low and the social and environmental costs for energy return both seem very high. While concerns about tar sand oil extraction are obvious, the environmental and social impacts of the other, extended, forms of oil mining are less visible but no less worrying.

The explosion and fire that destroyed the Deepwater Horizon oil rig in the Gulf of Mexico in April 2010 caused one of the world's worst environmental disasters of all time with nearly five million barrels of oil spilling into the sea and washing up on the coast of Mississippi and Louisiana. Deepwater Horizon is located in deep sea – 1,259 metres – and it is 400 kilometres south-east of Houston. It might seem that distance from human settlements would make this a relatively safe industrial operation. However, 11 workers died in the explosion and oil gushed into the sea for 87 days before the broken well could be successfully capped. The extensive oil slick damaged marine and coastal environments and the coastal and estuarine fishing industry in Louisiana. Tar balls were still washing up on the coast three years after the explosion. The disaster exposed the dangers of drilling in deep water and yet Brazil, in particular, has plans for even deeper water drilling.

The use of biofuels to supplement or even replace oil and gas would seem to be environmentally benign. However, a growing global market for ethanol has resulted in deforestation and the conversion of productive farmland for sugarcane production in countries such as Brazil or corn production in the USA.

PATHWAYS OUT OF OIL DEPENDENCY

Efforts are being made to increase the use of **renewable energy** sources such as solar, wind and geothermal power. Countries ranging from China to Germany

tar sands (also known as 'oil sand') refers to loose sand that contains bitumen, which is a viscous form of petroleum.

fracking refers to the process of injecting water under high pressure into deep layers of shale rock in order to create fissures for release natural gas embedded in the rock into collecting wells.

ethanol and biofuels, ethanol – or ethyl alcohol – is a volatile and flammable alcohol that can be extracted from starches and sugars. It is the best-known of a range of 'biofuels' which are fuels extracted from living organisms.

shale oil refers to the extraction of liquid hydrocarbons from shale rock; a different form of hydrocarbon to 'crude oil' or petroleum found in naturally occurring oil deposits.

coal seam gas refers to any deposits of gas trapped within coal seams. Efforts are increasing to tap into such deposits associated with coal seams which may not be big enough to support coal mining.

renewable energy relates to using sources of energy that are in unlimited supply – such as solar power or wind energy – and which do not result in the emission of greenhouse gases.

have set ambitious targets for the proportion of base-load electricity emanating from renewable sources by 2020[10] and efforts have gone into the development of solar-powered or hybrid motor vehicles. Efforts are being made to defeat car dependency in many cities around the world, with Copenhagen continuing to lead the way. However, it is very difficult to even imagine a future without hydrocarbon motor vehicles or without all the other products emanating from the petrochemical industry. Imagine a world, for example, in which it was either very difficult or very expensive to travel significant distances for work or leisure or to have access to food and goods imported from distant parts of the world. John Urry (2011) has suggested that we may learn to rely on communication technologies to maintain our sense of belonging to the world at large even when physical mobilities have become constrained. However, the transition to 'post-carbon' economies and ways of living is not likely to be that easy. It will require major changes in assumptions, beliefs and practices. In other words, economic and social transition require cultural changes that have barely been considered to date.

Cuba provides an important example because it was forced to shift away from oil dependency when the Soviet Union collapsed (see box). At a global level, the promotion of urban agriculture has been part of the international 'permaculture movement' since the 1980s and many cities around the world are trying to facilitate urban agriculture. The need to reduce '**food miles**' has been circulating in sustainability literature since it was introduced by Tim Lane of the UK's Sustainable Agriculture Food and Environment (SAFE) Alliance in the early 1990s. The focus on reducing 'food miles' has been branded as simplistic by food and agriculture writers who argue that transport is only one aspect of food production that needs to be rethought. A wider focus on 'localising' food production has been promoted by the international **Transition Towns** movement, initiated by permaculture practitioner Rob Hopkins.[11] Furthermore, the growing popularity of 'farmers' markets' – especially in the USA – suggests that the desire to eat 'fresh' food that has not been transported and stored for any length of time is gaining some momentum.[12] Indeed, the concept of 'relocalisation' has begun to move out of the popular literature on sustainability and into more scholarly discourses and we will return to this topic in Chapter 8.

food miles refers to the distance travelled by food items or components from where they originated as agricultural products to where they are consumed as food products.

Transition Towns refers to an international network initiated in 2005 by UK-based permaculture designer Rob Hopkins; it aims to make particular towns or settlements much more self-sufficient in terms of energy use and food and water consumption.

However, oil dependency needs to be seen as a 'wicked problem' with no easy or single 'solution'. First, we need to fully understand that some level of complexity is valuable: our technological advances have allowed us to improve our lives immensely. At the same time however, dependency on cheap oil has come at considerable environmental cost and globalisation has come at considerable social cost as well. As John Urry (2011) has argued, we do not need to dispense with all the benefits of globalisation in order to reduce carbon dependency but we will need to make substantial social and cultural changes to reduce our dangerous dependence on hydrocarbons. This will undoubtedly require a degree of 'relocalisation' of economic and social life – especially in the global north.

Discussion questions

1 Why has human society become so oil dependent?
2 What are some of the environmental and social costs of oil dependency?
3 Why is the link between energy consumption and 'progress' problematic?
4 Why are Hubbert's warnings about Peak Oil still relevant?
5 Why do we need to think more about expenditure of energy for food production?
6 What can be done to make food production more sustainable?
7 What are some of the costs involved in extending the search for hydrocarbons?
8 Why should we think of oil dependency as a 'wicked problem'; what are some of the implications of radically reducing oil dependency?
9 What is meant by the concept of 'relocalisation'?

KEY READINGS

Bayliss-Smith, Tim (1982) *The Ecology of Ecological Systems*, Cambridge: Cambridge University Press.

Brown, Lester (2008) *Plan B 3.0: Mobilizing to Save Civilization*, New York: W. W. Norton.

Pfeiffer, Dale Allen (2006) *Eating Fossil Fuels: Oil, Food and the Coming Crisis in Agriculture*, Gabriola Island, BC: New Society.

Tainter, Joseph (1990) *The Collapse of Complex Societies*, Cambridge: Cambridge University Press.

Tainter, Joseph and Tadeusz Patzek (2012) *Drilling Down: The Gulf Oil Debacle and Our Energy Dilemma*, New York: Copernicus/Springer.

Tverberg, Gail (2012) 'Oil Supply Limits and the Continuing Financial Crisis', *Energy*, 37: 27–34.

Urry, John (2011) *Climate Change and Society*, Cambridge: Polity.

Energy, thermodynamics and complexity

thematic essay

Modern science explains the concept of **entropy** through the Second Law of Thermodynamics which states that 'in a closed system over time energy irreversibly dissipates across energy gradients and entropy is a measurement of such dissipation'. In layperson's terms this means that concentrations of energy inevitably disperse, much as a glass of hot water (removed from any other sources of energy) will eventually cool to room temperature over time as the energy irreversibly dissipates into the surroundings. The famous physicist Arthur Eddington called this the 'arrow of time' – i.e. it goes in just one direction – towards dissipation. This inescapable law has consequences for our use of

entropy refers to the steady dissipation of energy across energy gradients.

Ilya Prigogine (1917–2003) was born in Moscow just before the Russian Revolution. His family left Russia in 1921 to live first in Germany and then Belgium where Ilya became a professor of chemistry at Brussels University. He was awarded the Nobel Prize for Chemistry in 1977 for his work on 'dissipative structures' that maintain themselves in a 'far from equilibrium' state.

Joseph Tainter (b. 1949) was trained in anthropology at the University of California, Berkeley, before going on to become a professor in the Department of Environment and Society at Utah State University. His best-known work is *The Collapse of Complex Societies* (1990) which examined causes for the demise of several ancient societies.

energy to power our societies; the phrase 'Nothing lasts forever' expresses Eddington's idea perfectly.

However, living organisms or social, technological or cultural systems do not seem to follow this law because they can seemingly sustain themselves and even become more complex over time. The solution to this apparent paradox was provided by the physicist **Ilya Prigogine**, who won the Nobel Prize in 1977 for his reformulated Second Law of Thermodynamics, commonly called 'non-equilibrium thermodynamics'. This considers complex systems – such as beehives, cities or multinational corporations – to be *open* systems that use energy from their environment to maintain or increase their ordered structure and function in some sort of steady state, 'far from equilibrium' (Prigogine 1997). However, it means that they can obtain a steady state by relying on a constant input of energy in the manner of a kettle of hot water on a stove top: unlike the glass of water on the bench, the constant heat keeps the water hot.

Starting in the first-quarter of the twentieth century, social scientists also began to think more seriously about the role of energy in the maintenance of human societies. For example, economists like Nicholas Georgescu-Roegen and Herman Daly began to focus on the limits to economic growth within systems that rely on the constant input of external sources of energy and raw materials (which also embody energy). The very idea of limits to growth is driven by an understanding of the Second Law of Thermodynamics but social scientists also began to consider the energy it takes to maintain our complex social and technological systems.

The rather iconoclastic historian **Joseph Tainter** has made a particularly important contribution to the question of complexity within human societies, starting with his idea that societies are 'problem-solving machines' which meet the challenges they face by implementing increasingly complex solutions. When faced with challenges like a famine, the need for a better-educated population, or even something as recent as the need for greater airline security following the 9/11 attacks, the response involves the creation of additional systems, such as new and extended food distribution system, greatly increased welfare systems or new security and surveillance systems at airports. A new level of complexity is added without necessarily solving the problem, yet the new systems then need to be sustained. According to Tainter (1990: 91):

> Energy flow and socio-political organisation are opposite sides of an equation … Not only is energy flow required to maintain a socio-political system, but the amount of energy must be sufficient for the complexity of that system.

However our complex societies are also subject to the Law of Diminishing Returns; the tendency for the return on investment in increasing complexity to decline over time. Here we can refer to the investment of both time and energy that is required to maintain the complexity of a system. This Law of Diminishing Returns is demonstrated well in the evolution of modern agriculture; i.e. we use more and more energy to produce our food so that while the total amount of food produced increases the energy cost for each increment in amount produced also increases. This leads to the situation, mentioned earlier in this chapter, whereby we are using ten units of energy to produce one unit of food compared to a 'hunter-gatherer' lifestyle which provides 30–40 units of food energy for every unit of energy invested. Furthermore, the energy efficiency of our food production continues to fall as we invest in more and more food production technologies.

A similar dynamic can be seen across a range of fields of human endeavour. For example, in the field of education it does not cost a lot to help children learn to read and write – and the benefits to the individual and society are enormous – while postgraduate tertiary education is very expensive and the return on investment is less. Similarly, in the field of health care, basic hygiene, such as teaching people to wash their hands, is critical and inexpensive while very sophisticated technologies for keeping people alive for longer offer a lower return on investment for society as a whole. This does not mean that we should abandon investments in higher education or sophisticated health care. It does not mean we abandon any sense of 'progress'. However, the spectre of Peak Oil means we will have to rethink our use of energy for meeting human needs and return on investment will become a more important consideration when we can no longer rely on cheap oil. If energy becomes more of a constraint then the drive towards more complex systems and increasing use of energy-hungry technologies becomes deeply problematic. The underlying principle of non-equilibrium thermodynamics will force us to rethink simplification and relocalisation.

NOTES

1 Tainter and Patzek (2012: 65–95) describe this dynamic as the *Energy-Complexity Spiral* – each drives the other. We increase our complexity to meet our needs and solve the challenges we face, meaning our energy use must increase. Yet, at the same time, any increase in energy supply (like the discovery of a new source) leads to increased complexity as we rush to exploit it.
2 See Korowicz (2010).
3 See Bayliss-Smith (1982); and Craumer (1979).
4 For example, Giampietro and Pimental (1994).
5 Brown (2008: 35).
6 Northrop and Connor (2013: 68).
7 Tverberg (2012).
8 Andrew Critchlow (2014) 'Age of $100 oil will return as energy industry cuts too deep', *The Telegraph*, 16 January 2015, www.telegraph.co.uk/finance/newsbysector/energy/11351126/Age-of-100-oil-will-return-as-energy-industry-cuts-too-deep.html (accessed 6 February 2017).
9 Writer Curtis Gillespie wrote about the devastation of the Alberta oil-sands operation in an edition of *Canadian Geographic* in 2008.

10 Note that there is considerable controversy about exactly what can be counted as renewable energy and even ambitious targets ranging from 15 per cent (China) to 35 per cent (Germany) do not mean that oil dependency has been overcome.

11 See Rob Hopkins (2008) *The Transition Handbook: Creating Local Sustainable Communities Beyond Oil Dependency*, Sydney: Finch Publishing.

12 US-based food access advocate Mark Winne has contributed some important writings on the topic – such as *Closing the Food Gap* (2008).

CHAPTER 6

Sustainability models and concepts

Key concepts and concerns

- shortcomings of the prevailing three-sector model
- on adding a fourth dimension
- the teaching value of the social ecology model
- the importance of systems thinking
- the largely unexplored importance of ecological thinking
- imagining the future

INTRODUCTION

The prevailing 'three-sector' model of sustainability – which aims to focus attention on finding overlaps between *environmental*, *economic* and *social* domains of thought and action – represents an attempt to tease out the notion of economically sustainable development (ESD) as it was introduced in the 1987 Brundtland Report. As articulated by John Elkington in 1994, this is also known as the **'triple bottom line'** model because it suggests that any economic development must not only satisfy the economic bottom line of profitability, but also demonstrate that it can be at least cost-neutral when it comes to environmental and social impacts. In other words, this model introduces two new areas of accountability for assessing the viability of all forms of human enterprise and it has been adopted very widely, to largely good effect.

triple bottom line suggests that conventional economic thinking on profit and loss needs to extend to a consideration of social and environmental outcomes of any activity or enterprise. Introduced by John Elkington in 1994 it was officially endorsed by the UN in 2007 and is sometimes referred to as People, Profit and Planet.

However, there are both transparency and equivalence problems that come into play when the 'triple bottom line' approach is used. For example, economic accountability relies on the use of quantitative indicators, while it is very difficult to come up with adequate quantitative indicators for monitoring social wellbeing, especially when it comes to considerations of affect, or feelings. Can we really measure the extent to which people feel happy or fearful, for example? We need to keep in mind that the very idea of a 'bottom line' comes from the field of economics, as does the thinking underpinning the setting of performance indicators. Every field of thought has its own language and it is not easy to find terms and language that can help us explore the intersections and overlaps of diverse fields of thought.

Efforts have been made to add other words and terms into representations of the 'triple bottom line'. However, it needs to be remembered that much of the language currently used in sustainability discourses originates in economics and carries with it the assumption that impacts and outcomes can be anticipated, measured, monitored and managed. Many commentators (e.g. Giddings *et al.* 2002; Dresner 2008) have argued that conventional economic thinking dominates the prevailing three-sector model to the extent that it marginalises key social considerations that do not impinge directly on the functioning of the economy, such as the desire for a secure sense of belonging somewhere. Such commentators also argue that a narrow focus on human economic systems prevents us from understanding the extent to which we are embedded in non-human ecological systems.

Social Ecology teaching and research programme at the University of Western Sydney emerged within the Agriculture School of what had been Australia's oldest agricultural college. In trying to respond to the complex needs of rural communities it adopted soft systems methodology and principles of community development.

As discussed in Chapter 2, this book works with the '**Social Ecology**' model which re-categorises the three sectors as *environmental*, *social* and *personal*. While the merits of this model have been discussed briefly, this chapter seeks to explain the value of this model for teaching sustainability. Most conceptual modelling draws either consciously or unconsciously on 'systems theory' or 'soft systems methodology' and this chapter seeks to acknowledge that influence. It touches on several concepts that can be used to amplify the Social Ecology model before turning its attention to the development of a set of 'guiding principles' that can underpin the broader notion of sustainability. In summary, the chapter aims to:

- explain the origins of the prevailing three-sector model;
- examine attempts to improve on that model before arriving at the choice of the Social Ecology model;
- acknowledge the ongoing importance of systems thinking;
- explain why 'ecological thinking' can help us reframe sustainability challenges; and
- introduce 'scenarios mapping' as a methodology for thinking more deeply about uncertain futures.

THE 'NESTED DIAGRAM' MODEL

Giddings *et al.* (2002) argue that problems arise as soon as we think of economy, society and the environment as having any degree of separation from each other. This, they suggest, reflects the way in which we separate the 'study of human life and the world around us' into distinct and separate disciplines (ibid.: 194). For this reason, they prefer a 'nested' representation of the relationships, in which the economy is seen as existing within the domain of the social which, in turn, exists within the wider setting of the environment (see Figure 6.1). According to these authors, the 'nested model' ensures that any consideration of the economy must be constrained by social and environmental considerations, rather than having any degree of autonomy. However, the unwanted effect might be to maintain a focus on the economy as the starting point of all sustainability considerations, with society and the environment being put into the background. While the intent of the model is commendable, it suggests a rather hierarchical and inflexible relationship between economy, society and environment whereas the earlier

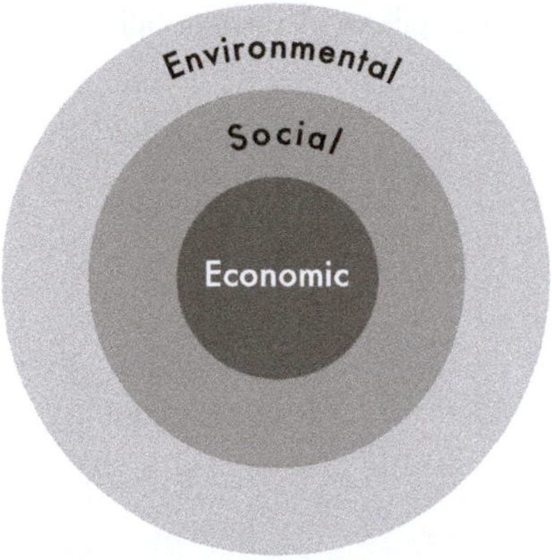

Figure 6.1 Nested diagram of sustainability
Source: adapted from B. Giddings, B. Hopwood and G. O'Brien 'Environment, Economy and Society: Fitting them into sustainable development', 2002, *Sustainable Development*, 10: 142

representation of overlapping circles allows for the fact that needs and considerations might arise separately within any of the three domains before being brought into interaction with the others. No model is perfect, but the suggestion that different considerations have to be brought into dialogue with each other has been useful. Economy may continue to dominate the other fields of consideration in prevailing discourses, yet the three-sector model was a breakthrough in suggesting that society and environment deserve equal and independent consideration.

ADDING A FOURTH DIMENSION

Another problem with the prevailing three-sector model is that it hard to know what is included or excluded from the broad domain of the 'social'. This has led to some proposals to add a fourth dimension or domain in order to tease out some things that might otherwise remain hidden within the broad domain of the social. For example, the Australian cultural development worker Jon Hawkes has argued that humans find a sense of personal and social worth by having opportunities to participate in cultural expression or production (Hawkes 2001). He suggested adding 'cultural vitality' as a '**fourth pillar**' of sustainability, alongside considerations of environmental, economic and social wellbeing (see Figure 6.2). Hawkes argued that local government authorities have a special responsibility for providing spaces and opportunities for community members to participate in cultural activities and cultural production and his argument has been accepted by a wide range of Local Government Authorities in Australia. The 'fourth pillar' has also been adopted by local government bodies in New Zealand, Canada and in parts of Europe.

fourth pillar former circus strongman and founder of Circus Oz, Jon Hawkes wrote *The Fourth Pillar of Sustainability* for Australia's Cultural Development Network in 2001. He has been pleasantly surprised by the enduring international interest in the rather low-profile publication.

The 'fourth pillar' model encouraged a group of social researchers in the Global Cities Research Institute at RMIT University in Melbourne to come up with another four domains approach (see Scerri and James 2010), which has been adopted as a useful instrument for sustainable urban planning in a range of cities, including Melbourne, Vancouver, Milwaukee and Porto Alegro. This model retains

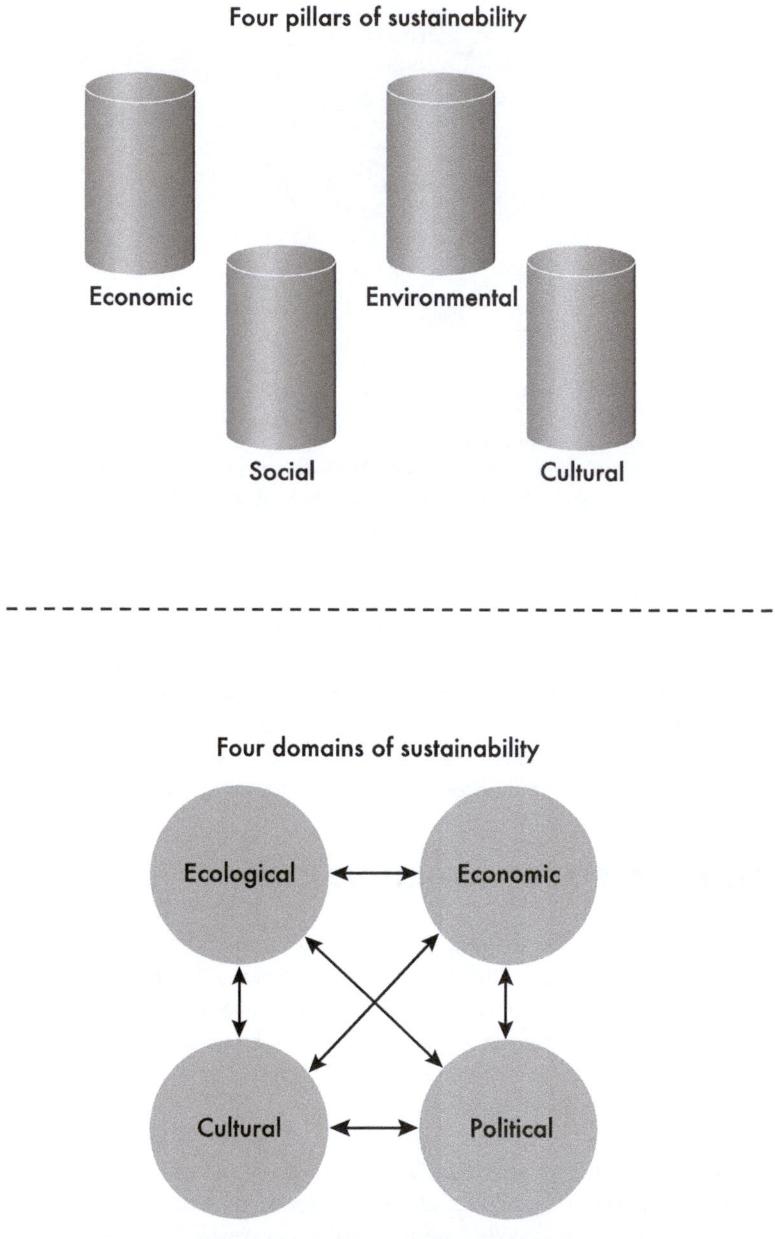

Figure 6.2 Four pillars model and four domains model
Sources: the graphic is an original by the author, representing the work of Jon Hawkes (2001) *The Four Pillars of Sustainability*, Cultural Development Network, Melbourne, and work on 'Circles of Sustainability' by Paul James and Andy Scerri, Global Cities Research Institute, RMIT University, Melbourne

the economic domain but it separates social into 'cultural' and 'political'. It renames environmental as 'ecological' to focus attention on interrelationships between human and non-human (see Figure 6.2). The model is now known as the '**Circles of Sustainability**' model because the four domains can be represented as equal sectors on a circle with sector divided into sub-sectors for each selected indicator. When a measure for each indicator is agreed, the circle representation makes it easy to identify areas of strength and weakness for a participating city.

Circles of Sustainability model was originally conceived by researchers at RMIT University in Melbourne as a four domains, rather than three sectors, model; it has been widely used in city planning in cities across the world.

The Circles of Sustainability model is essentially understood as a tool that generates conversation between a wide range of organisations and agencies involved in city planning, social welfare and environmental sustainability. Within the four domains, workshop participants are encouraged to select indicators related to the domain sub-themes, noting that data to construct indicators can be hard to obtain. Participants to the exercise are encouraged to think beyond the most obvious and easy-to-measure indicators in order to grapple with the tensions that might exist between, for example, forms of participation and the exercise of authority, or between a need to increase social inclusion whilst allowing different cultural groupings to maintain separate and diverse practices. Processes of negotiation are as important as the final selection of indicators and the model is based on principles of 'deliberative' or 'participatory' democracy. Selected indicators are not set in concrete and can be revisited at suitable intervals. According to Scerri and James (2010: 47–50), the 'background considerations' for a useful dialogue on indicators are:

- What kinds of things indicate that a community is sustainable?
- What kinds of things indicate that (when present or missing) a community is unsustainable?
- Who benefits and who loses in the current situation, and how might that be changed?
- What does it mean, in relation to current norms, to negotiate these matters?

THE SOCIAL ECOLOGY MODEL

As mentioned in Chapter 1, this book advocates use of the 'Social Ecology' model – as developed in teaching and research programme at the University of Western Sydney in the 1990s – as a valuable teaching heuristic. This model folds economic considerations into the social domain – on the assumption that economic development needs to be geared to social wellbeing – and it introduces a new focus on the personal dimensions of sustainability (see Figure 6.3). Arguably, this model makes the social domain even more cumbersome by adding economic considerations to a host of other indicators of social wellbeing. However, the elegant simplicity of the prevailing three-sector model probably explains its enduring appeal and we may be tempted to overcomplicate it by adding more and more sectors or dimensions. By folding 'economic' into the social domain, the Social Ecology model enables us to add in the 'personal' dimensions of the challenges we face globally while retaining the notion of the 'triangulation' that occurs when we look at a challenge from three different starting points. The model encourages us to consider impacts between people, society and environment and

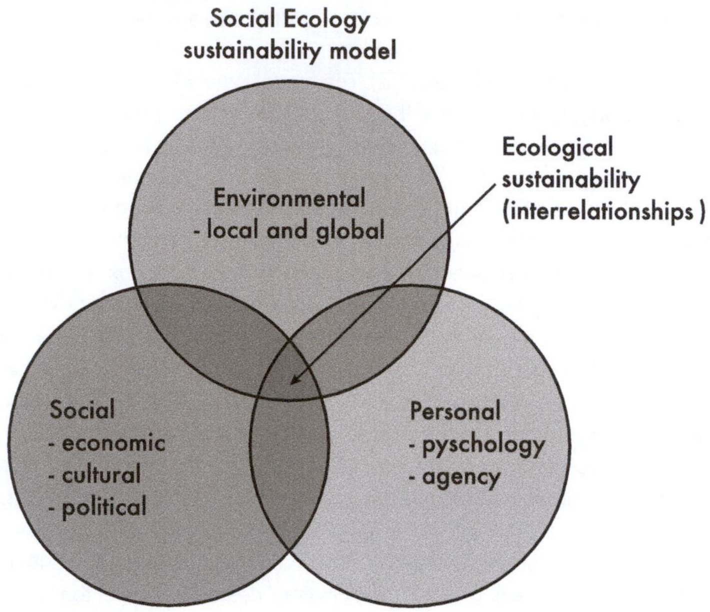

Figure 6.3 The Social Ecology model

it has played an important role in underpinning the design of the introductory course on sustainability at RMIT University in Melbourne which, in turn, led to the development of this book. Students in this course have welcomed the opportunity to contemplate what the big challenges of global sustainability might mean for them both personally and professionally.

The focus on the personal helps to bring the big concerns of sustainability back home without losing sight of the big global picture. It dispels the perception that sustainability is a matter for experts, governments or authorities, because it really is a matter of enduring concern for all of us. In introducing this model to students in the Social Ecology programme at the University of Western Sydney, Stuart Hill stressed that big global challenges require bold and creative responses, yet none of us can avoid the responsibility of thinking about the kinds of 'meaningful changes' that we can adopt and sustain personally.

Stuart Hill and the Social Ecology model

Stuart Hill was born in England and educated at Swansea University before going to McGill University in Montreal to complete his Ph.D. With a background in ecology and chemical engineering, his Ph.D work examined 'whole system ecology' with fieldwork carried out in a bat-inhabited cave in Trinidad. Having won an award for the best Ph.D thesis in 1969, Hill went on to establish Canada's leading research centre on sustainable agriculture at McGill University in 1974, and in 1977 he was awarded the Queen's

Silver Jubilee Medal for outstanding community work. He moved to Australia in 1996 to take up the position of Foundation Chair in Social Ecology at the University of Western Sydney. With a strong personal interest in psychotherapy he began to promote the Social Ecology model of sustainability in his teaching and research work. We have to get beyond work which will do little more than monitor our extinction in order to think about the small but meaningful changes we can each embrace, he was fond of telling his students. He has worked as an environmental consultant in Canada, the West Indies, West Africa, Asia, Australia and New Zealand, and from 2005 to 2007 was employed as a professional 'Provocateur' by the Department of Primary Industries and the Department of Sustainability and Environment in Victoria, Australia.

FROM 'EFFICIENCY' TO 'REDESIGN'

As a complement to the Social Ecology model, Stuart Hill has argued that we need to get beyond a focus on *efficiency* or *substitution* in order to look at ways to *redesign* unsustainable processes or systems. We might, for example, try to reduce the energy consumption of a household by using more insulation, closing up gaps beneath doorways and being cautious about the use of heaters or air conditioners. We might go a step further by replacing the existing heating system and other household appliances with more energy-efficient appliances. However, we could go even further by installing solar panels and passive insulation systems, rethinking other aspects of house design and function, and possibly even deciding to move to a smaller house closer to shops and work. Once we are on this track we might find permanent ways to reduce car use in order to reduce our household carbon footprint.

We can all begin by thinking about how we might be able to redesign our personal or household practices. Beyond that we can choose to participate in wider local community projects aimed at developing new systems for producing food and energy and for dealing with waste. We can participate in non-localised 'communities of practice' which share ideas about how to live more sustainably and we can try to take some of these ideas into our workplaces. We can play a role in convincing our workplace organisations to truly embrace the challenges of sustainability rather than try to deflect criticisms with minimal changes or token responses. In our own professional practice we can look for ways to help other people take on board key concepts of sustainable living.

SYSTEMS THINKING

Much of the thinking about sustainability is influenced by an approach to complexity known as 'systems thinking'. In essence, this approach is based on the idea that the whole is always greater than the sum of its parts and it encourages us to step back in order to get a bigger picture of how things work. The causes of malfunction may originate far from where the malfunction has its most serious consequences; for example, when job losses are caused by a decision of a multinational corporation to shift some of its operations from one country to another. We cannot hope to fix malfunctions unless we understand the functioning of the system, it this case the functioning of a globalised economy. Similarly, we need an understanding of global climate systems to imagine what the consequences of global warming might be in any particular area or region.

It appears that systems thinking emerged within the separate fields of engineering and biology (ecology) at a similar time in the 1920s. Engineers were interested in the functioning of complex machinery or human-made systems while ecologists were interested in the function of integrated communities of plants and animals (ecosystems). However, the benefits of thinking holistically were put into a comprehensive theoretical framework by the Austrian-born biologist **Ludwig von Bertalanffy** in the 1940s when he suggested that natural and constructed systems share some discernible properties. In advocating his General Systems Theory, Bertalanffy noted that all systems require a range of inputs and produce various outputs but they can only be called systems when they become largely self-regulating because they have built-in 'feedback' mechanisms that can trigger functional changes. Bertalanffy drew a distinction between 'closed systems', which operate within clearly defined boundaries, and 'open systems', which are open to many more inputs and disturbances. Engineers are more likely to be dealing with relatively closed systems than biologists or social planners yet systems thinking makes it clear that very few systems are really self-enclosed or operate as predictably as we might hope. For example, the very best technology for operating s system of trains will not guarantee that an urban mass transport system will function well.

Ludwig von Bertalanffy (1901–72) was born in Vienna and died in Buffalo, New York. Initially schooled at home he lived near a famous biologist, Paul Kammerer, who acted as a mentor. Von Bertalanffy began his university studies in philosophy and art history before turning to biology.

Systems become much more complex when subjectivity comes into play; for example when humans or other animals make individual decisions or judgements that will have consequences for others. To cope with this level of unpredictability, **Peter Checkland** and others introduced a distinction between 'hard' and 'soft' systems in the late 1960s and this developed into a 'soft systems methodology' for making sense of complex and largely unpredictable, systems.

Peter Checkland was born in Birmingham in 1930 and originally trained as a chemist before working as a chemical engineer. He took up a position as 'professor of systems' at the University of Lancaster in the 1960s, where he developed the 'soft systems methodology' that is now in use globally.

In essence, soft systems methodology begins with a mapping exercise aimed at creating a 'rich picture' of all the factors that might need to be considered in understanding the current behaviour of the system in question. In the case of a multinational corporation closing a particular part of its business, for example, the mapping would include the overall operations of the corporation and the factors that might influence decisions about continuing, expanding or closing particular operations. An initial mapping – or rich picture – is likely to be rather messy and it is followed by an attempt to create a map that highlights flows of inputs and influences in a linear flows diagram. This kind of mapping may already reveal opportunities to rethink influences and redesign the system to avoid undesirable outcomes. However, more work may be required to develop 'conceptual models' of the system that might suggest unforeseen ways to make an improvement, as illustrated in Figure 6.4. Soft systems methodology, it should be noted, is overtly interested in redesigning systems that are seen to produce undesirable outcomes.

A key concept in all systems thinking is that of 'feedback loops' and it is assumed that systems will function better if they have lots of 'inbuilt' feedback

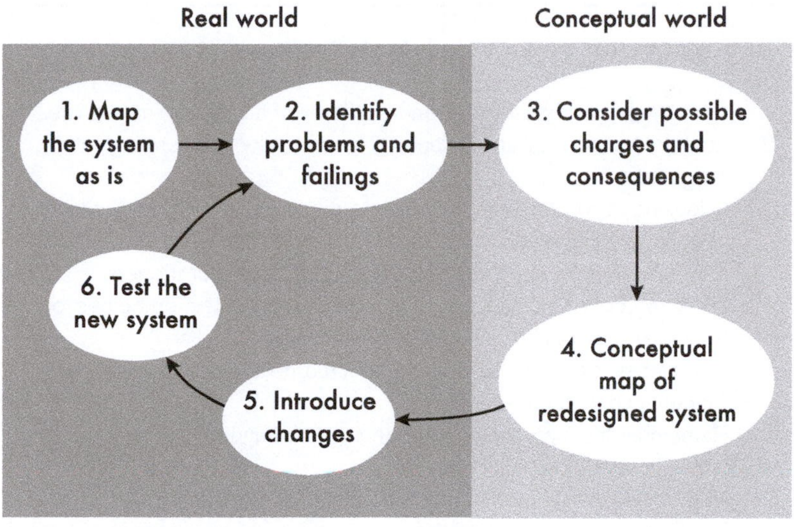

Figure 6.4 Soft systems methodology

loops. Broadly speaking, feedback can be either 'reinforcing' – i.e. encouraging the system to continue the way it functions – or 'balancing' – suggesting that something needs to change. In soft systems methodology the focus on feedback loops has been extended to an interest in the operation of 'double feedback mechanisms' which suggest that feedback mechanisms themselves need to be influenced by different sources of feedback. For example, the commander of a fire-fighting team that is trying to prevent a bush or forest fire from destroying homes or settlements deploys his/her team on the basis of information received about how the fire is burning. However, he/she also needs to be informed by weather forecasts that can provide prior warning of a change in wind direction or the arrival of rain. The work of John Ehrenfeld on 'addictive consumption', which was discussed in Chapter 3, made use of systems theory to contemplate the need for a second feedback loop on the meeting of human needs which would encourage the consumer to contemplate the 'authenticity' of the need being addressed by particular forms of consumption.

Donella Meadows and Diana Wright (see Wright and Meadows 2012) have suggested that there is a veritable 'zoo' of models and practices related to systems thinking and that practitioners need to use them thoughtfully. However, a number of key concepts have emerged in the field of systems thinking which aim to encourage a more holistic understanding of the complex interactions among the components of the system under review and these are summarised in the box below.

Donella Meadows (1941–2001) was a Harvard-trained biophysicist who taught systems dynamics alongside her husband Dennis at Massachusetts Institute of Technology (MIT). She was a member of the MIT team that undertook computer modelling for the famous *Limits to Growth* publication of the Club of Rome in 1972, with Donella named as the lead author. Shortly before she died she worked on a 30-year update of *Limits to Growth* by the same authors, which was published after her death, in 2004. She is primarily responsible for the leading 'primer' on systems thinking, published in 2008.

Key steps in system analysis

1. Start by mapping the 'inflows' and 'outflows' of the system as a whole.
2. Look for 'reinforcing' and 'balancing' feedback loops operating within the system.
3. In looking at how the system functions, step away from linear thinking about cause and effect to focus on 'unintended consequences' which may seem out of proportion to the apparent causes or triggers.
4. Look for both 'resistances' which reduce expected outcomes or 'escalations' which amplify expected outcomes.
5. Remember that there can be unexpected delays between causes/ triggers and their consequences.
6. Remember that no system is self-enclosed (bounded) and it interacts with a host of other 'unbounded' systems.
7. Remember that an apparently functioning system can be pursuing inappropriate goals or encouraging uncritical addictive behaviour.
8. Consider if the espoused goals/aims of the system remain fresh and relevant or have been 'eroded' by malfunction or loss of relevance.

It can be very difficult, of course, to represent a complex system in a two-dimensional system, maps and representations can make some things visible whilst making other things less visible. Indeed any attempt to represent relationships between components of a system can encourage a degree of linear thinking about cause and effect. On the other hand, the suggestion that all systems operate in a borderless world (see step 6 in the box above) can make it very hard to distinguish one system from other related systems. It is also very difficult for system mapping to factor in the values and assumptions that underpin the development of the system under consideration. However, as long as it is remembered that any attempt to map a system will be an approximation of complex reality, systems thinking remains a very important methodology for thinking holistically and for highlighting malfunctions or problems in a way that can suggest some practical changes.

Arthur Tansley (1871–1955) was a student at University College London, Cambridge University and Oxford University who eventually taught botany at all three of these prestigious universities. He also spent a year studying psychology under Sigmund Freud in Vienna. Through his work on plant ecology he became an ardent conservationist.

ECOLOGICAL THINKING

It is not really surprising that biologists were among the pioneers of systems thinking in the 1920s because this was the time when the study of ecology began to take off through the influence of the pioneering plant ecologist **Arthur Tansley** and animal ecologist Charles Elton. It was Tansley who coined the term 'ecosystem' to distinguish one biological community from another although it has always been understood that the boundaries between one system and another are very porous and that every ecosystem is embedded within much bigger flows of energy and materials. While integrated communities of plants and animals develop high levels of mutual dependence and, over time, become self-regulating to a significant degree, it is impossible to think of an ecosystem as being self-contained or closed.

Humans are unique in being able to impose fairly high levels of control and design on the systems within which we operate on a daily basis. However, we are beginning to pay a high price for imagining that we have been able to put ourselves above the 'laws of nature' and it is instructive to compare the kinds of principles that underpin the functioning of relatively undisturbed 'natural' ecosystems with the kinds of principles that are reflected in many of the systems created by humans. The differences are particularly stark when we examine the assumptions underpinning growth-oriented economic systems but they are much more far-reaching than that. Of course, humans are embedded in ecological systems and it is a rather contrived to draw a distinction between 'human systems' and 'ecological systems'; however the exercise in itself is quite revealing (see Table 6.1).

As mentioned in Chapter 2, Rachel Carson demonstrated how much we humans can learn about our unintended impacts on the planet's life support systems by developing a stronger understanding of ecological systems and processes. Very few people would have even heard the word '**ecology**' when Carson was writing in the early 1960s and now it is used very widely, if often rather loosely. Key ecological concepts – such as 'food webs' and energy flows – are much more widely understood today. However, David Orr (2011) is prominent among those who have argued that 'ecological literacy' has not been given the priority it deserves and we will continue to pay a price for widespread ecological ignorance.

ecology German biologist Ernst Haeckel coined the term *écologie* in 1866 but it takes its inspiration directly from the work of Charles Darwin on natural evolution. Although the term appealed to biologists, it struggled to establish itself as a field of study until the 1920s and 1930s when Arthur Tansley, Charles Elton and Frederic Clements developed the core concepts and terminology that helped researchers make sense of complex natural systems.

Table 6.1 Comparing prevailing assumptions (column 1) with what happens in natural ecosystems (column 2)

Source: adapted from Mulligan and Hill (2001)

Prevailing assumptions of human systems	*What happens in natural ecosystems*
Wait for crises	Responsive to early indicators
Unlimited growth	Growth is subjected to limiting factors
Reliant on fossil fuels or nuclear power	More directly reliant on solar energy
A focus on linear material flows	Cyclical flows and regenerative relationships
Competition is emphasised	Mutualism is favoured
Production is emphasised	Most resources are used for maintenance
Simplified and often hierarchical systems with an emphasis on control	Stability stems from 'functional diversity' and internal complexity
Heavy reliance on specialists with specific expertise	A diversity of roles for specialists and generalists in complex adaptive systems
Little awareness of time and place	Every place is unique and no moment in time will be repeated
Fast changes that benefit a minority, with many 'casualties'	Gradual co-evolutionary change with occasional bursts of rapid change

WORKING ACROSS SCALES FROM THE LOCAL AND THE GLOBAL

As Rachel Carson demonstrated so eloquently in *Silent Spring*, an understanding of ecological flows dissolves the boundaries between the local and the global. It is still useful to distinguish scales ranging from local or regional, to global or 'biospheric'; but the boundaries between them are contingent, approximate and porous. By contrast, we humans have developed social and political systems which operate at scales that tend to be more bounded in thought and practice. Sharp boundaries distinguish one local or regional government area from another while nations have fiercely guarded borders in an age of increasing global mobility of people, goods, information and ideas. Human systems of governance often undermine the operational integrity of what biologists would call 'biogeographic regions', with rivers and mountain ranges commonly being used to designate separating borders when they might better be seen as standing at the heart of the regional ecosystem. Environmental writers Peter Berg (in the 1970s) and Kirkpatrick Sale (in the 1980s) are probably the best-known advocates of the notion of '**bioregionalism**' which seeks to align human systems with local and regional ecological realities.

bioregionalism was first promoted by environmental writer Peter Berg in the 1970s and advocated by writer/activist Kirkpatrick Sale in the 1980s. It suggests that the governance of human communities and societies needs to start with an awareness of natural systems which may be depicted with reference to watersheds, terrain and soil characteristics and dominant plant or animal communities.

The notion of a bioregion can exaggerate the self-sufficiency of local eco-systems when no such self-sufficiency exists in practice. Nevertheless, various conceptions of biogeographic regions have been used in different parts of the world to find a better match between the needs of local and regional human and non-human systems. The '**Regional Natural Parks**' system in France provides one model for matching the preservation of human cultural diversity to the preservation of regional biodiversity and adaptations of the model have been implemented in a wide range of other nations. Of course, France has a long history of regional differentiation which is not found in many other countries, especially those in which indigenous societies were largely displaced by European settlers in the colonial era. Yet the work must continue to find a better match between biodiversity conservation and human settlement at regional levels in all parts of the world.

Regional Natural Parks (France) the first Parc Naturel Régional was set up in France in 1967, and by 2011 there were 45 of them covering 13 per cent of French territory with three million people living within their boundaries.

In focusing on the phenomenon of '**globalisation**', prominent sociologists – including Ulrich Beck, Saskia Sassen and Manuel Castells – have noted that old hierarchies of human governance have been radically destabilised. Sassen, for example, argues that nation states have largely lost their ability to regulate the ways in which 'sub-national sectors' – including relatively small organisations and communities – can now operate globally, while Castells has argued that new communication technologies have fostered the rise of a globally linked 'network society'. Internet communications have brought obvious benefits to people in all parts of the world. However, a weakening of regulating hierarchies also enables large and powerful corporations to operate anywhere in the world with very few impediments and they can withdraw or relocate their investments as quickly as they can make them.

globalisation as a term used to indicate increasing connections between systems and processes which once operated within national jurisdictions has been prominent in economic literature since the early 1980s. However, it came to have a wider meaning in the 1990s, and in 1992 UK sociologist Roland Robertson defined it as 'the compression of the world and the intensification of the consciousness of the world as a whole'.

It has become harder to hold large corporations to account for their social and environmental impacts, posing a need for stronger global systems of regulation and governance. The rise of corporate power may be matched, at least to some extent, by an increase in global political activism and by the emergence of globally connected civil society organisations. In the early 1970s, the new established environmental organisation Friends of the Earth popularised the slogan 'Think global, act local'. It has become more apparent now that we need to think and act locally and globally all at the same time, yet that imperative is more difficult to turn into a catchy slogan. In later chapters we will discuss further what it means to live in a world of global ecological flows that are impacted by global flows of people, goods, money, information and ideas.

Discussion questions

1. Why does the Social Ecology model fold economic considerations into the social domain of sustainability?
2. What are some strengths and weaknesses of the Social Ecology model of sustainability?
3. Is it feasible or necessary to redesign processes and practices rather than focus on efficiency or substitution?
4. Why is it important to think about 'feedback loops'?
5. What are some of the key considerations in system analysis?
6. What are strengths and weaknesses of systems thinking?
7. Is it relevant and useful to compare principles underpinning 'ecological systems' and 'human systems'?
8. What is meant by the concept of 'bioregionalism' and does it have practical relevance?
9. How can we think across boundaries from the local to the global?

KEY READINGS

Dresner, Simon (2008), 2nd edn, *Principles of Sustainability*, London: Earthscan.

Ehrenfeld, John (2008) *Sustainability by Design: A Subversive Strategy for Transforming Our Consumer Culture*, New Haven, CT: Yale University Press.

Giddings, Bob, Bill Hopwood and Geoff O'Brien (2002) 'Environment, Economy and Society: Fitting Them Together into Sustainable Development', *Sustainable Development*, 10: 187–96.

Orr, David (2011) *Hope is an Imperative: The Essential David Orr*, Washington, DC: Island Press.

Washington, Haydn (2015) *Demystifying Sustainability: Towards Real Solutions*, Abingdon: Earthscan/Routledge.

Wright, Diana and Donella Meadows (2012) *Thinking in Systems: A Primer*, London: Routledge.

thematic essay

Imaging the future

Climate models that have featured so strongly in the reports of the IPCC – as discussed in Chapter 4 – have focused our attention on our human ability to predict what might happen well into the future. Climate scientists routinely warn that their predictive models can only ever be approximate in a world of growing climate uncertainty and yet fierce public debate has emerged over the accuracy of their predictions. Clearly, we have acquired a much stronger global capacity to predict the future and even if the accuracy of the predictions falls as we look further into the future we are enticed by the possibility of being forewarned about what may lie ahead. Growing concern about what the future might hold has given rise to a range of modelling techniques and prominent among them has been a set of techniques that are most commonly called 'scenarios mapping'. The key principle in this approach is to imagine an array of plausible future scenarios in order to think about what can be done in the present to ensure that preferred scenarios are realised.

It has been noted that planning for an array of scenarios has long been a feature of military planning but the adoption of the practice for civilian use may have originated with the Royal Dutch Shell oil company at the time of the first big global 'oil shock' in the early 1970s.[1] The corporation developed techniques for generating conversation within the organisation about how it might adapt and survive in a world of growing oil shortages and this led to the appointment of trained 'scenarists' who could lead groups of people through exercises aimed at developing their capacity to think boldly, yet plausibly about the future. Such a scenarios mapping workshop should be informed by existing data and future modelling and it needs to have a particular time frame in mind; perhaps 20 or 50 years into the future. Importantly, the exercise must result in the formulation of a number of possible scenarios – commonly four – so that attention can then turn to what can be done in the present to steer in the direction of preferred outcomes.

As a member of a research team at RMIT University, the author was involved in an innovative scenarios mapping project in the western districts of Victoria in the period between 2007 and 2009. The research team had already worked with the regional community on a range of research and development projects when public alarm about the consequences of climate change escalated. Aware that the national scientific research organisation – CSIRO – was predicting an increase in the frequency and intensity of droughts for this part of Australia, community leaders wanted to stimulate discussion about what could be done regionally to either mitigate the local impacts or adapt to changing conditions. In this case, the community in and around the regional centre of Hamilton was the 'stakeholder' organisation and considerable thought went into selecting 40 community members – representing a range of sectors – to participate in a two-day workshop. A trained scenarist was employed and RMIT researchers were briefed on how to act as group facilitators.

The community representatives decided to work on the development of four diverse scenarios that might unfold within 30–50 years from the present and a report on the exercise was distributed within the district. What made this project innovative, however, is that an experienced creative writer was invited to participate in the workshop and then employed to turn some of the workshop outcomes into a range of future narratives featuring fictional yet plausible local characters dealing with largely unforseen challenges. The writer and a writing colleague worked with workshop participants to refine the stories based the imagined scenarios and the unfolding of the stories over a period of 20 years – i.e. 30–50 years hence – meant that some of them began to interact with each other. The stories were eventually published in a monograph titled *Unexpected Sources of Hope* (Nadarajah *et al.* 2008) with the title reflecting the fact that the authors themselves were surprised to discover which of the imagined characters managed to cope best in difficult and changing circumstances. The experience suggested that there is an interesting distinction to be made between future scenarios and compelling future stories that can give readers a glimpse of what it might *feel* like to be living in the imagined futures.

NOTE

1 See www.shell.com/global/future-energy/scenarios.html

CHAPTER 7

Risk and resilience

> **Key concepts and concerns**
>
> - risk aversion
> - increasing need to embrace risk
> - hazard exposure and risk tolerance
> - risk and innovation
> - personal and 'socio-ecological' resilience
> - characteristics of resilient systems

INTRODUCTION

In recent decades, the word 'resilience' has cropped up in numerous fields of policy and practice internationally, with variants including 'disaster resilience', 'urban resilience', 'community resilience', 'climate resilience' and 'personal resilience'. The growing popularity of the concept has led some scholars to suggest that it appears to have more practical relevance than the more abstract concept of 'sustainability' (e.g. Zolli 2012).[1] However, this probably reflects the fact that sustainability implies transformations which are harder to implement than many had imagined and the popularity of the word 'resilience' may, in part, reflect the fact that it can be used to shift responsibilities from governments to individual people and communities (see Chandler and Reid 2016). Properly understood, resilience thinking can serve the wider agenda of sustainability and the starting point here is to acknowledge that we need to think differently about the growing prevalence and complexity of risks we are facing globally.

Derived from the Latin word *resilire* – meaning to 'spring back' – the word gained currency in fields such as engineering and physics before being applied in relation to the capacity of people and communities to withstand stress at the time of an earthquake in the USA in 1854 (Alexander 2013). The concept of 'personal resilience' emerged strongly in 'developmental psychology' in the 1950s through the work of **Norman Garmezy** on the capacity of children to deal with stress. In 1973 the Canadian ecologist Crawford Stanley **'Buzz' Holling** published a very influential paper suggesting that humans have much to learn from the capacity of non-human ecosystems to 'absorb changes and still persist' although he subsequently stressed that it refers to the 'magnitude of disturbance' that can be

Norman Garmezy (1918–2009) was a clinical psychology who turned from early work on schizophrenia to thinking in the 1950s about the 'protective factors' that might enable people to avoid mental illness. Having had an alcoholic mother and an absent father, and after serving in the US army during the Second World War he argued that resilience could be acquired. He was dubbed the 'grandfather of resilience theory' by *The New Yorker* magazine.

'Buzz' Holling (b. 1930) gained a Ph.D. at the University of British Colombia in 1957, and served in the Canadian Department of Forestry. His 1973 paper on 'Resilience and the Stability of Ecological Systems' sparked much more interest than he could have imagined. He went on to become a pioneer of 'socio-ecological resilience', serving as the founding editor of the *Ecology and Society* journal.

Resilience Alliance was formed in 1999 at the instigation of 'Buzz' Holling to develop and promote the 'socio-ecological' model of resilience thinking. Based in Sweden, it publishes the influential *Ecology and Society* journal. Key figures have been Carl Folke and Lance Gunderson.

absorbed before a 'system changes its structure'. Given that his 1973 paper was published in a relatively obscure ecological science journal, Holling could not have imagined the impact it would have. The idea that we need to take the concept of resilience beyond its use in engineering and psychology to consider what makes some 'socio-ecological systems' more resilient than others eventually spawned the formation of the international **Resilience Alliance** in 1999 with a wide range of researchers building on the Holling's foundational ideas. Resilience is often discussed in relation to other terms such as 'vulnerability' and 'exposure to hazards' (Adger and Brown 2009) while its relationship with risk-taking is largely neglected. Of course, psychologists have long noted that resilient people are likely to have a high level of risk tolerance, however a growing interest in 'risk management' seems to encourage the view that resilience can be achieved by finding ways to avoid risk.

In a book published in German in 1986 and in English in 1992, Ulrich Beck pointed out that western societies are becoming increasingly 'risk averse' at the very time when human activities are making exposure to various forms of risk more widespread and pervasive. For example, the catastrophic accident in the nuclear power plant at Chernobyl in Ukraine in 1986 may have begun locally but its effects spread across many neighbouring countries and made the region surrounding the plant uninhabitable for humans. The increasing mobility of people and domesticated animals means that viruses and diseases can spread with unprecedented speed while the widespread use of dangerous chemicals and the generation of many forms of toxic waste mean that rising risks can rarely be contained within national boundaries. Increasing exposure to risk calls for greater awareness of the dangers posed – i.e. risk assessment – and it is obviously important to look for ways to minimise risk and **hazard exposure**. However, Beck warned that people living in western societies have been lulled into a false sense of security about the capacity of their governments and public authorities to manage risk. Rather than contemplate risk more fully, we have seen a marked increase in risk denial or aversion, he noted. In a follow-up book published in 2007, Beck found that risk aversion has become even more entrenched, especially in the wake of the terrorist attacks on the USA in September 2001. However, he argued that risk denial will become increasingly untenable in a 'world at risk' and that a need to grapple with risk will eventually trigger big changes in prevailing cultural beliefs and practices.

hazard exposure refers to human exposure to materials or processes that have a known potential to damage health or cause injury.

This chapter will consider some of the personal and social costs of risk aversion and focus attention on the relationship between risk and resilience. It notes that a measure of risk-taking is essential for innovation, although the distinction needs to be made between unconscious exposure to hazards and knowing acceptance of risk. Many studies have demonstrated that people living in poor countries or poor communities – with inadequate public health systems – are most likely to be exposed to 'natural' or human-induced hazards and this is a form of inequity that needs urgent and enduring attention. While resilience thinking can be used to shift coping responsibilities to 'vulnerable' people and communities, it also asks why some people and communities of people are more vulnerable than others and resources can be mobilised to address such vulnerabilities before they are exposed by unexpected shocks or accumulating stresses. At the same time, the chapter will argue that people living in western societies have something to learn from people living in non-western societies where risk aversion has had much less cultural influence. Arguably, post-Enlightenment confidence in the ability of humans to use scientific rationality in order to assert a new dominance over nature has made western societies more vulnerable to risk than they care to imagine and 'modern' society may have lost sight of the cultural roots of resilience.

While psychologists can describe attributes that make some individuals more resilient than others, ecologists have focused on the kinds of properties that make some 'socio-ecological' systems more resilient than others and some of their key findings have been summarised in an influential book by **Brian Walker** and **David Salt** (2006). Walker and Salt argue that principles of systemic resilience can be designed into the systems we create for human communities and the relevance of those principles will be explored in relation to the impact of **Hurricane Katrina** on the city of New Orleans in 2005 which exposed major faults in the city's disaster management plans. We need to learn the lessons of past disasters in order to give more substance to the rhetoric about 'disaster resilience' and the onset of global climate change makes this even more urgent.

The chapter begins by highlighting some of the dangers associated with prevailing risk management strategies before considering the benefits of embracing, rather than avoiding, risk. This chapter aims to:

- explain key shortcomings in prevailing western thought on risk management;
- consider some of the benefits that might flow from a significant cultural shift in the perception of risk;
- highlight some of the ways in which some people can become more resilient than others; and
- expand on the ideas of Brian Walker and David Salt (2006) in relation to systemic attributes that can make some human systems and settlements more resilient than others.

RISK MEASUREMENT AND MANAGEMENT

Scholars ranging from the psychologist Paul Slovic to the sociologist Ulrich Beck have noted that a very large risk management industry has emerged within western societies as the feelings of **risk exposure** have grown (see Photo 7.1). As Beck, in particular, has argued, there are good reasons for the rising concern because human-induced environmental hazards can no longer be contained to local regions, the increased mobility of people is increasing the threat of epidemics or pandemics of disease, and social conflicts have increasingly spilled over national boundaries and have become 'globalised' in their impacts. We can add to this the assessment that global climate change is already increasing the frequency and intensity of extreme weather events and that this climate volatility will grow. Beck has also pointed out that another factor driving the development of the risk management industry is that insurance companies cannot cope with the increasing levels of hazard exposure, while public authorities have become increasingly concerned about being held accountable – legally, morally and politically – for increasing risk exposure. National governments, in particular, are

Brian Walker began his career in biology and ecology in Zimbabwe (then called Rhodesia) before completing his Ph.D. in plant ecology in Canada. He moved from South Africa to Australia in 1985 to take up the position of Chief of the Division of Wildlife and Ecology at the Commonwealth Scientific and Industrial Research Organisation (CSIRO). He has been active in the international Resilience Alliance.

David Salt has served as editor of *Decision Point*, the monthly magazine of the Environment Decisions Group at the Australian National University. He has created and produced magazines for ANU, CSIRO and *Australian Geographic*.

Hurricane Katrina hit the coast of Louisiana on 29 August 2005, breaking flood protection levees in New Orleans and resulting in around 1,800 deaths and the displacement of 250,000 people.

risk exposure refers to human exposure to situations which may or may not damage health or cause injury.

Photo 7.1 Sign erected by protesters in New Zealand to warn hikers of an unexpected poison hazard
© Yva Momatiuk & John Eastcott/Minden Pictures/Corbis

trying to shift responsibility for risk management to private sector or community-based organisations.

The key thinking behind the growth of the risk management industry is that risks can be identified in advance and that detailed 'risk assessment' can identify categories of risk so that risk reduction strategies can be put in place. This approach encourages the view that risks can be anticipated and measured and the prevailing assumption is that risk is inherently bad. People organising public events, for example, are required to develop comprehensive risk management strategies which aim to take decisions about risk out of the hands of people attending such events. The author initiated a public festival to celebrate the work of the leading Australian poet and nature conservationist Judith Wright which included guided walks on the bushland property where the poet had been inspired to create some of her best-known work. While these walks were rated by festival attendees as a highlight of the first festival they were banned for the second edition because public liability insurers decided that the risk of injury was too high.

Of course, it is important for people to be informed about their exposure to hazards and risks and the risk management industry has developed some important techniques for anticipating and assessing risks in advance (see Chapter 12). However, it has encouraged a culture of extreme risk avoidance as it seeks to take decisions for risk-taking out of the hands of individuals and communities. It fosters the illusion that risks can always be anticipated and effectively managed out of existence.

CULTURAL DIFFERENCES ON RISK AND RESILIENCE

People living in western societies only have to visit big cities in Asia, Africa or Latin America to know that it is very risky to get into a moving vehicle or cross a busy road. People in many parts of the world use infrastructure that would be deemed to be unsafe in the west. There is a much lower emphasis on public safety and risk avoidance. In such countries, risk management is commonly thought to be the responsibility of individuals rather than public authorities. Obviously we can go from one extreme to another here when little attention is paid to hazard exposure or the risk of death or injury. However, people who live with significant levels of risk on a daily basis may well be more resilient than those who have been led to believe that risk can be managed out of existence. Paul Slovic (2000) has noted that cultural differences in regard to the perception of risk not only operate between one society and another but also within a complex, multicultural society such as that of the USA, and his work will be discussed later.

As mentioned in Chapter 1 and discussed below, the author has gained an insight into cultural perceptions of risk by comparing reactions to the 2004 **tsunami disaster** in Sri Lanka with responses to the 2009 **Black Saturday** bushfire disaster that took place close to his home city of Melbourne. In general the tsunami victims accepted that the benefits of living near the sea brought unavoidable risks while an inquiry was held in Melbourne to attribute blame and work out ways to avoid such a disaster in the future. Few Australians can tolerate risk in the manner of Sri Lankans, just as few people living in the west would be comfortable with the levels of hazard exposure experienced by people living in a city such as Mumbai. However, we are likely to learn more about resilience by reading a novel by a writer like **Rohinton Mistry** than by reading a western disaster management manual.

tsunami disaster, Sri Lanka refers to tsunami waves triggered by an undersea earthquake that occurred near Sumatra in Indonesia which travelled across the Indian Ocean to reach Sri Lanka and southern India (26 December 2004).

Black Saturday refers to 7 September 2009, when temperatures of over 46°C and winds of over 120 kph combined to create fierce forest fires which destroyed 2,030 houses and claimed 173 lives in an area stretching from the edge of Melbourne to cover a range of small towns.

Rohinton Mistry was born into the minority Parsi-speaking Zoroastrian community of Mumbai. He emigrated to Canada in 1975 where he became a writer. His first two novels – *Such A Long Journey* (1991) and *A Fine Balance* (1995) – were both shortlisted for the prestigious international Booker Prize. His third novel, *Family Matters*, was published in 2002.

HAZARD EXPOSURE AND RISK TOLERANCE

International disaster management literature commonly makes the point that poor people and communities tend to live in areas where they are exposed to 'natural' hazards. For example, people living in shanty settlements close to the sea bore the brunt of the Indian Ocean tsunami in December 2004 (see Mulligan and Nadarajah 2012). People living in rather flimsy housing will suffer the most in extreme weather events or natural disasters and poor people and communities lack the economic resources to 'bounce back'.[2] People who are struggling to feed themselves and their families before the onset of a natural disaster – such as a prolonged drought – struggle to survive when an environmental disaster arrives.

The disaster management literature tends to focus on exposure to environmental hazards or to the consequences of wars and conflicts. Yet the Bophal chemical factory disaster of 1984 – when 2,259 people died after toxic gas leaked out of a plant owned by Union Carbide – should never be forgotten. Similarly, it should be remembered that relatively poor people who depended on fishing for their livelihoods bore the brunt of the crisis when overfishing triggered a dramatic collapse in populations of Atlantic Cod off the coast of Newfoundland in the summer of 1992.

As Adger and Brown (2009) have stressed, much can be done to reduce the hazard exposure of vulnerable people and communities across the globe, and the urgency to do so has increased when we know that global climate change is going to increase such hazard exposures. At the same time, exposure to risk can enable individuals and communities to develop their own risk management strategies because, as Slovic has said, it is probably the feeling of risk that enables people to decide when the benefits of risk are worth taking. When people have an opportunity to assess risks for themselves they may well decide that the benefits outweigh the threats. For example, people may decide to accept the risk of living near the sea or near a forest that can erupt in fire in order to enjoy the benefits. Self-reliance can be a significant factor in the development of individual or community resilience and Adger and Brown found that people living in the remote Orkney Islands north of Scotland probably have a greater 'adaptive capacity' than people living elsewhere in the UK.

BACK TO BECK AND THE RISK SOCIETY

As mentioned above, the German sociologist Ulrich Beck offered a fresh perspective on the experience of risk in his provocative and influential book *The Risk Society,* which was first published in English in 1992. Having been born near to the end of the Second World War in a part of Germany that was absorbed into Poland, Beck had known risk as a child and he began to study the transformations of post-war German society as a sociologist in the late 1960s. Germany had proceeded rapidly from post-war uncertainty into rapid reindustrialisation and Beck became interested in how the new kind of modernity brought new kinds of risk. The scale and scope of industrial society introduces a host of 'manufactured risks', Beck argued, and the **Chernobyl nuclear plant disaster** of 1987 served to highlight the fact that human-induced hazards can no longer be confined to local areas or within national boundaries. Yet, at the very time in history when all people on the planet are being exposed to more complex and ever-present human-induced hazards, risk denial is on the increase as authorities try to downplay the extent of the challenge.

Chernobyl nuclear plant disaster occurred in Ukraine on 26 April 1986, when a fire and explosion in a nuclear power plant killed 31 workers; it resulted in the release of radiation, and affected 500,000 people in and around Chernobyl, with radioactive particles being carried into Russia and across much of Europe.

Ulrich Beck

Ulrich Beck was born in 1944 in a Pomeranian town that was incorporated into Poland at the end of the war. He studied sociology at Munich University and after gaining his Ph.D. in 1972 he took up a position as a lecturer at the university in 1979. Beck's thesis about the rise of the 'risk society' was first published in German in 1986, just a few months before the nuclear accident at Chernobyl in Ukraine that brought his work to public attention in Germany. German-speaking American sociologist Scott Beck introduced

Beck's work to the leading English sociologist Anthony Giddens and together the three of them produced an influential book entitled *Reflexive Modernization* (1994). As well as his work on the rise of the risk society, Beck has argued that globalisation is forcing individual people to make a 'life of their own in a runaway world', and he has suggested that the global movement of people, goods and ideas has brought about a 'banal cosmopolitanism'. In his later years Beck divided his time between Munich University and the London School of Economics. He died in Munich in 2015.

Rather than admitting that we have little choice other than learn how to live with increasing levels of risk, Beck argued that the response within western societies has been: a) to 'externalise' risk through the implementation of management plans; b) to 'individualise' risk by using legal processes to settle questions of responsibility; and c) for authorities to 'minimise' risk by suggesting that risk can be adequately managed. The prevailing response to the globalisation of risk, Beck concluded, was the implementation of a system of 'organised irresponsibility'.

Although Beck painted a rather bleak picture of western responses to the globalisation of risk, he was surprisingly upbeat about the possible longer-term consequences. The inadequacies of prevailing risk management strategies will become increasingly apparent, he predicted, and this will prompt a widespread desire to rethink attitudes to risk. It will become apparent that we cannot leave risk to the experts and there will be a growth in public understanding about the strengths and weaknesses of science. While increasing requirements on corporations and authorities to reduce public exposure to hazards is obviously a good thing, Beck noted; no one should be exposed to new hazards without being told and there is clear distinction between unconscious hazard exposure and conscious risk taking. However, his key argument was that we live in an inherently risky world and we might be exposed to risks that originate very far from where we live. The mobility of risk might lead to greater ecological awareness, Beck suggested, recalling the public impact of Rachel Carson's book on the global spread of organic pesticides (see Chapter 2). To an extent, the recent rise of 'resilience thinking' confirms many of Beck's predictions.

RISK AND INNOVATION

Major breakthroughs in human history have involved risk. Travellers and explorers venture into the unknown. Christopher Columbus risked sailing off the edge of the earth to prove that it did not exist. **Orville and Wilbur Wright** backed their judgement to get into the machine they designed to take them into the air. Medical scientists have run the risk of infection to develop new vaccines. Normally conservative economists have even invented the term 'risk capital' to encourage risk-taking for the sake of economic innovation. It is important to note that innovation often requires a leap of imagination – a willingness to imagine the seemingly impossible. Leonardo da Vinci imagined the possibility of a flying machine long

Wright brothers
Wilbur (1867–1912) and Orville (1871–1948) turned from manufacturing bicycles to the construction of a 'flying machine'. In 1903 they became the first humans to test the theory of flight in a heavier-than-air machine first imagined by Leonardo da Vinci 400 years earlier. They subsequently developed systems that would enable pilots to control such machines in flight.

before a successful one was built, and people experimented imaginatively with the use of bacteria and viruses to fight infection long before Edward Jenner developed his smallpox vaccine in 1796. Plato is credited with saying that necessity is the 'mother of invention',[3] while Thomas Eddison added that any inventor needs a good imagination.[4] However, risks must always be taken to turn ideas into practice and innovation mostly occurs when curiosity overrides the avoidance of risk. Of course, repeated failures can be disheartening. However, successful innovation reminds us that risk-taking can be very rewarding.

Nassim Nicholas Taleb was born into a Greek Orthodox family in Lebanon in 1960. He studied science at the University of Paris before moving to the USA where he has attracted attention for his rather provocative scholarly essays.

Nassim Taleb (2007) has taken the criticism of risk management a step further by suggesting that a desire for control is the enemy of invention. Noting that Europeans were certain that all swans are white until the encountered black swans in Australia, he has introduced the concept of the 'black swan effect' to argue that we need to be much more attuned to the 'highly improbable' or unforeseen 'outliers'. Extraordinary events such as the rise of Hitler in Germany, or the terrorist attacks on the USA in September 2001, Taleb argued, remind us that we can never really know in advance what might happen and we need to focus more on things we do not know and can only imagine rather than what we think we know. We need to embrace unpredictability rather than fear it.

PERSONAL RESILIENCE

Early work by Norman Garzmezy in the 1950s on the resilience of children, in particular, continued grow in the 1970s, especially through the work of US developmental psychologist Emily Werner. However, psychologists have been somewhat divided over the extent to which individuals can *acquire* an ability to cope relatively well with stress or adversity. Considerable attention has focused on childhood experiences or the ability of parents to help their children learn how to cope with stress.[5] It is widely accepted that individuals can become more resilient by developing their self-esteem, problem-solving skills, emotional awareness and social support networks.[6] However, in noting that there are gender differences and a range of cultural factors associated with perceptions of risk, Paul Slovic (2000) pointed that the perceptions can be 'socially amplified' in the way that risk is discussed publicly in any particular society or culture. Slovic later stressed (2010) that feelings associated with lived experiences of risk play a significant factor in the ways in which people weigh up the dangers and benefits associated with risk-taking. It is the feeling of risk more than knowledge of possible dangers that influences risk tolerance, Slovic argues, and this suggests that prevailing risk management or avoidance strategies are largely ineffective. The renowned scholar of personal resilience, **Michael Rutter**, has argued that the experience of a relatively good outcome in risk experience is a major factor in building personal resilienc.[7]

Michael Rutter was born in 1933 and has been described as the 'father of child psychology' in the UK. He became professor in the Institute of Psychiatry at Kings College, London, and has been a consultant psychiatrist at Maudsley Hospital since 1966.

Paul Slovic

Paul Slovic was born in 1938. A after completing his undergraduate studies at Stanford University, he gained his Ph.D. at the University of Michigan in

1964. He founded the non-profit Decision Research foundation in 1976, and in 1993 he received the Distinguished Scientific Contribution Award from the American Psychological Association. He is a professor of psychology at the University of Oregon, and has been awarded honorary doctorates from universities in Sweden and the UK.

A focus on personal resilience can underplay the importance of the many social and cultural factors that help to shape attitudes to risk. However, the work of Slovic shows that there is an interesting interplay between the personal and social dimensions of risk taking. If prevailing risk management strategies are doing more harm than good in learning how to live in a risky world, then there is a need for a cultural shift in the way that risk is perceived within western societies, in particular. However, cultural change is driven by innovators and risk-takers; by people who can first imagine and then realise the highly improbable.

INSIGHTS FROM ECOLOGY

Whereas psychologists have focused on individual resilience, ecologists have long been interested in why particular *communities* of plants and animals are more resilient to changing circumstances or perturbations than others. The focus here may be on a particular species of plant or animal but more likely it is on the interaction between all the components of a particular ecosystem. For example, Australian forests are well adapted to regular fire events and the Indigenous people learned how to take advantage of this through the sustainable use of controlled burning – also dubbed 'firestick farming' – to keep the forests flourishing (Flannery 1994). By contrast, the European settlers saw little benefit to them in the fire-prone forests and they struggled to produce food by using farming methods that were developed in the relatively wet conditions of Europe. Efforts to employ European farming methods in Australia have caused widespread soil erosion, high levels of species extinction and unsustainable use of freshwater supplies. What the European settlers did not appreciate is that the ecosystems of Australia and Europe are radically dissimilar because they have become resilient within very different circumstances. An ecological framework highlights our human dependence on a host of non-human elements while the socio-ecological concept of resilience, pioneered by C. S. Holling, reminds us that all systems involve complex interactions and interdependencies.

Building on the work of other leading thinkers in the international Resilience Alliance, ecologist Brian Walker and science writer David Salt set out to depict the key characteristics of resilient ecosystems (Walker and Salt 2006). They note, for example, that such systems tend to be non-hierarchical in form and yet they also feature high levels of mutual dependence between the different plants and animals that constitute the system.

Walker and Salt note that no living systems are static because they must be able to deal with daily, seasonal and 'incremental change' over time; with the latter sometimes reaching a '**tipping point**' when the system dynamics are thrown

tipping point is a term taken from ecology, it refers to a point at which incremental changes trigger a major change in the system.

completely out of balance. The ability to adapt to changing conditions requires some internal diversity within the system and in nature this requires genetic variability which can result in the creation of new 'hybrid' species. However, Walker and Salt note that too much diversity can be deleterious to communities of plants and animals that have high levels of interdependence and clear and distinct 'roles' for different species within the ecosystem. So it is not diversity for its own sake that is important but rather enough '**functional diversity**' to allow for changes in how the system functions if and when conditions change. Natural ecosystems tend to operate as interconnected nodes to allow for adaptation to localised conditions combined with systems of flow and connectivity between the localised systems that provide a bigger resource base.

functional diversity is a term taken from ecology where it refers to the level of diversity required to give a particular ecosystem a capacity to adapt to change.

In thinking about how the principles of resilience might be applied to the planning of human systems ranging from individual farms to large settlements, Walker and Salt insist that there are some characteristics that have widespread relevance, as summarised below (see box).

Characteristics of resilient systems

- Resilient systems will always incorporate a fairly high degree of *diversity*, even if such diversity sometimes seems redundant to the immediate needs of the system. Diversity provides alternatives if particular features of a system fail to function effectively.
- A resilient system will sustain its *functional diversity* even if this might appear to be wasteful in the short term. The danger created by not sustaining 'functional diversity' can be illustrated by noting that '**monocrop**' **agriculture** leaves crops vulnerable to insect attacks and it depletes the fertility of the soil over time.
- Resilient systems display ***modularity*** rather than forms of hierarchy so that the system as a whole can continue to function even if particular parts of it fail. It makes sense, for example, to ensure that power supply to a big city is not centralised in particular forms of infrastructure in case any of it fails.
- It is important to know the difference between incremental changes – or 'slow variables' – and 'thresholds' of tipping points. Resilient systems can cope with the former but not necessarily the latter.
- A resilient system needs to have ***tight feedbacks*** so that all changes in circumstances and function are monitored. The wellbeing of all depends on knowing when a system is beginning to show signs of stress that might indicate an approaching threshold.

monocrop agriculture refers to the practice of growing a single crop in a large area, year after year.

modularity refers to the extent to which a system's components can be separated and recombined.

tight feedback refers to a close relationship between feedback received and the capacity of the system to adjust its performance accordingly.

DESIGNING RESILIENT HUMAN SYSTEMS

In thinking about how humans can consciously work with the characteristics of resilient ecosystems in order to design more resilient human systems, Walker and Salt note that humans have a particular – if not unique – capacity to learn from the past and from past crises in particular. Of course, we know that human subjectivity – manifested as competing values, beliefs and interests – can make it difficult to reach a consensus on what we want our systems to do for us. For example, people living in a large city will have many different views about what kind of transport infrastructure will best serve their needs and aspirations. Nevertheless, the characteristics identified by Walker and Salt are a good starting point for thinking more consciously about resilient systems. We need a mindshift – especially in western societies – to work with the assumption that change and uncertainty are the norm and they cannot be designed out of existence. At the same time, we humans have a unique collective ability to think our way into an uncertain future by employing what resilience thinkers have called 'strategic foresight'. Taking into account what was said earlier about the link between risk and innovation, we need to make room for creativity and experimentation and this has led to the suggestion that we need to combine experimental and experiential knowledge (Folke *et al.* 2003). Of course, resilience cannot be achieved by abandoning what has worked well in the past, and ecologists have suggested that resilient ecosystems develop a kind of embedded 'memory' (ibid.). In human terms this can mean that 'old ways' and accumulated local knowledge should never be ignored. **Jack Ahern** (2011) has added the important observation that human communication systems enable us to transcend the boundaries of place and space and he has stressed the importance of 'multiscale networks and connectivity' in learning from the past and in developing strategic foresight. The suggestion that the principles of resilience can be adapted from one context to another became the key motivation for the New York-based **Rockefeller Foundation** when it decided to mark its 100th anniversary by helping 100 cities across the globe to develop resilience plans that could enable them to cope better with both unexpected shocks and accumulating stresses (Rodin 2014). Adding later thinking on human resilience to the principles articulated by Walker and Salt in 2006 suggests the following principles for resilient design:

Professor Jack Ahern from landscape architecture at the University of Massachusetts has promoted the concept of 'multiscale networks and connectivity' in a series of publications and lectures since 2011 under the title 'Safe-to-fail'.

Rockefeller 100 Resilient Cities programme aims to encourage participating cities to address vulnerabilities to unexpected shocks (such as earthquakes or floods) and accumulating socio-economic stresses (such as high levels of unemployment). The programme began in 32 selected cities in late 2013 and reached the quota of 100 in May 2016.

1 *Avoid inflexible hierarchical structures* by decentring the distribution of resources, knowledge and power – and by encouraging lateral connections. This is relevant to the operations of large human organisations, of any kind, but it even enters considerations of basic logistics, as in the supply of electricity or water to a major city.
2 *Introduce modularity* to ensure that malfunctions within the system do not paralyse other parts or functions. This is what lies behind the notion of urban 'hubs' in urban planning and design and the idea of semi-autonomous 'business centres' within large organisations.
3 Create physical *spaces* and allow *time* for people to *think creatively* about their roles and functions or even the purpose of their work. This is what lies behind the creation of 'business incubators' but more broadly it underlines the importance of artistic 'precincts' which can trigger reflections and conversations about the culture of the communities in which they are located.
4 Ensure good *monitoring* of performance and effective communication of monitoring outcomes.

5 Give all people time to think and *reflect* on what they are doing and ensure that people can learn from each other's experiences. Respect experiential, experimental and expert knowledge.
6 Take advantage of communication technologies to create 'multiscale networks and connectivity' in order to share knowledge and create agile support networks.
7 Seek a *balance between conservation and innovation*; remembering that some old ideas and practices may have enduring relevance. Here we can note that community 'engagement' strategies which are aimed at getting target communities to adopt new practices may neglect the importance of local knowledge and enduring traditions.

LESSONS FROM HURRICANE KATRINA

When Hurricane Katrina slammed into the city of New Orleans in late August 2005 it caused unprecedented damage and loss of life. Around 1,800 people died and the damage was estimated at $US125 billion. Around 250,000 people were displaced; the highest number for any natural disaster in US history. Many of those who left the city never returned. The response to the disaster was poorly coordinated and widely criticised. The hierarchical command structure of the Federal Emergency Management Authority (**FEMA**) did not cope well with the breakdown of communications and it was relying on data collected at the time of Hurricane Betsy which occurred 40 years earlier in 1965. A fleet of buses that had been brought to a central location in order to evacuate people from flooded areas was itself submerged in flood waters.[8] The city came to regret the demise of coastal wetlands and mangroves that might have helped to dampen the impact of the storm.

FEMA is the Federal Emergency Agency of the USA.

Organisations that operated in a more modular way than FEMA were more effective. This included the US Coast Guard and, rather unexpectedly, the Walmart chain of stores where local managers were asked to make their own judgements about emergency distribution of goods and equipment.[9] It is also interesting to note that a time when most storm-affected neighbourhoods were abandoned the Vietnamese community in an area called **Versailles** set up its own Community Development Corporation which called for volunteers with relevant skills and experience to begin immediate reconstruction. The Versailles community was able to rely on cash donations coming from the far-flung Vietnamese diaspora and by January 2006 more than half the neighbourhood had been rebuilt. Other flood-affected communities did not have multiscale support networks.

Versailles, Louisiana is an area on the banks of the Mississippi River about seven kilometres from the outer limits of New Orleans where there is a large community of Vietnamese Americans.

New Orleans is built in a location where there have been 27 major flooding events in 290 years yet it was caught unawares by the intensity of Katrina. No lateral thinking had been put into the possible consequences of such an extreme weather event. The city has also been famed for its cultural diversity and for the world-famous music emanating from the black American community. Yet poor black American communities in the city fared the worst in the disaster and in the largely bungled recovery efforts and many commentators accused the city and federal government authorities of racism in their failure to target assistance to those who were in the greatest need. The city community was fractured by the

Photo 7.2 Residents rifling through relief supplies in the wake of Hurricane Katrina: the relief effort was poorly coordinated
Photo by Mark Wolfe (Wikimedia Commons)

disaster partly because it failed to treat its social and cultural diversity as a priceless asset. An inflexible, hierarchically organised, disaster response effort reduced community resilience at local and city-wide levels. In a negative sense, the experience of Hurricane Katrina confirms the importance of the resilient design principles outlined above.

Disaster preparation and recovery work is never easy and Hurricane Katrina struck with unprecedented force. Operating in the wake of a disaster presents a host of major challenges and it is easy to be critical from afar or to be wise in hindsight.[10] However, it is important to learn the lessons of past mistakes and in relation to the principles of resilient design listed above, key lessons of the Hurricane Katrina experience are:

- Hierarchical disaster planning and management failed.
- Little attempt was made to stop and think about what could go wrong before Katrina arrived.
- Monitoring systems were not in place to ascertain whether the needs of the disaster-affected people were being addressed.
- Communication systems were hierarchical and there were few opportunities for affected communities to learn from each other's experiences.
- As emergency services and systems struggled to cope, disaster-affected communities were left to fend for themselves in trying to find sources of support outside the city.
- The social and cultural assets of a culturally diverse urban community were not sufficiently valued.
- Top-down approaches to the rebuilding effort divided the multiracial community, which exacerbated racial and cultural divisions.

Discussion questions

1. What are some problems associated with western approaches to risk management?
2. What distinction needs to be drawn between hazard exposure and risk-taking?
3. According to Ulrich Beck, what factors are resulting in the rise of the 'risk society'?
4. What does Beck mean when he says that western responses to increasing risk amount to 'organised irresponsibility'?
5. What links does Paul Slovic make between the feeling of risk and decisions people make about taking risk?
6. How relevant and useful is it for humans to try to emulate the characteristics of resilient ecosystems?
7. Is the growing interest in 'resilient thinking' an admission of defeat of something more positive than that?
8. What do you consider to be strengths and weaknesses in 'resilience thinking'?
9. What are some of the key lessons from Hurricane Katrina in relation to risk and resilience?
10. What can be learnt by comparing the responses to the tsunami disaster in Sri Lanka to the Black Saturday bushfire disaster in Australia?

KEY READINGS

Adger, W. Neil and Katrina Brown (2009) 'Vulnerability and Resilience to Environmental Change: Ecological and Social Perspectives', in Noel Castree, David Demeritt and Diana Liverman (eds), *A Companion to Environmental Geography*, Oxford: Wiley-Blackwell, pp. 109–22.

Beck, Ulrich (1992) *The Risk Society: Towards a New Modernity*, London: Sage.

Beck, Ulrich (2007) *World at Risk*, Cambridge: Polity.

Folke, Carl (2006) 'Resilience: The Emergence of a Perspective for Socio-Ecological Systems Analyses', *Global Environmental Change*, 16(3): 253–67.

Mulligan, Martin and Yaso Nadarajah (2012) *Rebuilding Communities in the Wake of Disaster: Social Recovery in Sri Lanka and India*, New Delhi: Routledge.

Slovic, Paul (2000) *The Perception of Risk*, London: Earthscan.

Slovic, Paul (2010) *The Feeling of Risk: New Perspectives on Risk*, London: Earthscan.

Taleb, Nassim Nicholas (2007) *The Black Swan: The Impact of the Highly Improbable*, New York: Random House.

Walker, Brian and David Salt (2006) *Resilience Thinking: Sustaining Ecosystems and People in a Changing World*, Washington, DC: Island Press.

thematic essay

Living with risk

Sri Lanka was completely unprepared for the tsunami waves that smashed into coastal communities around two-thirds of the island's coastline on 26 December 2004 (Mulligan and Nadarajah 2012). The disaster-affected areas included some that were still in the grip of a long and debilitating civil war and yet the national community responded magnificently to the crisis and the most pressing problems caused by the disaster were dealt with surprising speed and efficiency.[11] Unfortunately, the lack of disaster preparation at local and national levels meant that many avoidable mistakes were made in the relief and recovery work. For example, poor coordination and needs assessments meant that a lot of the relief funding that flowed into the affected communities was wasted and the national government deepened the trauma of many who had lost their houses by announcing, within days of the disaster, that they would not be allowed to return to live in areas within 100–200 metres of the sea (ibid.). Hasty efforts to relocate disaster survivors into new permanent settlements often exacerbated the problems for those who were left without functioning social networks or opportunities to generate household livelihoods (ibid.). Token efforts to assess and respond to complex community needs increased the tensions and divisions within some of the affected communities (see Photo 7.3).

Photo 7.3 RMIT University researcher Yaso Nadarajah (right) consults community leader Ashraff Mohammed, among tsunami-ravaged houses at Sainthamuruthu in south-east Sri Lanka. Anger rose in this area when it received much less assistance than many others (October 2007)

Given that many of them derived little obvious benefit from the vast sums of relief money that reached Sri Lanka after the disaster, the author and his co-researchers expected to find considerable anger among the survivors during a study conducted from 2005 to 2009.[12] Yet most of the survivors were surprisingly sanguine about the disaster and its consequences. Some had participated in protests against particular decisions made by local authorities or aid agencies, yet there was no inclination to point a finger of blame at anyone in particular. Many people expressed the sentiment that if you live by the sea you have to expect danger and the occasional anger of the sea should not blind us to the fact that it gives so much to coastal communities. Life before the tsunami had been a struggle for many of the survivors and few of them expected government authorities to solve their problems. Resettled communities quickly began to rebuild social networks even when they had been resettled alongside people they did not previously know.

The reaction to the tsunami disaster contrasts strongly to the reaction in Victoria to the Black Saturday bushfire disaster of February 2009, where 173 people died and 2,030 houses were destroyed when intense bushfires swept through a string of communities not far from the northern edge of Melbourne. The firestorm erupted on a day when temperatures reached 46°C at the end of two weeks of extreme heat. Air humidity was very low at the end of nearly seven years of drought conditions and wind speeds reached 120 kph (75 mph). The Australian Weather Bureau accurately predicted the disastrous conditions and advised people to leave areas where bushfires might erupt. Yet the disaster prompted widespread calls for a public inquiry to find out who was responsible for what went wrong and to make recommendations to ensure that the disaster would not be repeated.

There was intense media interest in the public hearings of the Royal Commission established by the Victorian government and at one point the High Commissioner for Victorian Police, Christine Nixon, was blamed for not taking the early emergency calls seriously enough. Eventually the electricity supply company SP Ausnet bore the brunt of blame for not adequately maintaining the power lines blamed for igniting the most damaging fires. Public commentary on the disaster noted that people put themselves at risk when they build, buy or rent a home adjacent to Australian eucalypt forests that are well adapted to the regular occurrence of fire in hot and dry weather conditions. Most people living in the areas affected by the Black Saturday fires enjoy their bushland environments and some of the areas attract many visitors. Yet there was a widespread assumption in Victoria that government authorities should take the responsibility for minimising bushfire vulnerabilities. There was very little focus on the fact that the conditions prevailing in many parts of the state on Black Saturday were consistent with predictions being made by climate scientists about the likely consequences of global climate change.

There can be little doubt that Australia has better disaster management plans and a much greater capacity to respond to disasters than Sri Lanka. Australians demand and receive much higher levels of public safety than those prevailing in Sri Lanka. However, when it comes to living with risk Sri Lankans are probably better prepared and more resilient.

NOTES

1 Andrew Zolli argued that 'resilience' has replaced 'sustainability' in an Opinion Piece in the *New York Times* in November 2012.

2 The terms 'bounce back' and 'build back better' are used widely in disaster management literature.

3 www.phrases.org.uk/meanings/necessity-is-th-mother-of-invention.html

4 www.goodreads.com/quotes/tag/invention

5 See Emmy Werner and Ruth Smith (2001) *Journeys for Childhood to Midlife: Risk, Resilience and Recovery*, Ithaca, NY: Cornell University Press.

6 Michael Ungar (ed.) (2012) *The Social Ecology of Resilience: A Handbook of Theory and Practice*, New York: Springer.

7 Michael Rutter (2012) 'Resilience as a Dynamic Concept', *Development and Psychology*, 24: 335–44.

8 Revkin, A. (2010) 'Lessons in Resilience From New Orleans', DotEarth NY Times blog http://dotearth.blogs.nytimes.com/2010/08/13/lessons-in-resilience-from-new-orleans/

9 Horwitz, S. (2008) 'Making Hurricane Responses More Effective: Lessons from the Private Sector and the Coast Guard during Katrina', *Policy Comment* No 17, Mercalus Centre, George Mason University, Arlington.

10 The difficulties involved in rebuilding New Orleans in the wake of the hurricane are well document in the book by Edward Blakely (2012).

11 See Martin Mulligan and Nelum Buddhadasa (2006) 'Sri Lanka: Great Achievements and wasted opportunities: a balance sheet of Sri Lanka's post-tsunami response', *Arena Magazine* 83, pp. 35–7, Melbourne.

12 The author was a lead investigator on a study funded by the Australian Research Council of the tsunami recovery effort in different parts of Sri Lanka (2005–9). A report of the study findings prepared for the Australian aid agency AusAID served as the basis for a book published by Routledge (Mulligan and Nadarajah 2012).

PART II

Finding focus and taking action

CHAPTER 8

Environmental dimensions of sustainability

Key concepts and concerns

- ecological flows
- biodiversity
- the biosphere
- ecosystem services
- resilient nature
- reinhabiting reality
- encountering wildness
- welcome to the Anthropocene

INTRODUCTION

Returning to the Social Ecology model of sustainability introduced in Chapters 1 and 6, we start a series of three chapters by drilling down first into the sector named 'environmental'. This is the obvious starting point for focusing on the challenges articulated in the Brundtland Report in 1987, even if the notion of sustainable development often begins by looking at economic policies and practices. Environmental considerations impose constraints on economic growth and development and we need to begin by understanding the nature of those constraints. This chapter will focus on three of the nine RMIT Guiding Principles introduced in Chapter 2:

- Acknowledge interconnectedness at all levels within the biosphere.
- Acknowledge that there are limits to growth.
- Respect diversity in both nature and culture.

The first of these three principles assumes knowledge of key ecological concepts and this chapter will work with the concept of '**ecological flows**' introduced in Chapters 1 and 6. This concept helps us to travel back and forth between local and global dimensions of environmental sustainability. The concept of the biosphere is important for understanding the limits to growth at a global level and it is interesting that the term has only really been in use since the 1920s. If we are going to work with the notion of the biosphere in order to better understand

ecological flows is a term used in this book to refer to the movement of water, nutrients and other materials through local and global ecosystems.

global limits we need to consider why it was introduced and how it is being used. The word 'biodiversity' is an even more recent invention which has gained considerable traction in conservation policies and in public education work. However, the two terms 'biosphere' and 'biodiversity' are rather abstract and seemingly remote for many people. How can such concepts be brought home to more people and how can they help people think more critically about their personal and professional practices? The concept of 'ecosystem services' has been introduced to highlight the extent to which we humans depend on functioning ecosystems for our own survival and wellbeing and while it is a rather human-centred way of valuing nature it can bring otherwise hidden dependencies into view. While biodiversity strategies commonly focus on action to preserve 'threatened' or 'endangered' species, this chapter aims to demonstrate that all of us have a responsibility for the preservation of biodiversity wherever we might encounter it. It is not enough to support the creation and maintenance of nature reserves or parks for city-dwellers have more encounters with 'wild' nature than they might think and this brings us to the notion of 'reinhabiting reality' proposed by ecophilosopher **Freya Mathews**. In sequence the chapter will:

Freya Mathews established her reputation as an ecophilospher with the books *The Ecological Self* (1991) and *Ecology and Democracy* (1996). She was associate professor in philosophy at Melbourne's La Trobe University in 2008 and is a co-editor of the *PAN Philosophy, Activism and Nature* journal.

- Demonstrate how 'ecological flows' can connect the local and the global, with particular emphasis on the flow of water.
- Explain the importance of biodiversity, properly understood.
- Consider the value of the concept of the biosphere and argue that the concept of 'the commons' can complement it nicely.
- Focus on the resilience of nature and opportunities to 'reinhabit reality', even in the midst of our cities.
- Consider the suggestion that we are entering a whole new era of human responsibility for nature.

However, in keeping with a tradition established by the Brundtland Report we will begin with a brief balance sheet of global environmental concerns and responses. Of course we can only include a selection of concerns and achievement.

Startling statistics

- 200 species of plants or animals are becoming extinct each year.
- From 2000 to 2010 global forest cover was reduced by 5.2 billion hectares.
- 52 per cent of land used for agriculture globally is affected by moderate to severe soil erosion.
- Water tables are falling in China, India and underneath the Great Plains of the USA.
- A coral bleaching event in 2005 affected 90 per cent of coral reefs in the Caribbean.

SOME CONTINUING AND RISING GLOBAL CONCERNS

1 Human activities are continuing to drive many species of plants and animals into extinction in what some scholars have called the sixth mass extinction in the history of the planet[1] (Leakey and Lewin 1996). Of course, different species of plants and animals come in and out of existence in the 'natural' processes of evolution; however, it has been estimated that current extinction rates are at least 1,000 times higher than any such natural rate, with at least 200 species becoming extinct every year.[2]

2 The UN Food and Agricultural Organisation has noted that global loss of forest cover was at its highest levels in the 1990s. Since then rates of ***deforestation*** have declined and some areas have been reforested (sometimes with plantation timber). Yet from 2000 to 2010 the annual loss of forest cover was still an alarming 5.2 million hectares per year with the biggest losses affecting tropical forests in Africa and South America.[3]

3 In 2012 it was noted that the world is continuing to lose around 12 million hectares of arable land in the process known as ***desertification***.[4] The United Nations *Convention to Combat Desertification* notes that 52 per cent of all land used for agriculture is either moderately or severely affected by soil erosion with direct consequences for around 1.5 billion people. Of particular concern is the southward expansion of Africa's Sahara Desert.

4 Increasing use of groundwater supplies for agriculture is causing an alarming *fall in underground* ***water tables***. There is particular concern about falling water tables in India, China and beneath the Great Plains of USA, while the use of aquifers for irrigation in Saudi Arabia and Iran threatens to make them dependent on importing freshwater. It is estimated that 70 per cent of freshwater available to humans is currently being used for irrigation.

5 An increasing concern arises from an increasing frequency and intensity of ***coral bleaching*** events globally. The Great Barrier Reef near Australia has experienced severe bleaching for two years in a row in 2016 and 2017, killing up to 50 per cent of the coral.[5] The increase in coral bleaching is associated with the onset of global climate change.

deforestation refers to the removal of forests to make way for other forms of human land use.

desertification refers to the conversion of land that can be used for agriculture into desert.

water table refers to the boundary between dry ground and ground that is saturated with water that has penetrated into the ground.

coral bleaching refers to the loss of pigmented microscopic algae normally residing in coral colonies, caused by excessive heat or acidification of the sea. Coral reefs struggle to survive repeated bleaching.

SOME GLOBAL ACHIEVEMENTS

1 The *Ramsar Convention on Wetlands*, which was first formulated in the Iranian city of Ramsar in 1971, has helped to protect and restore around over 200 billion hectares of wetlands globally. As of May 2013 there were 2,123 registered Ramsar wetlands covering 208.38 million hectares in and across 167 nations.[6]

2 As mentioned in Chapter 4, a 1987 protocol for phasing out the use of the gases responsible for the appearance of holes in the global *ozone layer* has been effective and an international Treaty on Persistent Organic Pollutants came into effect in 2000, targeting the use of nine damaging POPs.

3 A *Convention on Biological Diversity* came into effect in 1992 and a *Treaty on Plant Genetic Resources* came into effect in 2001. As of 2013, 193 nations were listed as parties to the convention on protecting biodiversity.
4 A *Global Environment Facility* was established in 1991 to raise money for environmental conservation projects in poor nations. By 2013 it had 183 participating nations with 3,215 projects in 165 countries.[7]
5 A UN *Convention to Combat Desertification* was established in 1994 and by 2012 it had 192 participating nations. It was a focus for discussion at the Rio+20 'Earth Summit' held in Rio de Janeiro in 2012.
6 A UN *agreement to establish rules for fishing in international waters* came into effect in 2001. Unfortunately, the agreement had the cumbersome name of Agreement for the Conservation and Management of Straddling Fish Stocks and Highly Migratory Fish Stocks and major fishing nations have largely ignored its existence.

FROM THE GLOBAL TO THE LOCAL

A focus on big global concerns and trends can obscure the need to take action at local levels. Most forms of environmental degradation – including the accumulation of greenhouse gases in the atmosphere – begin with local human activities, particularly those related to agriculture and industrial production. Furthermore, changes occurring at a global level have consequences for particular local ecosystems on which we depend for our survival, even if the era of global trade means that some of those local systems are remote from where we live. Yet policies formulated at national or global levels often lose sight of local ecological realities. For example, carbon pricing schemes – while important – can deflect attention from the local sources and consequences of greenhouse gas emissions while carbon offset schemes can provide an excuse for continuing with activities that generate CO_2.

As argued in Chapter 2, increasing global awareness contributed strongly to the emergence of the concept of sustainability as we know it today. It is critically important to have a good understanding of big global challenges, such as those discussed in Chapters 4–5 and Chapters 13–16. However, we need to then trace those challenges back to localised point sources because that is where the changes need to be made. We need, for example, to trace the greenhouse gas emissions back to the source of the emissions. As argued, in Chapter 3, we also need to focus on per capita use of energy and resources rather abstracted categories such as national averages. We need to reduce waste streams at source and repair degraded habitats. We need to stop plastics from flowing into the Pacific Ocean where no national government is prepared to take responsibility for the problem.

Rachel Carson's famous book – *Silent Spring* – helped a lot of people understand the links between local impacts and their widespread, even global, consequences. Climate scientists are now helping a new generation understand that localised activities are resulting in global warming and the onset of unpredictable climate change; noting that localised human activity can trigger extreme weather events at remote locations. We understand linkages between the local and the global by understanding the functioning of 'ecological flows'.

ECOLOGICAL FLOWS

As mentioned in Chapter 7, ecologists in the 1920s coined terms such as ecosystems and food chains or webs, with an underlying understanding of energy and material flows through living systems. It has subsequently become popular to think about various cycles that link local systems into wider cycles of things like water and nutrients. Such cycles can be represented diagrammatically and this enables the viewer to visualise the flow of otherwise hidden elements such as nitrogen or carbon between land, sea and atmosphere. This also helps us see that the flows can result in imbalances so that farmers and gardeners know that soils can easily lose their life-enhancing balance of carbon compounds, phosphates and nitrogen. The onset of global climate change has focused increasing attention on 'the carbon cycle' as represented in Figure 8.1, and this has popularised associated concepts such as 'carbon sinks'. The point about flows and cycles is that they are dynamic and terms such as 'storage' or 'sinks' can be a little misleading. However, they help to highlight problems of imbalances within a cycle.

In the case of the carbon cycle, human activity is altering the balance between carbon 'stored' in the form of marine and terrestrial plant matter and fossil fuels within the lithosphere compared to the carbon 'stored' in the form of greenhouse

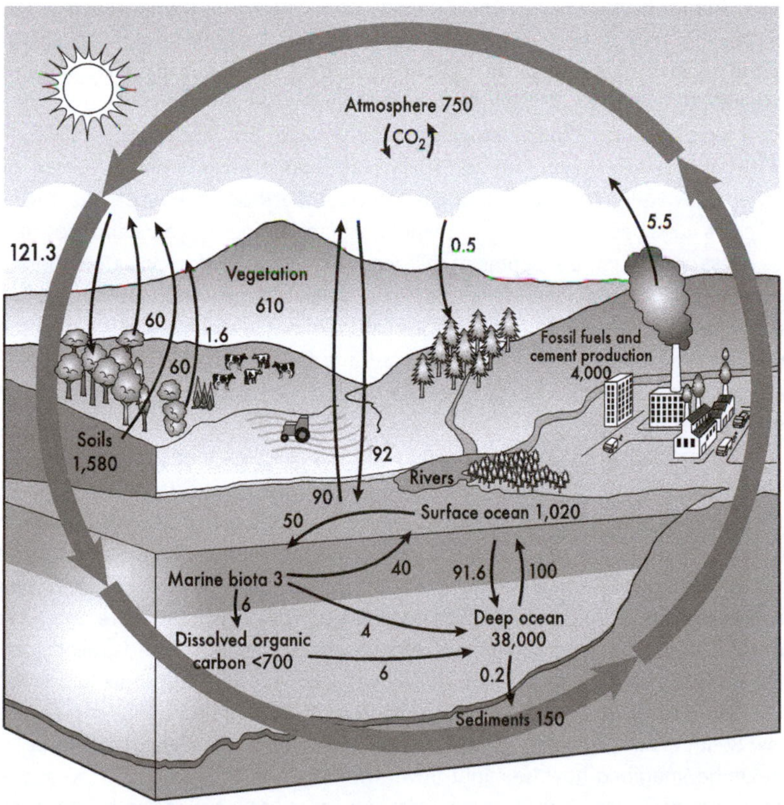

Figure 8.1 The carbon cycle
Source: NASA

gases in the atmosphere. We can take steps to return atmospheric carbon to land- and sea-based 'carbon sinks' yet we also need to understand that human activity is continuing to accelerate the flow of carbon back into the atmosphere. The accumulation of greenhouse gases in the atmosphere alters the movement of solar energy to the surface of the planet and back out again and we understand that it is the interaction between the flows of carbon and energy that has rather profound consequences for the global climate and the weather patterns that we experience locally. A diagrammatic representation of the carbon cycle enables the viewer to see how he/she is personally linked into the largely unseen movements of carbon atoms and this can help to make sense of concerns about increasing emissions of CO_2. All such diagrams simplify the functioning of complex natural systems, however they provide a good entry point for understanding connections between the local and the global.

FOLLOWING THE FLOWS OF WATER

The hydrological cycle is a particularly good starting point for understanding ecological flows because we can all visualise the movement of water into and out of our bodies and into and out of the households in which we live. Water makes life on Planet Earth possible and Chapter 13 will demonstrate that deceptively simple water molecules have a wide array of dazzling capabilities; yet most humans tend to treat it with relative disdain. Those of us living in western societies generally assume that it is freely available to us whenever we turn on a tap. Few of us stop to contemplate the journey that water takes to reach our mouths in a safe form for drinking and few even want to think where it goes when we flush our toilets. The restless water molecules that pass through our bodies, households, towns and cities have been circulating on Planet Earth for millions of years and they may have passed through the depths of the oceans or spent time in polar ice-shelves before reaching us or even after they have been with us. Individual molecules might travel vast distances within various cloud formations before returning to the surface as precipitation and once they get into the sea they might again travel vast distances within the 'global conveyor belt' of ocean currents (see Figure 8.2 and Chapter 4).

Contemplating the long journeys of water molecules that pass through our own bodies helps us to imagine our links to global systems of circulation. However, it still requires a leap of imagination to realise that we are more directly linked to creatures living in the sea than we might think. The various bits of plastic trash that are killing birds and marine animals in the middle of the vast Pacific Ocean have come out of our towns and cities; washed down through rivers and bays before getting caught up in the movement of ocean currents. An Australian poet, Michael Patterson, once recalled a time when he was standing beside a small mountain stream that he knew to be a source of the Clarence River in northern New South Wales, Australia. As he bent down to take a sip of water from the fresh stream he imagined how he might travel with the moving water to arrive at the coastal city of Grafton. It then struck him that he might not stop at Grafton because the very water that was passing his lips might just as well end up in the mouth of a distant whale and he contemplated the thought that he was metaphorically

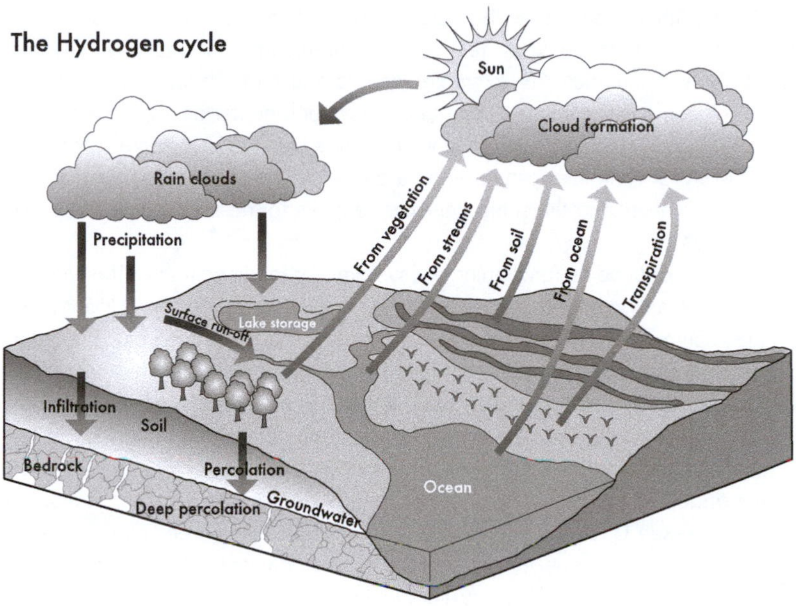

Figure 8.2 The hydrological cycle

'kissing the lips of whales'.[8] Global fisheries are in trouble – as we will see in Chapter 13 – yet the movement of water links us to them in ways we rarely imagine.

UNDERSTANDING BIODIVERSITY

Biologists have long been interested in the diversity of species on Planet Earth and Darwin's theory of evolution explained how such diversity emerged. However, the term 'biodiversity' came into popular use in the late 1980s to refer to understandings that have emerged within ecological science about the function of diversity within biological communities or ecosystems. Miller and Spoolman (2010) have noted that biologists are interested in at least four different forms of diversity and they list: *genetic diversity* (within a population or species); *species diversity* (between species); *ecological diversity* (referring to the diversity of habitats across the planet); and ***functional diversity*** (referring to the diversity within particular living communities that can make them adaptable and resilient).

functional diversity is a term used by ecologists which refers to the level of diversity required by a biological community to make it resilient to disturbance or capable of change and adaptation.

The notion of 'functional diversity' is particularly important here because it is not diversity per se that serves biological communities well but rather the presence of sufficient diversity to enable the community to respond to changes or disturbances. For example, particular species may cope better than others with floods or fires or the arrival of new species from elsewhere and ecologists note that 'hybridisation' often occurs in areas where one kind of ecosystem overlaps with another and new 'hybrid' species might be able to move into an area where there has been a major disturbance of some kind. Australian forests are well adapted to fire partly because there are high levels of hybridisation among the prevailing eucalypt trees.

On the other hand, too much diversity might not serve a biological community well because a functioning system requires predictable interactions between robust sub-communities. For example, insects and birds of various kinds play critical roles in the pollination of plants as they seek nectar as a source of food and such mutually beneficial interactions require a balance between diversity and predictability. Communities can only operate when there is a degree of conformity as well as diversity and the same principles applies to the functioning of human communities.

Humans depend on functioning ecosystems for food and many other 'natural resources', clean water and the balance of oxygen in the atmosphere. Plant communities can reduce soil erosion, water run-off and flooding, and coastal erosion caused by tides and storm surges. Many of our medicines and pharmaceutical products come from particular plants and animals – many of them in endangered tropical forests – and we enjoy nature for recreation or for what might be called 'spiritual renewal'. The term '**ecosystem services**' has been coined to refer to all the benefits humans derive from the existence of biodiversity and functioning ecosystems (see Costanza 2016). It is a rather human-centred term. However, it has been used to argue for the protection of biodiversity globally and will be discussed again briefly in Chapters 13 and 14.

ecosystem services is a term used to refer to all the benefits humans derive from the presence of healthy ecosystems.

THE BIOSPHERE

The term 'biosphere' is used to refer to the zone encircling the planet within which life can exist. It encompasses part of the planet's atmosphere, part of the solid crust – or 'lithosphere' – and much of the movement of water molecules in the 'hydrosphere'. However, it is more difficult to comprehend than 'atmosphere' or 'lithosphere' and it is often used rather vaguely. While the word was probably coined by the Austrian geologist Eduard Suess in 1875, it only gained traction after it was picked up by the Russian geophysicist Vladimir Vernadsky in 1926, around the time when ecological science was also emerging from the shadows. The notion of the biosphere helps to highlight the fact that we live on a planet with ultimately finite 'natural resources' within a single living system. UK scientist James Lovelock tried to make this point even more strongly during the 1970s when he suggested that we hark back to Greek legends of the goddess **Gaia** to think of the whole planet as a single, self-regulating living system. Angered by the fact that humans have continued to ignore warnings about human-induced global climate change, Lovelock returned to this theme in 2006 with the book *The Revenge of Gaia*.[9]

Gaia, in Greek mythology Gaia was the personification or primordial being of Earth, seen as being the mother of all. James Lovelock's way of thinking about the biosphere as a single living system came to be known as the 'Gaia hypothesis'.

In 1971, the United Nations Educational, Scientific and Cultural Organization (**UNESCO**) set up a Man and the Biosphere Programme to foster interdisciplinary research on ecosystem conservation. More broadly the programme aimed to popularise understanding of the concept of the biosphere and this eventually led to the setting up of 'biosphere reserves' in a wide range of countries in order to protect the planet's biodiversity. UNESCO reports that there are now 621 such reserves in 117 countries, with 12 of them straddling national borders. They now operate as a World Network of Biosphere Reserves.

UNESCO emerged as an idea at a conference of national education ministers held in England in 1942. It was formalised at a UN-sponsored conference held in 1945 and by the end of 1946 it had the active support of 30 national governments.

A problem with a term like 'biodiversity' is that it may only seem to operate at a global scale and for this reason the environmental education scholar and writer

Mitchell Thomashow contributed a book *Bringing the Biosphere Home* (2002).[10] Thomashow argued that all people have embodied interactions with the bio-sphere through the food we eat, the water we drink, our felt experiences of weather and seasons. We need to extend our embodied perception to a wider understanding of how the biosphere operates, he argued, in order to 'assess [my] own action and practices and those of my neighbors'[11] in relation to biospheric wellbeing.

Mitchell Thomashow was the Chair of Environmental Studies at Antioch University New England (1976–2006). He left Antioch to take up the position of Director of Unity College Maine, and in 2011 he became Director of the Second Nature Presidential Fellows Program which aims to bring a comprehensive sustainability agenda to US colleges and universities.

REVALUING 'THE COMMONS'

UNESCO established its network of 'biosphere reserves' in order to popularise the idea that certain areas within the biosphere need to be set aside for the conservation of global biodiversity. In a sense, this harks back to a much older human practice in which particular areas were set aside for the sustainable harvesting of food and natural resources. Although the tradition arose in many different settings and forms – from the mediaeval English village 'common' to communal forests in India – the concept of 'the commons' has been used to refer to areas set aside for public benefit rather than private use. In an essay that is widely considered to have been seminal for the rise of modern environmental scholarship, Garrett Hardin (1968) argued that a steady rise of self-interest has replaced earlier forms of communal interest and this has led to the overexploitation of agricultural lands even if they are still held as communal property. A major transformation occurred in Britain in the period 1760–1820 when 'enclosure laws' turned the widespread 'commons' – communal land that had been widely used for collecting or growing food, timber and other resources – into freehold title. This sparked a mass migration of rural people into the emerging industrial cities or overseas to countries like the USA, Canada and Australia. The enclosure of the commons began in Britain but it quickly spread to other parts of Europe. It meant that far fewer people were involved in the production of food and other agricultural products but Hardin suggests that it also led to a major shift of consciousness in western thinking about land and nature.

The enclosure of the commons has continued in non-western nations right up to the present. In March 1974, a group of peasant women in the northern Indian village of Reni went into communal forests to put their arms around trees in an effort to prevent them being felled by logging contractors and their action sparked similar protests in numerous communal forests in nearby regions in a movement that became known as the Chipko movement. It is a little sad to think that the brave action by the Reni women was later turned into a demeaning epithet used to question the sanity of environmental campaigners who are labelled as 'tree-huggers'. However, the idea of 'the commons' is proving to be more resilient than Hardin imagined. For example, lobster fishermen operating off the coast of Maine established the Maine Lobstermen's Association in 1954 in order to look after their shared resource and it is now the largest fishing industry association on the east coast of the USA. The idea of a 'global commons' has also been invoked to negotiate an international agreement for the protection of Antarctica's extraordinary biodiversity and a new protective treaty came into effect in 1998. Clearly the notion of 'the commons' can apply equally in relation to areas of land and sea and at levels ranging from a village to biospheric regions. It may be a more flexible and evocative term than 'biosphere reserve'.

RESILIENT NATURE

The global environment movement has made much in recent decades of the fact that growing numbers of species are facing extinction. While this has undoubtedly helped to mobilise support for conservation work it has probably encouraged a lot of concerned people to think of nature as being highly fragile. Furthermore, the international emphasis on establishing reserves or national parks to protect biodiversity has probably encouraged city-dwellers to imagine that biodiversity is something that exists only in rather remote areas. A range of writers[12] have argued that a relatively recent emphasis on the value of 'wilderness' protection has made it seem that some nature – often described misleadingly as 'pristine' – is worth preserving while the nature we are likely to encounter close to our human settlements is not as valuable. At a time when the majority of people on the planet are living in cities it is easy for city-dwellers to think that nature conservation is something they might support but not participate in.

Yet it is not hard to show city-dwellers that there is much greater biodiversity in and around their homes than they had imagined and that 'wild nature' is much closer than they think. Wild birds of prey take refuge in high city buildings or in city parks in major metropolises like New York; wild foxes come out at night in central London; colonies of native flying foxes have taken up residence in botanical parks in Australian cities, while other native birds have been lured back to central city areas by the growing abundance of native vegetation (see Photo 8.1). Wildness is very visible when bears come to forage in urban waste bins in the USA or Canada; what is much less visible is the fact that urban and suburban homes and gardens provide homes for a plethora of wild spiders and insects. If a city block is left vacant for any length of time, it will be recolonised by plants and the Australian branch of the international Seed Savers network has reported finding rare and endangered plant species within such spontaneous colonies.

English nature writer Robert Macfarlane (2007) has written very evocatively about the 'wild places' that exist in some surprising locales across the British Isles, while the Australian nature writer Tim Low (2002) has noted that some Australian animals and plants are thriving in towns and cities were they find new habitats inadvertently created by humans. Low also pointed out that there are ancient trees in city parks and gardens that can evoke a distant past; providing a living link, in the case of Australia, to what existed before the arrival of European settlers. It can be exciting, Low insists, to become aware of thriving communities of plants and animals that exist in our midst, often without our knowledge.

Macfarlane and Low both insist that nature is often more resilient than we imagine and this also became the theme of a set of images taken by photographer Sergei Gaschaks in 2012 when he visited the forests surrounding the Ukrainian town of Chernobyl which was abandoned after an explosion and fire in a nuclear energy power plant in 1987. While the area is still deemed to be unfit for human habitation 25 years after the nuclear disaster, Gaschaks reported that the forests are alive with wild animals.

Photo 8.1 Wild animals can be closer than most city-dwellers think: a fox in London
Source: © Terry Whittaker/Alamy

Reinhabiting reality

Picking up the theme that city-dwellers are much closer to wild nature than they imagine, the Melbourne-based ecophilosopher Freya Mathews (2006) has argued that it requires a conscious effort to look through the built infrastructure of the city in order to see the diverse communities of plants and animals that live in the same spaces as us. Mathews once took a very long walk with a group of friends in order to follow a particular urban creek from its destination near the centre of Melbourne to its source beyond the city limits; she argues that such journeys of discovery are available to all of us, as long as we make the time for them.

For most city-dwellers, daily routines are largely shaped by the way the built infrastructure operates and we become blind to the deeper reality in which we are immersed. That is why Mathews uses the term 'reinhabiting reality' for the conscious practice of reconnecting with the non-human beings that coexist with us. She describes a process of 'becoming native' to the places in which we dwell and she suggests that this amounts to a 'recovery of culture' that can give our lives a deeper sense of purpose.

A WHOLE NEW ERA OF HUMAN RESPONSIBILITY

While non-human nature can be more resilient than we might have imagined, US environmental writer **Bill McKibben** (1989) has argued that human activities have altered the conditions of life for all other animals and plants on Planet Earth, no matter how remote they might seem to be from the centres of human settlements. Pollutants produced locally can be carried far and wide by wind and water currents and the onset of human-induced climate change makes it even more apparent that nothing can escape our influence (McKibben 2010). According to McKibben, we have already witnessed the 'end of nature' to the extent that it cannot exist independently of us humans. This means that we have a greater responsibility than ever before for the fate of all other plants and animals on our planet in what some have dubbed the Anthropocene era.[13]

This watershed moment in the history of life on Planet Earth may seem rather scary. However, McKibben and others[14] argue that a growing awareness of this new era of co-dependence could also make us finally see the folly in trying to assert a perceived superiority over the non-human domain. Rather than exert a mastery over nature, we will be obliged to figure out how to ensure mutual coexistence and, according to **Thomas Berry**, this will give us a stronger appreciation for remarkable evolution of life on Earth. Berry and **Brian Swimme** worked collaboratively for ten years on ways of telling the story of the universe in order to engender a much deeper appreciation for the evolution of life on Earth and Swimme has continued that work with a wide range of books and videos. Starting with the big bang that created our expanding universe, we share a deep 'kinship' with all the planet's lifeforms and, according to Berry and Swimme,

Bill McKibben discovered a passion for journalism by becoming editor of the Harvard University student newspaper during his time at the prestigious university. He has combined his career as a freelance journalist with the position of Schumann Distinguished Scholar at the liberal arts Middlebury College in Vermont. He founded the climate change action organisation 350.org in 2007 and was called the 'world's best environmental journalist' by *Time Magazine* in 2009. In 2013 he won the international Gandhi Peace Prize.

Thomas Berry and Brian Swimme Thomas Berry had a long career in both

scientific accounts of *The Universe Story* eventually lead us to the conclusion that we belong to a 'communion of subjects'. There is no need for us to deny our own subjectivity or self-interest, the argument goes, but we need to acknowledge that other forms of life have their own subjective interests in order to work through the requirements of coexistence.

western and Asian cultural and religious studies when he met Brian Swimme in 1982. He worked for 20 years as the Director of the Riversdale Centre for Religious Research and served as President of the American Teillhard Association (1975–87). Berry introduced Swimme to the work of French theologian and philosopher Teillhard de Chardin, while Swimme was able to bring his studies in mathematics and cosmology into their decade-long collaboration that resulted in the publication of *The Universe Story* (1992).

Discussion questions

1. Why is it important to trace global environmental concerns back to local ecological realities?
2. What is meant by the concept of 'ecological flows' and what can we learn by focusing, in particular, on flows of water?
3. Why do ecologists talk about the importance of 'functional diversity' within natural ecosystems?
4. Discuss the proposition that we need to find a balance between diversity and conformity within both 'natural' and human communities.
5. What are some strategies for making the concept of the biosphere more accessible?
6. Why is it important to focus on resilience as well as vulnerability in relation to nature?
7. Why does Freya Mathews talk about 'reinhabiting reality'?
8. Why does Bill McKibben suggest that we have entered a whole new period of human responsibility or non-human life – and what good might come of the new imperative?
9. What did Henry David Thoreau have in mind when he suggested that 'in wildness is the preservation of the world'?

KEY READINGS

Berry, Thomas and Brian Swimme (1992) *The Universe Story: From the Primordial Flaring Forth to the Ecozoic Era – A Celebration of the Unfolding Cosmos*, San Francisco, CA: HarperCollins.

Low, Tim (2002) *The New Nature: Winners and Losers in Wild Australia*, Melbourne: Viking/Penguin.

Macfarlane, Robert (2007) *The Wild Places*, London: Granta Books.

McKibben, Bill (1989) *The End of Nature*, New York: Random House.

Mathews, Freya (2005) *Reinhabiting Reality: Towards a Recovery of Nature*, Albany, NY: SUNY Press.

Miller, G. Tyler and Scott E. Spoolman (2010), 13th edn, *Environmental Science*, Belmont, CA: Brooks Cole.

Thomashow, Mitchell (2002) *Bringing the Biosphere Home: Learning to Perceive Global Environmental Change*, Cambridge, MA: MIT Press.

thematic essay

Encountering wildness

The much acclaimed Scottish born American naturalist John Muir first became aware of the powerful nature writing of Henry David Thoreau in the same year that Thoreau died (1862). Muir said that the work made a huge impression on him. Yet whereas Muir went on to campaign for the protection of magnificent wilderness areas – like the area that became Yosemite National Park in 1890 – Thoreau actually preferred to stay at home in Concord where he had been born and where he returned in 1837 after studying the classics at Harvard University. He conducted a kind of experiment in living in a small hut adjacent to Walden Pond, outside Concord, and wrote about it in his most famous work *Walden: Life in the Woods* published in 1854. However, he stayed in and around Concord until his death, keeping a journal of his daily walks which was eventually published as *Walking* in 1861. He only left Concord for fairly short trips; to nearby rivers, Cape Cod, several months on Staten Island and several trips to the forests of Maine. Perhaps the Maine woods were his favourite because he wrote about his encounters with wild nature in the forests. However, he also insisted that you could find wild nature in and around Concord if you were attentive, for example, to all the life you might find in a single pond. Towards the end of his life he famously suggested that 'I have travelled the world ... without leaving Concord',[15] by which he meant that he had seen enough and had a strong enough imagination to visualise all the places he read about. He was also interested in the wildness that we might find within ourselves as humans.

In the latter stages of his life Thoreau became famous for public lectures that he gave in the Lyceum Theatre in Concord where he would pace up and down the stage sharing his thoughts on ways to live with, rather than in fear of, nature. On at least one such occasion he bellowed to his audience: 'In wildness is the preservation of the world!'[16] This famous saying has often been misquoted by replacing the word 'wildness' with the word 'wilderness' when that is almost the opposite of what Thoreau wanted to convey. Wildness is not only to be found in remote and awe-inspiring places but close to where we live and even within us. It is this wildness that gives us creativity and a capacity to deal with challenges and changes. It helps to dissolve our sense of separation from non-human nature and to accept that it is foolish to even think about asserting a mastery over nature.

Technologies that can make our lives more comfortable also enforce a sense of separation from nature. We tend to think of our homes as safe havens and our cities and towns as fortresses. Most of us dwell within the 'built form' with little awareness of the natural landscapes or the flows of energy, water and materials that continue to filter through our bodies, homes, towns and cities. This is a sharp contrast to the ways in which Indigenous people in all parts of the world lived in close relationship with what David Abram has called the 'more-than-human' world (Abram 1996). According to Paul Carter (1996) we moderns tend to have our eyes set on destinations as we travel in corridors cut through the land, while Indigenous people followed 'drift lanes' that can be understood as a kind of 'dialogue between foot and ground' (ibid.: 360). The word 'songlines' has been coined to refer to the ways in which Indigenous Australians travelled through familiar territory. Stories were associated with every single place in those landscapes and they could be chanted as people travelled to maintain orientation and enchant the journey. Most of us now separate our feet from the ground with layers of concrete, timber and shoe rubber. Yet we can use our imagination to reconnect with the land beneath and remember that all places have a multitude of stories accumulated over great expanses of time, before and after human settlement. We are much close to 'wild nature' that we often think and, like Thoreau, we can use our imagination to put our feet to the ground in storied landscapes (Mulligan 2003).

NOTES

1 See Leakey and Lewin (1996).
2 www.panda.org/about_our_earth/biodiversity/
3 www.earth-policy.org/indicators/C56/forests_2012
4 www2.unccd.int/
5 www.barrierreef.org/6 www.ramsar.org/
7 www.thegef.org/
8 The unpublished poem by Michael Patterson was shared with students and staff attending a postgraduate conference at the University of Western Sydney in January 2000.
9 James Lovelock, *The Revenge of Gaia: Earth's Climate Crisis and the Fate of Humanity*, New York: Basic Books, 2006.
10 Mitchell Thomashow, *Bringing the Biosphere Home: Learning to Perceive Global Environmental Change*, Boston, MA: MIT Press, 2002.
11 Thomashow (2002: 2).
12 For example, William Cronon.
13 The term Anthropocene may have been coined by ecologist Eugene Stoermer, www.wikipedia/wiki/Anthropocene
14 For example, Thomas Berry and Brian Swimme.
15 As cited by Simon Schama, *Landscape and Memory*, London: Fontana Press, 1996, p. 576.
16 Ibid.

CHAPTER 9

Social dimensions of sustainability

Key concepts and concerns

- environmental economics
- the economics of happiness
- values-based policy
- social inclusion and the politics of participation
- cultural vitality
- community formation

INTRODUCTION

The Social Ecology model of sustainability moves the functioning of the economy into the social domain rather than allow it to sit outside, or even above,[1] the functioning of society. Although this is seen as a rather radical move by many economists it harks back to the influential work of the Hungarian economist **Karl Polanyi** in the 1940s, in which he argued that economics must be embedded in culture and society. The social framing of economics helps to create a stronger link between economic development and the social equity outcomes of that development and this, in turn, links back to the considerations of both intragenerational and intergenerational equity that are highlighted in two of the nine RMIT Sustainability Principles. Focusing on the social outcomes of economic development also brings into play the principle that prevention is better than cure because it can be difficult and expensive to wind back economic developments that are having harmful social consequences for significant numbers of people. A focus on equity suggests that economic planning needs to have social inclusion as an important benchmark and this imperative needs to be a starting consideration.

Karl Polanyi (1886–1964) was born in Vienna of Hungarian parents. His expertise covered economic history, economic anthropology, political economy and historical sociology. He gained a position at Columbia University, New York, in 1947 but after 1953 had to base himself in Canada after his wife was denied a visa to the USA because of her past as a communist.

From the perspective of the global environment, economic planners need to put aside their discipline's obsession with growth to consider limits and constraints. The riposte of economists is often to warn that only growth-oriented economies can deliver good social outcomes in terms of employment and remuneration. However, Chapters 3 and 4 have demonstrated that prevailing economic development models are failing to close the gap between the rich and the poor while they also fail to satisfy the 'authentic' needs of people who find themselves on the treadmill of hyperconsumption. Narrow ways of assessing economic performance deliver forms of growth that are not only damaging to the natural environment but also socially divisive and we need to find new ways to ensure that economic development can deliver much better equity and wellbeing outcomes. This includes a need to ensure that poor people and communities are not exposed to dangerous forms of environmental pollution and other forms of environmental degradation. This chapter will argue that the functioning of the economy is only one dimension of social planning because it is also important to focus on cultural vitality and the politics of participation. The RMIT Principles that underpin this discussion are:

- Acknowledge that there are limits to growth.
- Remember that prevention is better than cure.
- Work to improve intragenerational equity.
- Face up the challenge of intergenerational equity.
- Respect requisite diversity in nature and culture.

The chapter begins with a brief review of the emergence of 'environmental economics' and the more radical 'ecological economics' before focusing on some of the key concepts used to broaden economic thinking in relation to both environmental and social impacts. Following discussion about the search for the 'good life' in Chapter 3, it will then focus on more recent attempts to promote an 'economics of happiness'. The economics of happiness is plagued by the fact that it is impossible to measure happiness and therefore set benchmarks for achieving it and this brings us to a discussion about the differences between 'evidence-based' and 'values-based' policy. Following the argument made in Chapter 4 that shifting the focus from income benchmarks to wider considerations of social inclusion, the chapter includes a very brief discussion of theories related to a politics of participation. This touches on the theme of human social and cultural diversity and the chapter picks up the argument that 'cultural vitality' can be seen as a 'fourth pillar' of sustainability.[2] The word 'community' is used widely yet loosely in literature on sustainability and the chapter will conclude with the argument that communities only exist in the contemporary world to the extent that they are created and constantly reinforced.

In summary, the chapter touches on:

- The need to widen prevailing economic thought and action to ensure that it can deliver better outcomes in relation to both environmental and social wellbeing.
- The need to make value judgements more transparent in policy-making, with a particular emphasis on increasing social inclusion and political participation.
- The importance of cultural vitality as a measure of social wellbeing.
- The need to constantly create and reinforce inclusive communities.
- Increased opportunities to engage in non-localised 'communities of practice'.

Kenneth Boulding (1910–93) born in Liverpool and educated at Oxford University, Boulding moved to the USA after the Second World War and became a US citizen in 1948. He argued that economics and sociology should be seen as a single field of social science. As a member of the Religious Society of Friends (Quakers) he was a persistent advocate for peace and non-violence.

BEYOND GROWTH ECONOMICS

Kenneth Boulding may have been the first economist to argue, in the late 1960s, that economic theory and practice needed to come to terms with limits to human use of 'natural resources' on 'spaceship Earth' yet a commitment to growth continues to lie at the heart of mainstream economics. US economist **Herman Daly** took up the battle in the late 1970s with the suggestion that we need to move from growth economics to 'steady-state' economics but even when he was appointed to a position in the World Bank he was not able to seriously shake the commitment to growth. UK academic and government adviser **Tim Jackson** tried a different tack in 2009 when he argued passionately that the time has come to decouple 'prosperity' and 'growth' because conventional economic theory and practice has not been able to improve social equity on a global scale. In 2016 the esteemed environmentalist David Suzuki released a YouTube video to argue that as long as it treats nature as an 'externality' economics is a form of 'brain damage' while Ozzie Zehner earlier tried to refocus the priorities of the environmental movement by arguing that 'We don't have an energy crisis; we have a consumption crisis.'[3] While efforts to dislodge growth from the heart of conventional economic theory and practice have had little success, the concerns expressed by Suzuki have been picked up in the emerging field of 'environmental economics'.

THE RISE OF ENVIRONMENTAL ECONOMICS

In arguing that there must be limits to economic growth on 'spaceship Earth', Kenneth Boulding drew on the work of Karl Polanyi in arguing that economic theory needs to be far more attentive to the long-term social consequences of economic development. Polanyi's work was also picked up by the German-born, UK-based economist Ernst Schumacher in his influential 1973 book *Small is Beautiful* which carried the rather provocative subtitle *Economics as if People Mattered.* At a similar time, the Romanian economist **Nicholas Georgescu-Roegen** was developing the argument that the Second Law of Thermodynamics – essentially indicating that useable energy slowly disperses – imposes unacknowledged limits on economic growth. In suggesting that economics must become more aware of 'biophysical constraints', Georgescue-Roegen is widely seen as being a 'father' of 'ecological economics'.

The concept of ecological economics gained momentum when Herman Daly put together an edited book in 1977 with the title *Towards a Steady-State Economics*; Daly subsequently went on to work for six years at the World Bank where he tried to build support for the reframing of economic theory and practice. In 1982 an international network was formed to promote ecological economics and key ideas of the movement were collated into a book by Juan Martinez-Alier published in 1987. However, ecological economics presents such a radical challenge to conventional economic theory that its influence has been limited and Daly's time as a senior economist at the World Bank ended in 1994 with little lasting legacy. A more moderate conception of 'environmental economics' has proved to be much more palatable to economists and policy-makers and it was boosted by the 1989 publication of a book by English economist **David Pearce** entitled *Blueprint for a Green Economy.* Although Pearce died in 2005 his legacy was honoured with the publication in 2012 of a book entitled *The New Blueprint for a Green Economy* by Edward Barbier and Anil Markandya.

Herman Daly was born in 1938 and as an academic economist he published a collection of writings under the title *Toward a Steady-State Economy* in 1973. He worked in the World Bank from 1988 to 1994 before returning to academia. Between 1992 and 2008 he was honoured with a string of international awards for his lifetime of work on 'ecological economics'.

Tim Jackson (b. 1957) first rose to prominence with work on 'preventative environmental management' after spending five years in the Stockholm Environmental Institute. This led to subsequent influential work on sustainable consumption. While he was serving as the Economics Commissioner on the UK Sustainable Development Commission he authored a rather controversial report that was subsequently published as *Prosperity Without Growth* (2009). As well as being professor of sustainable development at the University of Surrey he has won awards as the author of radio drama scripts performed on BBC radio.

Nicholas Georgescu-Roegen (1906–94) was born

in Romania and educated in mathematics at Bucharest University. He won a scholarship to study in Paris and also spent time in London before returning to Bucharest University. He was professor of economics at Vanderbilt University in Nashville, Tennessee, where he mentored Herman Daly as a student.

David Pearce (1941–2005) studied at both Oxford University and London School of Economics. He had a range of academic positions before beginning a long tenure at University College London, where he undertook his work in environmental economics. In 1989 he was appointed to the Global 500 Roll of Honour by the United Nations Environment Programme.

relocalisation of economic policies and practices is a better established discourse in France than in the English-speaking world although it gained traction in the UK through the promotion of the concept of 'food miles'. It lies at the heart of the Transition Towns movement initiated in the UK by Rob Hopkins based on 'permaculture design' principles invented in Australia.

The preoccupation of environmental economics has been to find ways to ensure that the environment can be given 'value' within economic policy and practice and that economic development should consciously aim to 'improve' the natural environment rather than result in resource depletion and environmental degradation. According to Pearce (1998: 21–30), a broader focus on costs and opportunities associated with economic production and distribution inevitably raises questions about 'higher- and lower-order rights and responsibilities' (ibid.: 26) and 'strategic values' (ibid.: 28). Such a focus on costs and opportunities has made cost–benefit analysis – first mooted by French economist Jules Dupuit in the 1860s – a mainstay of environmental economics in practice. Other approaches that have been adopted, with varying degrees of success, are life cycle analysis (LCA) and contingent valuation (CV).

The concept of LCA also pre-dates its use in environmental economics and is responsible for introducing the term 'cradle-to-grave' into economic thinking. Given that its products are seen as being largely deleterious to human health, it is rather ironic that the Coca-Cola corporation in the USA is credited with using LCA to think about the environmental impacts of its production processes in 1969. LCA has become a powerful tool for thinking about a wide array of both environmental and social consequences flowing from resource extraction, production processes and the disposal of waste material (to which we will return in Chapter 12). As will be discussed in Chapter 16, the focus on whole-of-life cycle production has boosted arguments for recycling much of the 'waste' products and by-products that otherwise go into environmentally damaging 'waste streams'. However, the 'cradle-to-grave' concept does not complete the cycle and industrial designers William McDonough and Michael Braungart have suggested that it should be replaced with an emphasis on cradle-to-cradle production.[4]

The emphasis in environmental economics on highlighting hitherto uncosted environmental impacts of production and transport has stimulated an interest in a degree of **relocalisation** of production, exchange and waste disposal. This includes efforts to reduce the 'food miles' in the transportation of food from sites of production to consumption that, in turn, has stimulated international interest in 'farmers' markets'. Other manifestations of relocalisation include localised recycling systems; the creation of urban 'hubs' to reduce use travel distances in cities; and the creation of local currencies aimed at encouraging people to purchase goods and services from local enterprises.

Although environmental economists insists that environmental impacts of production processes should be considered *before* the damage occurs – in line with the principle that prevention is always better than cure – it is ironic that the collapse of heavy industry in a range of 'developed' economies has opened the door for more environmentally-friendly enterprises and the city of Cleveland, Ohio, stands out as a model in this regard (see box)

The greening of Cleveland Ohio

Situated on the banks of Lake Erie, Cleveland, Ohio was once a major industrial centre of the USA with a thriving steel industry and large oil refineries. It is where John D. Rockefeller got his start as an industrialist and where he founded the leading petrochemical company Standard Oil. However, Cleveland was hit hard by the demise of manufacturing in the USA in the late 1970s and by 1983 unemployment in the city had reached 13.8 per cent. The population fell from nearly one million to below 400,000. A major response to Cleveland's economic decline has been the formation of a number of worker-owned cooperatives modelled on the famous cooperatives that were founded in the Mondragon, Spain, in 1956. The interesting thing about the Cleveland cooperatives is that they aim to build a green economy in the former heartland of steel and oil. The Evergreen Co-operatives include Ohio Co-operative Solar and the Evergreen Co-operative Laundry. In 2012 Evergreen Co-operatives decided to emulate a successful urban agriculture enterprise begun in Boston in 2008 under the name Green City Growers. In February 2013, the food-producing cooperative was able to open a massive hydroponic greenhouse covering 3.25 acres in what was once an industrial estate in the central district of the city; making it the largest urban food production business in the USA. All the Evergreen cooperatives favour the employment of local people in order to deliver both social and environmental benefits to the city.

Photo 9.1 An employee in the Evergreen Co-operative Corporation in Cleveland, Ohio
Photo by John McMicken

Genuine Progress Indicator is a term that was coined by the US organisation Redefining Progress in 1995. The GPI is probably the most prominent attempt to develop an alternative to the narrow income-based GDP index. It draws on the work of a range of economists – including Herman Daly and Marilyn Waring – and appears to have been taken most seriously in Canada.

Bhutan's Gross National Happiness Index began as a casual remark by the nation's Dragon King Jigme Singye Wangchuk in 1972 when he said that 'gross national happiness' will be the best measure of the nation's attempt to modernise its economy. The idea was picked up by the nation's newly formed Centre for Bhutan Studies in 1999 and a mix of quantitative and qualitative measures have subsequently been used in the development of Bhutan's Five Year Plan.

Brookings Institution is a Washington-based think-tank that specialises in social science research, especially in economics, urban planning, governance, foreign policy and global economy. It was formed in 1916.

THE ECONOMICS OF HAPPINESS

Sustainability scholars have long focused on the shortcomings of GDP as the indicator of choice for measuring the economic performance of nations and regions. A lot of work has gone into replacing GDP with something like a **Genuine Progress Indicator** and the OECD is supporting such initiatives. The Canadian Index of Wellbeing is seen as being a good model and other nations have been encouraged to undertake processes of consultation to develop an equivalent of their own. A key concept here is to shift the focus from production to the improvement of social 'wellbeing'.

The search for alternatives to GDP as a measure of economic success has focused global attention on the tiny Himalayan nation of Bhutan which has adopted a **Gross National Happiness index** for guiding the nation's development. Until recently Bhutan was only loosely integrated into the global economy and it remains to be seen if Bhutanese will continue to value the emphasis on national happiness over the consumerist allure of a more fully integrated economy. However, growing concerns about the social and personal impacts of hyperconsumption – discussed in Chapter 3 – have put the achievement of happiness on the agenda of economists and policy-makers in a range of highly developed nations. According to Washington-based **Brookings Institution** researcher Carol Graham (2011), the 'pursuit of happiness' is a founding goal of the USA as a nation – being enshrined in the nation's constitution – and she has argued that the time has come to revisit this goal as a framework for economic policy and practice. Noting that 'happiness' is a far more emotive term than something like 'wellbeing', Graham suggests that conversations about the pursuit of happiness should frame policy development more often. She notes that such conversations may rarely result in consensus about what is required for happiness to prosper but she argues that the dialogues in themselves will ensure that economic development policy is properly embedded within social development policy.

A more populist account of the economics of happiness is presented in a film put together by the well-known critic of western models of development Helena Norberg Hodge (2012). Norberg Hodge spent 35 years living as an outsider in the Himalayan province of **Ladakh** before she became a globe-trotting environmental activist and writer, driven in large measure by her alarm about increasing incursions into Ladakh by global corporations. The film features interviews with many of the world's leading green economists. However, the most telling scenes may be those which focus on a visit to London by a delegation of Ladakhi women. Not surprisingly the women are amazed at all the goods on display in glitzy Oxford Street shops. However, they are less impressed when Norberg Hodge takes them to see the mountains of trash in a waste disposal facility and they are positively alarmed when she takes them to visit old people living in an aged-care facility. They are visibly saddened when they meet a man who spends his days lying in bed watching television with no family to visit him. These scenes alone raise many questions about the social and personal costs of 'modern' economic development.

EVIDENCE-BASED AND VALUES-BASED POLICY

Work on the economics of happiness highlights the need to rethink the social values underpinning economic and social policy development. This poses a partial challenge, at least, to prevailing thinking within western nations that policies must always be based on clear and reputable 'evidence'. The international move to '**evidence-based policy**' – which began in the early 1980s – has undoubtedly helped to make policy-makers more accountable for the decisions they make. Making policy-making more transparent reduces the dangers of political corruption or the arbitrary use of political power and influence. However, the emphasis on 'evidence' has encouraged the illusion that policy-making is a rather technical process that deals only with 'objective' facts in order to achieve practical outcomes. Of course, 'evidence' can come in many forms but 'evidence-based policy' tends to favour supposedly unbiased facts and figures over perceptions, feelings or sentiment.

A leading critic of narrow and technical approaches to policy formation has been **Giandomenico Majone** who tried moderate the rise of 'evidence-based policy' with a book in which he argued that 'facts and values are intertwined in policy making' (1989: 8). Data used to support one policy option over others always reflects the assumptions and presuppositions of people who have collected the data, Majone argued. There is no such thing as an 'objective' fact and 'Argumentation is the key process through which citizens and policy-makers arrive at moral judgements and policy choices' (ibid.: 8).

While Majone focused on ways of addressing complex and sometimes contradictory social needs, similar considerations come into play in the formulation of environmental policy. This must also come down to a careful consideration of competing values and argumentation aimed at arriving at moral judgements about environmental and social wellbeing. The difference, however, is that non-human beings do not have their own voice in such processes of argumentation and Robyn Eckersley (2004) has argued that liberal democracies need to introduced new mechanisms to ensure that people with relevant knowledge are charged with the responsibility to advocate for the rights and interests of the non-human.

Ladakh is a region in northern India that lies between the Kunlun Range in the north and the Himalayan Range in the south. A rather remote area, it is known as the 'land of high passes'.

evidence-based policy was popularised by the UK Labour government led by Tony Blair in the late 1990s before being picked up by governments all over the world. It is based on the view that good policy needs to be based on rigorously researched 'objective' evidence.

Giandomenico Majone was born in 1932 and educated in Italy and the USA, where he gained his Ph.D. in statistics in 1964. In 1986 he became Professor of Policy Analysis at the European University Institute in Florence.

Selective use of 'evidence'

Despite the obvious fact that an expansion of coal mining to supply coal-fired power stations in Asia will undermine efforts to reduce global greenhouse gas emissions and despite the fact that ships carrying the coal from a special purpose port at Abbot Point in north Queensland to destinations in Asia will pass through a section of the World Heritage Great Barrier Reef, national and state governments in Australia have ignored scientific advice to approve development of the world's biggest single open-cut coal mine on the grounds that it will create new jobs. While the Indian company, Adani – which submitted plans to develop and operate the mine from 2017 onwards – has scaled back its proposals due to falling coal prices and repeated legal challenges by Australian environmental organisations, the two levels of government have sought to 'fast-track' the development, even at a time when the Great Barrier Reef has been experiencing its worst ever coral bleaching event (in 2015–16). Before announcing cuts to the scale of the operation in September 2017, Adani had promised that the project – which involves the construction of a 382-kilometre railway line to connect the mine to the port – would create 4,000 permanent jobs and around that number again in the construction phase. This 'evidence' was enough to entice relevant government ministers to ignore competing evidence about increasing greenhouse gas emissions and serious threats to the fragile coral reefs in order to rule that Adani had met all environmental management criteria in its development proposals. While marine biologists expressed grave concerns about the risk of oil spills on the reef, the relevant ministers ruled that all environmental risks were negligible. This case demonstrates that voter sentiment is bound to matter more to politicians than wider environmental considerations when it comes to weighing up the 'evidence'.

SOCIAL INCLUSION AND THE POLITICS OF PARTICIPATION

Blair government social inclusion agenda, soon after being elected as UK Prime Minster in 1997, Tony Blair announced that his government would reduce poverty by focusing on factors which prevent some people and communities from participating fully in British society. He established a Social Exclusion unit in his own office and continued to pursue a social inclusion agenda during his ten years as prime minister.

John Dryzek born in England and educated in England and Scotland before completing his Ph.D.

As suggested in Chapter 4, the '**social inclusion agenda**' that was popularised by the Blair Labour government in the UK in the late 1990s promises to put a broader framework around otherwise narrow framing of economic development. While the Blair government had limited success in implementing this agenda, it immediately posed important questions about the kinds of barriers that make it harder for some people and groups to achieve personal or social success compared to others. This, in turn, focuses attention on the complex needs of people and groups who feel socially excluded. It also highlights the need to sometimes slow down the development of economic and/or social policy in order to ensure that such complex needs are at least considered. The need to make policy development more socially responsive is the key concern of the 'deliberative democracy' school of political theory. According to this line of thought, it is better to take time to ensure wide participation in the development of policy rather than implement policies that may favour some people over others, or divide people and communities. A key principle is that decision making needs to be as transparent as possible in order to reveal any influence that may be exerted on the policy-makers by interest groups or lobbyists. Critics of deliberative democracy argue that it is too slow and cumbersome to achieve clear and efficient policy outcomes. However, its proponents argue that it is better to take time to consider a range of policy options rather than implement bad policy.

John Dryzek (2005) has applied the principles of deliberative democracy to the formulation of environment policy. The upsurge in environmental awareness that began in western countries in the 1970s has led to a variety of environmentalisms, Dryzek argues, and environmental pragmatists have very different assumptions and values compared to those who may be driven by radical green philosophies. Even those who disparage environmentalism have their own assumptions and values when it comes to considerations of human responsibilities for the non-human environment; no one has a values-neutral position on the environment. However, prevailing political processes rarely even try to bridge the gaps between competing environmental 'discourses', Dryzek argues. The starting point should be genuine respect for the diversity of views and approaches – even within the environment movement – so that efforts can be made to find some common ground. Of course, policy formation cannot be inhibited by the difficulties involved in reaching a consensus. However, the advocates of deliberative democracy argue that a deliberative process is likely to reduce polarisations in policy-making debates and also reduce resistance to the final outcomes.

in government and politics at the University of Maryland, near Washington, DC. He has been Head of the Department of Politics at both the University of Oregon and the University of Melbourne. He is currently the Centenary Professor in the Centre for Deliberative Democracy and Global Governance at the University of Canberra.

Opponents of deliberative democracy tend to argue that representative democracy is far more efficient because elected representatives can speak on behalf of their constituents without resorting to cumbersome processes of consultation. However, elected representatives cannot fully represent the complex needs of their electorates and they rarely include people who really know what it is like to feel excluded or marginalised. Despite the emergence of 'green politics' (see below), questions remain about who will represent the interests of the non-human or the interests of people yet to be born.

THE POLITICS OF SHARED SPACE

Increasing migrations of people – both within and between nations – mean that most local communities include significant numbers of people who have come from elsewhere and most nations, especially western ones, have become much more multicultural. Of course, the coexistence of groups of people with different beliefs and practices can cause division and conflict. However, UK geographer **Doreen Massey** (2005) has pointed out that it can also force people to openly negotiate terms for peaceful coexistence and this, in turn, can create more tolerant and culturally diverse local communities. There are some obvious benefits for people living in multicultural local communities – such as access to a diversity of foods and other cultural products (see Photo 9.2). What may be less appreciated is that a diversity of past experiences may give the community an increased capacity to adapt to changing circumstances. In Australia, for example, migrant communities often have more experience in growing their own food and they are at the forefront of many local community garden projects.

Doreen Massey (1944–2016) was born in Manchester and spent much of her childhood in a council housing estate before going on to study at Oxford University and the University of Pennsylvania. She worked at the Centre for Environment Studies in London until it was closed by the Thatcher government in 1979. She went on to become a professor in geography at the Open University, retiring in 2009.

New communication technologies have greatly increased our capacity to communicate regularly with people who are far away from us and we have more opportunities than ever before to participate in 'communities' that are not associated with any particular places in the world. However, environmental sustainability forces us all to think about our impacts on both the local and non-local ecosystems from which we draw resources and into which we dump waste materials. Our ecological impacts begin locally, even if they reverberate way beyond the local. While our attention has shifted to the global flows of people, goods, money, ideas and information, sustainability forces us to return also to the ecological flows that pass through our bodies, households and neighbourhoods.

Photo 9.2 Community festivals make communities of place more visible: Llanwrtyd Wells food festival
© Jeff Morgan 02/Alamy

As Massey has argued, our relationships with space are coming to the fore once again as few people can ignore the fact that space is being shared with an increasing diversity of humans. The onset of global climate change may also bring to our attention the fact that we also share space with a host of increasingly vulnerable non-human life forms.

CULTURAL DIVERSITY AND CULTURAL VITALITY

As indicated above, locally experienced cultural diversity can be a source of division and conflict but it can also give people access to a much greater array of cultural products and services. Culturally diverse communities can have a wealth of knowledge and experience to draw on in order to adapt to changing circumstances. However, diverse cultural practices cannot survive as memories alone and culture in general has little meaning unless it is practised and communicated.

If we think of culture as being the beliefs and practices that are in use within particular human communities – often passed from one generation to the next – we can see it as a source of resistance to change. Acquired beliefs and practices may rarely be questioned by those within the community concerned and those who do question them may become marginalised or even excluded by the community. At the same time, the culture of a community can be seen as the conscious representation – in forms ranging from works of art to magazines, popular films, representations within digital media or 'street art' – of prevailing or alternative beliefs and assumptions. Cultural representations may reflect the way in which the nation is constantly imagined and enacted in the daily practices of its citizens or they may reflect a diversity of subcultures or, as the author has found in a number of studies,[5] efforts being made by a local community to develop a deeper sense of belonging to place. While cultural representations may have the intent, or effect, of reinforcing existing beliefs and practices they can also generate conversations about the ongoing relevance of particular beliefs and practices; thus opening a door for cultural change. When reflective conversations about culture are carried out with an inclusive intent they can greatly strengthen a sense of belonging to vibrant and tolerant communities and this brings us back to the suggestion – discussed above and in Chapter 6 – that 'cultural vitality' should be seen as a 'fourth pillar' of sustainability.

The complex relationship between culture and art is beyond the scope of this book. However, art can make us think more deeply about otherwise taken-for-granted cultural beliefs and practices and it sometimes enables us to imagine what it might feel like to experience things we would prefer to avoid. The Nobel Prize-winning novelist J. M. Coetzee has noted that fiction writers often put their characters into morally challenging positions to explore their coping mechanisms.[6] We may be better prepared for challenging circumstances if we have at least had an opportunity to imagine them first.

Celebrating cultural inclusion

In conducting research for the Australian health promotion agency VicHealth (see Mulligan *et al.* 2006), the author was pleasantly surprised to find that a particular Melbourne neighbourhood that was widely perceived as being highly dysfunctional was remaking itself through diverse array of cultural celebrations and projects. For example, efforts being made by the local government authority in the area centred on the suburb of Broadmeadows to involve residents in environmental restoration work turned into an annual Multicultural Planting Festival in which the planting work culminated in a shared feast featuring a diversity of culinary traditions. When the international 'war on terror' sparked an upsurge of anti-Muslim sentiment in Australia, leaders of the area's different 'faith communities' made conspicuous efforts to attend each other's significant events, and a festival to celebrate Eid at the conclusion of the Muslim world's Ramadan month of fasting was opened up for participation by non-Muslim residents. A youth worker at the Victorian Arab Social Services decided to tackle the rise of anti-Muslim sentiment by forming the Anti-Racism Action Band (ARAB) which soon included dancers, musicians and comedians from a wide range of cultural backgrounds and the group was soon being booked for public performances right across the city. Through the efforts of local community leaders Broadmeadows became the home of a very innovative Global Learning Centre with a well-stocked and heavily-used public library.

CREATING MORE INCLUSIVE COMMUNITIES

sociology of community, the idea of community has divided western sociologists ever since Emile Durkheim criticised the seminal book on the topic by Ferdinand Tönnies in the early years of the twentieth century. There has never been a consensus on what community really means but a range of sociologists have argued that there has been a turn to community in a world of growing uncertainty.

The word '**community**' is often used simplistically in literature on sustainable development. For example, the term 'community engagement' often implies that there is a clearly identifiable community that needs to be educated or worked with. The word may be seen as being interchangeable with words like neighbourhood or town; it is still treated as a 'given' in a world of global flows.

Sociologists have long complained that the word can mean different things to different people and Raymond Williams wryly noted that it is commonly invoked as a 'warmly persuasive' word that 'never seems to be used unfavourably'.[7] Feminist scholar Iris Marion Young[8] went as far as saying that appeals to community often mask racist exclusions of those who are treated as 'outsiders'. The best explanation of community in the contemporary world comes from Gerard Delanty (2003). 'Community is relevant in the world today', he wrote, 'because, on the one side, the fragmentation of society has provoked a worldwide search for community, and on the other ... cultural developments and global forms of communication have facilitated the construction of community.'[9] Delanty notes that we can participate in the 'communicative construction' of many kinds of community – both place-based and spatially extended. However, he noted that many virtual communities are ephemeral and 'thin' in their consequences for participants and he concludes his book by saying 'the revival of community is undoubtedly related to the crisis of belonging in relation to place'.[10]

As mentioned above, the author has been involved in research on community wellbeing in a wide range of local Australian communities[11] and he was a lead researcher on a study focusing on the rebuilding of local communities in the wake of the tsunami disaster in Sri Lanka in 2004. The studies conducted in Australia confirm Delanty's suggestion that a sense of belonging to community only exists to the extent that it is 'wilfully constructed', while the Sri Lanka study confirmed the fear that narrow projections of community identity can cause social division and even conflict. Indeed the author has concluded that there is a 'dark side' to the desire to belong to community if the orientation is not to include social and cultural diversity and to embrace a range of cross-cutting sub-communities (Mulligan 2015). Delanty has emphasised the point that there is no need at all to counterpose the formation of place-based or local communities and the increasing opportunities afforded by new communication technologies to participate in spatially extended or 'virtual communities'. The proliferation of opportunities to participate in both real and/or virtual communities can create dilemmas for individuals having to decide where they might direct their time and effort. However, communities of place are likely to become more important in the context of global climate change and new restrictions on the use of fossil fuels for energy.

communities of practice is a term coined by anthropologists Jean Lave and Étienne Wenger in 1991 to refer to the ways in which people learn particular crafts. However, it soon gained a much wider meaning and Wenger has said that it can refer to 'groups of people who share a concern or passion for something they do and learn how to do it better as they interact regularly'.

In 1991, anthropologists Jean Lave and Étienne Wenger coined the term '**communities of practice**' to refer to consciously created communities of people who share a passion for certain practices and a desire to help each other refine their related knowledge and skills. While they initially used the term to refer people interested in particular 'crafts' they subsequently widened the meaning to include any kind of practice and noted that people do not need to meet in person to form a community of practice. Continuing advances in communication technologies have made it much easier for people to set up or join a host of such communities and while practice is the motivating force such communities they often discuss the values or ethics which might underpin the commitment to the selected practices.

Discussion questions

1. Why is the commitment to growth in conventional economic theory and practice being subjected to increasing criticism?
2. What have been key preoccupations of environmental economics since the late 1970s?
3. What is LCA trying to achieve?
4. What would have to change to put 'happiness' at the core of economic policy and practice?
5. What criticisms does Giandomenico Majone make of evidence-based policy?
6. What are some key principles of 'deliberative democracy' and how might they help the quest for sustainability?
7. What is valuable about cultural diversity?
8. Why should 'cultural vitality' be considered a 'pillar' of sustainability?
9. Why do communities need to be 'wilfully constructed' in the contemporary world and what is meant by the 'dark side' of community?
10. What is meant by the term 'communities of practice' and how relevant can they be for you?

KEY READINGS

Delanty, Gerard (2003) *Community*, London: Routledge.

Dryzek, John (2005), 2nd edn, *The Politics of the Earth: Environmental Discourses*, Oxford: Oxford University Press.

Graham, Carol (2011) *The Pursuit of Happiness: An Economy of Well-being*, Washington, DC: Brookings Institute Press.

Hawkes, Jon (2004) *The Fourth Pillar of Sustainability: Culture's Essential Role in Public Planning*, Melbourne: Common Ground Publishing.

Jackson, Tim (2016) 2nd edn, *Prosperity Without Growth: Foundations for the Economy of Tomorrow*, London: Routledge.

McDonough, William and Michael Braungart (2002) *Cradle to Cradle: Remaking the Way We Make Things*, New York: North Point Press.

Majone, Giandomenico (1989) *Evidence, Argument and Persuasion in Policy Processes*, New Haven, CT: Yale University Press.

Massey, Doreen (2005) *For Space*, London: Sage.

Mulligan, Martin (2015) 'On Ambivalence and Hope in the Restless Search for Community: How to Work with the Idea of Community in the Global Age', *Sociology*, 49(2): 340–55.

Norberg Hodge, Helena (2012) 'The Economics of Happiness', www.theeconomicsofhappiness.org

Pearce, David (1998) *Economics and Environment: Essays on Ecological Economics and Sustainable Development*, London: Edward Elgar.

thematic essay

The rise of green politics

People living in the Australian island state of Tasmania insist that the first green political party in the world was formed at a public meeting held in Hobart Town Hall on 22 March 1972. The meeting was held as part of a last, desperate, attempt to stop the construction of a large hydro-electricity dam that eventually flooded beautiful Lake Pedder in a rather remote wilderness zone of south-west Tasmania. The meeting resolved to stand a number of anti-dam candidates in the forthcoming state election under the name United Tasmania Group (UTG). Eventually, it is argued, the UTG morphed into the Tasmanian Greens and leaders of this party played a critical role in the formation of the Australian Greens in 1992. New Zealanders object to the Tasmanian claim because they insist that they had an even earlier political party – the Values Party – which had a core interest in environmental protection. Settling competing claims about the origins of green parties may be impossible and rather pointless because adoption of the word 'Greens' seems to owe its inspiration to use of the term 'green bans' by an Australian building workers' union in the early 1970s (see Mulligan and Hill 2001, chapter 10). Furthermore, the name was adopted in Germany following a visit to Australia of German Greens founder **Petra Kelly** in 1977 before it was used in Australia. What is clear from all this, however, is that the idea arose more or less simultaneously in a range of countries where strong environmental movements saw a need to exercise more direct political influence.

Petra Kelly (1947–92) was born in Bavaria and changed her name to Kelly when her mother married a US Army officer. She lived and studied in the USA (1959–70) where she was an admirer of Martin Luther King. She was one of the founders of the German Greens in 1979 and was in the German parliament (1985–90). She was shot dead by her partner, a fellow Greens politician and former army general, Gert Bastian in a murder-suicide.

Whereas the Australian Greens originated in campaigns to protect remote areas of wilderness, the German Greens largely grew out of their national campaign to stop and reverse the use of nuclear power. It is tempting to conclude that the Australian party was more deeply rooted in nature conservation while the German party was more social in its outlook. However, this neglects the fact that the charismatic leader of the Tasmanian Greens, **Bob Brown**, was also a committed social activist and that both Petra Kelly and Bob Brown have acknowledged the influence in their thinking of the Sydney-based trade union leader and Communist Party member **Jack Mundey** who had been primarily responsible for the concept of 'green bans' (Mulligan and Hill 2001). The first 'green ban' imposed by the NSW Builders Labourers Federation was aimed at 'remnant area of bushland' in a harbour-side Sydney suburb but such bans were soon being used to protect heritage areas and urban parks from 'greedy' property developers. While wanting to protect green spaces within the city the green bans also aimed to prevent the demolition of affordable housing for working-class communities and it was this mix of environmental and social aims that attracted the interest of both Kelly and Brown. Bob Brown was first

Bob Brown was born in 1944 in Oberon, NSW, where his father

elected as a 'Green Independent' to the Tasmanian Parliament in 1982 and even after he was joined by other elected representatives they continued to use the name Green Independents until 1992. Nevertheless the Australian Greens shared much of their history with their German counterparts and they shared the same foundation principles that focus on both ecology and social justice.

The German Greens grew more quickly and had more electoral success than their counterparts in Australia, partly because Germany's proportional representation electoral system that guarantees representation for minority parties. Petra Kelly was elected to the European Parliament in 1979 in the same year that the party had success in state elections in Bremen. The party had its first member in the federal German parliament in 1983 and by 1985 it was in a coalition government at the national level with the Social Democratic Party. The rather spectacular rise of the German Greens triggered the formation of Green parties in other European countries, while the Ecology Party in the UK changed its name to Green Party in 1985. A Green Party was formed in Canada in 1981.

After the early success Kelly continued to describe the party as being more like a movement than a party.[12] However, the rapid and increasing electoral success opened up divisions between the more radical wing of the German Greens – tagged the 'fundis' – and the more mainstream 'realos', with the latter gaining the ascendancy. As party representatives entered coalition governments at provincial and federal levels they softened the party's signature opposition to nuclear power and contravened its strident anti-war rhetoric.[13] Nevertheless the party continued to grow in membership and influence because it focused on the overlap of environmental and social concerns.

In recent decades Green parties have become significant political actors in some countries and not others. They have become most influential in some countries – such as Germany and New Zealand – which have proportional representation electoral systems which ensure that minority parties can have candidates elected to legislative assemblies. Nevertheless there is a global network of Green parties and they have risen to become a credible 'third force' in many parts of the world. Their combined environmental and social platforms reflect the core messages of the 1987 Brundtland Report in arguing for a strong nexus between the environmental and social dimensions of sustainability.

However, green politics is not just about the formation of Green political parties. As John Dryzek has noted (2005), environmental concerns have been firmly on the agenda of political debate in most parts of the world since the early 1990s at least. All political parties are expected to outline their strategies for dealing with such concerns and elections have been won and lost on this basis. Attempts have also been make political theory more environmentally sensitive through the pages of journals like *Environmental Politics*. Robyn Eckersley (2004), for example, has argued that representative democracy probably works better for the environment than any more authoritarian political models, as long as steps are taken to ensure that some people or agencies are

was a policeman. He became a medical doctor and worked in London before taking up a position as a GP in Launceston, Tasmania, in 1972. He fell in love with the Tasmanian wilderness and led the successful campaign to prevent the construction of a dam on the wild Franklin River in the early 1980s. He helped to establish the Wilderness Society in Australia and was elected to the Tasmanian parliament in 1983. He was elected to the Australian Senate in 1996 and became the first openly gay member of the Australian parliament.

Jack Mundey was born in rural Queensland in 1929 before rising to prominence as the leader of the Builders Labourers Federation in Sydney in the 1960s. A member of the Communist Party of Australia he broke with trade union tradition to place a work ban on an area of bushland in a harbour-side suburb in Sydney before turning this practice into a series of 'green bans' aimed at protecting open spaces and natural heritage of the city. His ideas on combining environmental care with social justice in a 'red–green' coalition directly influenced Petra Kelly.

charged with the responsibility of representing the interests of the non-human. Tim Hayward (2005), on the other hand, has argued that liberal democracies struggle to overcome 'short-termism' in dealing with complex and enduring challenges and also struggle to get beyond the conceptual framework of nation states in developing responses to big global concerns. As Dryzek reminds us, there is a rather fraught relationship between policy and politics and the most important gains may have been made through the slow development of policy that can transcend the theatre of politics. Nevertheless, the challenges of sustainability have served to highlight the need for patient policy work and for developing new forms of consensus politics and global governance.

NOTES

1 Noting that discussion of sustainability often begins with a focus on economic development.
2 See Jon Hawkes, *The Fourth Pillar of Sustainability*, Melbourne: Common Ground Publishing, 2001.
3 Ozzie Zehner made this argument in a book entitled *Green Illusions* published in 2012. A focus on unsustainable consumption has also been a preoccupation of Australian environmental economist Clive Hamilton with books entilted *Growth Fetish* and *Affluenza*.
4 William McDonough and Michael Braungart, *Cradle to Cradle: Remaking the Way We Make Things*, New York: North Point Press, 2002.
5 For example, Martin Mulligan *et al.*, *Creating Community: Celebrations, Arts and Wellbeing within and across Local Communities*, Melbourne: VicHealth, 2006.
6 See Jonathon Lamb '"The true words at last from the mind in ruins": J. M. Coetze and Realism', in Graham Bradshaw and Michael Neill (eds), *J.M. Coetzee's Austerities*, Farnham: Ashgate, 2010.
7 See Raymond Williams, *Keywords: A Vocabulary of Culture and Society*, New York: Oxford University Press, 1983.
8 Iris Marion Young, 'The Ideal of Community and the Politics of Difference' in L. J. Nicholson (ed.), *Feminism/Postmodernism*, New York: Routledge, 1990.
9 Delanty (2003: 193).
10 Ibid.: 195.
11 See Mulligan *et al.* (2006); Mulligan and Smith (2011).
12 See Werner Hulsberg, *The German Greens: A Social and Political Profile*, London: Verso, 1988, p. 124.
13 See Joachim Jachnow 'What's Become of the German Greens?', *New Left Review*, 81, May–June 2013, pp. 95–118.

CHAPTER 10

Personal dimensions of sustainability

Key concepts and concerns

- personal resilience
- taking and sustaining action
- from individual sense-making to collective endeavour
- opportunities in the 'digital age'
- communities of practice
- arguments for hope
- entering a new era in the history of humanity

INTRODUCTION

Throughout this book there is an emphasis on what individuals can do to respond to big global sustainability challenges and the personal benefits that may come from participating actively in the global movement for sustainable living. This orientation is facilitated by the Social Ecology model for sustainability, which brings the 'personal' dimension into play. The challenge to live more sustainably confronts every person on Planet Earth. It is not something we can leave to 'experts' or governments or society at large. Clearly there is a critical role for expert knowledge and for policies and systems that encourage, enable and enhance individual action. However, in suggesting, rather provocatively, that society as we have known it is dead, **Nikolas Rose** (1996) has argued that it has become critically important for individuals to create the communities that can give each of us a sense of belonging and purpose and this suggests that the construction of society begins with individuals rather than the society shaping the emergence of mature individuals. At the same time, every individual has a personal relationship with the non-human, ecological, systems that make life possible. The Social Ecology model encourages us to examine the categories of 'environmental' and 'social' from the perspective of individual responsibility and action.

Nikolas Rose was born in London in 1947. Originally trained in biology, he studied political theory at London School of Economics. He has held senior academic positions at Goldsmiths College, University of London, London School of Economics and King's College, London. His sociological work is heavily influenced by the work of Michel Foucault.

The danger in bringing everything back to individual responsibility and action is that individuals can feel overwhelmed by the scope and complexity of the big global challenges discussed in earlier chapters. This is where the 'death of society' argument – that has come from political conservatives such as Margaret Thatcher as well as political radicals like Nikolas Rose – has gone too far. Possibilities for personal action on sustainable living have already been raised in earlier chapters and this will be the specific focus of Chapter 11. The key aim of this chapter is to consider how individuals can create the kinds of communities and societies that can rise to the challenges we face globally. As discussed in Chapters 4, 5, 7 and 9, we need to start by rethinking our prevailing cultural beliefs and attitudes on living with risk and uncertainty and this chapter begins with a discussion of personal resilience introduced in Chapter 7. However, 'resilience' is often perceived as being a rather passive capacity to withstand change so this chapter begins a discussion on taking and sustaining action that will be taken further in Chapter 11. At the same time, it is important to understand the limits to individual action and a starting point for this is the pioneering work of English sociologist **Anthony Giddens** on 'structure and agency', which notes that individual beliefs, attitudes and practices are largely shaped by those of the societies into which those individuals are born.

Anthony Giddens was born in London in 1936. He studied at the University of Hull, London School of Economics and King's College, Cambridge. He established his reputation as a leading sociologist in the 1970s with the books *Capitalism and Modern Social Theory* (1971) and *New Rules of Sociological Method* (1976).

individualisation refers to the widespread observation that individual people are increasingly being expected to attend to their own needs and desires rather than look to the state, community or society.

The sociology of structure and agency notes that prevailing cultures tend to resist change because beliefs and practices are upheld by a wide range of social institutions, such as those established to educate the young, teach people how to do their jobs or perform their designated roles, or introduce people to systems of religious or secular beliefs. However, Giddens is among those sociologists who have noted that the increasing global movement of people, goods, information and ideas is undermining the influence of local or even national institutions. Increasingly, Giddens has noted (1994), we live in 'post-traditional' societies that do less to socialise individuals into particular ways of thinking and acting and this is both rather scary and exciting in regard to the possibilities for individual and collective action. The process of '**individualisation**' – which was discussed in Chapter 3 in relation to the perception that we can all consume our way individually towards health and happiness – has undermined traditional modes of social action. However, increasing global flows of people, goods, information and ideas have opened up new possibilities for taking action on a wider scale. New communication technologies have made it easier for individuals to join non-local communities, some of which can be described as 'communities of practice'.

The weakening of traditional social institutions makes it harder for individuals to make sense of their own lives and Richard Sennett (2006) is prominent among sociologists who have suggested that more and more people are trying to make sense of their diverse lived experiences by trying to weave them into a coherent life narrative or autobiography. The author's own research on the 'well-being' of local communities in Australia has noted a growing interest in storytelling and this helps to explain the interest shown in the use of new communication technologies to create and share stories in the practice referred to as 'digital storytelling' (Mulligan and Smith 2011). This chapter will explore some of the opportunities for taking action that have been facilitated by new digital communication technologies before it returns to the suggestion raised in Chapter 1: that we all need to learn how to 'travel hopefully' in a world of growing risk and uncertainty. The chapter aims to give substance to the last of the nine RMIT Sustainability principles, namely:

1 Learn how to travel hopefully in a world of uncertainty.

In summary, the chapter will focus on:

- Possibilities for taking individual action in a 'runaway world'.
- The creation and sharing of life stories.
- Opportunities presented by the 'digital age', including possibilities for joining communities of practice.
- Some reasons for feeling hopeful about the future.

PERSONAL RESILIENCE

As noted in Chapter 7, psychologists have long observed that individuals who are prepared to take risks and live with fairly high levels of uncertainty are the ones who will cope best with unexpected changes. While some psychologists have argued that the concept of 'personal resilience' overstates the ability of individuals to act independently, others have argued that individuals can consciously work on their capacity to cope with change and unpredictability, even if this involves the creation of strong networks of family and friends that help to take the emphasis away from individual resilience. All of us can embrace the understanding that life is often much less predictable than we might hope; we can never really know what the future might hold. Rather than focus our thoughts on where we want to be – personally or professionally – at some point in the future we can focus more on the journey we are already making and the unforeseen challenges or opportunities that might come our way.

Chapter 3 focused on the idea that the search for the 'good life' might involve a conscious rejection of prevailing social expectations or prevailing perceptions about what constitutes personal 'success'. The suggestion that we need to look inside ourselves to find a sense of self-worth touches on Abraham **Maslow's** decision to make 'self-actualisation' the top of his pyramid of needs. As Epicurus put it, 'If you live according to opinions you will never be rich.' However, self-actualisation underplays the fact that our very sense of self is strongly influenced by prevailing cultural beliefs and practices. For example, individualism was valued more highly in western societies than in non-western societies long before the accelerating processes of 'individualisation' that have been discussed in Chapter 3 and above. A dangerous belief in human mastery over nature is also deeply embedded within western cultures and this has created a form of human hubris that undermines the capacity of individuals to cope well with environmental risk and uncertainty. Personal resilience cannot ignore the influence of culture. At the same time, the global challenges discussed in this book are raising many questions about individual resilience and this, in turn, raises questions about the beliefs and practices that have given rise to widespread risk aversion. Personal resilience (in the personal sphere) and cultural change (in the social sphere) cannot avoid each other.

Maslow's hierarchy of human needs was developed by the American psychologist in the 1960s. Although criticised for positing a rather inflexible relationship between diverse and intersecting needs, the concept of basic and 'higher' needs has stood the test of time.

TAKING AND SUSTAINING ACTION

The big global challenges that are discussed in this book can leave individuals feeling rather insignificant and powerless. At one extreme, a sense of powerlessness encourages some individuals to throw themselves into a frenzy of activities – or activism – that cannot be sustained for long periods of time and which often has little lasting effect. At the other extreme, individuals can decide that personal action is insignificant and worthless. Inaction is irresponsible while effective action is elusive and this poses deep dilemmas that **Stuart Hill** – the leading advocate of the Social Ecology model of sustainability – has addressed with his work on 'meaningful change'.[1] No individual action should be dismissed as being insignificant, Hill has argued, as long as it is part of a broader action plan. However, in Hill's view, personal action only becomes meaningful if it can be sustained, and for this reason individuals need to build up a body of sustainable practices. At the same time, it is easy to become complacent or rather unimaginative about what we think we can achieve and in workshops on meaningful action, Hill challenges his audiences to think boldly and imaginatively about big change projects that might not seem realistic or feasible. As discussed in Chapter 7, innovation is often driven by people who dare to think the unthinkable or strive for something that seems beyond reach.

Stuart Hill was born in England and educated in England and Canada. He worked at McGill University in Montreal before taking up the position of Foundation Chair in Social Ecology at the University of Western Sydney in 1996.

There is an obvious danger in working for a particular change that either remains unachievable or fails to live up to expectations. For this reason, Hill has invented a personal planning tool that encourages the user to plan for a suite of activities or practices; both big and small and with time horizons ranging from the immediate present to more than the individual's own lifespan. The tool encourages the user to think big without being paralysed by complex challenges. However, it is only effective if the action plans are reviewed periodically in relation to the effectiveness of actions already taken. It is important to think strategically about opportunities to take action as they arise and it is also important to be pragmatic about taking action that can make a difference, even if it is a small step on a long journey.

Effective action requires effective monitoring as to outcomes or effects and this is why systems theory – also discussed in Chapter 6 – suggests the need for 'feedback loops' that provide some kind of performance feedback. In relation to personal action this might involve something as simple as taking the time to reflect on the effectiveness of any action taken or it might involve conscious consultation with other people to get their views on the effectiveness of actions taken. Very often we can only undertake meaningful action by working with other people; perhaps in project teams. Effective project management requires the setting of clear goals and some kind of outcomes or 'performance indicators' and the implementation of monitoring or evaluation processes and techniques. Collaborative action can be more effective and more enjoyable than individual action but similar principles apply in regard to monitoring effectiveness. Positive feedback sustains the motivation to persist or even expand on action already taken while negative feedback provides the opportunity to redirect energy and resources. Sustainability requires effective monitoring and this will be discussed further in Chapter 11.

Ulrich Beck was born in 1944 in a German province which became part of Poland at the end of the Second World War. He studied at the University of Munich where he went on to have a long and distinguished academic career. His work on the risk society was published in German in 1986 and in English in 1992.

'A LIFE OF ONE'S OWN IN A RUNAWAY WORLD'

The pre-eminent English sociologist Anthony Giddens undoubtedly knew of the work that **Ulrich Beck** was undertaking on the rise of the 'risk society' in the 1980s because he was thinking along similar lines. However, Beck's work was not translated into English until the early 1990s and around this time the US-born, UK-based sociologist Scott Lash facilitated a dialogue between Beck and Giddens which led to the publication in 1994 of the influential book entitled *Reflexive Modernization.* Giddens and Beck had come to similar conclusions about the demise of old social institutions in a world of accelerating global flows and both had focused on the destabilising influences of the risks associated with such global flows. Beck probably encouraged Giddens to focus more on the ecological dimensions of rising global risk but they shared optimism about how the shifting relationships between self and society might promote deeper reflection about risk and responsibility. Beck, in particular, had focused on the processes of 'individualisation' that were discussed in Chapter 3, yet they both argued that individuals have greater opportunities to become the authors of their own stories. In later work, both have used the term 'runaway world' and Beck has suggested that we all face the need to find a 'life of one's own in a runaway world' (2001). In a similar vein, Richard Sennett[2] has suggested that individuals are increasingly obliged to make sense of their own life experiences and they do so by trying to weave diverse experiences into a coherent narrative. Research conducted by the author on community art practices in Australia[3] revealed a growing interest in storytelling as a way of developing a sense of belonging and purpose in a rather confusing world. Community art practices are often targeted at individuals who feel socially excluded and the author's research suggested that an ability to share life stories can help to overcome social isolation (see box).

Social isolation and storytelling

In research conducted for the Australian health promotion agency, **VicHealth**, the author and his co-researchers talked to a wide range of people in four diverse local communities who spoke passionately about the importance of storytelling for overcoming social isolation. However, one rather unexpected example helps to illustrate the claim. This focused on the experiences of a man who was living in a boarding house with other people who, like him, had experienced prolonged periods of drug use; many of them having spent time in prison. We interviewed this person because he had written a number of stories that had been published in a magazine called *Roomers* which enjoyed widespread local circulation. The interviewee suggested that we talk to him in his boarding house room where we were surprised to find piles of his stories, some of them tacked to the walls. Why so many stories and what do you do with them all?, we asked. The answer was that for health reasons the man had taken up the practice of jogging every day and after being encouraged to write a story for *Roomers* he decided to dredge his memory for particular stories as he jogged. Once he got home from his run he sat down to commit the story to paper so that it would not be lost.

Some of the stories were submitted to *Roomers*, some selected to go on his walls and some were given to other people in the boarding house.

VicHealth is a government-funded health promotion agency in Victoria, Australia. Its innovative work has included the funding of community artwork to foster social inclusion and personal wellbeing.

The running writer insisted that he was very selective about giving his stories to other residents in the boarding house because he knew that some would see it as an intrusion. The stories enabled him to mediate his relationships with people who had similar life experiences but he insisted on maintaining tight control over how and when he might share his stories. The stories were primarily written for the author to make sense of his own life but they gave him greater agency in his dealings with other people.

Blair Labour government came into being after the British elections of 1997 when Tony Blair became the youngest British prime minister since 1812. Initially seen as a breath of fresh air, the government lost popularity when it decided to support the US-led invasion of Iraq in 2003.

social inclusion became a policy orientation of the Blair Labour government after leader Tony Blair gave a famous speech titled 'Bringing Britain Together' in London in 1997. The government established a special Social Inclusion Unit. The government's ability to build a more inclusive society did not live up to Blair's rhetoric but the 'social inclusion agenda' had a significant influence on public policy in many other countries.

In the late 1990s Anthony Giddens became an enthusiastic supporter of the **Blair Labour government's** '**social inclusion** agenda' and he suggested that old forms of adversary politics might give way to new forms of social consensus. The Blair government failed to live up to the promise of its early rhetoric and politics has continued resumed normal transmission. Giddens resumed his scholarship on individual agency in a world of growing risk and he became convinced that conditions for social life had changed more radically that he and Beck had imagined in their 1994 collaboration (see box). New communication technologies, he has argued, increase both the possibility and the imperative to make a life of our own in a runaway world. Given his early work on structure and agency, Giddens is aware that individuals have limited abilities to shape their own lives. However, we have unprecedented opportunities to share stories and insights and thus become more conscious of the challenges and opportunities that we face.

Anthony Giddens: *We are off the edge of history*

Anthony Giddens was born into a lower-middle-class London family in 1938. He completed his undergraduate studies at the University of Hull in 1959 and went on to complete postgraduate studies at London School of Economics and King's College, Cambridge. He worked for many years as a fellow at King's College and served as Director of the London School of Economics (1997–2004). Giddens was famous for his early work on structure and agency, which helps to explain the possibilities for, and limits of, individual action to change society. He was one of the first significant sociologists to grapple with the profound consequences for human societies of communication technologies that have overcome barriers of space and time in regard to ways in which we relate to other people. In his collaborations with Ulrich Beck he has turned his attention, increasingly, to the rise of global risk. He was given a life peerage in 2004 in honour of his distinguished career.

In recent times Lord Anthony Giddens has turned his attention to the implications of global climate change (2009). In a public lecture at Cambridge in October 2012 he noted that no previous human society has 'interfered in nature' the way we do today. This means that we are 'off the edge of history' in knowing what will come of our meddling. This is a scary thought, Giddens admitted, but we are slowly coming to understand that 'interdependence enters into our personal lives and biographies', especially with the continuing emergence of communication technologies that make time and space less of a barrier to our interactions with others.

NEW OPPORTUNITIES IN THE 'DIGITAL AGE'

The author's research on community art in Australia has highlighted the fact that digital storytelling technologies and techniques have greatly increased the capacity for people to create and share short stories based on lived experiences. These might end up in local repositories – as was the case in the creation of a **Memory Bank** of community history stories in the fast-changing Australian regional city of Geelong in 2009 – or they might be shared widely through social media outlets such as YouTube. Not everyone has the capacity to turn fragments of a story into a compelling video narrative and some digital stories are more finely crafted than most. However, there seems to be an appealing immediacy and accessibility about this mode of storytelling, as shown by the global popularity of YouTube. Particular YouTube clips can suddenly 'go viral' bringing individual people and their stories to the attention of a worldwide audience, if only fleetingly.

Geelong's Memory Bank was set up in July 2008 as part of a larger community art project called 'Connecting Identities'. It is a repository for a host of short 'digital stories' curated by film-maker Malcolm McKinnon.

In a world that seems to be suffering from an oversupply of accessible information and opinions it is interesting to note that the ancient practice of storytelling is enjoying something of a revival. We are mesmerised by the success stories of people have risen from relatively humble beginnings to make a big impact on our lives. We are fascinated to learn, for example, that Mark Zuckerberg's 'irresponsible' decision to play with his computer rather than focus on his studies in dentistry at Harvard University led to the creation of Facebook. Of course, very few people can emulate the rapid success of people like Zuckerberg, Steve Jobs, Bill Gates, or follow the long road of people like Nelson Mandela. It is easy to be distracted by 'celebrity culture'. People who have grown up the world of the internet and 'smartphones' – sometimes called 'digital natives' – must learn how to distinguish between good information and informed opinion, on the one hand, and the circulation of dubious information and prejudicial opinion, on the other. In a world of constant distraction it has become harder to learn how to concentrate and use one's time well. However, powerful communication tools create new possibilities for individual agency. Global connectedness should survive the resource constraints imposed by the need to reduce greenhouse gas emissions and move beyond oil dependency. New communication technologies make it easier to build the global movement for sustainable living that **Paul Hawken** has called the largest movement in the history of humanity (2007).

Paul Hawken was born in San Francisco in 1946 and attended both San Francisco State University and the University of California at Berkeley without completing a degree. He left university to work in the burgeoning civil rights movement. He established his reputation as an environmental writer with the 1983 book *The Next Economy*.

From local action to global presence

350.org is a global organisation campaigning to reduce global greenhouse gas emissions to avoid dangerous climate change. It takes its name from the target set by James Hansen in 1988 for an acceptable level of greenhouse concentrations in the upper atmosphere and even though the target of 350 ppm has already been exceeded, the organisation argues that the target is still achievable. The organisation was started by the prominent US environmental writer and journalist Bill McKibben in conversation with his students at Middlebury College in the Champlain Valley of Vermont. McKibben had already undertaken a well-publicised walk across Vermont to raise public concern about escalating climate change and he initiated a protest movement called Step It Up in 2007 which organised protests at 1,400 sites across the country. However, 350.org represented an attempt to turn this into a global protest movement by making more use of social media outlets. The organisation now has a presence in many countries and its activities are focused around the multifaceted Global Power Shift campaign. In 2012, 350.org was awarded an international prize by the UK-based non-government organisation Katerva for its work on behaviour change.

Jean Lave and Étienne Wenger are an unusual pairing in that Lave studied social anthropology at Harvard University before going to work at the University of California at Berkeley (UCB), while Geneva-born Wenger studied computer science before coming to work in that area at UCB. Lave and Wenger met in UCB's Institute for Research of Learning.

As discussed in Chapter 9, new communication technologies enable us to participate in a host of 'virtual' 'communities of practice'. According to the anthropologists who coined the term, **Jean Lave and Étienne Wenger**, such communities will only endure if key participants share core values and beliefs. In contrast to more ephemeral networks, communities of practice seek to enact shared beliefs and values.

Carlo Petrini (b. 1949) had been a political activist in Rome for many years before he got involved in food politics through the campaign to block the opening of an outlet of McDonald's hamburger chain near the city's famous Spanish Steps in the early 1980s. He initiated the formation of the Slow Food movement in Italy in 1986 and helped to write a manifesto for launching the international Slow Food movement in 1989.

Slow Food as an international community of practice

As discussed in Chapter 3, the international Slow Food movement grew out of a successful 1986 campaign to prevent establishment of a McDonald's fast food outlet near Rome's famous Spanish Steps. The campaign had been organised by an organisation named Arcigola which had the broader aim of celebrating centuries-old Italian tradition producing and enjoying locally produced food. The leader of Arcigola, **Carlo Petrini**, used the success of the local campaign to organise an international gathering in Paris in 1989 which adopted a manifesto focusing on the social importance of locally produced food. By 2011 Slow Food International claimed to have more than 1,300 local groups in over 150 countries, with local groups known as 'conviviums' to suggest that vibrant local communities can form around the ancient art of feasting. Local Slow Food groups can be seen as communities of practice in that they exist to develop and promote particular practices. However, the international movement can also be seen as a community of practice in that it is clearly underwritten by shared values, beliefs and practices. Communication technologies facilitate the construction of multilayered communities of practice.

ARGUMENTS FOR HOPE

In thinking about sustainability at a global scale it is hard to avoid feeling rather overwhelmed by the scale of the challenges we face. While the challenges we now face – notably human-induced global climate change – are unprecedented we can draw on other dark times in human history to consider how people have been able to sustain and build hope rather than give in to despair. The German philosopher of Jewish descent, **Ernst Bloch** faced overwhelming despair when he narrowly escaped the Nazi Holocaust in his homeland, and he used that experience to subsequently create a seminal body of work on the 'principles of hope'. Hope that is not built on deep reflection amounts to little more than 'enervating escapism' he wrote, while 'educated hope' is not content to accept the world as it appears. 'Only thinking directed towards changing the world and informing the desire to change it does not confront the future … as embarrassment and the past as spell', he argued.[4] Another German philosopher of Jewish descent, **Hannah Arendt**, also had a close encounter with the Nazi Holocaust and although there is no evidence of direct contact between these two Holocaust

Photo 10.1 Outsized protesters confront an oil drilling ship near the coast of Aotearoa New Zealand: hope driven by courage
Photo by Nick Tapp

Ernst Bloch (1885–1977) was the son of a Jewish railway worker who studied and taught philosophy before fleeing Germany to escape the Nazi regime in 1934. He lived in exile in the USA from 1938–48 where he worked on the manuscript for his epic work *The Principle of Hope*. As a committed Marxist he returned to East Germany (German Democratic Republic) in 1949 to take a position at the University of Leipzig. He fell out with the GDR regime over the Soviet invasion of Hungary in 1956 and was forced to resign his university position in 1957. He went to live in West Germany in 1962 where he actively supported the youth 'radicalisation' of the 1960s.

Hannah Arendt (1906–75) was born into a secular Jewish family in Hanover. She studied philosophy at the University of Marburg where she had a romantic relationship with her teacher and mentor Martin Heidegger. She left Germany for Czechoslovakia in 1933 and lived for a while in Paris where she worked with Jewish refugees from the Nazi regime which stripped her of her German citizenship in 1937. She moved to

New York in 1941 where she worked as a leading political theorist until her death in 1975. She came to public attention when she covered the 1963 trial of former Nazi functionary Adolf Eichmann in Jerusalem for *The New Yorker* magazine.

refugees their work on hope in dark times complements each other. While Bloch wrote on the transformational power of 'educated hope' Arendt stressed the need to take collective responsibility for things that might be done in our name and, according to Claus Wrangel, the 'political force' of hope for Arendt 'depends on the possibility of acting out-of-hope; to step outside the moment of hope, to change the present rather than remain hopefully in it'.[5]

Returning to our contemporary global challenges we can take hope from the fact that humanity has only really been thinking about global sustainability challenges for just over a quarter of a century and that is a short time within the long span of human history. Scientific processes have given us an unprecedented understanding of how planetary systems work and we are now aware that humans are capable of exceeding the 'carrying capacity' of some of those systems. We know that the future wellbeing of humanity requires significant changes in our beliefs and practices and we are becoming more aware of our increasing responsibility for the future wellbeing of other living things. We know a lot about the changes we need to make to live more sustainability on this planet; we now need to summon the global will to make the difficult changes happen. We need to use 'educated hope' in order to work tirelessly for the scale of changes that are required.

Unbridled consumption simply cannot be sustained and addictive consumption on the part of a global minority threatens to trap the majority in endless cycles of poverty. However, addictive consumption does not lead to self-fulfilment and we know that we might actually attain a better quality of life by stepping away from the treadmill of consumption. Hawken's analysis of the 'largest' movement in human history starts with the suggestion that many local communities in the global south can only survive if they rehabilitate practices of self-reliance but their efforts are now being lauded by many people and organisations in the global north. Communication technologies have broken down old forms of isolation and new forms of global solidarity have been forged.

Robert Louis Stevenson (1850–94) is the author of some of the most popular classics of Scottish literature, including *Treasure Island*, *Kidnapped* and *The Strange Case of Dr Jekyll and Mr Hyde*. The son of devout Presbyterian parents who expected their talented son to become a respected lawyer, Stevenson instead adopted a rather Bohemian lifestyle and made a name for himself as a travel writer.

There can be no guarantee that will succeed in our global endeavour to find ways to live sustainably on a warming and potentially overpopulated planet. We know more about what the future could hold than ever before and yet that future looks more uncertain than we had imagined. We have to learn how to live with increased levels of risk and uncertainty by becoming more adaptable and resilient and by worrying less about what the future might hold. This is a scary yet exciting time to be alive and, as mentioned in Chapter 1, we might take solace from the rather counter-intuitive sentiment expressed by **Robert Louis Stevenson** when he said: 'To travel hopefully … is better than to arrive.'

Seven arguments for hope

1 The biggest challenges sometimes bring out the best in people; we can be surprisingly compassionate, innovative and resilient in a crisis.
2 We have unprecedented global awareness and incredible powers of communication.
3 Growing global challenges may mean that the imperative to cooperate may overtake self-interest and competition.

4 A lot of the intellectual work for knowing how to live more sustainably has already been done; we need to focus now on building social and political will to change direction.
5 We have enhanced capacities to become the author of our own stories.
6 Social and political change can come quickly after a long build-up.
7 We have the exciting opportunity to participate in the biggest social movement in history.

ENTERING A NEW PHASE IN THE HISTORY OF HUMANITY

The suggestion – most commonly attributed to Paul Crutzen – that we have entered the new era in the history of life on Earth has attracted very strong interest. Efforts are underway to officially endorse the argument that we have seen the end of the Cenozoic era, which endured for the last 65 million years, and have entered the Anthropocene era, in which a single species – i.e. *Homo sapiens* – has already changed the conditions of life for all other living things. This is a scary thought and yet a number of writers have suggested that the big evolutionary picture of life on Planet Earth can actually be a source of great inspiration. A key argument is that evolution has imparted on living systems a tendency towards self-organisation.[6] It is rather ironic that the big picture of evolution starts with the very, very small because microbiologist **Lynn Margulis** has been given credit for a revolution in thinking about evolution when her studies of micro-organisms – reported in the early 1970s – showed a tendency towards cooperation and self-organisation (see Phipps 2012). In 1994 the theologian **Thomas Berry** and mathematician/cosmologist **Brian Swimme** released a book which argued that the biggest picture of all – i.e. the story of the creation of our universe and the evolution of life on our planet – can inspire us to feel a deep sense of solidarity with all other forms of life. The emergence of human consciousness, the authors argued, is part of that unfolding story and Berry has suggested that we might eventually learn to think of life on Earth as a 'communion of subjects rather than a collection of objects'. Earlier, Berry had written: 'To learn how to live graciously together would make us worthy of this unique, beautiful blue planet that evolved in its present splendour over some billions of years.'[7]

Ten years later the biologist **Ursula Goodenough** expressed a similar thought when she wrote:

> If we can revere how things are, and can find a way to express gratitude for our existence, then we should be able to figure out, with a great deal of work and good will, how to share the Earth with one another and with other creatures, how to restore and preserve its elegance and grace.[8]

Lynn Margulis was born in 1938 and gained her Ph.D. in botany at the University of California in Berkeley in 1963. She published her first theoretical work on the origins of symbiotic eukaryotic cells in 1966 while working as a young academic at the University of Boston in 1966 but she had to show fierce determination to continue this work against strong opposition. Eventually she was recognised for her role in shifting the focus of evolution to the emergence of symbiotic micro-organisms.

Thomas Berry (1914–2009) was a vastly experienced theological scholar when he met the much younger mathematician with an interest in the origins of the cosmos – **Brian Swimme** – in 1982. Berry introduced Swimme to the philosophy of Pierre Teilhard de Chardin and they worked together for ten years to write *The Universe Story* in 1992.

Ursula Goodenough (b. 1943) studied zoology at Columbia University before completing her Ph.D. at Harvard University in 1969. She was an associate professor in biology at Harvard before taking up a position at Washington University in 1978. Highly regarded for her textbooks in genetics, her 1998 book *The Sacred Depths of Nature* is considered to be the seminal text of the 'religious naturalism' movement.

Discussion questions

1 What experiences have you had in finding inner strength and what have you learnt about how you might find it again?
2 What is meant by the suggestion that we need to make 'a life of one's own in a runaway world'? What might create the feeling of living in a 'runaway world'?
3 Is it useful, or even possible, to aim at becoming the author of your own life story?
4 What might be some communities of practice that you have joined and why can they claim that name?
5 Do the seven arguments for hope articulated in this chapter make you feel any more hopeful? If so, why?
6 Does the concept of the Anthropocene fill you with hope or fear or a mixture of both?
7 What do you think of the suggestion that we humans may be obliged to nurture new forms of trans-species solidarity? How and where might this emerge?
8 Is the concept of travelling hopefully useful to you? If so, why?

KEY READINGS

Beck, Ulrich (1995) 'A Life of One's Own in a Runaway World…', in Ulrich Beck and Elisabeth Beck-Gernsheim (eds), *Individualization: Institutionalized Individualism and its Social and Political Consequences*, London: Sage, pp. 22–9.

Berry, Thomas and Brian Swimme (1992) *The Universe Story: From the Primordial Flaring Forth to the Ecozoic Era*, San Francisco, CA: HarperCollins.

Giddens, Anthony (1995) 'Living in a Post-Traditional Society', in Ulrich Beck, Anthony Giddens and Scott Lash (eds), *Reflexive Modernization: Politics, Tradition and Aesthetics of the Modern Social Order*, Cambridge: Polity Press, pp. 56–109.

Hawken, Paul (2007) *The Blessed Unrest: How the Largest Social Movement in History is Restoring Grace, Justice and Beauty to the World*, New York: Penguin.

Mulligan, Martin (2015) 'On Ambivalence and Hope in the Restless Search for Community: How to Work with the Idea of Community in the Global Age', *Sociology*, 49(2): 340–55.

Phipps, Carter (2012) *Evolutionaries: Unlocking the Spiritual and Cultural Potential of Science's Greatest Idea*, New York: HarperCollins.

thematic essay

From human compassion to trans-species solidarity

At a time when Australia had adopted a particularly harsh policy for deterring refugees and asylum seekers from trying to reach the country by boat, the Melbourne writer Arnold Zable visited the Greek island of Ithaca, the birthplace of his wife. He was struck by the contrast when he heard that when a ship carrying refugees and asylum seekers got into trouble nearby, the islanders rushed to the rescue, bringing some 700 passengers back to land in their fishing boats and making sure that they all received food and dry clothes. The islanders opened their homes, gave the unfortunates their own clothes and a bakery set about baking 700 rolls to feed them (Zable 2004). When Zable asked the islanders why they had been so compassionate towards 'illegal' migrants they told him that, as people who depend on fishing, they know that anyone can get into unforeseen trouble whenever the wind changes, thus needing to find safe refuge. Zable wrote up the story under the title 'Any Time the Wind Can Change', which, in turn, gave birth to a song with the same title by singer/songwriter Kavisha Mazzella. The story and song featured in a performance tour featuring Zable and Mazzella which focused on the extraordinary contribution that so many migrants have made to Australian social and cultural life.

The crux of the story is that it can be in our own self-interest to show compassion towards other people in a volatile world. It touches on the need to develop personal resilience – as the fishing folk of Ithaca know only too well – yet it reminds us that we are never really alone. As we enter into what many are calling the Anthropocene era of planetary history it should become more evident that we humans need to show much greater compassion towards all other forms of life which collectively create the living systems on which we depend. Furthermore, as Anthony Weston has stressed, we need to show compassion for non-human life forms that may be living closer to us than we often think, even when we live in the midst of cities.[9] We should not only be concerned about the future for endangered polar bears or Tasmanian devils but for the wellbeing of habitats and ecosystems that penetrate our cities and towns. However, as Freya Matthews has argued, this requires a new kind of attentiveness to the life worlds of birds, insects, small animals and plants that we might otherwise take for granted within our urbanised environments.[10]

It was a special kind of attentiveness to non-human life worlds that enabled Charles Darwin to develop and refine his ground-breaking theory of natural evolution. Darwin's journey on *HMS Beagle* and his eye-opening encounters with stunningly diverse, yet sometimes brutal, regimes of life on the Galapagos Islands have been well documented. We know that 24 years passed between the time when Darwin visited the islands and the time when his theory of natural evolution was finally published in 1859. We also know that he laboured and agonised over the articulation of the theory for nearly 20 of those years. He finally agreed to the publication only after hearing that his meticulous work might be upstaged by the publication of a similar theory by Alfred Wallace.

Darwin agonised over his emerging theory because it challenged his own religious beliefs and because he knew that it would highly controversial. He continued to formulate his theory by examining variations and adaptations in organisms ranging from beetles to barnacles and by engaging in his parallel interest in geology. His attention to detail enabled him to publish a theory robust enough to withstand the inevitable backlash – certainly more robust that the theory articulated by Wallace – even if he had to anticipate later work on genetic variability. Tim Flannery (2011) has suggested that Wallace developed a richer understanding of the broad implications of the theory of evolution but Darwin's theory changed the world because it was based on detailed and accurate observation coupled with a brilliant imagination. The fact that it caused him such personal discomfort only made the work more praiseworthy.

It is interesting to note that it took Darwin's great work of science to challenge the assumption – championed by such fathers of European Enlightenment as Francis Bacon and René Descartes – that we humans will be able to use our unique powers of rational thinking to finally make nature bend to our human will. Of course, belief in human 'mastery' is such a seductive delusion that it can continue to defy deeper rational thought. We continue to ignore our own long-term self-interest by disturbing the functioning of the planet's ecological systems. However, Darwin's basic theory has been refined and taken into new areas of thought (Phipps 2012), with some of this work extending to the evolution of the human psyche. We now understand that the evolution of life on Earth is part of the bigger story of the creation and evolution of the universe. Carter Phipps (ibid.) has suggested that evolutionary thinking has been the real revolution of the modern era of human thought and the sense of being part of a miraculous community of life on Earth can fill us with hope as we journey into the turbulent conditions of the Anthropocene. We humans can be more compassionate and resilient than we often think. However, we might need to modify Thoreau's famous dictum about the importance of wildness for the preservation of the world to say that, 'In solidarity with other life forms is the future of humanity.'

NOTES

1 See www.stuartbhill.com/index.php/meaningful-change
2 Richard Sennett, *The Culture of the New Capitalism*, New Haven, CT: Yale University Press, 2006.
3 See Mulligan *et al.* (2006).
4 See Ernst Bloch, *The Principle of Hope, Volume 1*, Boston, MA: MIT Press, 1986.
5 See Claus Wrangel (2014) 'Hope in a time of catastrophe? Resilience and the future in bare life', *Resilience: International Policies, Practices and Discourses*, 2(3): 194.

6 See Stuart Kauffman, *At Home in the Universe: The Search for Laws of Self-Organization and Complexity*, Oxford: Oxford University Press, 1995.
7 Thomas Berry, *The Dream of the Earth*, San Francisco, CA: Sierra Club Books, 1988, p. 12.
8 Ursula Goodenough, *The Sacred Depths of Nature*, New York: Oxford University Press, 1998, p. 74.
9 Anthony Weston, *A Practical Companion to Ethics*, 4th edn, Oxford: Oxford University Press, 1997.
10 Freya Mathews, *Reinhabiting Reality: Towards a Recovery of Culture*, Albany, NY: State University of New York Press, 2005.

CHAPTER 11

Taking action

Key concepts and concerns

- working with key actors and stakeholders
- policy cycles
- performance indicators
- regulations and market mechanisms
- community engagement
- fostering sustainable behaviour
- a narrative approach to culture change
- on being a change agent

INTRODUCTION

The Social Ecology model of sustainability used extensively in this book highlights the need to bring big sustainability challenges back to a consideration of things that individual people can do; at home and in the various organisations and communities to which they belong. The model brings the 'personal dimensions' of sustainability into view and this was the focus of Chapter 10. This chapter reverses the direction of that line of argument to consider what individuals can do in wider organisational, social and cultural settings. It starts by focusing on the seemingly simple task of building relationships with other 'actors' within organisational or community settings before considering how change proposals might be 'enshrined' within adopted policy. However words like 'actors', '**stakeholders**' and even 'policy' are used rather loosely in the literature on sustainability and this chapter argues that we need to distinguish very carefully between different modes of engagement and consultation. We need to understand that policies can be seen as 'issue-attention cycles' (Portney 1992) that can never be fully completed. They articulate transitional outcomes of ongoing dialogues and debates.

stakeholders are those who have a 'stake' or interest in a particular project or enterprise. The term was first used in the Stanford Research Institute in 1963.

Many concepts and terms that circulate in the literature on sustainability come from the fields of economics and business management and while there is nothing wrong with that in itself we need to understand their origins and limitations. As noted in Chapters 4 and 9, growth-oriented, free market economic theories and practices have generally failed to address the big global challenges identified in the 1987 Brundtland Report but that should not rule out the judicious use of concepts and tools taken from economics and business management.

Chapter 9 noted that the word 'community' is particularly open to abuse and misuse and yet community development practice and meaningful community engagement work can build momentum for wider social and cultural change. The chapter looks at the influential work by **Douglas Mackenzie-Mohr** and William Smith on fostering behaviour change within communities but it goes on to suggest that we also need to focus on wider cultural change and here we return to the importance of storytelling that was raised in Chapter 10. Social and cultural change, it will be argued, are never linear and only rarely predictable. However, individuals can consciously hone their ability to act as change agents in contexts ranging from a workplace organisation to the virtual world of social media.

Douglas Mackenzie-Mohr, after *Time* magazine rated the first edition of *Fostering Sustainable Behaviour* (1999) as 'required reading' for anyone interest in sustainability, its lead author has risen to international prominence winning major awards in Canada and being cited in *The New York Times*.

KEY ACTORS AND ACTOR NETWORKS

As mentioned above, it is useful to draw a clear distinction between 'actors' – who may be able to play an active role within a particular scenario – and 'stakeholders' – who may have an interest but little capacity to act. Of course, some stakeholders can be actors or even 'key actors' and it is important to remember that particular stakeholders have the ability to change the direction of a project or proposal even if the personal or professional consequences may be much less significant for them than other stakeholders who may have much less influence. Stakeholders can be categorised in terms of both their exposure to the consequences of the project/proposal and in terms of their ability to change its direction. A further distinction can be drawn between actors and 'key actors' and we will start with the latter because anyone who assumes – or is given – responsibility to implement change within an organisation or community needs to identify a range of people who could have important roles to play. The selection of key actors should not be based solely on old friendships or associations; rather, it requires careful, strategic, consideration of roles that need to be played to win support and build momentum for change. If they are not already committed to the intended change then such key actors need to be recruited to the cause and this may only happen if they are given a chance to amend or develop the change proposals. Any change proposal that fails to convince key actors is doomed to failure and this may reflect the fact that the changes have been poorly conceived or poorly researched. The rationale for change needs to be cogent and convincing and the key actors need to work together with a shared understanding of the rationale.

At one level the idea of creating a network of key actors is fairly a simple one. However, key actors who have been recruited to a cause must then work with a wide array of people who need to enact changes; the deeper we dig into these layers, the more likely we are to face forms of inertia or even outright resistance. Cultural change within an organisation or community of people is difficult to achieve because, as sociologist **Pierre Bourdieu** has put it, we all operate with a 'habitus' of acquired dispositions and unconscious assumptions. People may react emotionally to a change because it is perceived as a threat to normality and 'irrational' responses should be anticipated. Patience is needed in promoting a disturbance to unconscious norms. Furthermore, people who are being recruited

Pierre Bourdieu (1930–2002) born of humble parents in southern France, Bourdieu carved out a career in philosophy, anthropology and sociology to become one of France's leading public intellectuals in his later life. His interest in anthropology – which stemmed from serving as a military conscript in Algeria in the 1950s – gave rise to his concept of 'habitus'. He initiated the argument that 'social' and 'cultural' capital are just as important as 'financial' capital for creating stronger societies.

to enact change will almost certainly have rather complex relationships with other actors. The sociologist Bruno Latour (2005) has popularised the notion of '**actor networks**' and yet he has suggested that the term network is also rather misleading because connections between different actors may be largely hidden from view – in the manner of a rhizome – and only become visible when the actors behave rather unexpectedly. Latour suggests that effective actor networks tend to focus on building robust relationships as much as they might focus on particular tasks or desired outcomes. Cultural change within organisations or communities of people is not likely to be linear or predictable and yet effective actor networks can bring about far-reaching changes that a key actor may not have imagined.

networks of actors/ actor networks actor network theory – which is most prominently associated with the work of French sociologist Bruno Latour – goes beyond the concept of networks of human actors in that it sees a role for non-human components in such networks. However, it has deepened understanding of the behaviour of human networks.

STAKEHOLDER CONSULTATIONS

The benefits of identifying and consulting various 'stakeholders' was first advocated in business management theory,[1] however it has been picked up very widely in public policy theory and practice. The '**contingent valuation**' approach for determining the value of non-market resources has also advocated widespread consultation with people who may have a direct or indirect stake in the preservation or exploitation of particular natural 'resources'. Although it can be very hard – sometimes impossible – to reconcile the competing interests of different stakeholders, the benefits of stakeholder consultations and negotiations are now widely accepted, even if the processes can be time-consuming and sometimes inconclusive.

contingent valuation was first proposed in 1947 as a survey-based technique for estimating the value of non-market resources, such as benefits derived from preserving the natural environment.

Because stakeholder consultations tend to be time-consuming and rather unpredictable they are often performed in rather shallow or tokenistic ways. For example, a narrow range of stakeholders may be consulted and the outcomes of consultations can be manipulated to justify a pre-existing proposal. Stakeholder consultations should aim to consider the interests of all categories of stakeholders

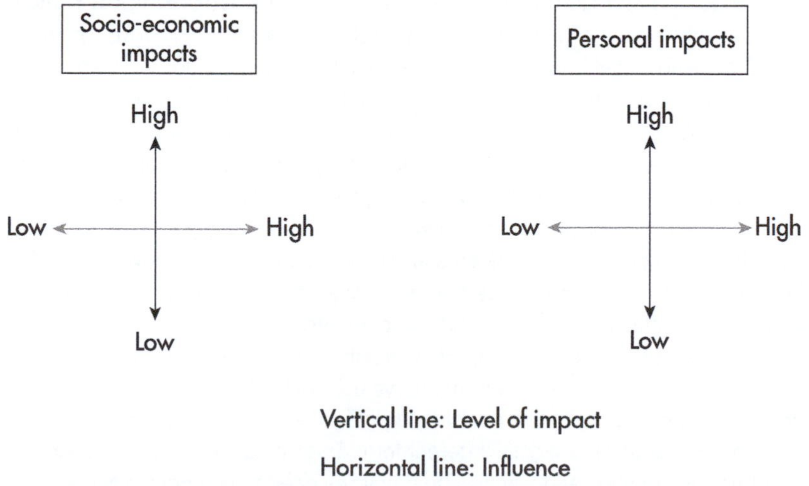

Figure 11.1 Matrices for identifying stakeholders in relation to professional interests, impacts and influence

not just those with obvious influence. Hasty, shallow or tokenistic consultation processes may cause deeper division and resentment among the wide array of stakeholders and this can rebound on those responsible. For example, the author found that hasty and narrow consultations around the delivery of aid to tsunami-affected communities in Sri Lanka in 2005 resulted in very unfair distribution of the aid and this commonly boiled over as anger directed at aid agencies and local government authorities. The author's study of post-tsunami recovery also highlighted the need to draw a clear distinction between stakeholders and communities, which is taken up later in this chapter.

MAKING AND MONITORING POLICY

The discussion above has focused on implementing change proposals within organisations or communities of people. However, to ensure that desired changes are sustained and/or integrated with other changes they may need to be set within policy frameworks which aim to articulate the orientation and commitments of the organisation or community in relation to the issues being addressed. The sustainability agenda that was fleshed out by the Brundtland Report of 1987 called for policy responses at all levels from localised communities and organisations to nation states and global systems of governance. Policy responses have ranged from new restrictions on the release of environmental pollutants to international protocols for restricting the emission of greenhouse gases. Environment policy has become an established field of practice at levels ranging from private corporations to various agencies of the United Nations. It is assumed that 'good policy' will drive changes in attitudes and practices.

Yet, as Thomas and Murfitt (2011) have stressed, the word 'policy' has many meanings. Vig and Kraft (1994, 1st edn: 5)[2] offered a rather 'common sense' definition in saying that 'policy states an intent to achieve certain goals and objectives through a conscious choice of means, usually within some specified time period'. Vig and Kraft have refined their work on **environmental policy** through eight editions of their seminal book on the topic. However, **public policies** are never set in stone for, as Considine has noted (2005: 1) 'The policies of governments and the counter-policies of agitators and special interest groups each offer to make tomorrow different from today. They do so in a world undergoing cataclysmic change.' The suggestion that policy formation should be strictly evidence based and values free was discussed, and dismissed, in Chapter 9. However, this does not diminish the importance of developing policies in order to highlight particular issues or concerns and build a consensus on how to address them, as long as we acknowledge that decisions about how to act always come back choices reflecting different values or priorities.

public policy and environmental policy, public policy normally refers to policies made by government or semi-government authorities and agencies. Environmental policy refers to policies adopted by government agencies to protect the natural environment but it also refers to policies adopted by private organisations to articulate their commitments to environmental protection.

Portney (1992) offered an important insight when he described environmental policy processes as 'issue-attention cycles', noting that the attention often fades once a policy has been formulated only to re-emerge when the issue or problem re-emerges in a slightly different form. This introduces a cyclical conception of policy formation and it implies that policies need to be constantly revisited and reassessed. Thomas and Murfitt (2011: 52) have presented this as a 'policy cycle' (see Figure 11.2) and cycles starting with 'agenda setting' and passing

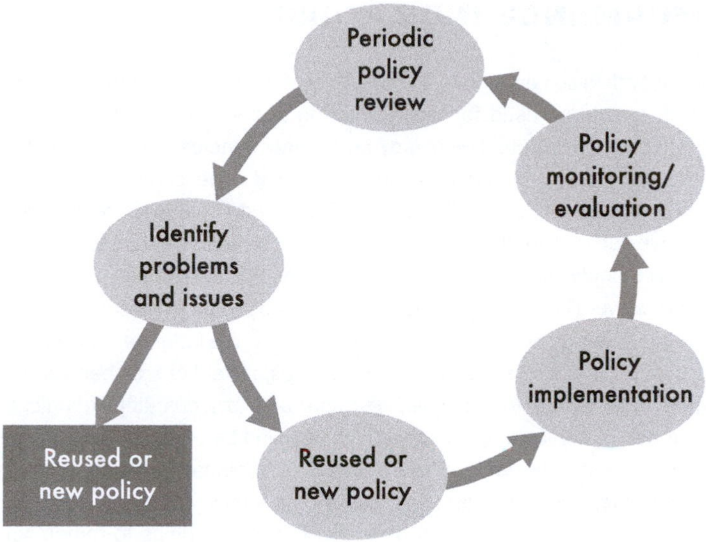

Figure 11.2 Policy cycles
Source: adapted from I. Thomas and P. Murfitt, 2nd edn, *Environmental Management: Processes and Practices for Australia*, Sydney: Federation Press, 2011, p. 52

through policy formulation, implementation, monitoring and review can be adopted by any kind of organisation, not just those responsible for public policy. As Thomas and Murfitt noted, a policy review may reprioritise the problem being addressed but this does not mean that the problem has been 'solved'. It simply highlights the fact that priorities must be chosen and this, again, comes back to choices based on values or priorities.

Efforts that have been made in a range of countries to radically reduce the number of people who become addicted to cigarette smoking provide a good example of the successful use of policy cycles. Although the national policy approaches have varied, the early cycles tended to focus on public education about health risks associated with smoking and the use of taxes to create price disincentives. A second wave of policy focused on banning cigarette smoking in a wide range of places and spaces where people gather and restrictions on cigarette advertising. A third wave of policy that has emerged in some countries has focused on ensuring that cigarettes are sold in unattractive packages, often with graphic representations of negative health effects. Each of these policy cycles has built on the success of the one before and it would have been unthinkable to introduce unattractive packaging without the shift in public sentiment that earlier policies achieved. The result is that public policy cycles have made cigarette smoking an exception in countries such as the UK, the USA, Canada and Australia while little progress has been made in a range of European countries. In the absence of any public policy on the matter, cigarette smoking grew rapidly where China became the biggest consumer of tobacco products. However, smoking in schools in China was banned in January 2014 and a ban on smoking in public places in Beijing was introduced in June 2015. It seems that the anti-smoking policy cycles have begun.

performance indicators are goals that are expressed as benchmarks against which actual performance can be measured.

PERFORMANCE INDICATORS

The policy cycle also come down to difficult choices about what the 'performance indicators' should be used for the monitoring and evaluation; with the choices being reflected in the selection of 'key performance indicators' (KPIs). For a long time, the language of indicators has focused on the choice of quantitative indicators – i.e. performances that can be measured in numbers or statistics. For example, we can monitor the health of a particular community of people by tracking the statistics on diseases and recovery. However, this tells us very little about the community's overall wellbeing or happiness. It has become more common to select a mix of quantitative and qualitative indicators – with the latter generally emerging out of qualitative surveys that focus on feelings, reflections or behaviours that defy quantification. So, for example, we might add to a quantifiable indicator on the incidence of particular diseases a qualitative indicator about how stressed or happy people might be feeling. The addition of qualitative indicators increases the choices available to the organisation or community wanting to set KPIs, yet values-based choices still need to be made. It probably helps to remember that the selection of KPIs can be revisited for any particular policy cycle. It is undoubtedly important to have an inclusive conversation about the choice of KPIs to be used in any particular cycle because the possibilities are endless.

Scerri and James (2010) have suggested that the setting of 'sustainability indicators' can become an important focus for conversation and negotiation within particular organisations and communities. Consensus may be very hard to achieve but the effort to reach agreement can be very informative for all involved. The process for choosing indicators, they argue, may be as important as the final choice because selected indicators will always have limited purpose and relevance.

REGULATIONS AND MARKET MECHANISMS

A perennial debate in countries with highly developed economies is whether it is better to rely on government regulation or market-based incentives to achieve environmentally sustainable development. For example, pollution emanating from economic enterprises – ranging from big industrial plants to small businesses – can be subjected to pollution control legislation. However, it can be expensive to constantly monitor pollution outputs and many economists argue that it is more effective to reward corporations and enterprises that monitor their own outputs or adopt less polluting modes of production. Economic incentives might include government subsidies or tax cuts but they might extend to labelling systems or public rewards for businesses and organisations that show 'corporate responsibility' in taking environmental sustainability seriously. **Ratings systems** that enable consumers to select products that are energy efficient, water efficient, or 'ethical' in terms of their use of products and raw materials have become more prevalent. However, this kind of consumer choice is not only achieved by giving certain products a market edge, it also relies on regulations which might, for example, require a producer to adequately label their products. In practice, a mix of regulations and incentives may be needed to move towards what many are calling the 'green economy'.

ratings systems refer to comparisons made between different items, products, performances that indicate performance in relation to particular goals, such as minimal use of energy.

Chapter 6 reviewed the concern that the prevailing 'triple bottom line' approach to sustainability separates economic development from social wellbeing and tends to make environmental considerations subservient to the assumption that economic growth is essential. Chapter 11 focused on efforts being made to reframe economics in relation to the natural environment – i.e. 'environmental economics' – and to refocus on human happiness rather than narrowly framed economic indicators such as GDP. However, it is important to remember that people who run private corporations are obliged to focus on the long-term sustainability of their 'business model' and a number of important sustainability concepts have been drawn from business management literature; such as 'stakeholder consultation' and '**scenarios mapping**' (see Chapter 6). Another valuable concept is that of developing a '**business plan**' or 'business case' for a project or initiative because this involves weighing up the costs and benefits involved. Economic costs and benefits will always be a consideration but they need to be contextualised within a wider consideration of social and environmental costs and benefits. Turning costs and benefits into numbers makes it easier to develop a project '**balance sheet**', provided the translation into numbers is meaningful and reliable. A business plan can provide a good foundation for a dialogue about the anticipated costs and benefits of a proposal. Meanwhile, the onset of global climate change has injected new urgency into the global debate about how to accelerate a transition towards a global 'green economy'. The need for such a transition was argued by a former World Bank economist **Nicholas Stern** in an influential 2006 report he wrote for the UK government on the economic consequences of climate change. Essentially Stern argued that the costs associated with maintaining an economy that is heavily dependent on the use of oil and oil-based products will steadily rise while corporations that make a shift to low-carbon production will eventually benefit economically, even if there is a short-term transition cost. The Stern Report urged the UK government, and other national governments, to develop policies that would encourage and reward the development of the low-carbon economy.

The conundrum is that there is a limit to what any national government can do to encourage global corporations to make such a shift. Individual businesses say that they want policy certainty before changing their long-term investment and development strategies while most national governments are reluctant to impose constraints on what businesses do. Meanwhile, some global schemes for encouraging investments in greenhouse gas reduction projects have come under fire for actually making things worse.[3]

US economist **Joseph Stiglitz** is probably the most influential critic of free market approaches to the development of a global economy and he has called for much stronger policy interventions on the part of national governments. The more radical German green economist **Wolfgang Sachs** (2015) has argued that market mechanisms will never make the big cultural changes that are needed because the challenge is to 'shake off the hegemony of ageing Western values' that underpin the very idea of development. For Sachs (ibid.), the time has come to reverse the trend of globalisation so that each society can develop 'indigenous models of prosperity' based on 'stable or shrinking volumes of production'. Clearly there is no consensus on how to best make the transition to a global green economy. In the meantime, governments at all levels will continue to work with a mix of regulations and incentives.

scenarios mapping was initiated separately by the US military and by Shell Oil in the early 1970s to encourage contemplation of different scenarios that might evolve in the future and the particular challenges they might pose for those involved in the contemplation.

business plan refers to the background research required to justify investments of money and/or time in a new or revised project or initiative, using a cost–benefit approach.

balance sheet of project costings normally refers to a concise presentation, usually in table form, of anticipated financial costs and incomes. However, the notion of 'balance sheet' has been extended to refer to any cost–benefit analysis.

Nicholas Stern (b. 1946) is an Oxford- and Cambridge-educated economist who worked as a chief economist and senior vice president of the World Bank (2000–3) and as a government economics advisor (2003–7). His report on the economics of climate change was delivered to the UK government in October 2007.

COMMUNITY ENGAGEMENT

It is widely assumed that any transition to more sustainable ways of living requires public education and/or 'community engagement'. It was noted in Chapter 9 that the word 'community' is widely used and frequently abused, with **Gerard Delanty** (2003) arguing that a sense of belonging to community only exists today if it is 'wilfully constructed' and that we can now belong to a variety of real and virtual communities. In sustainability literature 'community' is often taken to mean local, place-based, communities yet Delanty, and many others, encourage us to pay attention to the formation of human communities in a wide variety of settings and contexts. We might think, for example, of communities that can form within large workplace organisations or spatially dispersed communities of people with shared backgrounds or interests. When it comes to the challenges of sustainability, particular people or organisations will have a duty or obligation to motivate sustainable behaviour yet many more could assume the responsibility to motivate behavioural or social change.

It is hardly surprising that prevailing discourses on sustainability have taken their core ideas and much of their language from environmental science, engineering, economics and psychology. This breadth of source material is a strength and yet it can foster the impression that strategies for achieving sustainability are a matter for relevant 'experts' and that the expertise must be taken *to* communities, rather than found within them.

A handbook produced by an international team of planning and community development professionals – *Kitchen Table Sustainability: Practical Recipes for Community Engagement with Sustainability*, by **Wendy Sarkissian** *et al.* (2009) – has stressed that the desire for sustainable living resides within communities and that 'people know more than they realize'. People will refrain from offering their opinions if they run the risk of appearing ignorant, the authors argue; people are likely to think that any communities they belong to are too weak or fragmented to take effective collective action. The authors note that action on sustainability requires an understanding of key concepts – such as 'social and biophysical realities' or the dangers of 'anthropocentrism'. However, once a motivation for change is firmly established it can become the incentive to build stronger communities, and the book includes examples of community building in places ranging from Minneapolis to Melbourne. Community engagement work is suited for people who might enjoy 'kitchen table conversations', the authors suggest, and it is essential to take time to build trust and turn ideas into action. However, patience can be rewarded with outcomes that are unexpected and delightful, the authors conclude. The book by Sarkissian *et al.* focuses on working with local communities but the key principles can be applied to community building in other settings and contexts, even if kitchen tables need to be replaced by other kinds of tables or by something as different as an online chat site.

FOSTERING SUSTAINABLE BEHAVIOUR

Douglas Mackenzie-Mohr and William Smith begin their influential book on fostering sustainable behaviour (first published in 1999) by arguing that regulations and

Joseph Stiglitz (b. 1943) is a Nobel Prize-winning economist at Columbia University in New York, who is well known for his criticism of free market fundamentalists. He has served as a chief economist and senior vice president at the World Bank.

Wolfgang Sachs (b. 1946) holds degrees in sociology and theology from Munich University. He has worked in a range of universities in Germany and the USA and was a co-author of a highly regarded book on global development – *The Development Dictionary* – in 1992. He has worked at the Wuppertal Institute for Climate, Environment and Energy since 2009.

Gerard Delanty is professor of sociology and social and political theory at the University of Sussex and editor of the *European Journal of Social Theory*. His work focuses on the implications of globalisation for the analysis of the social world.

Wendy Sarkissian was born and educated in Canada but has spent most of her professional life in Australia. She has a master's-level qualification in

information have never been enough to entrench behaviour change because it is very easy to slip back into old habits and behaviours, especially when the old behaviours deliver some personal benefits. For example, Mackenzie-Mohr notes that when he moved to a new house in 1993 he was determined to walk to work because it was good for the environment and for his personal health. However, the walk took 30 minutes and his resolve weakened when he began to think that he would prefer to spend more of that time with his family. Of course, it is easier to sustain a behaviour change when other people are making a similar effort; when it becomes a social activity rather than an individual effort. The book by Mackenzie-Mohr and Smith looks at ways to make behaviour change a community activity. They suggest that the chances of success are boosted when there has been a collective effort to identify the 'barriers and benefits' and when a selected initiative or programme is piloted and evaluated before being properly launched, or dropped.

English literature and Town Planning and a Ph.D. in environmental ethics. She has worked for 30 years as a social planning consultant in both North America and Australia.

Mackenzie-Mohr and Smith argue that sustainable behaviour can often be motivated on the basis of long-term economic self-interest and they borrow from the language of economics in using the term 'community-based social marketing'. However, like Sarkissian *et al.*, they also draw from the international practice of community development. Community development practice originated in the UK and spread to other countries in the late 1960s and early 1970s. The *International Journal for Community Development* celebrated its 40th anniversary in 2012 and it has been an important forum for swapping insights derived from an international field of practice that has probably not been given the respect it deserves.

From race riots to community power

In 1985 the inner-urban London suburb of Brixton was plunged into 48 hours of 'race riots' following the shooting by white police of black resident Dorothy Groce while they were looking for her son. Brixton is an area with extensive public housing and after the riots it was widely considered to be one of London's worst suburbs in which to live. By 2013 Brixton was home to one of the UK's most active Transition Town groups campaigning for community-based responses to the challenges of climate change and Peak Oil. Recognising that there are many economic benefits to the local community in adopting sustainable living goals, Brixton Transition Town formed itself as a Community Interest Company in 2010. In 2013 the company initiated the UK's first community-owned power station with 82kW of solar panels installed on the roofs of a public housing estate, with funding coming from 103 local investors. The success of this project has encouraged similar initiatives in other parts of London under the banner **Repowering London** (see www.repowering.org.uk).

Repowering London is a not-for-profit organisation which aims to build on the success of the Brixton community power project to support and seek funding for similar projects in other parts of London.

While Mackenzie-Mohr and Smith focus on strategies for motivating behaviour change from the ground up, others have focused on the kinds of public policies that might foster behaviour change at local levels. Here the focus has also shifted to incentives and barriers and an interesting model emerged out of the work of the UK Department for Environment, Food and Rural Affairs (DEFRA 2005, as

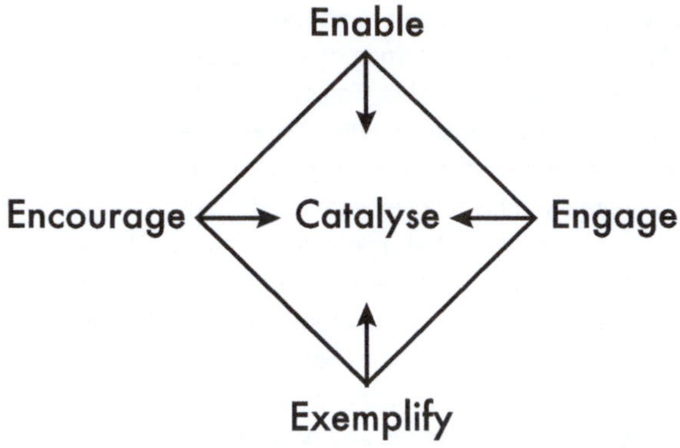

Figure 11.3 Behaviour change model
Source: adapted from T. Jackson, 'Challenges for Sustainable Consumption Policy', in T. Jackson (ed.), *The Earthscan Reader in Sustainable Consumption*, London: Earthscan, 2006, p. 123

cited in Jackson 2006). This model recommends an equal emphasis on policies and initiatives that *enable*, *encourage* and *exemplify* sustainable behaviour while also *engaging* communities to take up such behaviours (see Figure 11.3)

Tom Wessels (b. 1951) is a terrestrial ecologist and professor of environmental studies at Antioch University in New England. His 2006 book on 'the myth of progress' was published in a second edition in 2013.

A NARRATIVE APPROACH TO CULTURE CHANGE

The US natural history academic and writer **Tom Wessels** (2006) has argued that all the rational, scientific, arguments for sustainability have failed to dislodge the persistent 'myth of progress' from the public imagination. Rising epidemics of asthma, obesity, diabetes and unipolar depression have not been enough to shake popular belief in unlimited human 'progress', he argues (2006: xxii–xxiii). The time has come, Wessels concludes, to shift the emphasis from behaviour change to deep-seated cultural change.

John Michael Greer (b. 1962) a graduate of the University of Washington, Greer's prolific freelance writing and public commentary has focused on what he considers to be the impending collapse of industrial society. Although from a non-religious background he joined the Ancient Order of Druids in 1995 and served as its American Grand Archdruid from 2003 to 2015.

In a similar vein, but from a very different perspective, the rather provocative freelance environmental writer **John Michael Greer** (2008) has argued that the myth of progress has emerged and persisted as a kind of antidote to the ancient myth of apocalypse, which suggests that the golden age of humanity is already in the past because we have set out on a path towards self-destruction. Believers in apocalypse may be widely disparaged in the contemporary world, yet Greer notes that the end of the world has become a popular topic of Hollywood movies; he suggests that fear of the apocalypse makes us cling to the myth of linear and limitless progress. Myths that are deeply embedded within any particular human culture are likely to have ancient and forgotten origins and they may be supported by a host of old stories passed from one generation to the next; such as enduring English 'fairy tales' about the eventual triumph of good over evil. As Greer points out (ibid.: 50), stories passed down in traditional oral cultures were never for entertainment alone and it is interesting to note how many of the old stories continue to circulate. Storytelling is intrinsic to what it means to be human and the rise of empirical science in recent centuries has only partially diminished their importance in communicating knowledge and cultural awareness.

After being dismissed for a long period as being 'unscientific', storytelling has attracted renewed interest within social science fields of study, ranging from sociology to psychology. Indeed, 'narrative inquiry' has become a specialised form of qualitative research operating across many social science disciplines. The ability of stories to motivate people has been acknowledged. Of course, it is important to examine the origins of stories that enjoy popular appeal and Greer has noted that the 'stories we tell ourselves' often have unknown ancient origins. However, the art of storytelling is open to all, and new communication technologies have opened up greater opportunities to make and share 'digital stories'. Stories are widely seen as being cultural artefacts but they can also be understood modes of persuasion for social and cultural change.

Believing in black swans

The polymath Lebanese American scholar and writer **Nassim Nicholas Taleb** began his book on the 'impact of the highly improbable' (2007) by noting that Europeans imagined all swans to be white before they encountered black swans in Australia. An unquestioned assumption was brought down by the first sight of a single black bird, Taleb exclaimed.

Taleb used the example of 'Black swan logic' to argue that the world is deeply unpredictable and that things that have not even been conceived, let alone understood, can have major consequences. A person waking up to the dawning of a new year in Europe in January 1914 could not have imagined the long and bitter war that would engulf the continent for the next four-and-a-half years. No one predicted the sudden demise of the Soviet Union in 1989 and global stock market crashes continue to catch the pundits by surprise. People with artistic genius – such as the poet Edgar Allen Poe or the painter Vincent van Gogh – have been dismissed as being mad during their lives. We need to be much more open to the unexpected and unorthodox, Taleb argued, because the desire to stay within the safety of the known is the enemy of insight and innovation.

Nassim Nicholas Taleb was born in 1960 in Lebanon and educated in Paris. His extensive interests range from mathematical finance and risk engineering to various literary traditions. He lives in the USA where he has built a reputation as a talented and thought-provoking essayist.

ON BEING A CHANGE AGENT

In teaching an undergraduate introduction to sustainability course at RMIT University, the author and his teaching team have regularly invited young people working as change agents in a wide variety of settings and contexts to speak to the classes. The presenters are asked to tell the story of how they became a change agent and then offer reflections on what they have learnt from the experience. It has been remarkable to observe the consistency of reflections across the presentations, and when these are translated into tips for budding change agents the most common ones have been:

- Focus on an issue or set of challenges that you really care about.
- Be bold but also realistic about your chances of success.

- Do your research and make sure you know the issues and concerns very well.
- Use the internet to find out what actions others have taken elsewhere in the world.
- Try to find people you can enjoy working with and pay attention to these relationships as well as 'the cause'.
- Try to find a role that suits your talents and temperament but do not underestimate what you can do.
- Work on your oral and written communication skills.
- Be creative in the way you do things; a little humour can go a long way.
- Always remember that good teams will achieve more than talented individuals working alone.
- Do not get demoralised when some things do not work; learn the lessons of failure.
- Keep a balance in your personal life and avoid 'burn-out'; you have your whole life of activism ahead of you.

Discussion questions

1. What distinctions need to be drawn between key actors, actors and different categories of stakeholders?
2. Why is it hard to predict what might emerge from the work of actor networks?
3. What are the dangers of a shallow approach to stakeholder consultation?
4. Why is it useful to think of policy as 'issue-attention cycles'; why the emphasis on cycles?
5. Why is it important to think of both qualitative and quantitative performance indicators?
6. In relation to action on sustainability what are some of the useful concepts that have emerged out of business management theory and what are some of the dangers in relying on market mechanisms?
7. What is required for effective community engagement work?
8. What are some of the benefits and pitfalls in working with storytelling to foster culture change?
9. Why does social change emerge in a non-linear manner?

KEY READINGS

Greer, John Michael (2008) *The Long Descent: A User's Guide to the End of the Industrial Age*, Gabriola Island, BC: New Society Publishers.

Mackenzie-Mohr, Douglas and William Smith (2011), 3rd edn, *Fostering Sustainable Behaviour: An Introduction to Community-Based Social Marketing*, Gabriola Island, BC: New Society Publishers.

Sarkissian, Wendy, Nancy Hoffer, Yollana Shore, Steph Vajda and Cathy Wilkinson (2009) *Kitchen Table Sustainability: Practical Recipes for Community Engagement with Sustainability*, London: Earthscan.

Scerri, Andy and Paul James (2010) 'Accounting for Sustainability: Combining Qualititative and Quantitative Research in Developing "Indicators" of Sustainability', *International Journal of Social Research Methodology*, 13(1): 41–53.

Thomas, Ian and Paul Murfitt (2011) *Environmental Management: Processes and Practices for Australia*, Sydney: Federation Press.

Vig, Norman and Michael Kraft (2012), 8th edn, *Environmental Policy: New Directions for the Twenty-First Century*, New York: Sage.

Wessels, Tom (2006) *The Myth of Progress: Towards a Sustainable Future*, Burlington, VT: University of Vermont Press.

thematic essay

Non-linear social change

On 1 December 1955, the rather quietly spoken **Rosa Parks** was arrested after she refused to give up her seat to a white person on a Montgomery bus. The bus boycott that began on the day she went to court to be fined for her 'offence' lasted for 381 days and made the Montgomery Baptist preacher Martin Luther King Jr a national figure. The Montgomery bus segregation laws were deemed to be unconstitutional in the US District Court in 1956 and the boycott victory gave great impetus to the nationwide civil rights movement. Just half a century later a black American was elected as the US president.

Two other Montgomery women had been arrested and fined for refusing to give up their bus seats before Rosa Parks. However, Parks was married to an activist in the National Association for the Advancement of Coloured People (NAACP) and it was a network of activists who initiated the effective boycott. As a dignified and eloquent person, Rosa Parks became a powerful symbol of resistance but the time was also right for the campaign. Slavery in the USA had been abolished 90 years earlier, following the passage of the Emancipation Proclamation championed by Abraham Lincoln. However, the national emancipation act came more than 60 years after slavery had been abolished in all the states north of the **Mason-Dixon Line** and the fight to end slavery was long and bitter. By contrast, the civil rights movement achieved rapid successes with minimal conflict and violence. Overt racial discrimination and exploitation – which had been largely unquestioned within human societies for thousands of years – quite suddenly became unconscionable in the USA. Social change was driven by a sweeping change of consciousness.

As mentioned in Chapter 2, Rachel Carson's book *Silent Spring* is widely seen as the spark that lit the green fire of modern environmentalism even though Carson herself did not live to see her book's full effect. Around 20 million Americans turned out for Earth Day in 1970. The international environment organisation Greenpeace was initiated in 1971 when a group of protesters used a ramshackle fishing vessel to protest against nuclear weapons tests on the island of Amchitka, Alaska; and Friends of the Earth was formed in the USA and the UK in the same year. It is more difficult to begin a protest movement against something as big and diffuse as global climate change.

Rosa Parks (1913–2005) was born as Rosa McCauley in Alabama with both black America and Native American heritage. She suffered poor health as a child and was raised on a farm by her mother and maternal grandmother. She married National Association for the Advancement of Coloured People (NAACP) member Raymond Parks in 1932 and was secretary of the Montgomery chapter of the NAACP when she triggered the bus boycott campaign in 1955.

Mason-Dixon Line was drawn up by Charles Mason and Jeremiah Dixon between 1763 and 1767 in order to resolve a border dispute between states to the north and south of the line. It has come to represent a deeper cultural divide between northern and southern states.

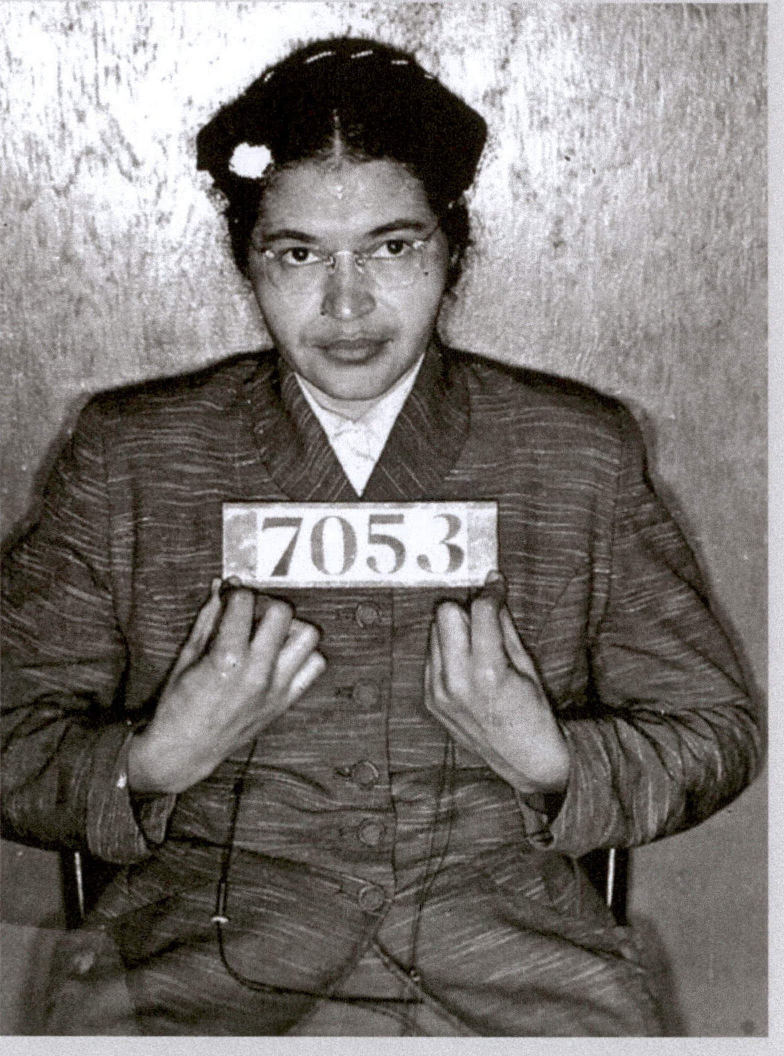

Photo 11.1 Rosa Parks: the woman who sparked a civil rights campaign by refusing to give up her seat on a bus
© Mug Shot/Alamy

Nevertheless, the US climatologist James Hansen sparked an escalation of public concern when he took the unusual step for a scientist of intervening in public debate on the matter during Congressional Hearings in 1988 and former US vice president Al Gore used his public profile to build on this concern with his 2006 documentary *An Inconvenient Truth.*

Action on global climate change cannot be simply oppositional because the causes are so complex and slow-burning. Not much can be achieved by changing specific laws or even by focusing on a narrow range of practices. Yet Paul Hawken (2007) has predicted that we are beginning to witness the emergence of the biggest social movement in human history with the proliferation of highly dispersed yet globally connected sustainable living groups and organisations. Public concern about global climate change undoubtedly waned after achieving its high tide mark in the period from 2006 to 2009. However, social, political and cultural change is rarely predictable or linear in its emergence and growth. The need to respond to global environmental challenges will continue to evoke responses and some people will be in the right place at the right time to make a big difference.

NOTES

1 R. Edward Freeman, *Strategic Management: A Stakeholder Approach*, London: Pitman Books, 1984.

2 Norman Vig and Michael Kraft, *Environmental policy in the 1980s: Reagan's New Agenda,* Washington, DC: Congressional Quarterly Press, 1994.

3 See, for example, Julia Dehm (2011) 'Tricks of Perception and Perspective: The Disappearance of Law and Politics in Carbon Markets', *Macquarie Journal of International and Comparative Environmental Law*, 7(2): 1–18.

CHAPTER 12

Introduction to assessment and monitoring tools

Key concepts and concerns

- footprint calculators
- risk assessment and management
- life cycle analysis
- cost–benefit analysis
- scenarios mapping
- unpredictability and the principle of emergence

INTRODUCTION

As we have seen in Chapter 11, there are many competing schools of thought on how to get people, organisations and communities to behave more sustainably. Some argue that we need a mix of economic penalties (e.g. taxes) and incentives (e.g. subsidies) to bring about sustainable behaviour change. Others suggest that we can rely on human curiosity and inventiveness to come up with new ways to meet our needs in regard to things like energy, food, water and shelter. Several scholars (e.g. Benyus 1997) have argued that we need to radically redesign most human systems so that they emulate natural processes in regard to functions like the total recycling of all waste. The term '**biomimicry**' has been used to suggest that close observation of nature might enable us to design things that function more sustainability and an example of this is in the design of wind turbine blades that generate 20 per cent more power because they have added bumps like those found on the tail of humpback whales.[1] However, it has been argued throughout this book that clever inventions will not be enough to create sustainable societies. We need to raise awareness at all levels of society about the personal, cultural and social changes we need to make to live sustainably and there are numerous environmental assessment and monitoring tools that can be used for this purpose.

biomimicry is a term that was coined by American nature writer Janine Benyus in a book with 'biomimicry' in its title (1997). It suggests strong benefits in learning directly from nature in designing products and processes.

This chapter can only provide an introduction to selected tools and assessment methodologies which all require more detailed explanation and practical experience to be used effectively. No attempt is made here to provide a comprehensive review of available methods and tools. Rather the chapter begins with some tools and methods that require little expertise before introducing some approaches that would require further study. The aim of the chapter is to draw attention to particular tools and methods that are known to be effective in raising awareness among those using them, even if they do not necessarily suggest clear solutions. The emphasis in this chapter is on assessing and monitoring the challenges we face rather than 'managing' them. As argued in Chapters 4 and 5, the big challenges of sustainability are interlinked and can be seen as 'wicked problems' that require constant and ongoing attention rather than 'resolution'. However, assessment and monitoring provides a good foundation for thinking about informed action and this chapter needs to be read in conjunction with Chapter 11.

Ecological footprint calculators provide a good starting point for thinking about environmental impacts related to social units ranging from households to organisations, cities and nations. There are many such calculators in circulation and most of them are suitable for use by novices, so the concept is discussed here rather than any particular calculator. Another good starting point for investigating environmental impacts is to compile an inventory of raw materials and waste or to conduct an audit of energy use. Inventories and audits are a common starting point for a lot of **Environmental Impact Assessment (EIA)** work but this chapter will stop short of introducing the much more complex task of compiling EIA or Social Impact Assessment reports.

Environmental Impact Assessment (EIA) refers to a study of all the possible environmental impacts of a proposed project to be carried out before the project begins. A requirement to conduct EIAs as a precondition for any new project was first enacted in the US National Environmental Policy Act of 1969 but the practice has now become widespread. The term Environmental Impact Statement (EIS) is often used to refer to the report of an EIA.

While the chapter introduces a particular tool for assessing risk, more attention is focused on the two processes of life cycle analysis (LCA) and cost–benefit analysis (CBA), which were mentioned in Chapters 6 and 9. Both of these processes tend to raise questions rather than provide answers but they play an important role in both widening and specifying our understanding of the environmental and social impacts and consequences of a project or enterprise. They provide a strong foundation for some of the forms of action discussed in Chapter 11. The chapter then returns to the relatively new 'scenarios mapping' approach to future thinking that was mentioned in Chapter 6. Scenarios mapping workshops, it will be argued, require a lot of thought and preparation to be successful but the underlying principles are not difficult to grasp.

All tools and methods have their strengths and weaknesses and this makes it important for sustainability practitioners to have a big toolbox and a working knowledge of diverse approaches. However, there is an underlying danger in thinking that complex challenges can be broken down and effectively measured. Assessment and monitoring can only ever be approximate and contingent because the world we live in is more unpredictable than we had imagined and that is the topic of the chapter's thematic essay. The key aims of this chapter are to demonstrate that:

- selected assessment and monitoring tools can raise awareness of environmental and social challenges; and
- assessment and monitoring can provide a strong foundation for the action strategies discussed in Chapter 11.

Mathis Wackernagel was born in Switzerland in 1962. He gained his Ph.D. at the University of British Columbia in Vancouver (1994) and worked with his Ph.D. supervisor to develop the first Ecological Footprint Calculator. He is president of the Global Footprint Network.

FOOTPRINT CALCULATORS

Ever since **Mathis Wackernagel** developed the concept and mechanisms used for estimating an 'ecological footprint' for his Ph.D. dissertation in the early 1990s the concept has been popular, and it has spawned the development of similar tools, such as 'carbon footprint' calculators or greenhouse gas emission calculators. There are many versions of ecological footprint calculators in use today, however the basic approach is to convert an estimate of raw materials used and waste generated by any unit of production and consumption – ranging from a household to an enterprise, a city or a nation – into an estimate of how much land is required to produce the raw materials and dispose the waste. The word 'footprint' was used to indicate a relative share of planetary resources needed to sustain the targeted unit of production and consumption and the most effective use of the tool has probably been to compare use of resources in the high consumption societies of the global north with those of the global south. The idea of the footprint has been extended to suggest that current rates of global resource depletion mean that by 2050 we would need more than two planet's worth of resources to sustain current levels of consumption with a growing global population (see Chapter 3).

It is not easy to quantify all the environmental consequences of consumption and production and available data may be rough or unreliable. Use of a calculator tool by novices can produce unreliable, yet seemingly certain, estimates of environmental impacts. However, the use of such tools can be a real eye-opener for people who have not contemplated environmental impacts before. As long as their limitations are clearly understood, footprint calculators have a big role to play in community education. They can bring in the personal dimensions of sustainability challenges by focusing on household footprints and they can provide a good very good *starting point* for thinking about sustainability challenges.

INVENTORIES AND AUDITS

Another good starting point for thinking about sustainable production and consumption is the compilation of an 'inventory' of raw materials used and waste generated or an 'audit' of energy or water use for the selected unit of production and consumption. The terms are borrowed from economic accounting and while the starting assumptions are similar to those of footprint calculators, the exercise can encourage a more thorough accounting of materials and energy used and waste generated. **Energy audits** have been used widely to work out energy efficiency plans for households and enterprises and it is not hard to find do-it-yourself energy auditing tools.[2]

energy audits refer to surveys and analysis of energy flows for particular buildings and they are usually conducted in order to reduce energy supply requirements. They became popular after the global oil crisis of 1973.

The compilation of inventories can be a consciousness-raising exercise and they can also be used as the first step for LCA or CBA. There is always a problem in allocating the use of resources and generation of waste to a particular enterprise or activity when resource use and waste generation cannot be determined so precisely. However, this only serves to remind us that no tool is without its limitations.

RISK ASSESSMENT AND MANAGEMENT

It was argued in Chapter 7 that western societies have probably gone too far in wanting to avoid or manage risk because a degree of risk-taking is essential to

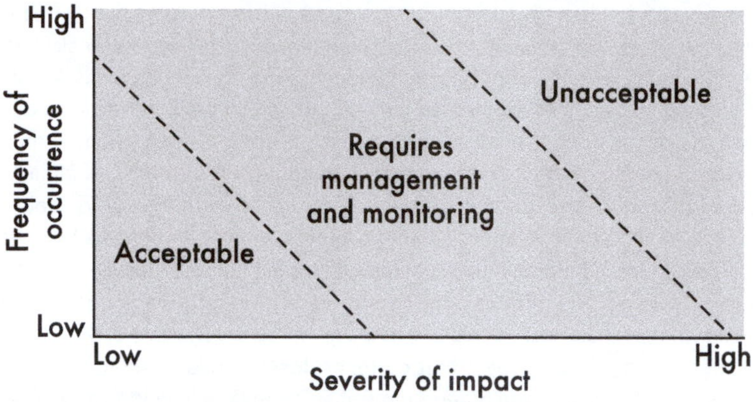

Figure 12.1 Risk assessment matrix
Source: adapted from I. Thomas and P. Murfitt, 2nd edn, *Environmental Management: Processes and Practices for Australia*, Sydney: Federation Press, 2011, p. 132

acceptable and unacceptable risk is a distinction commonly made in risk management literature, however, cultural beliefs play a big role in determining socially acceptable levels of risk. Risk avoidance is a relatively new preoccupation of 'western' societies.

build resilience in an uncertain world. Nevertheless, it can be valuable to compile an inventory of the risks to which people and communities are being exposed so that there can be conversations about what might constitute **acceptable and unacceptable risks**. As demonstrated in Figure 12.1, acceptability of risk may be determined, in part, by anticipating the frequency of occurrence and there is often a large grey area between risks that are clearly acceptable or unacceptable.

Rather than leaving risk management to designated people or 'experts' it is probably better to use an inventory of risks to generate conversations about which risks need to be avoided or managed. According to Thomas and Murfitt (2011: 130), it is critical to avoid trivialising risks in any communication aimed at raising awareness but, at the same time, it is important to talk about the risks in plain language and in a calm manner. In the end, risk management requires the conscious cooperation of all those who may be exposed to risks or who may expose others to risks.

LIFE CYCLE ANALYSIS

William McDonough is an American architect and designer who teamed up with German industrial chemist and former Greenpeace activist **Michael Braungart** to write *Cradle to Cradle: Remaking the Way We Make Things* in 2002.

As mentioned in Chapter 9, LCA has been around since the 1960s and it is responsible for the notion of thinking through the consequences of production or activity cycles from 'cradle-to-grave'. Environmentalists have extended this idea to suggest that we need to build in a much stronger emphasis on recycling by looking at the possibilities for turning this into genuine cycles from 'cradle-to-cradle'. An influential book by industrial designers **William McDonough** and **Michael Braungart** (2002) suggests that we have only begun to scratch the surface in regard to the possibilities for recycling. More attention needs to be paid to exciting and fulfilling redesign work because, the authors argue, 'cradle-to-cradle' outcomes can be both morally satisfying and aesthetically pleasing. Following the release of their book, McDonough and Braungart set up a certification procedure for products that met their criteria and the first set of certificates issued in 2005 went to products that included a Think Chair by Steelcase which claimed to use 99 per cent of recyclable material with minimum generation of waste in production and minimal transport from sites of production to the consumer. While it may be impossible to fully close the life cycle loop of any product or service it helps to link the 'technical' cycles of production, use and disposal to more slow-moving 'biological' cycles of decomposition and nutrient release in order to encourage the use of materials that can be recycled by nature.

LCA for environmental sustainability has become an increasingly sophisticated field of practice with efforts being made to underpin the spreading practice through the adoption of international standards. However, introductory versions of the tool can be used for awareness raising and community education work, provided they are portrayed as being introductory and incomplete. Arguably, LCA is primarily a diagnostic tool because it tends to pose many questions without providing answers.

Thomas and Murfitt (2011: 139) have amended the prevailing model of LCA stages[3] to end with an emphasis on action rather than interpretation. Their recommended stages are:

- The *scoping* stage, in which goals and system boundaries need to be agreed.
- The *inventory* stage, in which all available data on raw materials or component parts, energy and waste need to be compiled.
- The *impact assessment* stage, in which flows of materials and energy are considered in relation to known environmental concerns or trends.
- The *improvement assessment* stage, which aims to identify better ways to use materials and energy.

The inventory stage is seminal for the process as a whole because the very process of collecting data on all the environmental inputs and outputs for a project, process or initiative raises many questions about its sustainability. The inventory stage can be seen as the brainstorming phase and impact assessments then shine a light on the things that most urgently need attention. No LCA can consider everything and available data may be patchy or unreliable. However, the step-by-step process makes LCA a powerful tool. The biggest challenge comes in the final 'improvement assessment' stage and this is where opportunities to complete the cycle of cradle-to-cradle need to be considered.

LCA AND SOCIAL SUSTAINABILITY

A strength of LCA is that it can also focus the mind on the social dimensions of sustainability for any particular production or activity cycle. This is achieved by focusing not only on where raw materials or component parts come from but on how they were extracted, grown or manufactured before reaching the nominated site of production or consumption. Furthermore, waste disposal decisions can have significant social implications, especially when waste is 'exported' to sites where environmental protection regimes are weak or not enforced.

A simple example illustrates how LCA can raise awareness about the social dimensions of sustainable production. An LCA conducted on a pair of Lee Cooper

Table 12.1 An LCA illustrated

Part/component	*Origin*	*Conditions of production*
Cotton for denim	Benin	Pickers earn 60p per day
Pumice used for stonewashing	Turkey	Taken from a volcano site
Denim dyed in Milan using synthetic German indigo dye	Germany	
Brass rivets	Namibian copper and Australian zinc	
Zip teeth	Japan	
Polyester tape for zip	France	
Sewing thread	Northern Ireland	
Thread dyed in Spain	Spain	
Garment sewn by a 21-year-old factory worker in Tunisia	Tunisia	Maker paid 58p per hour

environmental costs include damage caused to natural systems by extraction and production processes; damage caused by the generation of streams of waste; and the less obvious costs resulting from the transport of raw materials, goods and waste.

Fair Trade the international fair trade movement was initiated by several Christian groups in the 1930s and 1940s before becoming part of a much bigger social movement in the 1960s. The movement was boosted by the introduction of fair trade certification in 1988. There are a number of international organisations involved in coordinating fair trade activities with the most prominent being Fair Trade International (www.fairtrade.net).

blue jeans on sale at a clothing store in Ipswich, UK, at just under £20 revealed the inventory of components (Crewe 2004: 195–214) as set out in Table 12.1.

In this exercise the focus was on social impacts of garment production, whereby consumers in the UK benefit from the exploitation of garment factory workers in Tunisia, in particular. Further research would be needed to add in the environmental impacts of cotton growing in Benin; mining operations in Australia, Namibia and Turkey; and dye manufacture in Germany. However, the example does highlight the extensive transportation of raw materials and components that end up in a pair jeans sold in the UK and this, in turn, hints at **environmental costs** resulting from the use of fossil fuels in such transportation. At the very least this inventory raises questions for UK-based consumers about the environmental *and* social sustainability of their consumption choices.

Using LCA to consider the social implications of production can lead to some disturbing findings. A fire that killed 117 workers in a Dhaka garment factory in November 2012 revealed some of the human horror that might lie behind a 'Made in Bangladesh' label on clothes bought in a shop in Europe or America. Even more sinister is that access to minerals that are used in the production of mobile cell phones and other electronic devices has triggered conflict in some of the source countries, as the box below suggests. Knowing the identity of sites of extraction or production can open the lid on a box of horrors but this is the starting point for ethical consumption, as discussed in Chapter 3. The often hidden social costs of globalised production and trade can be partially addressed by consumers seeking to avoid products with 'tainted sources'. However, it may be more important in the long run for consumers to support campaigns aimed at ensuring much better international minimum standards in relation to the environmental and/or human costs of extraction and production. The international **Fair Trade** movement seeks to coordinate efforts to improve the social impacts of global trade.

Mineral wealth and social misery

Congo is a country that is rich in minerals – including diamonds and gold – and yet that mineral wealth has often brought misery to the Congolese people. For example, when the deadly civil war in neighbouring Rwanda spilt over the border in 1996 the Rwandan army occupied part of the country and refused to leave even when Congolese rebel forces that they had supported deposed the dictatorship of Mobuto Sese Seko in 1997. Uganda also took advantage of the civil conflict in Congo to occupy another part of the country. Rwanda took its opportunity to loot the country of diamonds and a huge stockpile of the mineral coltan while Uganda loaded up planes with stolen gold, coffee and timber (Kern 2007: 131–2). Officially the 'first' Congo war (beginning in 1996) was followed by a 'second' war beginning in 1998, but they can be seen as two phases of the same war. Coltan is of particular interest because it is used to extract the mineral tantalum which is, in turn, used to manufacture tantalum capacitors that are a key component of mobile or cell phones, laptop computers and a range of other electronic devices. Rwanda benefited from a global price increase from $US40 to $US380 per kilogram for its ill-gotten Congolese coltan in the period between 1998 and the end of 2000. Other minerals mined in mineral-rich Congo – including gold and tin – are also used in the production of electronic devices and a number of multinational mining corporations are involved in these mining operations.

The International Rescue Committee has estimated that the death toll from the 'second' Congo war (starting in 1998) could be as high as 5.4 million with a further two million forced to flee their homes. While these figures have been disputed there is no doubt that if you add the tolls from the first and second wars together the combined total make this the deadliest war since the end of Second World War and there is also no doubt that it involved the widespread use of rape and torture. Whole areas of the country were evacuated and many people were forced to move into poorly constructed refugee camps. Some of the worst violence was perpetrated by Rwandan soldiers who had already been responsible for genocide in their own country (ibid.: 129–30). Yet there was remarkably little coverage in western media of the deadly conflict or its consequences. Kern argues that western mining companies – especially the Canadian company Barrick Gold – had a strong interest in deflecting global attention away from the conflict. Kern also suggests that many people would have been unaware that relatively cheap minerals extracted from the Congo helped to keep the price of their mobile cell phones low. An international campaign eventually forced some leading manufacturers of electronic devices to avoid using raw materials from 'tainted sources' and to be more transparent about where the raw materials came from. Civil war in the Congo had shocking social impacts and it also had bad environmental consequences resulting from warfare and the displacement of millions of internal refugees. A thorough LCA on the sourcing of raw materials used in the production of a particular electronic device would expose these kinds of consequences.

LCA AS AN EDUCATIONAL TOOL

In its most simple form, LCA can be a valuable education tool. A group of people can be asked to focus on any product they may take for granted and be asked to consider the production and use cycle of that item, as illustrated in the example portrayed in Figure 12.2

An exercise like this, focusing on the overall cycle of production and consumption of a particular item, can only be a starting point, however, because it does not factor in energy flows or the social costs of different stages of production or use. The simple model introduces underlying cycles and connections that can extend like far-reaching tentacles. However, it can be kept simple in order to serve as an introductory exercise and participants can be asked to consider the following questions:

- What raw materials or components go into the product and where do they come from?
- What environmental impacts arise from the extraction of the raw materials, production of components, transport to place of assembly, assembly process and transport to site of purchase?
- What are the working conditions and pay rates for all those involved in the extraction, production and transport of the product?
- What environmental impacts – e.g. emissions – result from my use of the product?
- What will I do with the product when I want to dispose of it? Can it be reused or can parts of it be recycled?

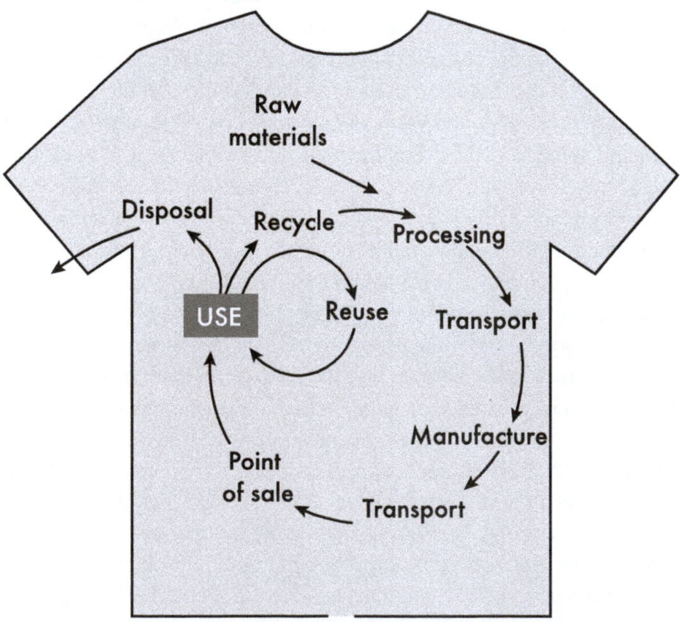

Figure 12.2 Life cycle of common clothing

- Have I purchased the product that has the best (or least bad) environmental and social impacts?
- Do I really need this product or can I consider alternatives?

Many organisations – including the US Environmental Protection Agency or the European Commission – offer tools and training in the use of LCA.

COST–BENEFIT ANALYSIS (CBA)

Cost–benefit analysis (CBA) was first used for environmental purposes as early as 1808 when the US Secretary of Treasury, Albert Gallatin, ordered its use in regard to water management projects. It had become a common practice in US water management by the 1930s, and in 1981 it was briefly adopted as an assessment guide for all publicly funded projects in the USA, before this requirement was abolished by President Ronald Reagan. It continues to be used widely by government agencies and private enterprises internationally for determining the economic viability of a particular project or activity and it is commonly used to assess the environmental sustainability of projects as well. CBA has grown to embrace a wide array of concepts and practices – as discussed by Boardman *et al.* (2010) – however, the principles are not complicated and it can be used in a simple form. At face value it appears to go further than LCA in turning assessments into recommendations. However, CBA has its critics because the assumptions that underpin the final conclusions are narrowly conceived.

As Table 12.2 illustrates, there are essentially six main stages for the conduct of a CBA.

Table 12.2 Main stages of cost–benefit analysis

Stage	*Sub-stages*
Project definition	■ set physical boundaries of the project ■ identify who and/or what will be affected ■ consider project options
Identify all the relevant costs and benefits	■ identify all possible and probably impacts arising from the project ■ exclude those that cannot be directly attributed to the project ■ finalise the inventory of costs and benefits
Value all the included costs and benefits	■ collect data on monetary costs and benefits of the project ■ award a monetary amount to costs and benefits that are more difficult to quantify in this way (see below)
Select and apply a discount rate for changes in value over the life of the project	■ choose between low (4%), medium (6%) or high (10%) discount rates ■ consider the possibility of new investment opportunities ('opportunity cost')
Assess the economic viability of the project	■ compile a final balance sheet of monetary costs and benefits ■ run the model with different sensitivities (e.g. who and what is included or excluded in the inventory of costs and benefits)
Make your recommendations	■ key factor is the final monetary assessment of costs versus benefits ■ exercise judgement as to the accuracy of estimates and margins of error

An obvious weakness with this tool is in the awarding of monetary values to things that may be very hard to quantify, such as the enjoyment that people might gain from being able to visit nature conservation areas or the cost to an animal of losing certain habitats. A number of **valuation methods** have been developed to assign monetary values to environmental assets and they include: a) *contingent valuation*, involving an estimation of 'willingness to pay' to preserve an environmental asset, e.g. preserving a forest for nature conservation; b) *travel cost valuation*, involving the cost people are prepared to pay to travel to a specified site, e.g. travelling to a national park; c) *hedonic pricing*, involving an estimation of the cost of preserving an asset for people to enjoy, e.g. the cost of maintaining a national park; and d) *opportunity cost*, involving an estimation of the value of the asset if it was to be used for a different purpose, e.g. the value of a forest if it was converted to farmland. Such valuation methods can help to bring environmental 'externalities' into the framing and language of economic policy and practice. However, they are commonly based on conjecture and personal judgements and they are all entirely human-centred in terms of what gives something value. The major criticisms of the use of CBA for considering the environmental and social impacts of any project or activity are as follows:

valuation methods that are discussed in this chapter aim to put a figure on values that are excluded from the dominant 'market value' framework. There is little consensus about the best approach.

1 There are great uncertainties in the awarding of monetary values for many of the costs and benefits and environmental valuing techniques, in particular, produce varied results.
2 The choice of the discounting rate is rather arbitrary.
3 No distinction is made between the people or non-human beings that may benefit from the project or activity and those that are likely to suffer.
4 The focus on units rather than systems – e.g. ecosystems – undervalues interactions.
5 The focus on a single project or activity excludes interactions with other activities or projects, for better or worse.
6 Because so many arbitrary decisions come into the awarding of values CBAs are open to manipulation or abuse.

These criticisms are very significant when it comes to environmental values, in particular. However, CBA is a very useful tool as long as the limitations are known and acknowledged.

SCENARIOS MAPPING

As mentioned in Chapter 6, contemplating diverse future **scenarios** is a good way of thinking more critically about what the future might hold. 'Scenario planning' was probably invented by the US military before being picked up by the Royal Dutch **Shell** petrochemical corporation at the time of the first global 'oil shock' in the early 1970s. It focuses on the understanding that future scenarios are not predictions of what *will* happen; but, rather, an effort to sketch out a range of possible settings in which designated actors will find themselves. While the crafting of future scenarios must rely on a deep understanding of current trends and the best available modelling of how these trends might evolve, it is important

scenario is defined by the *OECD* as a 'postulated sequence of development of events'.

Shell Oil has been working with future *scenarios* since the global oil crisis of 1973.

to contemplate a range of possible scenarios in order to develop a capacity to adapt to changing and largely unforeseen circumstances. While the point of the exercise may be to work for *preferred* scenarios – rather than allow 'worst case' scenarios to emerge unchecked – the term 'scenario planning' probably exaggerates the possibilities for determining outcomes and the term 'scenarios mapping' may be less misleading.

A scenarios mapping workshop can focus minds on the future and generate conversations about how to work for preferred outcomes. However, such workshops need a lot of thought and preparation to even achieve these modest goals. The following steps are recommended for preparing and running scenarios mapping workshops:

- Turn the starting concern into a *strategic question* which can focus the minds of participants on taking action and which also helps to determine who needs to participate in the exercise.
- Set the scope (e.g. geographic scale) and time frame (i.e. how far into the future?).
- Carefully *select participants* in relation to the focusing question and the possibilities for taking action.
- Ensure that all participants are provided with the *best available data on relevant trends and predictions* about the future well *before* they attend the workshop.
- Allow *plenty of time* for the workshop – possibly more than one day – in order to work through the process steadily and deliberately.
- After clarifying the aims and processes of the workshop the first task needs to be the identification of *key uncertainties* because this makes it possible to contemplate a range of scenarios.
- Ensure that facilitators understand the process and the need to ensure that it is not rushed.
- Use the work on 'key uncertainties' to identify some starting points for developing diverse scenarios. It may be useful to map out the starting points for each scenario to ensure that they each focus on a different combination of factors and/or actors.
- It may help to break into small groups to craft the diverse scenarios independently of each other. Each such working group will need a properly prepared facilitator.
- The *key outcome* of a scenarios mapping workshop is the articulation of a range of possible future scenarios.
- The workshop might conclude with a discussion about research and action plans related to the choice of preferred scenarios. However, it is critically important to avoid imposing a sense of control or predictability about such outcomes because the key aim of the exercise is to increase *adaptive capacity* combined with greater *foresight*.

Scenarios mapping is good for extending time frames well into the future. As mentioned in Chapter 6, the author was involved in running a scenarios workshop in a rural Australian town which focused on the consequences of climate change over a period of 30–50 years from the present. Participants in this workshop decided to identify fictional – yet plausible – characters who may find themselves living and working within the imagined scenarios and this led to the development of future stories that were set within the challenging future scenarios.[4]

Discussion questions

1 What are the key strengths and weaknesses of ecological footprint calculators?
2 How useful is it to distinguish between acceptable and unacceptable risks, and who should decide where the boundary might lie?
3 Why is LCA better understood as a diagnostic tool rather than a problem-solving tool?
4 Why is LCA a particularly valuable tool for exploring both the environmental and social dimensions of sustainability?
5 What is involved in shifting the emphasis from cradle-to-grave to cradle-to-cradle thinking?
6 What are the key strengths and weaknesses of CBA?
7 How can scenarios mapping help us to think further into the future?
8 What are the key ingredients for a successful scenarios mapping workshop?
9 Why has it been suggested that we need to embrace uncertainty and what is meant by the concept of 'emergence'?

KEY READINGS

Bauman, Henrikke and Anne-Marie Tillman (2004) *The Hitch-Hiker's Guide to LCA: An Orientation to Life Cycle Analysis Methodology and Application,* Lund: Studentliteratur.

Boardman, Anthony, David Greenberg, Aidan Vining and David Weimer (2010), 4th edn, *Cost–Benefit Analysis: Concepts and Practice,* Upper Saddle River, NJ: Prentice Hall.

Crewe, Louise (2004) 'Unravelling Fashion's Commodity Chains', in Alex Hughes and Suanne Reimer (eds), *Geographies of Commodity Chains*, London: Routledge, pp. 195–214.

Kern, Kathleen (2007) 'The Human Cost of Cheap Cell Phones', in Stephen Hiatt (ed.), *A Game as Old as Empire: The Secret World of Economic Hit Men and the Web of Global Corruption*, San Francisco, CA: Berrett-Koehler, pp. 93–112.

Thomas, Ian and Paul Murfitt (2011), 2nd edn, *Environmental Management: Processes and Practices for Australia*, Sydney: Federation Press.

McDonough, William and Michael Braungart (2002) *Cradle to Cradle: Remaking the Way We Make Things*, New York: North Point Press.

Woolcock, Michael (2009) *Towards a Plurality of Methods in Project Evaluation: A Contextualised Approach to Understanding Impact Trajectories and Efficacy*, Manchester: Brooks World Poverty Institute, University of Manchester.

thematic essay

Understanding unpredictable systems

Between 1905 – when Albert Einstein published his first great work – and 1922 – when Niels Bohr won his Nobel Prize for Physics – a quiet revolution took place within the physical sciences. Einstein, Bohr and Ernest Rutherford had led the way in challenging the severe limitations of Isaac Newton's mechanical physics. Even non-living systems are more deeply unpredictable than scientists had imagined, these great thinkers pointed out. This, in turn, highlights the folly of assuming that systems created and sustained by unpredictable humans behave in inherently rational and predictable ways. The need to embrace unpredictability in trying to understand the behaviour of any system was probably best captured in the articulation of the 'uncertainty principle' by German physicist Werner Heisenberg in 1927, although this work was not published in English until the 1950s.

Of course it is one thing to acknowledge deep uncertainties and another thing altogether to know how we can work with this understanding. In 1987 New York-based science journalist James Gleick was able to explain that scientists operating in a range of fields were focusing on the idea that the world around us is driven by a complex interplay between chaos and order and the **Santa Fe Institute** was formed in 1984 by several Nobel Prize-winning scientists in order to swap understandings on 'patterns' that emerge at the 'edge of chaos'. The term 'strange attractors' was coined to identify the origins of new patterns out of chaos and attention then shifted to understanding the *emergence* of new 'complex adaptive systems'. Predictability had been replaced by an appreciation of **emergence** – or 'immanence' – with a new emphasis on the unique qualities of any emergent system.

The death of certainty presents a major challenge for people and organisations who are trying to predict and manage the behaviour of systems ranging from the global climate to systems designed to meet human needs in relation to things such as food or energy. Indeed much of the language of environmental management – including the use of the word 'tools' – suggests that the desire for certainty is pervasive, even if we do acknowledge that all tools have their weaknesses. Complexity science – most evident in the work of the Santa Fe Institute – suggests a need to focus instead on the emergent qualities of adaptive systems. This understanding lies at the heart of the critique of 'development' theory and practice articulated by Harvard University social scientist and World Bank employee Michael Woolcock.[5]

Michael Woolcock admits that it is rather unusual for a person with a Ph.D. in sociology to be working within the World Bank. He took up the role as the Word Bank's Lead Social Development Specialist in 2010 after serving as the founding Research Director of the Brooks World Poverty Institute at Manchester University in the UK. His influential line of argument is that a lot of 'development aid' funding is being wasted on schemes and projects that focus on desired outcomes rather than the unique local conditions and contexts in which they are operating, or the *quality* of the work as it is being implemented. Development work needs to be more context sensitive, he argues, and we need

Santa Fe Institute in New Mexico was set up in 1984 by a diverse array of leading scientists including Nobel Prize-winning physicist Murray Gell-Mann. It aimed to share insights across scientific disciplines on the behaviour of complex systems in order to articulate a new 'complexity theory'.

emergence, the evolution of complex systems out of a multiplicity of interactions has intrigued philosophers since the time of Aristotle; however, its current meaning was captured well by economist Jeffrey Goldstein in 1999: 'the arising of novel and coherent structures, patterns and properties during the process of self-organization in complex systems'.

to understand that token forms of community consultation or participation do more harm than good. Evaluation of projects or programmes, Woolcock argues, is often aimed at establishing their 'external validity' – or generalisability – rather than their 'internal validity'. Yet the reality of development work is that the context in which it is being undertaken may be so complex that it is impossible to even determine the boundaries of a particular project or intervention.

A focus on 'internal validity' shifts the emphasis from 'outcomes' to the evolution of a project or intervention over time. Performance indicators emerge from within the project rather than from an external agency. According to Woolcock (2009), effective project evaluation work needs a 'plurality' of evaluation methods, ranging from quantitative assessments of impacts to ethnographic observation of processes and comparisons with comparable case studies. In Woolcock's words we need 'more concerted attempts to understand mechanisms driving impact trajectories over time, in different places, at different scales, and in accordance with how well they are implemented' (ibid.: 15).

social impact assessment emerged alongside EIA, arguably as a result of the 1969 US National Environmental Protection Act (NEPA). It is not easy to reach agreement on what constitutes good or bad social outcomes of any change and a lot of work has gone into negotiating key principles and 'variables' to be assessed for international SIA practice under the auspices of the International Association for Impact Assessment.

Woolcock's work has focused on development 'interventions' in countries with a complex mix of social and environmental challenges, such as Indonesia. It is obviously more difficult to put boundaries around such projects compared to some of the production cycles discussed elsewhere in this chapter. However, LCA brings long distance supply and production chains into view and all of us participate – for better or worse – in international 'development' work. In a globalised economy, development 'aid' cannot be separated from daily practices of production and consumption.

Environmental and **social impact assessment** tools provide a good starting point for thinking about environmental and social impacts but Woolcock's work on evaluation highlights the need to focus on context, quality of work and the evolution of a project over time. The focus on quality reminds us that we should never lose sight of the personal and social *values* that people bring to their work. The long-term effectiveness of any project or human endeavour will depend more on the values that underpin the work rather than measurable outputs at any particular point in time.

NOTES

1 www.bloomberg.com/slideshow/2013-08-18/14-smart-inventions-by-nature-biomimicry.html#slide10
2 See, for example, http://energy.gov/
3 Based on the phases: project description; inventory; impact assessments; interpretation.
4 See Nadarajah *et al.* (2008).
5 See, for example, Patrick Barron, Rachael Diprose and Michael Woolcock (2011) *Contesting Development: Participatory Projects and Local Conflict Dynamics in Indonesia*, New Haven, CT: Yale University Press.

PART III

Key challenges and applications

CHAPTER 13

Focusing on water

Key concepts and concerns

- value of water
- the hydrosphere and hydrological cycle
- freshwater ecology
- environmental flows
- pressure on marine environments
- water waste and pollution
- catchment management

INTRODUCTION

It is commonly said that Planet Earth might better be called Planet Water because the abundance of surface water makes it the only planet in our solar system that is capable of sustaining life. As Steven Solomon (2010: 9) has put it: 'Water's pervasiveness and indispensable capability to transform and transport other substances played a paramount role in forging Earth's identity as a planet and the history of life upon it.' Paradoxically, access to freshwater has caused conflict and tension within and between human societies and yet it is impossible to avoid the conclusion that it has not been valued sufficiently. This chapter argues that the science of water is a good starting point for rethinking the value of water to humans. We can follow the flow of water to understand how freshwater and marine ecosystems work and to recognise that the very water molecules that pass through our own bodies may end up in a tropical cyclone or in the gullet of a deep sea fish. The concept of '**ecosystem services**' has been introduced to make our human dependence on the wellbeing of complex, multilayered ecoystems (Costanza 2016) and it is being applied in new approaches to river basin management, for example. However, this chapter will suggest that we need a more fundamental starting point for thinking about the neglected importance of water.

ecosystem services is a term used in environmental management to refer to anything that can contribute to environmental wellbeing. It emerged from the field of 'ecological economics' as a way of ensuring that the benefits of healthy ecosystems can be factored in to all thinking about economic development.

The concept of 'environmental flows' has helped to highlight human responsibility for the wellbeing of freshwater ecosystems, however we need to follow the flow to accept much greater responsibility for increasingly stressed marine environments. Putting a higher value on water highlights the need to reduce water waste and pollution. However, we need to look beyond streams and water deposits to understand the vital functions of water, and in this regard the concept of catchment management has been a major advance. The main aims of this chapter are to:

- Highlight the importance and value of water as it moves through the global hydrosphere.
- Introduce some concepts that can help us rethink our relationships with water.

Startling statistics

- Just over 70 per cent of the planet is covered by water and this is mirrored in the fact that about 70 per cent of the human body is water.
- Over 97 per cent of surface water is in the world's oceans and only 2.5 per cent is in the form of freshwater.
- Between 2000 and 2010 two billion people gained access to clean drinking water.
- There are still 783 million people without adequate drinking water and 2.5 billion people live without adequate sanitation because of water scarcity.
- On average a child dies every 20 seconds because of water scarcity.

Grand Renaissance Dam is under construction on the Blue Nile in Ethiopia, about 40 kilometres from its border with Sudan. When it is completed it will be the site of the biggest hydroelectricity power station in Africa.

Darfur region war, Darfur is a region that was incorporated into Sudan in 1916. War broke out in 2003 when the Sudan Liberation Movement/ Army declared war on the government of Sudan over the treatment of non-Arabic communities in Darfur. A ceasefire was negotiated in 2010 and South Sudan became a separate country in 2011.

'WATER'S FOR FIGHTING OVER'

Because humans cannot survive without access to freshwater for more than a few days, human settlements have always clustered around rivers and water sources and ancient civilisations rose up along great rivers like the Nile in northern Africa, the Tigris and Euphrates in the Middle East, the Indus and Ganges in Pakistan and India, and the Yellow River in China. Some civilisations were able to extend their global reach because they developed the capacity to travel long distances by boat, seizing control of global trade. The power of steam began the industrial revolution in Europe and the harnessing of hydroelectricity enabled a great expansion of industrial society, especially in North America. As Solomon shows (2010: ch. 13), the construction of dams and canals enabled a rapid expansion of the US settlement 'frontier' after 1865 and yet battles over water rights caused conflict and prolonged feuds, leading the celebrated writer Mark Twain to comment wryly: 'Whiskey is for drinking, water is for fighting over.'

Population growth in some of the more arid regions of the world is increasing tension and conflict within and between nations. For example, Egyptians – who have always been anxious about their heavy dependence on the Nile – are now angry about Ethiopia's upstream construction of its so-called **Grand Renaissance Dam**. Water security has long been a factor driving conflict between Israel and its hostile neighbours while prolonged drought played a major role in sparking the deadly civil war in the **Darfur region** of South Sudan that continued from 2003 until 2010. Access to water is even causing concern in regions that always seemed to have abundant supplies. For example, the management of water flows in the Indus River catchment continues to be a bone of contention within simmering relationships between Pakistan and India while the building of hydroelectricity dams on the upper reaches of the Mekong River threatens water supplies in four nations that lie further down the river (see Figure 13.1). The melting of glaciers in

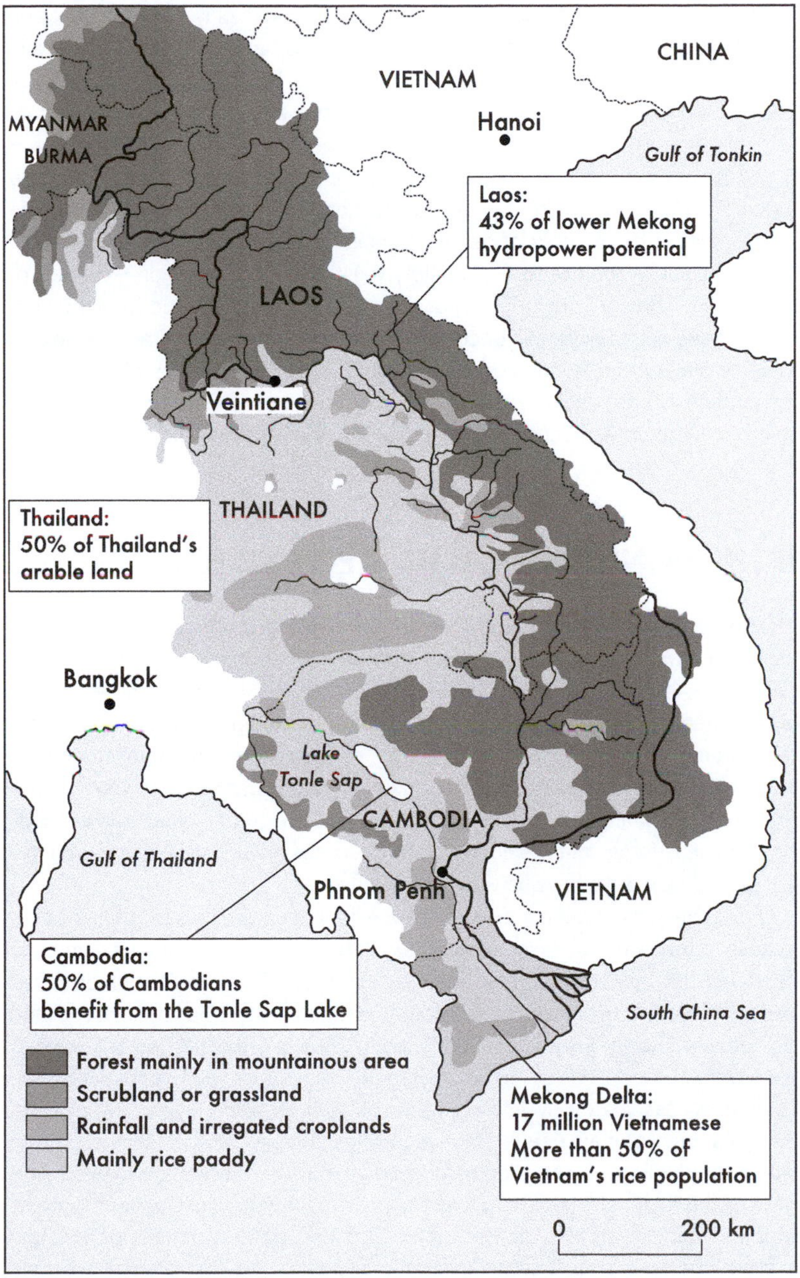

Figure 13.1 Five nations have an interest in the management of water flows in the Mekong river basin
Source: Mekong River Commission (www.mrcmekong.org)

the Himalayan Mountains as a result of global climate change poses a long-term threat to flows of water in the major rivers of surrounding countries, which contain nearly 50 per cent of the world's population. Many writers have suggested that access to water in 'the age of scarcity' will come to rival access to oil as a source of tension and conflict.[1]

While water is the key defining feature of our planet, only a tiny fraction of it is in a form that can be accessed by humans and other forms of terrestrial life. While people living in affluent societies give little thought to the supplies of freshwater that reach their homes by pipe or to the streams of waste water that are flushed away down drains and toilets, an estimated 783 million people – 11 per cent of the global population – live without adequate drinking water and around 2.5 billion live without water for sanitation.[2] There has been a marked improvement in the number of people gaining access to safe drinking water in the first decade of the twenty-first century – estimated at two billion – yet lack of water for sanitation in and around growing cities has been blamed for a 130 per cent increase in the incidence of cholera.[3] Diarrhoea continues to be the biggest cause of illness and death in the world and, according to the World Health Organization, 88 per cent of diarrhoeal deaths have been linked to water access problems. Differential access to water is a major cause and indicator of social inequity in our world.

RETHINKING THE VALUE OF WATER

This chapter focuses on big global water challenges and some of the emerging solutions. However, the biggest problem may be that for many people in the world – who have not yet experienced water scarcity on a regular or prolonged basis – water is seen as a free and inexhaustible resource. Growing public concerns about the pollution of waterways, rising costs for maintaining water supplies and for dealing with streams of waste water, and new efforts to put a price on water access rights, may be shifting public opinion slowly. Yet we encounter water so constantly and in so many forms that it is difficult to think of it as an exhaustible resource. We need to find new ways to value water more highly.

Fortunately, there are rich cultural resources that can help us to 'rethink water' because many writers have noted that water has had enormous symbolic importance for humans since our species emerged. Since ancient times it has been the subject of myths and rituals, poetry, art and music.[4] It has been associated with purity, with vigorous and young life, and with a sense of feeling calm and at peace with the world. It is at the heart of many religious or spiritual traditions. We are eternally fascinated by flowing water as well as lakes, rivers and oceans. Feelings about water are deeply embedded within our psyche. Our fascination with water is partly driven by our dependence on it, but the fascination may also be driven by the fact that it is so hard to grasp in its entirety, because water has many forms and moods. As Philip Ball has noted (2000: ix), water continues to fascinate us even when we strip it of its 'symbolic trappings'. 'At first glance a simple molecule,' Ball continues, 'water still offers up profound challenges to science.'

The science of water is a good starting point for rebuilding public respect for water. As discussed in Chapter 10, the 'restless molecules' of water have unique and seemingly contradictory capacities that make life on Earth possible and Ball (2000) and Perkowitz (2001) say that scientists never tire of delving into water's mysteries. However, this chapter will argue that we need a wider understanding of the ecology of water flows. A basic understanding of the hydrological cycle is the point of departure here but we need to expand the usual models of that cycle to appreciate the ecological flows of water on a global scale. We need to follow the flows of water to appreciate that the molecules that pass through our bodies and households might end up in distant marine environments for it is water that makes the connections between terrestrial and marine life forms and ecosystems. The fact that water respects no boundaries blurs the distinctions we make between different terrestrial ecosystem and between terrestrial and marine ecosystems.

Revaluing water means that people in affluent societies need to take more personal responsibility for reducing water waste. We have much to learn from people who have learnt to cope with water scarcity and yet there is much more we can do to radically increase water security for the world's poor. We also need to take more personal responsibility for reducing water pollution and here our concern for water security must extend to non-human life. New discourses on 'environmental flows' and 'marine protected areas' help us to avoid anthropocentrism in our ecological understanding of water. While much of our attention focuses on the growing challenges of water scarcity, we need to note that climate change predictions suggest that some parts of the world will experience more frequent and prolonged droughts while other areas will experience more frequent flooding. Flood mitigation schemes will not be enough to prevent more frequent and intense flooding experiences and here we can learn from people living in countries like Bangladesh where flooding is a very regular occurrence.

THE HYDROSPHERE

Because water comes in many forms and circulates between oceans, land and air, the **hydrosphere** is more difficult to visualise than the **atmosphere** or **lithosphere**. There is no evidence to suggest that water molecules escape from the atmosphere into space and this suggests that the total volume of water has remained the same since geological times. Water is found as vapour in the atmosphere; in the world's vast oceans; in groundwater aquifers; in lakes, rivers and streams; as frozen deposits of ice or snow in the polar caps, on high mountain ranges, or as extensive areas of 'permafrost'. Only 2.5 per cent of water on the planet is in the non-saline form needed by non-marine forms of life and nearly 69 per cent of that is in the ice caps or mountain glaciers.[5] A tiny 0.26 per cent of freshwater is found in the world's lakes, rivers and streams.

hydrosphere refers to the layer below and above the surface of the planet where bodies of water are found.

atmosphere refers to the layer of gases that surrounds the planet.

lithosphere refers to the outer crust of the rocky planet.

The restless movement of water molecules means that the water in rivers and lakes is turned over in a matter of days or weeks. By contrast, it has been estimated that it takes 1,500 years to replace water in deep groundwater deposits or mountain glaciers; 2,500 years to replenish the oceans; and about 10,000 years to replace the water in the frozen deposits of ice caps or permafrost.[6] The operation of the hydrological cycle – see Chapter 9 – means that water molecules circulate globally. The speed of movement varies from fast-moving clouds and streams to very slow-moving ice sheets and glaciers. Yet the concept of the hydrosphere enables us to think of water movement as a single planetary system. As Marq de Villiers (2001: 26) famously remarked, 'Water can be polluted, abused and misused, but it is neither created nor destroyed, it only migrates.'

While it is obvious that weather is affected by the movement and precipitation of water vapour in the atmosphere, few people appreciate the extent to which water operates as a kind of global thermostat, keeping temperature fluctuations within a reasonable range. On the one hand, water has an unrivalled capacity to absorb heat and, on the other, water vapour in the atmosphere operates as an insulator to reduce fluctuations in surface temperatures. The oceans play a particularly significant role in absorbing and distributing solar heat from the equatorial regions towards the north and south. Shallow, fast-moving ocean currents are driven by prevailing winds. However, an even more significant flow is created by the fact that cold, salty water sinks and warmer, less dense, water rises, in a movement known as '**thermohaline circulation**'. This sets up the movement of warm water away from the equatorial regions towards the poles. The movement of the warm water creates an undercurrent of cold water moving in the opposite direction and this sets up what has been called the 'great conveyor belt' of ocean currents (see Figure 4.3, p. 57). The global flow carries warm water from the Pacific into the Atlantic and cold water from the Atlantic into the Pacific.

thermohaline circulation refers to ocean currents that are generated by differences in the density of sea water.

Temperature differentials within the atmosphere set up faster moving atmospheric currents which are largely responsible for the weather patterns we experience. However, the interplay between atmospheric and oceanic currents causes longer term climate shifts; for example, the oscillation of wet and dry periods across the Pacific Ocean that goes by the name of the '**El Niño Southern Oscillation**'. Warm ocean currents play a significant role in triggering the formation of tropical cyclones and climate scientists predict that rising sea temperatures – caused by global climate change – will make the interplay between ocean currents and atmospheric weather events even more volatile.

El Niño Southern Oscillation is the term used to describe fluctuations in ocean temperatures in equatorial region of the Pacific Ocean caused by the movement of warm ocean currents. El Niño refers to a relatively dry period while La Niña refers to a relatively wet period.

FRESHWATER ECOLOGY

Access to freshwater is obviously critical to the species of plants and animals that followed the evolutionary path out of the seas to colonise the lands. While some plants and animals have become highly adapted to arid environments – developing ways to maximise the internal circulation of water and minimise water loss from their bodies – most need ready access to surface or groundwater supplies. While plants depend mainly on rainfall and the movement of rainwater through the soil, sources of water serve as focal points for overlapping animal habitats, as is illustrated in the congregation of animals around the famous African 'waterhole'. Moving water also creates new habitats by turning rock into soil – primarily through the action of glaciers – and by transporting fertile soils from one location to another. Humans have been able to increase their range by developing technologies for transporting water over increasing distances. However, this has probably made us more complacent about the importance of water and so streams have commonly been turned into waste disposal systems or used as separating boundaries rather than as focal points.

Cambridge University botanist Arthur Tansley has been credited with coining the term 'ecosystem' in 1935 and its subsequent rise in popularity shows that it helps us to think about the interactions between plants, animals and a range of 'resources' within a shared physical space. We can think about the ecosystem of a particular forest, valley or even a cave, or we can think about the ecosystem centering on a particular lake or stream. In the case of a stream we can focus on the organisms that dwell within the main currents, on the edges of the stream, in the 'riparian' zone, or in the wider 'catchment'. However, any notion of a self-contained community breaks down when we take water as its central element because the movement of the water can bring in 'outside' elements – ranging from nutrients and food to toxins – while insects, birds and animals will travel far to reach a stream or lake. Nevertheless, it is still useful to think of streams and lakes as being the focus for an interacting community of plants and animals, as illustrated in Figure 13.2.

As noted in Chapter 2, readers of Rachel Carson's 1962 *Silent Spring* were shocked to learn that inorganic compounds used as pesticides on North American

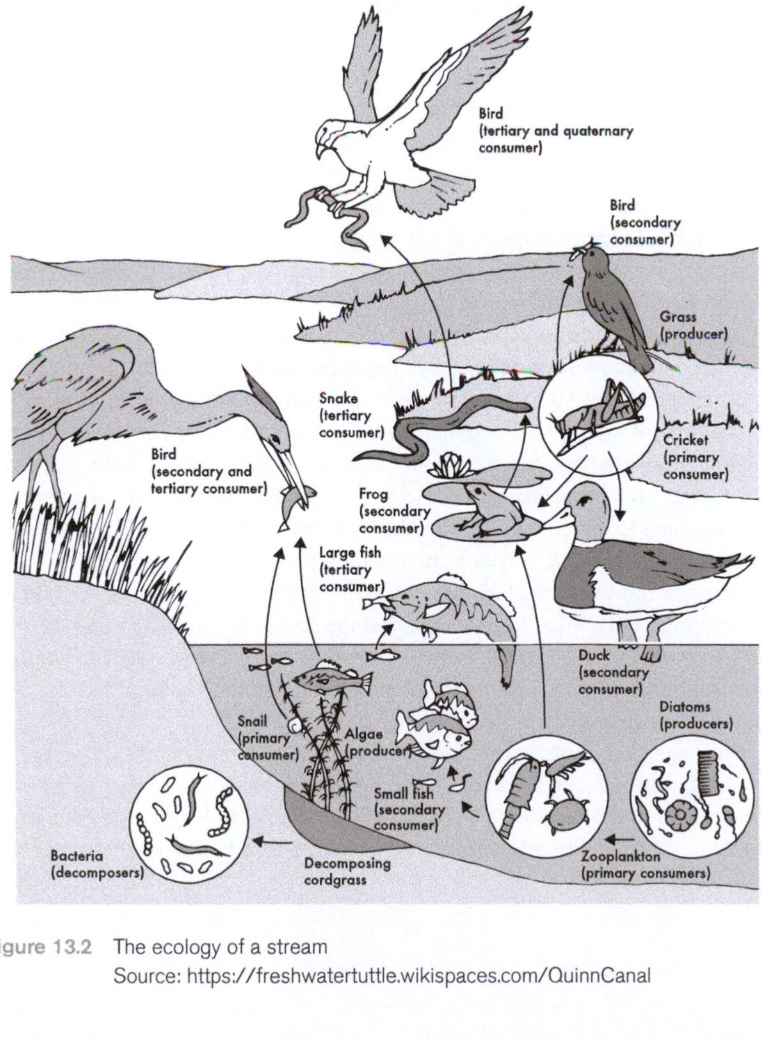

Figure 13.2 The ecology of a stream
Source: https://freshwatertuttle.wikispaces.com/QuinnCanal

farms were travelling far and wide through expansive food webs and by being absorbed and transported by water. The study of the biodiversity within a particular body of water can help us see if it is 'healthy' – i.e. capable of supporting life – or 'polluted' – i.e. capable of destroying life. Given the importance of water for all forms of life, water quality testing in particular streams or bodies of water can serve as a great starting point for understanding how ecosystems work. However, water dissolves boundaries and connects ecosystems. For this reason we need to balance the conception of ecosystems with an understanding of ecological flows. As Carson pointed out, inorganic compounds sprayed on crops in North America were starting to show up in the fatty tissue of penguins in the Antarctic before their use was banned and this reminds us that freshwater pollution is connected to the pollution of marine environments. As mentioned in Chapters 2 and 8, plastic waste is forming floating islands of trash in the vast Pacific Ocean and bits of plastic are killing marine creatures and sea birds that are far away from where the waste originated.

ENVIRONMENTAL FLOWS

Ecological science has highlighted the need to think of streams and lakes as sites for important non-human living communities rather than just as reservoirs containing water for human use. The volume of water in any particular stream or lake can fluctuate seasonally, or from one year to the next, and most of the organisms living in or around the stream or lake can cope with these kinds of fluctuations. However, ecologists have demonstrated that chronically low levels of water can make the water toxic to some or many of the organisms and they have also demonstrated the importance of periodic inundations, or floods.

At first ecologists began to focus on the minimum volumes of water needed to sustain endangered species but this focus proved to be too narrow and in the 1990s attention shifted to the flow regimes – 'environmental flows' – required to sustain plant and animal communities. The concept of environmental flows enables relevant authorities to impose limits on the amount of water that can be extracted from particular waterways and it also helps to determine when the time has come to release water from dams or storages back into the waterway. Efforts can be made to simulate inundations and floods by ordering a major release of stored water to 'flush out' the river system. A new attempt to monitor environmental flows has, for example, helped to rescue endangered river red gum swamp forests adjacent to Australia's heavily exploited Murray–Darling river system, although the ending of a prolonged drought may have been the defining factor in this success.

Prolonged droughts – predicted to be more common and more severe in many parts of the world as a result of climate change – will always test policy commitments to the maintenance of environmental flows. However, science has provided a model for long-term sustainable management; the rest is a matter of social and political will.

MARINE ENVIRONMENTS UNDER INCREASING PRESSURE

Understandably, humans – gazing out to, or across, the seas – have imaged that the oceans are an inexhaustible source of food. Coastal fisheries have been a critical resource for many thousands of years and local fishing fleets have steadily increased their range to operate beyond the edge of their continental shelf and well out into 'international waters'. However, the United Nations Food and Agriculture Organization (FAO) now estimates that 69 per cent of global fish stocks are either fully exploited or overexploited; i.e. being exploited beyond 'sustainable yields'.[7] Alarmingly, the FAO has estimated that around 90 per cent of big ocean fish have been effectively 'fished out'. Concern about the future of global marine environments ensured that 'Life Below Water' was separated from 'Life on Land' when the UN **Sustainable Development Goals (SDGs)** replaced the earlier **Millennium Development Goals (MDGs)** in 2015, however enforcement of the agreed goals is the biggest problem.

Not only are the fishing fleets operating further and further into international waters, they are also using the indiscriminate 'longlining' technique in which they put out lines up to 130 kilometres long, hung with thousands of baited hooks.[8] Longlining can catch a wide array of fish, including swordfish, tuna, sharks and bottom-dwellers such as halibut and cod. However, they also snare unintended targets such as dolphins, endangered turtles and seabirds. Even more destructive is 'drag-net fishing' in which nets up to 15 metres deep and 64 kilometres long are dragged across an area catching almost everything in their path and often scraping clean the floor of the ocean.[9] A 1992 UN ban on drift nets longer than 2.5 kilometres in length has significantly reduced the practice but it is very difficult to enforce such regulations and the ban on drag-netting has probably increased the use of 'longlining', which is almost as destructive. A wide array of nets and cages are also in common use. It seems that very little has been learnt from the dramatic collapse of Atlantic cod stock in 1992 which severely damaged the economy of Newfoundland (see Chapter 8)

It is, of course, very hard to establish the rule of law on the open seas even if organisations such as the International Maritime Organization and the International Seabed Authority are able to impose an array of penalties for breaches of international agreements. Some success has been achieved by using various United Nations forums to name and shame national governments that fail to impose sanctions on vessels operating in violation of global agreements. A growing desire to cooperate and take marine protection more seriously is reflected in the increasing number of marine protected areas (MPAs) being established in both national and international waters. The first such marine sanctuary was established by the **International Union for the Conservation of Nature (IUCN)** in 1986 and there are now more than 4,000 MPAs in the world. The biggest MPA surrounds the Pacific Island nation of Kiribati and it is the size of California.

As mentioned above, water flows do not end when freshwater streams enter the ocean. The hydrological cycle means that we are closer to marine creatures than we often imagine and protection of global fisheries is not something we can leave to international agencies. Marine environments are not the inexhaustible resource we imagined and marine protection begins with what we consume and

Sustainable Development Goals (SDGs) are a 2015 extension of the UN's 2000 Millennium Development Goals (MDGs) which largely aimed to eradicate extreme poverty and disadvantage by 2015. Eight MDGs were expanded into 17 SDGs and they strongly reflect the principles outlined in the 1987 Brundtland Report.

Millennium Development Goals (MDGs) are eight goals that were adopted at a special UN Millennium Summit held in New York in May 2000.

International Union for the Conservation of Nature (IUCN) is an international organisation that fosters scientific research and supports the development of nature conservation projects globally. It was formed in 1948 and its headquarters are in Switzerland.

our relationship with the water that flows through our bodies, homes, farms, neighbourhoods and cities.

Run-off woes

hypoxia is a term widely used to refer to oxygen deficiency; here it is used to refer to low levels of dissolved oxygen in the sea.

Every year in spring and summer, the coastal waters in the Gulf of Mexico suffer from oxygen depletion, leading to the suffocation of bottom-dwelling fish, crabs and shrimp that are unable to move to less polluted areas. The condition known as ***hypoxia*** occurs when oxygen levels in the sea fall below two parts per million and the annual hypoxic zone in the Gulf of Mexico is the third largest in the world after those that recur in the Baltic and Black Seas (Miller and Spoolman 2010: 25).

In recent years the National Oceanic and Atmospheric Administration (NOAA) in the USA has established Hypoxia Watch in the Gulf of Mexico and data on oxygen levels is made available through the internet. However, the condition is difficult to reverse because it is largely caused by nutrient run-off from agricultural activities in the vast Mississippi river basin. Although hypoxia can occur naturally as a result of the decomposition of organic matter accumulating in the oceans, the use of farm fertilisers containing nitrogen and phosphorous compounds results in the process known as eutrophication, in which nutrient-rich water causes algal 'blooms' that deplete the levels of dissolved oxygen. Only a sustained reduction in the use of agricultural fertilisers could prevent the regular occurrence of

Photo 13.1 Algal blooms resulting from hypoxia intersect with sediment churned up by storm activity to radically disrupt the ecology of the Gulf of Mexico
Photo by Jeff Schmaltz (Wikimedia Commons)

the hypoxic zone and the problem here is that the Mississippi basin contains some of the most important agricultural zones in the USA.

This run-off problem highlights the fact that water defies the conventional boundary between terrestrial and marine 'resource management'. We cannot treat the oceans as a bottomless 'sink' for dumping polluted water because pollution does not stop when rivers meet the sea.

REDUCING WATER WASTE

Outside arid regions of the world, water awareness tends to be rather low. It is widely assumed that freshwater supplies will be replenished on a regular basis by rainfall and that we can also turn to vast groundwater aquifers or even resort to desalination of sea water if necessary. A combination of climate change and population growth is making reliance on rainfall more difficult; groundwater supplies are already being depleted and water tables are falling in many parts of the world (Miller and Spoolman 2010: 24); and desalination poses other problems because it currently relies on intense use of fossil fuels for energy. Attention needs to shift towards strategies for using finite supplies of freshwater more efficiently and more selectively.

Given that irrigated agriculture accounts for around 70 per cent of global freshwater use[10] this is the obvious place to start in looking for reductions in water use. Stronger restrictions need to be imposed on the use of water for irrigation and a preference established for drip irrigation, especially in areas where evaporation rates are high. More needs to be done to reduce inefficient use of water in agriculture. Market opportunities cannot be the sole determinant of agricultural production because they are largely blind to long-term environmental costs. On the global scale, industry accounts for around 20 per cent of water use[11] and stronger restrictions need to be imposed here as well, especially in the use of water for waste disposal (resulting in water pollution). Much more can be done to increase the use of recycled water in industrial production.

Increasing urbanisation presents both problems and opportunities when it comes to reducing water use. As discussed in Chapter 10, it can be difficult for city-dwellers to perceive the problems involved in guaranteeing a supply of freshwater and in disposing of waste water. On the other hand, efficiencies of scale can be achieved in both supply and treatment of waste water and public education campaigns can be effective in reducing waste and in encouraging forms of recycling. For example, a prolonged drought in south-eastern Australia, leading up to 2010, triggered a successful public education campaign to reduce household water use in Melbourne, with strategies focusing on increased use of 'grey water' and the collection of rainwater and reductions in water used in washing and toilet flushing.[12] Strategies for reducing domestic and industrial use of water can range from increasing prices to introducing new water-saving and recycling technologies. However, the biggest challenge may be to shift the entrenched perception of water as being a largely free and inexhaustible resource.

REDUCING WATER POLLUTION

Water pollution can be understood as any change in water quality that can harm humans or other living organisms and it can either come from single (point) sources or more diffuse (non-point) sources. Point sources – as in a particular factory of farm – are relatively easy to identify and control through environmental pollution laws and policies. Non-point sources include more diffuse run-off from agriculture in general or from the streets and public spaces in a city and responses can range from trapping and treating the polluted water to public education campaigns about the harmful effects of largely unseen pollutants. Public education on water pollution has been enhanced in many developed nations through the implementation of '**streamwatch**' water quality testing projects in particular schools or communities. More people are learning that plastic waste discarded on city streets can end up in marine environments, killing birds and marine animals and forming floating islands of waste.

streamwatch is a term used widely in Australia and to a lesser extent in the USA to refer to programmes aimed at monitoring water quality in streams.

As discussed in Chapter 16, more can be done to reduce the volume of waste materials that might enter our waterways and more can also be done to collect and recycle waste materials. Water pollution is particularly severe in heavily populated and under-resourced cities of the world but the mobility of water guarantees that the problem is not contained within those cities. There is a rising global imperative to reduce water pollution within bodies of water that either pass through, or adjoin, more than one nation.

As Miller and Spoolman have noted (2010: 257–8), we are becoming more aware that many streams have a capacity to 'cleanse themselves' as long as they are not overloaded with pollutants. Riparian vegetation and natural wetlands have a capacity to extract chemicals – such as nitrogen and phosphorous – from water and degrade harmful bacteria. A diversity of organisms within the streams themselves can restore pH levels (i.e. acidity) and the balance of dissolved oxygen. If we know how streams work as ecosystems we have more chance of helping them cleanse themselves.

CATCHMENT MANAGEMENT

An extension of the capacity to understand how streams can cleanse themselves is to understand what constitutes a healthy catchment for a particular river system. We understand better than ever that forest clearing results in the build-up of life-destroying sediments in streams and bays and we know that run-off from urban streets and paved areas dramatically increases the load of pollutants within the waterways. In 1992, **Carolyn Merchant** suggested that 'catchment consciousness' can be a starting point for ecological awareness and since that time catchment management has gathered force as a policy framework for restoring the health of degraded waterways and river systems. Of course, many river catchments are so vast that no single community, authority or even nation can assume responsibility for its wellbeing. This makes it necessary to identify 'sub-catchments' within the wider catchment, or river basin. However, the wellbeing of the catchment as a whole must always frame the work that is done within any particular sub-catchment; often suggesting a need for increased international collaboration.

Carolyn Merchant (b. 1936) is a well-known US-based science historian and environmental writer. Her books include *The Death of Nature* (1980), *Ecological Revolutions* (1989) and *Radical Ecology* (1992).

Catchment consciousness has helped to reframe flood mitigation strategies because the speed and volume of run-off water can be reduced before it impacts on areas of human settlement. At the same time, periodic floods and the creation of '**floodplains**' are integral to the ecology of river systems and flood mitigation also needs to be informed by a better understanding of 'environmental flows'. Climate change predictions make it clear that flood mitigation work will become increasingly important in many parts of the world and we can improve our capacity to predict and manage 'catastrophic' flooding. At the same time, many communities will need to increase their capacity to cope with periodic flooding and in this regard the developed world may have much to learn from people living in flood-prone areas such as Bangladesh and southern Vietnam.

floodplain is the area adjacent to a river or stream from the banks of the channel to the base of enclosing valley walls.

Discussion questions

1. What do you think of the suggestion that water scarcity can pose increasing problems for international peace and security?
2. What can be done to get more people to value water more highly?
3. What can be gained by thinking about the global mobility of water molecules within the hydrosphere?
4. What key insights emerge from focusing on freshwater ecology?
5. What can be done to increase public awareness of the rising stresses on marine environments and what could come from increased awareness?
6. What is meant by the notion of 'environmental flows'?
7. What strategies are needed to reduce water waste and water pollution globally?
8. Why is 'catchment consciousness' rated so highly by scholars like Carolyn Merchant?

KEY READINGS

Ball, Phillip (2000) *H_2O: A Biography of Water*, London: Phoenix (Orion).

De Villiers, Marq (2001) *Water: The Fate of Our Most Precious Resource*, Boston, MA: Houghton Mifflin.

Miller, G. Tyler and Scott E. Spoolman (2010), 13th edn, *Environmental Science*, Belmont, CA: Brooks/Cole, chapter 11.

Perkowitz, Sidney (2001) 'The Rarest Element', in David Rothernberg and Marta Ulvaeus (eds), *Writing on Water*, Cambridge, MA: MIT Press (Terra Nova), pp. 3–14.

Solomon, Steven (2010) *Water: The Epic Struggle for Wealth, Power, and Civilization*, New York: Harper Perennial.

Learning from the Aral Sea disaster

The Aral Sea – lying between the Central Asian republics of Khazakstan and Uzbekistan – was once one of the four largest lakes in the world. However, a poorly conceived attempt by the former Soviet Union to use water from the lake and its two feeder rivers to create one of the world's largest areas of irrigated farming ended in disaster. Between 1976 and 2006 the lake lost 90 per cent of its water with the water level dropping by 22 metres, roughly the height of a six-storey building (see Photo 13.2). Salinity levels rose sevenfold and the lake lost 85 per cent of its associated wetlands. At least 26 of the lake's 32 native fish species became extinct and local birds and mammals disappeared. The irrigated area turned to dust with the Aral Sea dust being blown as far as 500 kilometres away; some of it settling in the ice and snow of the Himalayan mountains. The loss of water changed the local climate, resulting in hotter and drier summers, colder winters and a very short growing season for the remaining farms.[13]

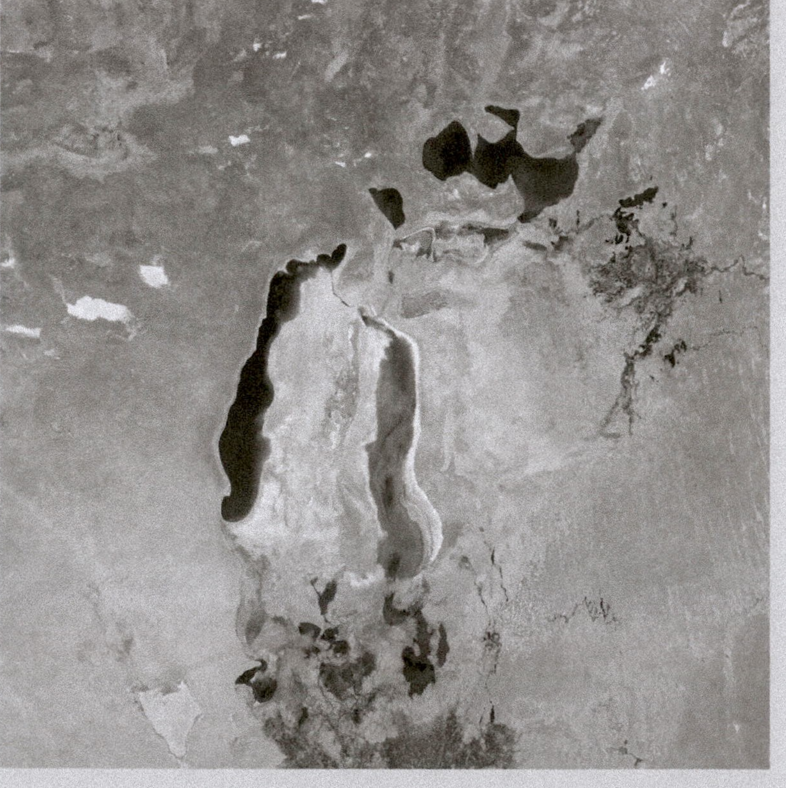

Photo 13.2 The Aral Sea disaster should stand as a reminder of what can go wrong when we use water wastefully: satellite image of what was left of the sea in 2012
© NASA/Corbis

The unprecedented disaster became an international concern, with the World Bank investing $US600 million in upgrading the irrigation systems and purifying drinking water for surrounding settlements. The five nations that are in the lake's vast catchment area agreed to reduce their water extractions and improve their irrigation efficiency so that more water would reach the sea and a dyke was completed in 2005 to raise the water level in the lake by about three metres. International agreements struck in 1992 and again in 2002 – involving five nations with a direct interest and three more with an indirect interest in the sea – helped to stabilise the falling water levels. However, doubts surround the capacity of the diminished lake system to survive future droughts and global climate change is likely to make that even more difficult. There is clearly no hope at all of returning the lake to its former glory.

The Aral Sea story points to the possibility of increased international collaboration to reduce unsustainable water use, even in parts of the world that regularly experience water shortages. Yet the action has come too late to prevent the lake system passing its ecological tipping point and the story should serve as a reminder of what can go wrong when communities and nations act out of profound ecological ignorance. The sorry state of the Aral Sea should serve as a constant reminder to all of global humanity that our attempts to assert dominance over nature can backfire badly.

Humans have been responsible for many previous environmental disasters, with the desertification of the area once known as the Fertile Crescent – in modern Iraq – serving as a reminder that it has been happening for thousands of years. However, opportunities to migrate away from degraded areas are diminishing and humans will be called on increasingly to care for degraded environments, such as that surrounding the Aral Sea. At the same time, startling images from the Aral Sea disaster should be used frequently with the simple slogan 'Never again!' We must learn to act within ecological limits and monitor levels of environmental stress so that we can act to restore stressed and degraded ecosystems before they reach a point of no return.

NOTES

1 See Solomon (2010: ch. 4).
2 www.unwater.org/
3 According to World Health Organization data.
4 See Ball (2000).
5 For key statistics and information about water, see www.unwater.org/statistics/en/
6 Ibid.
7 www.fao.org/docrep/009/y582e00.html
8 For information on longlining, see FAO Fisheries and Aquaculture www.fao.org/fishery/
9 Ibid.
10 www.unwater.org/statistics_use.html

11 Ibid.

12 The success of the campaign was reported in *The Age* newspaper on 3 March 2011, at a time when a new state government abandoned household consumption targets.

13 See Miller and Spoolman (2010: ch. 11).

CHAPTER 14

Food and agriculture

Mel Neave and Martin Mulligan

Key concepts and concerns

- agricultural productivity
- different modes of agricultural production
- Green Revolution
- food security
- inequities in global agricultural trade
- natural resource and biodiversity depletion
- soil erosion and degradation
- agriculture-related pollution
- non-industrial food production alternatives

INTRODUCTION

Agriculture refers to the cultivation of crops and the rearing of animals to provide food and other products for human use. It is both a major consumer of the planet's natural resources, including land, water, soil, energy and biota, and a supplier of various environmental and social 'services'. Benefits for humans – i.e. 'social services' – include the production of food and the generation of employment, while **ecosystem services** include the release of oxygen, the pollination of plants, carbon storage and even the preservation of some forms of biodiversity (Costanza 2016). At a global scale, agriculture faces the ongoing challenge of providing greater food security for a growing population yet expanded production in the second half of the twentieth century has failed to seriously close the gap between rich and poor nations and in some areas food security even fell. Expanded production has, however, increased the environmental impacts of agriculture, some of which are relatively obvious, for example the clearing of forests or the release of pollutants, included greenhouse gases. This chapter will show that agriculture also generates environmental and social impacts that are less obvious and sometimes quite unexpected. Thus, agricultural production has major implications for global sustainability.

ecosystem services is a term used in environmental management to refer to anything that can contribute to environmental wellbeing. It emerged from the field of 'ecological economics' as a way of ensuring that the benefits of healthy ecosystems can be factored in to all thinking about economic development.

This chapter begins by looking at global trends in food production and productivity before investigating some of the complexities that affect the global distribution of food. It considers the challenges involved in providing food security for an increasing global population and examines why the gap in food security between rich and poor nations is not closing. The chapter also explores how existing agricultural systems impact on the environment and notes that agriculture is contributing to the phenomenon of climate change while the onset of global warming makes it harder to deliver global food security. While most current agricultural practices are causing negative environmental and social impacts there are some initiatives that focus on sustainable food production and distribution. Work on the concept of 'ecosystem services' offers new ways to strike a much better balance between economic development and ecological conservation (Potschin *et al.* 2016), however a detailed consideration of ecosystem services concepts and methods is beyond the scope of this book. The chapter closes with an essay that discusses some of the key principles of ecologically sensitive agriculture.

Startling statistics

- Between 1990 and 2010 global population and cereal yields both rose by 30 per cent but the percentage of cereal produced for food increased by less than 25 per cent.
- 223 million people in sub-Saharan Africa were considered undernourished in 2013.
- 4,000 plant and animal species are currently endangered by agricultural practices.
- 90 per cent of calories consumed by the world's people come from just 30 crop species.
- 14 species of animals account for 90 per cent of livestock production.
- Globally, nearly 1 in 8 (or 852 million) people are undernourished, whereas over 500 million people are classified as obese.

GLOBAL AGRICULTURAL PRODUCTION AND PRODUCTIVITY

Food and Agriculture Organization (FAO) is a UN agency that was mooted at a conference held in 1943 and formally established in 1945. Its main aim is to reduce global hunger and malnutrition and its headquarters are in Rome.

On a global scale agricultural productivity has increased considerably over the past five decades. The **Food and Agriculture Organization (FAO) of the United Nations** estimates that global cereal production increased from less than 900 million tonnes in 1961 to over 2,500 million tonnes in 2012. Likewise, total global food supplies from crops rose from approximately 390 million tonnes in 1961 to nearly 1,000 million tonnes in 2012. Thus, today we are generating more agricultural outputs in general and more food in particular than we have in the past and the FAO predicts that this trend will continue into the future (FAO 2013a).

Agricultural productivity increases are typically achieved in two ways: (1) by increasing the area of land that is used for agriculture; and (2) by increasing the yields generated per unit area. Although the observed global growth reflects a combination of these factors, they play out differently in different parts of the world (see Figure 14.1). While certain regions or countries in the developed world have achieved increased yields (e.g. the USA, Europe and Australia), others have seen production increases largely through the physical expansion of agricultural land area (e.g. Latin America, south-east Asia and **sub-Saharan Africa**). At the global scale, however, the majority of the increase observed since the middle of the twentieth century is attributed to improved yields, which are estimated to account for 78 per cent of the increased output. Increasing yield has largely resulted from the mechanisation of agricultural production, although other contributing factors include improvements in crop science, the development of effective fertilisers and increasing investment in large-scale production methods.

sub-Saharan Africa refers to a band of countries – from Mauritania to Somalia – that are located south of the Saharan desert and north of sub-tropical forests and savannahs.

TYPES OF PRODUCTION

In 1987 the Brundtland Report identified three basic systems of global agricultural production:

- resource-poor;
- industrial; and
- **Green Revolution**.

Green Revolution refers to agricultural research and development that occurred between the 1940s and late 1960s with the specific aim of increasing crop yields in countries where hunger is prevalent. It was led by US agricultural researchers and featured the use of synthetic fertilisers. The name was coined in 1968.

These three systems differ in terms of their current spatial distribution – i.e. certain regions tend to adopt certain approaches – and in terms of their environmental and social impacts. Understanding these different agricultural systems is a good starting point for examining some of the sustainability challenges related to global food production.

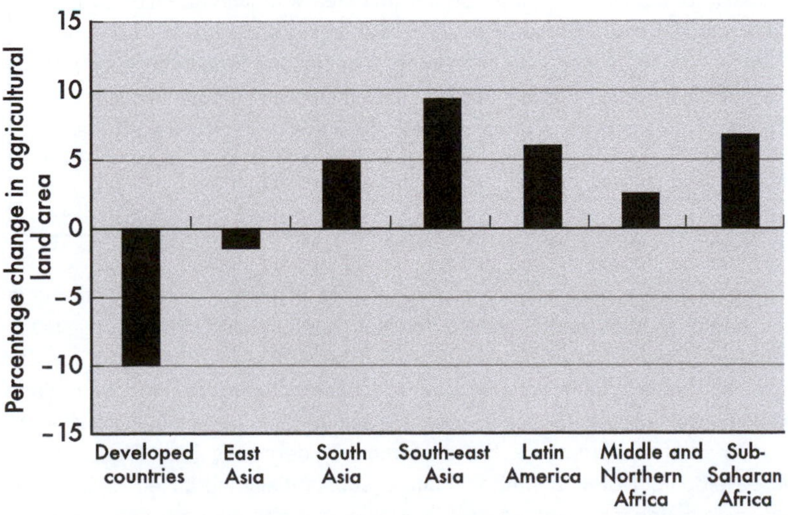

Figure 14.1 Change in percentage of agricultural land area for the major global regions
Source: adapted from FAOStat (http://faostat3.fao.org/faostat-gateway/go/to/home/E)

Prevailing modes of agricultural production

Resource-poor agriculture refers to low external input, traditional or unimproved agriculture, and is also commonly known as subsistence farming. It typically requires large inputs of human labour and is relatively low in production intensity. In other words, the yields per unit area from this approach tend to be low. It is commonly rain fed, making it extremely vulnerable to climatic perturbations. It is also often undertaken on poor or 'marginal' land that is prone to degradation, such as semi-arid to arid environments, higher elevation regions and forests with fragile soils. This means yields can decline over time as the environmental resources on which resource-poor agriculture depends deteriorate.

In contrast, *industrial agriculture* is capital and input intensive. It is usually undertaken on a large spatial scale and is widely used in the developing world, including in North America, Europe, Australia and New Zealand. Industrial agriculture dominates in wealthier and more developed countries where farmers have sufficient economic resources to implement it. It aims to achieve intense productivity and is typified by large single-crop (or 'monoculture') farms and concentrated animal production facilities. As well as requiring high capital investment it can be labour intensive, although labour inputs will decline as production tasks are mechanised. Industrial agriculture also includes the widespread application of pesticides and fertilisers.

Green Revolution agriculture refers to the outcomes of the so-called Green Revolution that unfolded in the developing world in the 1960s and 1970s. This involved the development of new plant and crop varieties that were explicitly designed to increase food yields. It represented an intensification of agricultural production per unit area with little attention paid to the specific environments in which it was being undertaken. The Green Revolution was a response to growing post-Second World War concerns about the capacity of Asian nations to feed their growing populations. It was feared that famine in some politically 'unstable' nations could threaten global security so agricultural researchers in the USA and Europe worked collaboratively to develop new high-yield crops.

At the global scale, resource-poor agriculture has resulted in a steady decline in per capita production, yet it is still the dominant agricultural method used in many underdeveloped countries, especially in sub-Saharan Africa and more remote regions of Asia and Latin America. Low agricultural productivity in these regions combined with population growth means that hunger is generally increasing as environmental resources are being continually degraded (see Figure 14.2). The development of industrial agriculture substantially increased global food production during the twentieth century. However, it also generates a wide range of environmental 'residuals' – or harmful by-products – that threaten the long-term sustainability of this mode of production and this, in turn, is reducing the capacity of the world to feed its ever-growing population. By the early 1980s in participating

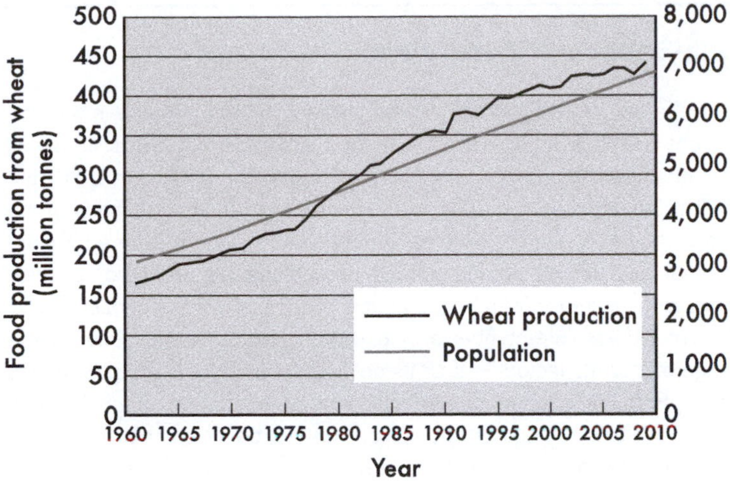

Figure 14.2 Global food produced from wheat and population (1961–2009)
Source: adapted from FAOStat (http://faostat3.fao.org/faostat-gateway/go/to/home/E)

countries, the Green Revolution had increased cereal yields by about 21 per cent and cereal production by about 17 per cent (Evenson and Gollin 2003). However, Green Revolution agriculture requires large inputs of water and inorganic fertilisers and pesticides. Although the techniques are still used in well-irrigated regions, especially in Asia where cereal production doubled between 1975 and 1990, they have been much less successful in Africa where water is often in limited supply.

PRODUCTION LAGS BEHIND POPULATION GROWTH

With enthusiasm for the Green Revolution waning there is rising concern that global productivity for certain crops may have reached a plateau. For example, global wheat yields increased by more than 160 per cent between 1960 and 1990 but have increased by only 25 per cent since the early 1990s. At the same time, the global population has more than doubled from a little over 3 billion to 7 billion. FAO predictions suggest that the gap between production and demand will continue to grow and this could result in increasing famines and a consequent destabilisation of global systems for the production and distribution of food.

What makes this worse is that the recent growth in agricultural productivity has been unevenly distributed across the globe. In the 1970s and 1980s, for example, productivity in Africa declined by about 1 per cent a year whereas outputs from other regions were increasing. In part, this reflects the continuing domination of resource-poor agricultural production in much of Africa, where rainfall is greatly affected by climate variability and change. Intense droughts in many parts of Africa in the 1980s brought this problem to the world's attention, with the onset of widespread famine which then triggered violent conflict in parts of Somalia and Sudan. Warfare and civil unrest, in turn, make it much harder to rebuild agricultural production when the droughts subside.

Sub-Saharan Africa alert

Global attention has focused on the persistent risk of famine in the arid regions of sub-Saharan Africa since the famines of the 1980s. However, the situation has shown very little improvement since then. In 2013 the FAO estimated that over 223 million people were undernourished in the region and this was an increase of nearly 50 million on the equivalent number for 1990–2. As a population percentage, the proportion showed a welcome decrease from 33 per cent in 1990–2 to 25 per cent in 2011–13, yet the absolute number of people to be fed increased. Obviously, a range of internal factors – such as political instability – have undermined attempts to introduce more efficient forms of agriculture in sub-Saharan Africa, but global focus on the region has not delivered the anticipated gains. The region continues to be a global 'hotspot' for issues related to food security and food-related social conflict.

Increased agricultural productivity over the last century has also been driven by changes in global diets. As countries become increasingly developed and urbanised, diets often shift from coarser grained cereals to rice and wheat and tend to include more meat and milk products. These shifts generate changes in global agricultural networks, with feed crops being increasingly diverted to support livestock production rather than directly providing for human consumption. Diets higher in animal products make a less efficient use of Earth's natural resources, with the FAO predicting that it takes approximately 3 kg of grain to produce 1 kg of meat (FAO 2013a). Thus, shifting diets have contributed to agricultural industries becoming less sustainable. Livestock expansion in some countries is also associated with intensive farming activities such as feedlots and sow stalls that have serious animal welfare concerns associated with their use.

tariffs are taxes imposed by a government on imports while *subsidies* refer to government support for domestic production.

Ironically, although many people now have access to improved diets, the gulf between the well-fed and the under-fed is widening. It is currently estimated that there are around 852 million undernourished people in the world while over 500 million people are classified as obese. The global imbalance in food availability is even more pronounced when the issue of food wastage is considered. A 2013 report produced by the Institution of Mechanical Engineers in the UK[1] estimated that between 30–50 per cent of all food produced is unconsumed due to a combination of factors including poor harvesting and transport practices and market and consumer waste.

General Agreement on Tariffs and Trade (GATT) is a multilateral agreement on the regulation of international trade that was first signed in 1947. In 1994 GATT became part of the World Trade Organization which set out to reduce international barriers to free trade.

COMPLEXITIES OF GLOBAL AGRICULTURAL TRADE

In turning our attention from food production to distribution we need to note that global trade in agriculture is complicated by long-running debates about 'free trade' versus national subsidies or **tariffs** (taxes or duties applied to imports or exports). While the **Global Agreement on Tariffs and Trade (GATT)** foresees a steady removal of national tariffs and subsidies many nations are concerned about their 'sovereign' food security and have defied free trade agreements when it comes to agriculture. The Australian Government's Department of Foreign Affairs and Trade has asserted that average tariffs for agricultural goods are more than three times higher than for non-agricultural goods.[2] The use of tariffs varies from country to country; for example, import tariffs on rice in Japan exceed 800 per cent compared to just 5 per cent in the US.[3] However, debate continues to rage about whether or not market forces can deliver long-term food security. Many farmers argue that short-term fluctuations in global food prices undermine the possibilities for long-term development of environmentally and economically sustainable production. Furthermore, farmers may not be encouraged to produce food for local or national needs when markets drive changes in production choices.

Nations with strong economies are more able to ignore demands to reduce tariffs and subsidies and therefore farmers in these wealthier countries have a greater capacity to withstand downturns in global market prices. This means that millions of farmers in poorer nations are disadvantaged by the terms of trade and the fluctuations in prices. Agricultural subsidies also tend to encourage excess production – i.e. production that exceeds demand – and this puts further downward pressure on global food prices. The **Common Agricultural Policy (CAP) of the European Union**, for example, has been widely criticised for inflating food prices and supporting product oversupply. The CAP operates by providing price guarantees and directing payments to landholders who produce certain products. In doing so, it promotes over production. Excess food generated as a consequence of this policy is either wasted or is delivered to poorer countries, thereby undermining their internal agricultural systems.

European Union Common Agricultural Policy (CAP) was first established in 1957 to build agricultural cooperation across Europe. Initially it focused on production but has recently focused on pricing mechanisms.

The application of tariffs and subsidies to the global trade in agriculture is actually reducing food security in many parts of the world and this is particularly so for poorer nations with higher food vulnerabilities. Increasing global demand for food requires a concerted effort to increase production and productivity, but this will not be enough unless there is a fairer distribution system to ensure that the food actually reaches those in need. The North American Free Trade Agreement (NAFTA) was implemented to enable free trade between the USA, Canada and Mexico, with the aim of reducing internal prices for products within those countries. Some argue that since it was signed in 1992, NAFTA has contributed to the disenfranchisement of Mexican farmers, with agricultural production systems in Mexico becoming increasingly driven by foreign capitalists producing for export markets. As long as food is treated as a global 'commodity' within a market economy, global food security is certain to decline, especially when richer nations can undermine 'free trade' with the selective use of subsidies and tariffs.

FOOD PRICES

FAO Food Price Index is a measure of monthly changes in the international price expressed in terms of the average price of a basket of food commodities.

To monitor global trends in food prices, the FAO compiles a **Food Price Index** (also known as the FFPI), which is a composite measure of the monthly change in a bundle of international food prices. Changes in the annual average Food Price Index over time indicate that real global food prices have declined since they reached a high in 2011, but that prices have been relatively high since they

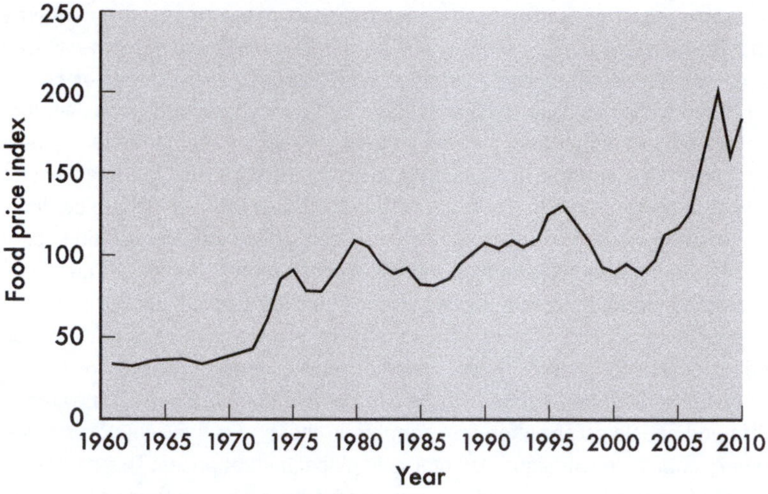

Figure 14.3 The Food and Agricultural Organization of the United Nation's nominal Food Price Index (1961–2010)
Source: data from FAO (www.fao.org/worldfoodsituation/foodpricesindex/en)

exhibited a dramatic rise in 2007–8 (see Figure 14.3). The elevated prices are creating food shortages in many parts of the world on a scale similar to the last global food crisis of 1974–5; yet this new crisis is largely escaping the attention of the developed world. The food crisis of 1974–5 was partly caused by a number of unfavourable weather 'events' that resulted in a decline in production. In particular, the Soviet Union – as it was then called – experienced a series of substantial crop failures between 1972 and 1975 and global food supplies consequently declined. This situation was exacerbated by a dramatic rise in oil prices that was triggered by conflicts in the Middle East. High prices for oil drive up the costs of petroleum, gasoline, farm equipment, pesticides and fertilisers; forcing producers to increase prices to cover increased production costs. Agriculture's heavy reliance on the petrochemical industry has created a dangerous vulnerability.

While there are some similarities between the 1974–5 food crisis and that of 2011–13, there are also marked differences. Whereas the earlier crisis was driven by a lack of supply, the later crisis can be attributed more to growing demand, made worse by the fact that food products, such as corn, are being diverted into other uses, such as biofuels. Population increases and the marketisation of agricultural production are combining to put demand and supply pressures on food prices. High food prices obviously have the greatest impact on those with little money and the global market then exacerbates the distribution of food in favour of those who can pay. Furthermore, high global prices for products such as biofuels are encouraging farmers everywhere to turn to 'cash crops', such as *Jatropha curcas,* that are aimed at that market. Ironically, farmers in Africa are exporting cash crops for biofuels at a time when their countries are struggling to feed themselves.

Food and social conflict

There is growing evidence to suggest that high food prices, and consequent food shortages, are triggering or exacerbating social conflict. For example, sustained high food prices since 2008 are thought to have been a contributing factor to the uprisings that are collectively known as the 'Arab Spring', which began in Tunisia in December 2010. Obviously this was not the only cause of the social unrest but anger at the inability of governments to control food prices meant that some governments – for example, in Egypt and Kuwait – used subsidies to keep internal food prices down and this, in turn, put new pressure on national budgets leading to cuts in jobs and services. Furthermore, countries of the Middle East are highly dependent of importing food from other countries and so efforts to keep internal prices low affected food imports and this had negative consequences for food exporting nations. This highlights the way in which one crisis can trigger others in relation to the production and distribution of food.

The Arab Spring began in Tunisia but quickly spread to countries ranging from Egypt to Bahrain, reflecting the global connectedness that is facilitated by global trade. Drought and related food insecurities in southern Sudan were significant factors in sparking a prolonged and costly civil war that split the nation and drought is also thought to have been a contributing factor to the widespread unrest and violent conflict that began in Syria in 2012.

NATURAL RESOURCE DEPLETION

Twentieth-century increases in global food production coincided with growing concerns about the environmental impacts of both industrial and Green Revolution agriculture. Techniques used to increase food production and productivity included the introduction of new varieties of crops and livestock; a large rise in the use of 'external inputs', ranging from fertilisers and pesticides to machinery and financial credit; and the provision of infrastructure support, such as new roads, markets and irrigation schemes. All of these have increased pressure on natural resources by depleting soil fertility; reducing local biodiversity; introducing new environmental pollutants; increasing pressure on local water supplies; and increasing the use of energy derived from fossil fuels. In response to the growing environmental impacts many governments have introduced measures to reduce pollution and conserve their soils, water and biodiversity. As a result 'primary production' in many countries has developed a close relationship with 'environmental management'. Thus, food production within these countries is increasingly framed by the need to maintain environmental health.

It is now widely recognised that sustainable farming practices are enhanced by the maintenance of 'healthy environments' that deliver a multitude of 'ecosystem services', such as healthy soils and robust water supplies. Yet the pressure to

United Nations Environment Programme was established in 1972 to promote environmental awareness and advocate for stronger environment protection policies internationally. It produces regular assessment reports and facilitates international negotiations and agreements. Its headquarters are in Nairobi.

Millennium Ecosystem Assessment was called for by UN Secretary Kofi Annan in 2000 and the assessment report was finally issued in 2005.

Millennium Development Goals (MDGs) are eight goals that were adopted at a special UN Millennium Summit held in New York in May 2000.

Sustainable Development Goals (SDGs) are a 2015 extension of the UN's 2000 Millennium Development Goals (MDGs) which largely aimed to eradicate extreme poverty and disadvantage by 2015. Eight MDGs were expanded into 17 SDGs and they strongly reflect the principles outlined in the 1987 Brundtland Report.

increase food production also results in competition for land, with the World Bank estimating that approximately 38 per cent of the total global land area is already devoted to pasture and crop use and that this proportion is increasing.[4] The environmental impacts of agricultural production are influenced by a range of factors, including the type and initial condition of the natural environment, the regional climate and the type and intensity of agriculture being undertaken. However, on a global scale the pressure on the planet's natural resources is increasing with particular concern focusing on the fact that a very high 70 per cent of freshwater used by humans is being for agricultural production (as discussed in Chapter 13). The use of freshwater for agriculture varies from one country to another but in some underdeveloped nations it is as much as 82 per cent and yet these are the countries where food and water security are both likely to be low for most people. In an effort to minimise water losses, some countries actively discourage the exportation of agricultural products that use large volumes of water. While water insecurity is a growing concern for global humanity, unsustainable use of freshwater is also reducing biodiversity, especially within freshwater habitats such as lakes, rivers and wetlands. Concerns such as these, call the sustainability of current agricultural practices into question, leading many to consider alternative farming methods, some of which will be discussed later in this chapter.

BIODIVERSITY IMPACTS

The most significant consequence of farmland expansion has been an associated reduction in natural biodiversity at local, regional and global levels. If we think of biodiversity as being measured in terms of genetic, species or ecosystem diversity we need to acknowledge that increasing agricultural production can have negative impacts on all of these. GRID-Arendal – a Norwegian centre established with support from the **United Nations Environment Programme** – estimates that over 4,000 plant and animal species around the world are currently threatened by agricultural intensification, and that approximately 87 per cent of the total number of threatened bird species are impacted negatively by farming activities. Furthermore, the 2005 **Millennium Ecosystem Assessment**[5] identified agriculture as the largest driver of genetic and species loss at both global and regional scales. According to this assessment, six out of 14 global biomes have seen 50–65 per cent of their land areas converted, primarily to agricultural land. Work on the Millennium Ecosystem Assessment reflected the fact that environmental sustainability was included as one of eight UN **Millennium Development Goals (MDGs)** adopted in 2000. When the MDGs were replaced by 17 **Sustainable Development Goals (SDGs)** in 2015, the focus on environmental sustainability was expanded to include one goal focusing on 'Life Below Water' and one focusing on 'Life on Land'.

Although recent trends suggest that overall rates of agricultural expansion are now declining, significant land clearance is still occurring in some of the world's most important biodiversity hotspots. In particular, increases in agricultural land area over the last century have occurred largely at the expense of primary forests in tropical regions. Indeed, it is estimated that as much as 70 per cent of the new agricultural land established in Asia over the past 150 years has become available through the clearance of tropical forests. Indonesia alone is estimated to have lost an average of 685,000 hectares of forest per year between 2005 and 2010 with much of that land being used to produce biofuels rather than food (Koh and Wilcove 2008). The loss of tropical forests is of particular concern because while they account for only about 6 per cent of the planet's surface area they contain somewhere between 50 and 75 per cent of its biodiversity. They also play an important role in balancing the global carbon cycle, as discussed in Chapters 4 and 10.

Growing trade in wild animals and products

Although humans have been using certain animals for food and medicines for thousands of years there has been a growing market for wild animals and their body parts in recent decades. In part this reflects an increasing demand for exotic pets but there is also a growing market for pharmaceutical and beauty products that make use of a range of wild plant and animal body parts. The illegal poaching of wild animals for human use is putting pressure on a range of endangered species, including Asian tigers. Although Asian tigers are now endangered, with as few as 3,200 remaining in the wild, they are still actively hunted for their skin, body parts and meat. Tiger hunting is a customary practice in certain parts of the world, which raises a more challenging issue of shifting embedded cultural views to become more sustainable within the modern world. Ironically the harvesting of wild animals has introduced new human diseases with the 2003 epidemic of severe acute respiratory syndrome (SARS) thought to have begun with the handling of wild animals, especially civet cats, that are traded in local markets in China. Wild animal trade and harvesting also raises animal rights issues. The use of bear bile in traditional medicines in Asia, for example, comes at a high cost for the individual animals that are held captive in cruel conditions. Furthermore, the reduction or loss of individual species can destabilise functional ecosystems.

LOSS OF DIVERSITY WITHIN FARMING

Modern forms of farming – which favour large-scale production of particular crops or animals – also reduce biodiversity within agricultural areas. Global agricultural systems are currently dominated by a small number of crop and animal species, with the FAO estimating that 90 per cent of the calories consumed by people today are provided by only 30 crop species, while just 14 animal species account for 90 per cent of all livestock production.[6] The loss of genetic diversity within agriculture reduces the capability of modern agricultural systems to adapt to environmental change by, for example, breeding new species to meet certain objectives, such as drought or salt tolerance. Artificial genetic modification is being used to replace natural genetic diversity but the use of genetically modified organisms has been opposed in many countries, particularly in Europe, because the long-term consequences for the environment and human health are largely unknown.

In addition to reductions of biodiversity within farming practices we are seeing a global reduction in the diversity of the practices themselves. Food production systems are becoming more uniform – at least within countries that have made the break from resource-poor agriculture – and this means that the resultant farming practices are much less likely to take into account local environmental conditions. This has resulted, for example, in the use of irrigation to produce 'thirsty' crops such as rice and cotton in parts of Australia where water supplies are limited. Irrigated farming in Australia's Murray–Darling river basin has not only caused a dangerous decline in water flows within the river system itself, but has also contributed to the problem of soil salinity by causing water tables to rise and transport salts to the soil surface. European settlers in Australia brought numerous farming practices that were better suited to the wetter conditions of their homelands. The imposition of these practices on the fragile Australian landscape has resulted in considerable environmental degradation, including widespread erosion, soil and water **salinisation**, soil acidification and biodiversity loss.

salinisation refers to the transport by water of soil mineral salts to the ground surface where it inhibits plant growth.

SOIL EROSION AND DEGRADATION

Soil erosion – understood as the loss of soil particles at a rate that exceeds any replacement process – is a major concern within all forms of agricultural production. It results primarily from the removal of protective surface vegetation, which leaves the soils exposed to wind and flowing water that are able to pick up loose particles. Certain grazing animals – such as sheep and goats – tend to eat plants down to their roots and those with hard hooves can kill off surface vegetation with their trampling. Such animal-induced 'devegetation' is particularly evident around sites where animals cluster, such as drinking wells. Native vegetation is actively removed when crops are planted and the exposure of the soil is subsequently repeated when the crops are harvested. Erosion occurs every time soils are exposed, even if this is for a relatively short time.

Over time, repeated episodes of erosion remove or reduce the 'topsoil', which is the most productive part of the soil profile. Consequently, erosion leads to an overall decline in the fertility of the soil. Furthermore, as crop plants grow they absorb nutrients from the soil that are subsequently exported out of the environment when the crops are harvested. This leads to a gradual reduction in certain soil constituents, such as calcium, magnesium and potassium that help neutralise soil acidity. Whenever soil acidity increases, the affected soil loses its capacity to support plant life, leading to reduced productive capacity. Some farming practices also result in an increase in soil salinity, especially in arid or semi-arid regions where the soils rarely experience natural inundation. Dry land salinity in Australia, for example, has been exacerbated by the replacement of deep-rooted native trees, which keep the water tables down, by shallow-rooted grasses for grazing animals. Rising water tables bring mineral salts to the surface. It has been estimated that 5 per cent of cultivated land in Australia is already affected by dry land salinity, with fears that this could rise to as high as 22 per cent.[7]

Soil as pollutant

While we tend to think of soil as an environmental asset, dislodged particles can also become a hazard. Intensification of farming activities on the prairies of the mid-west USA, for example, resulted in a series of devastating 'dust storms' in the 1930s that prompted a major rethink of regional agricultural practices. Indeed, the US EPA has identified sediment that began as dislodged soil particles as the most common 'pollutant' in surface water bodies. Sediment within water bodies can reduce visibility for aquatic animals, overwhelm the habits of bottom-dwellers and block the gills of many of the fish. Sediment suspended in water can also prevent sunlight from penetrating the water, which reduces the growth of aquatic plants. This, in turn, reduces food supplies for other aquatic organisms.

CHEMICAL POLLUTANTS

Agricultural production results in the generation of a variety of pollutants, many of which enter the environment as '**nonpoint source**' contaminants. Nonpoint source pollutants do not have a clear point of origin and are often comprised of a variety of materials, making them difficult to regulate and manage. Stormwater run-off from a collection of farms in a region, for example, will carry a combination of sediment, nutrients and chemicals depending upon when and where the run-off occurs. Although much of this material is non-toxic, some of it is extremely harmful to the environment, even in very small concentrations. Pesticides – which are described as a type of 'agro-chemical' – are designed to be toxic to certain living organisms and although they may be applied selectively to particular plants or animals, they are commonly diffused into soils and groundwater from where they travel into streams and rivers. Agro-chemicals may also be dispersed by the wind during the application process. The transportation of agro-chemicals by wind or water means that they can have negative impacts on living organisms a long way from where they were released.

nonpoint source pollution refers to pollution that cannot be traced to a single source. It contrasts with point source pollution.

A study of pesticide occurrence in streams and groundwater in the USA over a ten-year period[8] demonstrated that pesticides are frequently present in water bodies, although at concentrations that are not generally considered to be harmful to humans. However, the study showed that concentrations of certain pollutants were high enough to endanger the health of aquatic organisms, with 56 per cent of sampled streams containing at least one or more pesticide at a level that exceeded agreed environmental standards. Among the pesticides identified in the water bodies was dichlorodiphenyltrichloroethane – or DDT – which had been banned for agricultural use in the USA nearly 20 years before the study began. The harmful environmental effects of DDT were detailed in Rachel Carson's highly influence 1962 book *Silent Spring* and the US ban on the use of DDT is thought to have saved a number of species – including the iconic bald eagle – from extinction. It now seems that the ban has not been as effective as hoped and despite global efforts to ban this extremely hazardous substance it continues to be used for disease vector control in several countries.

In addition to being costly for the environment, the use of pesticides is also costly for farmers, with a study of cotton production in five countries estimating that in the 1990s $US2–3 billion worth of the chemicals were used on cotton farms in those countries every year.[9] While the financial cost of using agro-chemicals can be rolled into the price charged, the negative impacts on human and environmental health cannot be offset. Excessive pesticide application in agriculture has also resulted in the development of '**pesticide resistance**' in certain pest populations. Pesticide resistance refers to a heritable change in the susceptibility of a pest population to a pesticide and is partially a consequence of the rapid reproduction capacity of certain pest species. Pesticide resistance is often countered by increased applications of pesticides or using combinations of pesticides, both of which have greater environmental impacts. Ultimately, however, resistance results in pesticides becoming ineffective and leads to reduced agricultural production.

pesticide resistance refers to decreasing susceptibility of a pest population to a particular pesticide.

NON-TOXIC AGRO-CHEMICALS

In contrast to pesticides, fertilisers are non-toxic products that are used to promote the growth of agricultural plants. Indeed, one of the major contributors to agricultural expansion in the twentieth century was the development of new fertilisers and fertiliser-making techniques, such as the Haber-Bosch process, that enabled fertilisers to be produced on an industrial scale. Productivity successes achieved by industrial and Green Revolution farming have entrenched the regular and persistent use of 'synthetic' – i.e. artificially manufactured – fertilisers in agriculture and it is estimated that 30–50 per cent of current global crop yields can be attributed to fertiliser applications. However, while fertilisers have substantially contributed to the global growth in agricultural production, their release into rivers, lakes and coastal waters can stimulate the growth of aquatic algae leading to what is known as 'algal blooms'. A blooming of naturally occurring algae might sound harmless but as the algae die and decompose they starve the water of oxygen, creating low-oxygen ***hypoxic*** 'dead zones' where aquatic and marine plants and animals 'die off'. The annual dead zone that appears in the Gulf of Mexico after algae bloom on fertilisers released by the mighty Mississippi River, that was discussed in Chapter 13, is just the tip of the global iceberg. These low oxygen conditions occur in many water bodies, both marine and freshwater. The difficulty with controlling the use of agricultural fertilisers is that an individual farm may not contribute greatly to the total volume of farm 'run-off' but the cumulative effect of multiple farms releasing fertilisers can be devastating for local and regional ecosystems.

hypoxia is a general term for low levels of oxygen; it is being used increasingly to refer to low levels of oxygen in bodies of water.

Ironically, global dependency on the use of fertilisers to boost agricultural production use can also contribute to global food insecurity. For example, phosphorous is the key ingredient of many of the most effective agricultural fertilisers and is typically extracted from naturally occurring phosphate deposits that are ultimately finite. Some estimates suggest that global phosphate supplies could be exhausted within a century and this would have particularly severe consequences for areas with relatively 'old' (i.e. not replenished by relatively recent geological or glacial activity) weathered soils that have low levels of natural phosphorous. A global shortage of phosphorous would, for example, seriously threaten agricultural production in Australia if existing systems of production are not changed.

OTHER PROBLEMS

Just as the release of non-toxic fertilisers has caused unexpected environmental consequences, farms emit other substances that can be more harmful than imagined. For example, manure from livestock farms causes pollution in local streams and waterways by contributing pathogens, such as *Cryptosporidium* and *Giardia* protozoa, that cause gastrointestinal illness and high levels of nitrates that cause a blood disorder known as 'blue baby syndrome' in humans. In addition, not all agricultural pollutants are waterborne. Agro-chemicals and dust particles can be carried long distances by the wind, generating health problems for people located many kilometres from the site of their application. A 2005–6 study of air quality at a remote site in the Yunnan Province in south-west China, for example, found that certain organo-chlorinated compounds, including the pesticides DDT and endosulfan, originated in agricultural regions in southern China, India and mainland south-east Asia.[10] Thus, these highly toxic and persistent substances travelled thousands of kilometres in atmospheric transport systems.

Globally, agriculture makes a significant contribution to the generation of greenhouse gases with the Consultative Group on International Agricultural Research estimating that agriculture is responsible for around one-third of greenhouse gas emissions resulting from human activity (Gilbert 2012). Within the overall array of human-induced greenhouse gases, agriculture makes a disproportionate contribution to the generation of the greenhouse gases nitrous oxide (N_2O) and methane (CH_4). In the UK, for example, it has been estimated that agriculture contributes 62 per cent of the country's nitrous oxide emissions and 37 per cent of its methane emissions.[11] Methane is a by-product of the animal digestion process known as enteric fermentation and this is particularly prevalent in ruminant animals, including cattle and sheep whose numbers have substantially increased through livestock farming. Methane is also produced in the decomposition of materials in rice paddies. Current estimates suggest that within a century methane could overtake carbon dioxide as the biggest contributor to global warming because it is more efficient in re-radiating absorbed solar radiation. Methane, nitrous oxide and carbon dioxide also contribute to the depletion of the planet's protective ozone layer.

While agriculture contributes to the generation of greenhouse gases it is also vulnerable to increasing climate change impacts. The Intergovernmental Panel on Climate Change (IPCC) Fourth Assessment Report suggested that global warming would reduce some crop yields while increasing the impact of weeds and pests. Increasing occurrences of extreme weather events – including droughts, floods, bushfires and cyclones – have already begun to disrupt farm production in vulnerable areas and a combination of extreme weather events and rising sea levels poses threats to many coastal regions and areas surrounding major river deltas in countries such as Vietnam and Bangladesh. Climate change also disrupts the normal seasonal cycles making it harder for farmers to plan ahead. In short, climate change threatens to impose new stresses on already stressed agricultural production systems.[12] This increases the need to redesign systems of production and distribution to reduce the vulnerabilities and impacts.

Discussion questions

1 Why have the global increases in food production in recent decades failed to deliver significant gains in global food security?
2 What are some of the factors causing food insecurity in much of Africa and in a range of impoverished nations around the world?
3 What are some of the negative consequences of selective use of agricultural tariffs and subsidies?
4 In what ways does a reliance on market mechanisms undermine the sustainability of global food production and distribution?
5 What are the key negative environmental impacts of industrial and Green Revolution agriculture?
6 What particular concerns have arisen in relation to the capacity of soils to support food production?
7 How can growth-stimulating plant fertilisers be bad for the environment?
8 What are some of the key principles for designing and implementing ecologically sensitive food systems?

KEY READINGS

Fargione, Joseph, Jason Hill, David Tilman, Stephen Polasky and Peter Hawthorne (2008) 'Land Clearing and the Biofuel Carbon Debt', *Science*, 319: 1235–8.

Food and Agriculture Organization of the United Nations (2012) *World Agriculture Towards 2030/2050: The 2012 Revision* (www.fao.org/docrep/016/ap106e/ap106e.pdf).

Food and Agriculture Organization of the United Nations (2013a) *The State of Food and Agriculture* (www.fao.org/docrep/018/i3300e/i3300e00.htm).

Food and Agriculture Organization of the United Nations (2013b) *Tackling Climate Change Through Livestock: A Global Assessment of Emissions and Mitigation Opportunities* (www.fao.org/docrep/018/i3437e/i3437e.pdf).

Gilbert, Natasha (2011) 'Summit Urged to Clean up Farming', *Nature*, 479: 279.

Godfray, C., J. R. Beddington, I. R. Crute, L. Haddad, D. Lawrence, J. F. Muir, J. Pretty, S. Robinson, S. M. Thomas, C. Toulmin (2010) 'Food security: The Challenge of Feeding 9 Billion People', *Science*, 327: 812–18.

Pretty, Jules and William Sutherland (2010) 'The Top 100 Questions of Importance to the Future of Global Agriculture', *International Journal of Agricultural Sustainability*, 8: 219–36.

Rockström, J., W. Steffen, K. Noone, Å. Persson, F. S. Chapin, E. F. Lambin, T. M. Lenton, M. Scheffer, C. Folke (2009) 'A Safe Operating Space for Humanity', *Nature*, 461: 472–5.

Ecologically sensitive agriculture

thematic essay

Organic farming – i.e. farming that does not make use of introduced or synthetic agrochemicals – was the only form of agricultural production for many thousands of years and its global dominance was only challenged in the second half of twentieth century. The negative environmental and human health impacts caused by the rise of industrial and Green Revolution agriculture is stimulating renewed interest in organic farming in many parts of the world, although it remains a rather marginal practice. An interesting new development, however, involves the use of scientific knowledge to design more intense forms of organic farming in the process that is widely known as '**permaculture**' (short for permanent agriculture). The key principles of permaculture design were worked out by Australian horticulture student David Holmgren in the early 1970s although Holmgren admits that effective promotion of the concept owes much to his early collaboration with high-profile Tasmanian psychology academic Bill Mollison (Mulligan and Hill 2001: 202–6). Holmgren also acknowledges that he borrowed heavily on the 'keyline' farming techniques that were developed in Australia by a mining surveyor-turned-farmer, P. A. Yeomans (ibid.: 193–202). Yeomans focused on detailed observation of the movement of water within the particular landscapes where a farming venture is located in order to work with, rather than try to alter, the natural flow. Holmgren drew on his own knowledge of horticulture and ecology to include a focus on the maximum use of solar energy and to 'design' in biodiversity by including an array of plant and animal species within the food 'system'. A major focus of Holmgren's permaculture design principles – first published in 1978 – was the maintenance of healthy soils without the use of synthetic chemicals and he showed that this could be achieved on scales ranging from a small urban plot to an entire farm.

organic farming refers to farming practices that consciously avoid using synthetic chemicals.

permaculture refers to a holistic approach to the design of food producing gardens which aims to work with, rather than against, natural systems and flows. The term was coined by Australians David Holmgren and Bill Mollison in 1978; permaculture associations run training courses and offer certification for trained practitioners in many countries.

Permaculture's emphasis on working with ecological flows shifts the emphasis from farms as distinct entities to food production systems operating within a particular area or region. It also blurs the boundaries between city and countryside in relation to possibilities for producing food. It is interested in radically reducing the distance between food production and consumption, and Rob Hopkins – an accredited permaculture practitioner based in the UK – used permaculture principles to underpin his influential *Transition Handbook* (2008) which focuses on strategies for reducing the dependence of neighbourhoods, towns and cities on the use of fossil fuels.

While permaculture began with an emphasis on food production, a number of other international movements have begun with a concern about perceived social and environmental costs of large-scale food distribution systems. For example, Community Supported Agriculture (CSA) was initiated in the USA in the 1980s by two farmers from Switzerland and Germany who brought biodynamic farming methods with them from Europe. CSA has grown to include a number of different schemes but key principles include consumers sharing risks with farmers by paying in advance for food to be produced and other techniques to get consumers interested in what the farmers produce.

A key aim of CSA is to help small-scale farmers resist the growing dominance of agricultural corporations on the grounds that farmers with a personal stake in the future of their own farms are more likely to take an interest in what they produce and the consequences for their properties of the production processes.

farmers' markets refers to markets at which food producers can sell the produce directly to the consumers. Although it is an ancient practice it has been consciously revived in recent times to reduce the distance between food production and consumption. There has been strong growth in new farmers' markets in the USA, Canada, the UK and Australia.

The same desire to support small-scale famers is underpinning the rapid expansion in the number of '**farmers' markets**' operating in towns and cities in many parts of the world, especially in the USA. A farmers' market that has been operating in central Los Angeles since 1934 claims to have coined the term as well as the idea, although the latter claim is disputed. However, the growing number of such markets has attracted the interest of the US Department of Agriculture which has reported that the number of such ventures has increased from 1,755 in 1994 to 8,144 in 2013.[13] Of course, the direct marketing of farm produce has never disappeared from local food markets of Europe and the developing world but such markets virtually disappeared in North America before a decline in the number and quality of food retailing options sparked the resurgence. Following the lead of the USA, farmers' markets have been growing in popularity in many other developed nations.

As mentioned in Chapter 5, the international Slow Food movement was also initiated by Italian community activist Carlo Petrini in 1986 as a form of resistance to the growing domination of industrial food production and distribution. While the international Slow Food movement shares the concerns of parallel international food movements with the environmental and social costs of industrial scale food production, it has also highlighted the fact that mass production and long-distance transport commonly undermine the quality of food available in the marketplace, in regard to both taste and nutritional value. The Slow Food movement has cleverly argued that the enjoyment of good food can drive a desire to become a more ethical food consumer, although this argument works mainly for people who have time and money to spend on more selective food purchasing. Selective food purchasing is not an option, for example, for people living in the growing number of so-called 'food deserts' in the USA; i.e. areas that lack any significant food retail outlets. A rather different approach is to bring food production closer to where low-income people are living in urban environments. As mentioned in Chapter 5, urban agriculture is emerging in some US cities that have experienced prolonged economic downturns but it is also expanding in many cities of emerging and underdeveloped nations. Space is an obvious constraint for growing food within urban environments but this is where the principles of permaculture can come into play and there is an obvious overlap between urban agriculture and permaculture.

The 'alternative' food production and consumption practices cannot compete economically with 'mainstream' industrial agriculture. However, as the environmental costs of industrial farming continue to mount, the alternatives will become more attractive. Furthermore, a growing need to reduce our dangerous dependence on fossil fuels will build incentives to reduce distances between the production and consumption of food. Market mechanisms alone cannot create sustainable global food systems and the emphasis needs to shift to a joint consideration of global food security and ecological impacts of production and distribution. The alternative practices discussed above share a number of key principles that could underpin a more sustainable approach:

- Reduce or eliminate the use of synthetic chemicals.
- Avoid waste of energy and water.
- Use biodiversity principles in diversifying farm production.
- Increase diversity in the scale and distribution of food production sites.
- Reduce the distance between food production and consumption.
- Ensure the delivery of food to those experiencing food scarcity.
- Reduce the generation of greenhouse gases in the production and distribution of food.
- Increase the capture and reuse of methane gas.

NOTES

1 Institution of Mechanical Engineers (2013) *Global Food: Waste Not, Want Not* (www.imeche.org/docs/default-source/reports/Global_Food_Report.pdf?sfvrsn=0).
2 DFAT: www.dfat.gov.au/trade/negotiations/trade_in_agriculture.html
3 WTO: www.wto.org/english/tratop_e/tariffs_e/tariff_data_e.htm
4 World Bank: http://data.worldbank.org/topic/agriculture-and-rural-development
5 Millennium Ecosystem Assessment (2005) *Ecosystems and Human Well-being: Synthesis* (www.unep.org/maweb/en/index.aspx).
6 United Nations Environment Programme (2006) *Africa Environment Outlook 2: Our Environment, Our Wealth* (www.unep.org/dewa/africa/docs/en/AEO2_Our_Environ_Our_Wealth.pdf).
7 *Australia State of the Environment Report* (2001) (www.environment.gov.au/about-us/publications).
8 Conducted by United States Geological Service (USGS).
9 Study conducted by International Cotton Advisory Committee.
10 Yue Xu, Gan Zhang, Jun Li, Paromita Chakraborty, Hua Li and Xiang Liu (2011) 'Long-range Atmospheric Transport of Persistent Organochlorinated Compounds from South and Mainland South-Eastern Asia to a Remote Mountain Site in South-Western China', *Journal of Environmental Monitoring*, 13: 3119–27.
11 Jeremy R. Franks and Ben Hadingham (2012) 'Reducing Greenhouse Gas Emissions from Agriculture: Avoiding Trivial Solutions to a Global Problem', *Land Use Policy*, 29: 727–36.
12 Derek Headey and Shenggen Fan (2010) *Reflections on the Global Food Crisis: How Did It Happen? How Has It Hurt? And How Can We Prevent the Next One*?, International Food Policy Research Institute Research Monograph 165. Washington, DC.
13 www.ams.usda.gov

CHAPTER 15

The urban challenge

Michael Buxton and Martin Mulligan

Key concepts and concerns

- the urban age
- diverse urban forms and convergent globalisation
- urban environmental impacts
- urban sprawl
- urban decline
- peripheral growth and urban slums
- privatised governance
- focusing on the hinterlands

THE CHALLENGE OF URBAN SCALE

Cities are the major sources for global production of economic and cultural goods and services, yet they inevitably cast a large ecological footprint in consuming what they cannot produce themselves. Modern world cities cannot be seen as sustainable in and of themselves, given that sustainable development is defined as development able to be continued indefinitely. Long ago, in human history, cities exceeded their capacity to produce their own food and water supplies and to provide all the other resources needed for sustaining life. As distinct entities cities are net consumers of natural capital and the continuing growth in the size and number of big cities is posing major challenges for sustainable use of the world's natural resources. Unbridled urban growth threatens to overwhelm the planet's capacity to support human life.

Assessing the sustainability of cities requires accurate calculations of their resource consumption related to the possibilities for replacing or renewing those resources as well as the capacity to absorb the resulting waste generated (see Chapter 16). Such calculations can be made in broad and abstract terms but cities are located in particular places in the world and we also need to consider their impacts on local environmental or ecological systems, such as the rivers, bays, or surrounding '**hinterlands**' (see Chapter 13). Cities also tend to foster a segregation of the rich and the poor with much better access to resources and

urban hinterlands refer to areas of land that are used to provide resources for the functioning of a city yet they are largely invisible to most city-dwellers.

amenities for those with the best supplies of financial capital. Cities can offer a rich cultural life for people with enough money to access it while the poor often live in degraded neighbourhoods or urban slums, which frequently pose a serious health threat. Well-off communities can avoid the worst impacts of urban pollution but not entirely. In other words, cities bring the environmental and social dimensions of sustainability into sharp relief because social wellbeing is ultimately linked to environmental health.

Startling statistics

- In 2008 we passed the point at which more than half of the world's population live in cities.
- 21 of 28 megacities are located in 'developing countries'.
- By 2015, 440 of the 600 cities making the biggest contribution to global GDP will be located in 'developing countries'.
- Between 1950 and 1990 the combined area of cities in the USA grew by 243 per cent.
- It is anticipated that 70 per cent of China's population will eventually be concentrated in cities along river valleys and the coast, many of which are vulnerable to sea level rises and flooding.

urbanisation refers to the increasing proportion of people living in urban, rather than rural, areas.

cultural amenity is a term used to cover cultural facilities and the mix of cultural activities that take place in a particular area.

Cities have emerged in different parts of the world in different periods of human history and the different trajectories of urban development have been influenced by culture, geography and world trade. Broadly speaking, we can distinguish a different pattern of urban development in the USA compared to Europe while countries such as Canada and Australia show a mix of European and American influences. Historically, the 'western' city has taken a different form to cities in Asia, Africa and some parts of Latin America. However, economic globalisation has begun to blur the distinctions between western and non-western cities and a similar trajectory of **urbanisation** has emerged within a host of underdeveloped countries. Urbanisation has proceeded at a faster rate in the developing world and it poses greater environmental and social challenges within the developing countries. At the same time, we have seen the emergence of a number of global megacities that interact more directly with each other than at any other time in human history. This chapter will trace different trajectories of urban development in different parts of the world in order to show that the 'urban challenge' takes different forms. At the same time, many of the environmental and social challenges posed by urban 'sprawl' are common and the chapter aims to demonstrate a universal need for much stronger city-wide planning and governance.

The global trend towards urban growth is not likely to be reversed even if it can be slowed (see Figure 15.1). However, well-planned urban 'consolidation' could lead to much more efficient use of energy, food, water and other natural resources while it could also help to ensure that people living in low-income households have better access to employment, social and recreational services and **cultural amenity**. Chaotic urban growth creates a host of environmental and

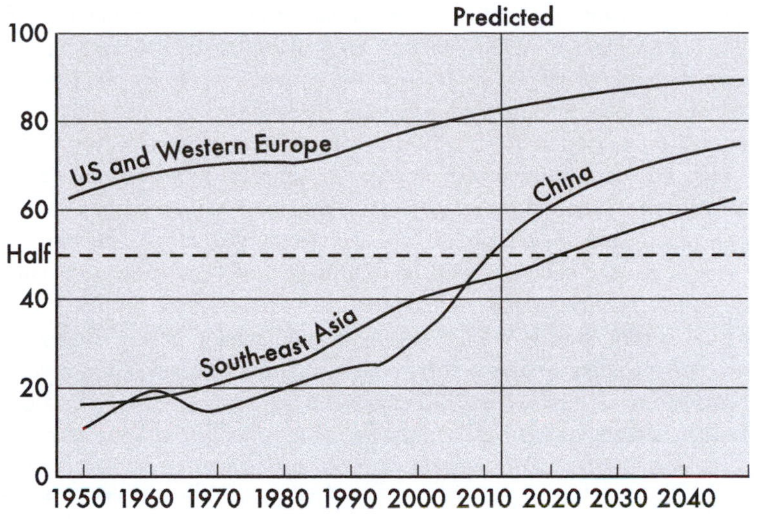

Figure 15.1 Percentage of population living in cities
Source: data from **UN Population Division** (www.fao.org/worldfoodsituation/foodpricesindex/en)

UN Population Division was established as a commission in 1946 and now operates as part of the Department of Economic and Social Affairs. Its key task is to produce regular demographic reports.

social problems yet cities can become hubs of innovation for environmental and social sustainability.

DEBATING THE MERITS OF CITIES

A range of debates continue to rage over the benefits and pitfalls of the **urban form**. One argument is that 'economies of scale' come into play both in supplying city-dwellers with food, water, shelter, energy and other essentials and also in dealing with waste streams. Urban enthusiasts argue that cities have always been the incubators of innovation, while others suggest that megacities tend to become global factories of production rather than centres of innovation. Many health workers argue that it is much easier to offer good quality health care services for people living in cities while others argue that cities have historically been the incubators for diseases that can turn into epidemics or even international pandemics.

urban form refers to the overall spatial arrangements in a city, taking into account built infrastructure and how it reflects the city's economic and social functioning.

More will be said about the debates over the benefits and pitfalls of the urban form in the essay at the end of this chapter ('For and against the city'). What cannot be avoided, however, is that the current combination of global population growth and urbanisation – i.e. migration into urban settlements – means that the cities of the world are sucking up the world's natural resources at an unsustainable rate. Loose talk about the development of 'sustainable cities' underestimates the scale of the challenge we face globally. Some of these challenges apply to all cities and yet the solutions must be grounded in the social and ecological realities of each city.

THE URBAN AGE

Cities of the western world grew rapidly towards the end of the nineteenth century. However, it is the rapid growth of many cities across all parts of the world in the last part of the twentieth century and early part of the twenty-first century that enables to now say that we have entered the global 'urban age'. According to the United Nations Population Fund, 2008 marked an important turning point because since that year more than half of the world's population is now living within urban centers. As mentioned above, opinions are divided as to whether or not this is a bad thing but continuing urban growth will undermine the possibilities for sustaining human populations and the urban age potentially carries the seeds of its own destruction. Global population is unevenly distributed between rural and urban areas and between developed and 'developing' countries. Yet the trend everywhere is for net migration from rural to urban and the migration into the cities of the developing world is the biggest human migration in history[1] Cities grow through both migration and 'natural' increase in population especially in developing countries. However, during the 1990s the world population increased by around 600 million and staggering two-thirds of this increase occurred within cities.[2]

The United Nations Population Division has estimated that on current trends the global population will grow by 3.7 billion in the period from 1990 to 2030, and 90 per cent of this increased population will be living in cities.[3] The same trends suggest that by 2050, a staggering 85 per cent of urban-dwellers will be those living within the cities of the countries currently classified as 'developing'. Already, 21 of the world's 28 megacities – defined as cities with more than 10 million people – are located in 'developing' nations. Megacities are growing much more slowly in the developed world and some cities are actually shrinking in size. The UN predictions suggest that the population growth for cities in the 'developed' world will be 'only' 150 million by 2050. Most of the shrinking cities are located in Eastern or Central Europe or northern Britain, while populations are shrinking within the inner zones of some old North American cities

China (1.35 billion) and India (1.28 billion) have the biggest populations in the world and the global hotspots for urbanisation are along the eastern seaboard of China and along an imaginary line that could be drawn from Mumbai to Kolkata in India, where distinct towns are beginning to merge to form urban conurbations. Already 40 per cent of India's population live within this 'line' of cities and it is predicted that the massive migration of people from rural parts of China into the coastal and riverside cities could mean that those cities will eventually contain 70 per cent of China's 1.35 billion people. A slowing of China's rapid period of economic growth has seen the migration into the cities fall below expectations – with unoccupied residential blocks being dubbed 'ghost cities' – however the central government remains determined to continue building bigger cities (see Photo 15.1).

SUSTAINABILITY IMPLICATIONS

Given that many cities in the developed world have either stabilised or even shrunk in size, many pundits suggest that urbanisation will result in a decline in birth rates within the 'developing' nations. This has led to the prediction that global population might peak at around 9.3 billion people by 2050 and thereafter it might begin to fall, reducing the pressures being exerted on food supplies and the world's natural resources. The more pessimistic view is that a global population of more than 9 million – with a majority living in cities – is already past the point of

Photo 15.1 Shanghai has grown exponentially in recent times
© Prisma Bildagentur AG/Alamy

sustainability. Historically, city-living tends to change food consumption habits because most people have more choice of food than those living in rural areas. This often sets up a trend towards increasing consumption of meat and this, in turn, means that more agricultural land is required to support the per capita food consumption of city-dwellers (see Chapter 14).

Urbanisation is currently increasing the global generation of greenhouse gases, given that fossil fuels are used for the collection and transport of the minerals and raw materials needed to construct and sustain the cities. As mentioned in Chapter 4, China recently overtook the USA as the world's biggest contributor to greenhouse gas emissions and much of this has been driven by the rapid growth of the country's cities. It needs to be noted that developed countries are 'outsourcing' the production of greenhouse gases by importing goods produced in 'developing' nations, including China. Nevertheless, urbanisation in the underdeveloped world has become a growing threat to global sustainability. Furthermore, the impact cannot be measured by the increase in urban population alone because, as noted above, city-dwellers in China consume much more food and energy than those living in rural areas, and urbanisation has led to a sharp increase in the use of motor vehicles. China was already producing more light motor vehicles in 2013 than either the USA or Japan, and on some predictions the country could have 200 million motor vehicles on the road by 2020.[4]

THE USA SETS THE TREND FOR URBAN SPRAWL

urban sprawl refers to the tendency for cities to expand in size in a largely unplanned way.

The end of the Second World War triggered a massive expansion in the size of cities in the USA because of a growing desire for detached housing with low population densities. New suburbs grew at the metropolitan edge and the lack of public transport development resulted in a rapid increase in automobile dependency. In the new urban zones land uses were largely segregated into residential, retail and industrial 'zones' and this exacerbated the problem of car-dependency. As Garreau (1991) has pointed out, US cities pioneered the development of large shopping malls, often situated at the intersection of major roads, and the development of such commercial 'hubs' then created further pressure for outward expansion. Gillham (2002) has demonstrated that during the 1970s and 1980s over 95 per cent of population growth in the USA took place in suburban areas. 'Urban sprawl' is characterised by high consumption of land for low population density. Kahn (2000) has shown that between 1950 and 1990, the population of urban areas in the USA grew by 92.3 per cent while urbanised land area increased by 243 per cent.

Many commentators associate urban sprawl with 'leap-frog' development in which there is a discontinuity of urban development with a distance of open space, or farmland, intervening before residential development recommences. This type of development is usually developer driven, and it can represent a strategy by private developers to negate policies of containment by government. It may also result from a lack of cooperation among government agencies in managing urban growth. However, sprawl can also be a conscious planning choice that results in growth in the size of cities and a decline in population within the older urban 'core'. Planned or not, sprawl is a form of urbanisation that creates a raft of environmental and social problems ranging from high levels of car-dependency and lack of waste management infrastructure to social isolation and the segregation of the city into rich and poor neighbourhoods. Urban sprawl also results in the loss of agricultural land within easy reach of the city and it can destroy the habitats of plants and animals already under stress. In other words, urban sprawl tends to increase the ecological footprint of the cities concerned and pose a greater risk to the maintenance of biodiversity.

URBAN DECLINE

megacity is a term normally used for cities with more than 10 million people.

The USA has its share of **megacity** conglomerations, such as extended New York City, the Los Angeles basin, and the connected settlements in the San Francisco Bay area. Yet most cities in the USA are middle-sized and many of them have either stabilised or shrunk in recent decades. Furthermore, while New York, San Francisco and Boston are famous for their thriving old city centres, there has been population flight from central business districts and inner residential areas of cities like Detroit, Cleveland and Buffalo. The picture is mixed for the nation's third biggest city, Chicago, with some inner areas thriving while others are declining.

A number of factors have coalesced to cause this urban decline. An obvious one has been the closure of big factories and traditional forms of industrial production while a less obvious factor has been the steady drift – since the 1960s – of white middle-income families from inner areas to new suburbs and the replacement of these families by low-income groups that cannot afford to live in the suburbs. Once it set in, this trend turned into a 'flight from blight' as crime rates increased in the inner-urban 'ghettoes'. This inevitably becomes a form of racial

Photo 15.2 Detroit, Michigan – Michigan Central train station, which has fallen into disrepair after closing in 1988
© Jim West/Alamy

segregation and 'flight from blight' becomes 'white flight' as white middle-class families head for the suburbs in search of 'quality' schools, 'decent' health care facilities and other services.

A third factor behind the fragmentation of many US cities is that one city can comprise many local government bodies. The municipal boundaries within old cities have been frozen since the 1930s while the local government bodies on the urban fringes tend to compete with each other to attract economic investments and population growth. Declining populations of inner-urban areas led to catastrophic crashes in revenues for those local authorities. In the absence of city-wide governance, few mechanisms exist for transferring incomes from relatively affluent outer urban areas to sometimes bankrupt inner-urban municipalities.

Norton (1979) has demonstrated that the process of urban decline began after the Second World War and that between 1950 and 1975 every 'old city' lost population while every 'young city' grew. Rusk (1993) demonstrated that central city income levels in some old cities fell below 70 per cent of suburban income, and passed the point of no return for investment and job creation. The trend has largely continued into the twenty-first century, with some cities deciding that inner-urban regeneration is so unlikely that housing has been cleared to make room for practices such as 'urban agriculture'. Some cities – including Pittsburgh, Philadelphia and Washington, DC – are showing signs of increasing public and private investment in the inner areas, while Harlem in New York City provides an example of an area that has been regenerated.

Reinvesting in mass transit in the USA

The problems with urban sprawl have encouraged a number of cities to reinvest in mass transit systems. Portland, Oregon has invested federal funding into mass transit to link higher density residential and mixed-use areas around light rail stations. This has helped promote a vibrant city core and suburban commercial centres. An extensive light rail system, the Metropolitan Area Express (MAX), and a commuter rail system, now link many suburbs. A long-standing urban growth boundary limits outer-urban growth as an essential tool to redirect investment into the existing city.

The San Francisco rail plan has extended the Bay Area Rapid Transportation (BART) and light rail systems, and has connected commuter rail lines to the downtown area. Costs have been shared between levels of government, rail bond funding, affected communities and taxes. A broader Municipal Railway (Muni) system includes bus, trolley bus and light rail lines.

The Massachusetts Bay Transportation Authority (MBTA) operates the Boston commuter rail, subway and bus systems. The system brings about 30 per cent of workers to the city and is the fastest expanding system in the USA. Elevated railways have been replaced and the Red and Green Lines extended, bringing economic benefits to connected commercial areas. Effective mass transit has made a major contribution to the vitality of the downtown and inner-urban neighbourhoods.

PERIPHERAL GROWTH IN PREVIOUSLY DENSE EUROPEAN CITIES

Historically, European cities have presented a very different form to that of post-1945 American cities. Densely populated old city cores, which tend to be well served by public transport, often have a mix of residential, retail, commercial and other land uses. In the 1960s, many high-rise residential structures began to appear on the fringes of some cities in an even higher density model. Over time, lower-income and immigrant groups became concentrated within these high-rise estates where there is often poor access to employment, retailing and other services. Middle-income housing on the urban fringe tended to replicate the housing model of traditional inner-urban areas, emphasising dense apartment construction up to six stories in height, sometimes with attached low-rise family housing.

Post-war European cities did not segregate land uses as extensively as was the case in the USA and there was more limited development of shopping malls or 'office parks'. Traffic was commonly diverted around the cities to avoid the construction of freeways in densely populated areas.

However, spatial development practices are changing in many European countries. Residential development on the peripheries – particularly in southern Europe – has increased substantially from the 1980s onwards. Development on the periphery has often featured medium density housing of about 45 dwellings per hectare. There has been an increase in the construction of detached housing on separate land titles but the average size of such lots is still well below lot sizes in North America. A number of Spanish cities – including Madrid, Bilbao, Valencia, Seville and Malaga – have seen a shift of population and economic activity towards outer suburbs and Hoffmann-Martinot (2004) has demonstrated that urban sprawl is now characteristic of many outer metropolitan areas across France. Paris alone now covers more than 14,000 square kilometres and Kraemer (2005) has pointed to a similar pattern of suburban development in a wide range of German cities with many outer areas becoming a stronghold of detached single-family houses on large allotments.

The preservation, or restoration, of historic character and protection of amenity has been the key to the success of inner-urban regeneration in many European cities with new high standards of 'liveability' attracting new economic activity and extensive tourism. Integrated regional planning – incorporating values and principles adopted by governments, business and communities over long time periods – has helped to facilitate economic investment and the development of new facilities. Some European countries – such as Germany – have managed to keep a lid on the kinds of real estate speculation that push up house prices while an oversupply of outer-urban housing in countries with more fragile economies – notably Spain and Ireland – has resulted in a dramatic boom-and-bust cycle.

Avoiding urban sprawl in Europe

Although some low-density sprawl has been built recently on the fringes of dense cities such as Barcelona, generally densities of 45–120 dwellings per hectare are used for new developments in Europe. In the UK attempts are being made to increase the traditional density of the fringes of cities and towns from 25 to 45 dwellings per hectare, almost four times the Australian average. Many European cities are also covered by wider regional plans that ensure that the urban fringe and adjacent rural areas are properly integrated with each other. A good example of this is the plan that covers the four largest cities in the Netherlands: Amsterdam, Rotterdam, the Hague and Utrecht, and adjacent towns. The region known as the Randstadt retains a non-urban 'green heart'. The green heart contrasts with 'green belts' that are usually situated on the fringes of cities and serve to protect agricultural and natural resources. Green belts are often used in association with urban growth boundaries and in England and Scotland they cover a total area of two million hectares. Fifteen green belts cover 14 per cent of England, with the London Green Belt now comprising over 486,000 hectares.

Planning in the area adjacent to the Dutch city of Utrecht is particularly instructive. Here a city 'extension project' (named Leidsche Rijn) was instigated in 1994 with the intention of housing 300,000 people. However, 770 hectares of the development's 1,790 hectares was zoned for uses such as horticulture, waterways and scattered residential precincts. The development is on track to provide nearly 30,000 new housing units by 2015 with gross residential density of 37.2 dwellings per hectare, and it will also include district parks, industrial sites and ecological zones. About 70 per cent of new housing will be medium-density, low-rise terraces with a 30 per cent component of affordable housing, both rental and owner occupied. The new district is partly located along an existing heavy rail line, which is being expanded from two to four tracks to separate local and intercity services and will offer metro-like frequencies. The remainder of the site is serviced by several dedicated busways enabling high-frequency services within Utrecht's existing urban bus system and the possibility for conversion to light rail in the future. A dense cycle path network connects Leidsche Rijn to the existing city of Utrecht.

URBAN 'SLUMS' OF THE 'DEVELOPING' WORLD

Most of the big cities of Asia, Africa and Latin America have become notorious for the emergence of sprawling low-rise, non-sanctioned, squatter communities or 'shanty-towns' (see Photo 15.3). In some cities – such as Mexico City – some such slums have been incrementally taken over by middle-income people while the former slum-dwellers have been forced to retreat to unoccupied land on the urban fringe. A wide range of commentators have suggested that urban slums in countries ranging from India to Brazil have developed strong social networks and quite vibrant small-scale entrepreneurial economic development that can deliver income for most slum-dwellers. Others, however, have said that such poorly

Photo 15.3 An urban slum in New Delhi, India
Wikimedia Commons

constructed settlements are incubators for disease and crime and Mike Davis (2006) is famous for suggesting that they represent the ultimate dystopia that could represent the future for increasing numbers of impoverished people. In many 'developing nations' – most notably China – there is a sustained push to relocate slum-dwellers into high-rise apartment blocks. Communities are being extensively relocated from one place to another, sometimes resulting in the fragmentation of old social networks.

While 'slum clearance' accounts for some of the urban growth in the developing world, most growth occurs on the urban fringes in 'extended' metropolitan regions.[5] In many of these cities population density is falling in the inner regions as they are being 'redeveloped' and people are being moved to make way for arterial roads and freeways. Both the affluent and the poor are migrating towards the peripheral urban regions although they live there in segregated areas. The fringes of expanding African cities tend to be populated with poor migrants from rural areas who often retain their rural connections. **'Informal'** and **low-income settlements** are also proliferating on the outskirts of many cities in Central and South America, although middle- and upper-income people migrating outwards from inner-urban areas account for the bulk of the fringe metropolitan population increase in South America and Asia. The latter trend is resulting in an increase in single-use, low-density residential development with outer-urban residents having a high level of car dependence. Manila probably pioneered this pattern of development with housing enclaves associated with shopping malls and connected to the city centre by freeways. Chang (1998) has shown that a high proportion of inner-urban migrants to Beijing also settle in outer areas and that these migrants comprise up to one-third of the population of some of these districts.

informal settlement is used to refer to any settlement that has not been officially planned or sanctioned. It is considered to have less negative connotations than the word 'slum'.

In the Maoist era, an effort was made to make Chinese cities more self-sustaining communities where work, housing and services were sited in close proximity to each other. However, this has changed radically to the point where housing has been separated from manufacturing and commercial land uses and increasingly both residential areas and workplaces have been relocated to outer urban locations. Large-scale redevelopment of the traditional *hutong* residential areas of Beijing[6] has occurred for commercial and residential development and only 50,000 residents are expected to be left in the redeveloped commercial core of Shanghai.

A similar pattern of outer-urban growth is occurring in Bangkok – even though large areas of land remain undeveloped in the inner-urban zone – and in Jakarta, where the total urban area – known as **Jabodetabek** – covers 6,392 square kilometres and has a population of around 28 million,[7] making it the seventh largest urban area in the world.

Jabodetabek is the name used for the greater Jakarta area. The name is an amalgamation of letters signifying the merging of five formerly separate municipalities and three regencies.

PRIVATISED GOVERNANCE

The new urban form that is emerging in many developing nations replicates much of what emerged earlier in western cities. It is possible today to drive out of a suburb in a city like Los Angeles and fly across the world to find replica houses in a new urban development in China; perhaps with a Spanish theme! Several scholars[8] have noted that in such countries local industrialists with close ties to political leaders have seen an opportunity to invest in real estate by creating or investing in urban development corporations. These developers have then set out to cater for – or stimulate – consumer demand for 'best practice' housing estates that are similar to those built on the peripheries of cities all around the world. A transnational design culture that created similar new estates in cities ranging from Shanghai to Vancouver.

In many Asian cities private developers have effectively taken over the governance of many new peripheral urban areas. For example, private corporations have not only built houses in the new 'towns' of Jakarta's Jabodetabek but have also built schools and a range of other community facilities. When private profit becomes the overriding imperative, the short- and long-term environmental consequences are rarely considered.

COMPARING AUSTRALIA AND CANADA

Australia has a long tradition of concentrating its population into a few large cities, making it one of the most urbanised nations in the world. Two-thirds of the total population live in the five biggest cities and two of them – Sydney and Melbourne – account for 40 per cent of the national population. According to the Australian Bureau of Statistics,[9] cities contribute 80 per cent of GDP in Australia and 75 per cent of all employment. In contrast to the trend in the USA, the inner areas of most Australian cities – above 100,000 people – have continued to be critical economic and cultural generators. In retaining relatively high-density residential areas and economically powerful central business districts, Australian cities resemble those of Europe and the trend is for the inner-urban areas – already the most densely populated in the country – to become even more dense. At the same time, Australian cities have also been expanding in geographic spread and it has been estimated that between 1945 and 1995, more than one million hectares were added to the cities.[10] A 2013 national government survey found that outer urban growth was occurring most rapidly in the city of Melbourne but the population growth has not been matched by a similar growth in employment opportunities.[11] The survey found that with less than one job for every three working people and little access to public transport, 84 per cent of outer Melbourne residents were using their private vehicles to travel to work.

gentrification is a term used to refer to the transformation of areas that were once clearly working class in character into areas that are better defined as being middle class.

urban heritage refers to historically significant urban buildings and infrastructure.

Australia's dual – inner and outer – model of urban growth has also led to a growing socio-economic segregation, with higher-income, tertiary educated, professional people congregating in the inner and middle ring and a much lower proportion of such people living in the outer suburbs. Such spatial segregation compounds the disadvantages for low-income households because they have less access to employment, transport and other services. A higher proportion of household income is allocated to transport, energy and food costs. Ironically, one of the factors that has driven the '**gentrification**' of the inner suburbs of Australia's biggest cities – Sydney and Melbourne – has been cultural 'amenity' and access to **urban heritage**. Yet the demand for inner-urban residences has sparked the development of high- and medium-rise residential towers which threaten to replace or overwhelm heritage areas or sites of cultural significance.

Many Canadian cities exhibit a combination of American and Australian trends. For example, in the period between 1961 and 2001, Toronto grew in area at a rate that was about 30 per cent faster than the rate of national population increase;[12] and from 2006 to 2011 its rate of growth was almost double the national rate, with more people moving into outer areas with low-density housing and poor public transport. Urban sprawl in Canada partly reflects the fact that a fragmented approach to urban governance has undermined integrated, city-wide planning. At the same time, Canadian cities have retained vibrant central business districts and recent attempts to impose urban growth boundaries have helped to contain the sprawl. Toronto still anticipates a population increase of about 2.5 million by 2036[13] with a significant expansion of the urban area. The city of Calgary has been the most proactive in adopting a sustainability agenda with a transportation plan that aims to create self-sufficient 'urban villages' defined as mixed-use activity areas with higher-density housing, local employment, street accessibility and improved transit options in both existing and newly developing suburban neighbourhoods.

Showing the way in Australia

While urban planning in Australia's fourth biggest city – Perth – has its critics it has led the way in Australia in the development of more intensive types of residential subdivision. This includes medium density inner-urban redevelopment, and the Liveable Neighbourhoods design code. The Subiaco Redevelopment Authority (SRA) led the regeneration of 80 hectares of former industrial land adjacent to the existing activity centre of Subiaco. The inner-city revitalisation project demonstrated that cities do not need to embrace high-rise development to gain significant increases in density. Meanwhile the outer-urban growth corridor between Joondalup and Clarkson-Jindalee has changed from being functionally segregated and car based to being better connected. Public transport has been essential to this new urbanisation, particularly with the addition of the new Joondalup and Mandurah rail lines and the development of the northern suburbs transit system. Passenger numbers are well in excess of those predicted, rising 67 per cent in the ten years to 2011, with 63 million people carried in 2012 alone. This high use has led to overcrowding of services and the 2013 public transport plan proposes further extensions.

Ellenbrook is a masterplanned 1,200-hectare greenfield development at the north eastern fringe of metropolitan Perth, some 25 kilometres from the CBD. By 2003 some 10,000 residents – about 35 per cent of the ultimate target population – inhabited the district. It served as one of the reference designs for the Liveable Neighbourhood code, which pioneered many innovations such as water-sensitive design, high-connectivity street networks, diversity of lot sizes, house design guidelines and integration of employment and commercial facilities within residential areas. There is an employment target of 0.75 jobs per household, equivalent to an approximate local job containment rate of 50 per cent. Every property has fibre-optic cable and there is also an NGO-run business incubator. Ellenbrook is organised in five separate villages, each with a distinct character achieved through design regulations and public art.

NEGLECTED HINTERLANDS

urban periphery refers to the outer edges of a city, where expansion is commonly occurring. The term 'periurban' is used to refer to the zone in which urban expansion is putting pressure on earlier forms of land use.

green belt refers to an area of land within an urban area that is deliberately preserved in a natural or agricultural state. The idea of having a green 'belt' to encircle urban growth emerged in the UK in the 1930s.

The emergence of 'global cities' – which tend to focus more on their connections with each other than their situation within a particular nation – has undermined the significance and value of urban 'hinterlands'. While many people continue to live in the **urban periphery** – up to 100 kilometres from the city centre – they journey to the city centre for work and recreation. Historically, hinterlands have been critical to the success of cities. They are often a mosaic of land uses – including residential, small rural lots and rural-residential pockets. They also host an array of commercial enterprises and government institutions and they offer a significant recreational amenity. They can also be a source of important environmental services, often including the city's water supplies. They produce more food than many city-dwellers realise and include an array of other 'natural resources, offering opportunities for recreation and inspiration to urban residents. Taken as a whole they are a vital, yet neglected, global resource. Cities are more dependent on their hinterlands than most urban planners and policy-makers acknowledge.

Yet the hinterlands are under enormous pressure from urban sprawl because their complex socio-ecological character does not give them high market value in comparison to their potential for residential development. Urban authorities, or higher levels of government, can intervene to protect such areas by setting city limits or by declaring '**green belt**' zones. The land market is a threat to the future of the hinterlands and yet history suggests that cities which have taken action to protect their hinterlands have performed better economically. The contribution of the hinterlands to future urban prosperity is likely to increase with the unfolding of global climate change, with food, water and energy security becoming harder to achieve.

Discussion questions

1. What are some of the key differences in the urban form as it has developed in the USA and Europe?
2. What are some of the key environmental and social challenges arising within the burgeoning cities of the 'developing world'?
3. What are the negative social and environmental consequences of urban sprawl?
4. What are some strategies for reducing car dependence within cities?

5 What are some of the strategies being implemented in particular cities in the USA, Europe and Australia to contain urban sprawl?
6 Within debates about the benefits and pitfalls of cities for social and environmental sustainability, what are the key arguments for and against the city?

KEY READINGS

Bernick, Michael and Robert Cervero (1997) *Transit Villages in the 21st Century*, New York: McGraw-Hill, chapter 2.

Davison, Graeme (2004) *Car Wars*, Sydney: Allen & Unwin.

Friedmann, John (2002) *The Prospect of Cities*, Minneapolis, MN: University of Minnesota Press.

Marcuse, Peter and Ronald van Kempen (2000) *Globalising Cities*, Oxford: Blackwell.

Nelson, Arthur (2013) *Reshaping Metropolitan America: Development Trends and Opportunities to 2030*, Washington, DC: Island Press.

Newman, Peter and Andy Thornley (1996) *Urban Planning in Europe*, London: Routledge.

Thompson, Susan (ed.) (2007) *Planning Australia: An Overview of Urban and Regional Planning*, Cambridge: Cambridge University Press.

For and against the city

thematic essay

The social and environmental benefits and pitfalls of urbanisation have been a matter for fierce debate in recent decades. Urban enthusiasts have long argued that cities are the generators of knowledge and innovation and many suggest that this contribution grows in proportion to the size of the city; i.e. 'bigger is better'. The counter-argument is that large cities tend to become 'world factories' that focus on production rather than innovation. Whatever knowledge is produced, this argument continues, is unevenly distributed and knowledge and power create new forms of hierarchy and spatial segregation of the rich and poor. Rather than breaking the boundaries of disadvantage, innovation can create hierarchies of opportunity.

Debate also rages on the extent to which cities have not only bred disease but even shaped modern human genetics. The congregation of people and domesticated animals within early towns and cities resulted in the emergence of new diseases but this also resulted in increasing human resistance to disease. Ancient cities were certainly a major health hazard until the Romans developed much better water supply and drainage systems. Nevertheless, cities tended to be giant incubators for the spread of old and new diseases right up until the late nineteenth century. New medicines and public health campaigns addressed many of the health challenges that emerge within large congregations of people. However, new pathogens and viruses – often arising from close human contact with animals – now threaten to gather momentum within particular cities before going global. Cities present both threats and opportunities in regard to health and health care.

land use mix refers to any policy which seeks to maintain a diversity of land uses in a particular area, as distinct from segregated zoning.

The term 'urban form' refers to the generalised shape of an urban region and the disposition of its major components. It is represented commonly by population density, land use types and the degree of **land use mix**. Other characteristics of the urban form include subdivision and building design, transport patterns and infrastructure provision. Cities have always cast an ecological footprint that extends beyond the defined city limits but increasing flows of people, goods, energy and materials make it harder than ever to define the city limits and depict where one urban area ends and another one begins. While it has become harder to think of a city as a single entity, city-wide planning and governance has become more important. Rather than focus on the city as an undifferentiated whole we can focus on the complex, interacting dimensions of the urban form. Manipulating the characteristics and functions of the urban form – with particular emphasis on density and land use – can deliver environmental, social and economic benefits. On the other hand, concentrations and interactions can also multiply the problems.

The focus on urban form as a way to achieve specific environmental benefits such as energy savings has also been disputed. Some have suggested that since many cities generally change only by 2–3 per cent a year, concentrating on urban form may have extensive cost and lifestyle implications for little benefit. Yet even at this level of annual change, efficient models of urban form can make a major contribution to urban environmental performance within a generation. However, it cannot only be a matter of focusing on energy supplies because up to 70 per cent of delivered energy is subject to the influence of land use planning. For example, Australian cities make the major contribution to the generation of transport-related greenhouse gas emissions nationally because land use planning has meant that 70 per cent of national road transport kilometres occur within urban areas.[14]

While the benefits and pitfalls of cities continue to be debated there is widespread agreement that compact models of urban form produce the best energy performance. According to Williams, Burton and Jenks (2000) a range of studies conducted in the late 1980s and early 1990s demonstrated that changes to urban form emphasising higher-density mixed uses close to public transport offer the greatest energy savings and positive environmental, social and economic outcomes. Identified benefits included reduced car travel and emissions, lower infrastructure costs, more varied and intensified social activities, better access to, and use of, services, and protection of the countryside.

There is considerable research to indicate that density and land use mix both lead to an increase in the use of public transport and walking as a mode of transport over single-occupant vehicle use. However, a number of variables affect this relationship, including the quality of public transport, the extent to which car-based retail malls are discouraged, the localisation of employment and services, and the design of subdivisions that allow walkable access to services. Some studies into the relationships between urban form and vehicle use have proved controversial, particularly the claim by ECOTEC (1993), and Newman and Kenworthy (1989) that transport energy use falls as dwelling density increases. Critics suggest that many other factors – including personal income, fuel prices, car parking provisions – influence rates of private vehicle use. Mees (2010) insists that the key factor is the quality of public transport provision.

While it may be harder than imagined to pinpoint the factors that can reduce private vehicle use, a reduction in urban sprawl is clearly a starting point and there can be no doubt that the biggest environmental benefit of more compact cities is, indeed, reduction of car-dependency. Stopping sprawl needs to be combined with a bigger effort to design cities that positively encourage walking, cycling and the use of public transport. A number of compact city models have emerged in recent times and they offer different mixes of low-, medium- and high-density housing stock. Much depends on the existing urban form and opportunities that may, or may not, emerge to shift public attitudes and practices.

Finally, it should be noted that the development of more compact cities is not all about novelty and innovation, because cities of the past were commonly more compact than those of the modern era. Traditional Asian cities, for example, were very dense and relatively low consumers of energy and yet this traditional urban form is giving way to high-rise construction with generally poor insulation, high rates of heat loss and capture, large empty internal spaces (such as atriums) and extensive use of artificial light and air conditioning. Some new forms of urban density are less sustainable than the old and in such cases it might be a case of going 'back to the future'.

NOTES

1 See www.un.org/en/development/desa/population/publications/
2 Ibid.
3 www.un.org/esa/population/
4 *China: Automotive Industry Handbook,* International Business Publications, Washington, DC, 2013.
5 Christopher Silver, *Planning the Megacity: Jakarta in the Twentieth Century,* London: Routledge, 2008.
6 Hutong refers to residential areas built around ancient city laneways.
7 See Singh, R. B. (ed.) (2013) *Urban Development Challenges, Risks and Resilience in Asian Mega Cities*, Tokyo: Springer.
8 See Fulong Wu (ed.) *Globalization and the Chinese City,* London: Routledge.
9 www.abs.gov.au/
10 *Green Cities,* Australian Urban and Regional Development Review, Canberra, 1995.

11 Study conducted by the federal Bureau of Infrastructure, Transport and Regional Economics.

12 www.statcan.gc.ca/

13 www.statcan.gc.ca/

14 www.infrastructureaustralia.gov.au/publications/files/Urban_Transport_Stategy_Paper.FINAL.pdf

CHAPTER 16

Rethinking waste

Ruth Lane and Martin Mulligan

Key concepts and concerns

- waste streams
- global material and waste flows
- waste as resource
- revaluing waste
- linear and circular material flows
- increasing the lifespan of goods
- historic shifts in perceptions, beliefs and practices

INTRODUCTION

Waste is commonly defined as matter out of place; the material residue of human activities which is either in excess of current needs, has no further use, or poses a potential hazard for environmental or public health. However, these meanings are subject to change over time and differ in different social and cultural contexts. Perceptions of waste are strongly linked to the creation and recognition of value within different societies and this emerges in everything from the way waste is treated within economic systems to wider ethical considerations about managing waste. For this reason some scholars have preferred to define waste very simply as 'any material we have failed to use' (Gille 2010: 1050). However, a focus on materials as end products will not help us understand the economic, technological or social practices that have created them, let alone the values that underpin such practices. Environmental scientists and social commentators agree that growing exploitation of the planet's ultimately finite natural resources is increasing the need to rethink the ways in which waste has been dealt with in industrial societies. Indeed, it is commonly suggested that 'waste' needs to be seen as a potential 'resource';[1] but this chapter will argue that we need to go further in seeking to understand the practices that are generating increasing volumes of waste.

It is important to begin by taking stock of global trends in the production and circulation of various types of waste – as reported by key international agencies – in order to discern the factors that are driving such trends. Because the generation of industrial waste is closely linked to the production and distribution of goods we need to focus on the role that waste plays – or could play – within our economic systems; with particular attention to efforts being made to turn waste into a resource through reuse or recycling schemes. While many such schemes operate at local levels we need to also focus on the circulation of waste within global trade networks. A global perspective enables us to understand the growing opportunities for recycling but – as we will see in a case study focusing on the reprocessing of electronic waste in Bangladesh (see box pp. 264–5) – this raises other concerns about the valuing of human labour and social wellbeing. The concentration of harmful waste processing activities among the poorer populations of the world is one of the concerns of global **environmental justice** movements. In this chapter we will review some of the efforts being made within economically developed nations to reframe waste as a resource, yet we have to remember that these never operate strictly within national boundaries. Because **waste flows** are no longer contained within local or national boundaries, this chapter argues that we need to better understand the diverse social, cultural and economic contexts within which global waste circulates.

environmental justice is a term that emerged in the USA in the early 1980s to suggest a need to ensure that all sectors of society can have access to healthy natural environments.

transborder waste flows refer to the fact that waste that is generated in one nation is often transported to one or more other nations for disposal or recycling; it flows from the site of production to other parts of the world.

THE CONTEMPORARY CHALLENGE

Globally, the volume of waste is increasing. This is driven by global changes in the pattern of resource consumption linked to population growth, urbanisation and economic development (UNEP 2010). Global trends towards urbanisation in both developed and developing countries are particularly significant in driving increases in municipal solid waste. There are also strong links between the level of economic development and municipal solid waste generation with the greatest per capita volumes found in the wealthiest countries; around 2.2 kg per person per day in OECD countries (ibid.). As well as the increasing *volume* of waste we also need to note an increasing *complexity* of materials used in manufactured goods that are now entering the waste stream. The fastest growing waste stream in both developed and developing countries is composed of electronic products or parts which, in turn, include some materials that are hazardous to humans or the environment (ibid.).

Increasing levels of consumption are also responsible for depleting and degrading natural resources worldwide. In mining, for example, the global trend towards ever increasing levels of production is compounded by increasing reliance on lower-quality ore bodies. As rich ore bodies are depleted mining operations are shifting from underground towards large open-cut mines that involve significant earth moving operations and big environmental rehabilitation challenges. According to environmental engineer, Gavin Mudd,[2] 'it is the environmental cost which will, in the medium to longer term, govern the real availability of metals and minerals'.

Food and Agriculture Organization (FAO) is a UN agency that was mooted at a conference held in 1943 and formally established in 1945. Its main aim is to reduce global hunger and malnutrition and its headquarters are in Rome.

Increasing global food production and consumption is also causing a depletion of natural resources. A recent report on food waste by the United Nations **Food and Agriculture Organization** (Gustavsson *et al.* 2011) highlighted a global trend towards the consumption of more resource-intensive foods and increasing amounts of wasted food in affluent countries. Paradoxically, food waste exacerbates the global problem of food security because resources are being depleted while global food distribution is inequitable. In 2011, the UN Food and Agriculture Organization estimated that 1.3 billion tonnes of food – approximately one-third of all food produced – was wasted at some point in the food supply chain stretching from the farm to the household (ibid.). On a per capita basis, significantly more food is wasted in the industrialised countries than in developing countries and much of this waste occurs at the consumption stage, in both retail outlets and in households.

Not only is the global volume of waste increasing, it is also becoming more globally mobile. Of particular concern is the flow of hazardous wastes from developed to developing countries where labour is cheap and regulatory protections for public environment and health less restrictive. While much attention has focused on the transborder flows of electronic waste, Crang *et al.* (2012) show that a vast array of waste products – ranging from rags to giant ships – end up in developing nations.

A BROAD UNDERSTANDING OF VALUE

Economics tends to dominate our thinking on how we might give value to things that are currently dismissed as waste. Yet the economics of reuse and recycling only partially explains changing attitudes to waste. Most people living in high-consumption societies are aware that earlier generations experienced times when thrift was the order of the day and we know that goods which are readily dismissed as waste in developed nations are often seen as valuable resources in poorer nations. The economics of supply, demand, utility and price help to explain such differences in attitude or perception. However, we also know that value is influenced by social or cultural beliefs and practices. For examples, attitudes may vary from one society to another, or from one time to another, on the value ascribed to old or 'antique' furniture; just as attitudes may vary on the value of particular building materials, foodstuffs or types of clothing. As discussed in Chapter 3, fashions are commonly driven by the marketing of economic goods and services through the 'generation of desire'. Yet, value can also relate to deep cultural beliefs about what is good, beautiful, or morally appropriate. While the globalisation of economic production is creating more common ground in relation to consumption, religious and cultural differences will continue to have a significant influence on value.

It is interesting here to contemplate the interplay between utility and aesthetics because some industrial designers (e.g. McDonough and Braungart 2002) are arguing that a growing need to reduce waste will increase the value attributed to products that are highly efficient and resourceful. The argument here is that aesthetics will change over time so that waste reduction comes to be equated with beauty and the argument is supported by growing interest in art that works with used goods and materials. To date this can best be described as a 'niche aesthetic' arising in the developed world and the prediction is rather speculative. However, it serves to remind us that attitudes to waste are probably more changeable than most people imagine.

From a social and cultural perspective waste might be defined as anything that is no longer valued by the communities in which it is circulating and we have noted that values can change over time. In historic terms, urbanisation has shifted the values that people ascribe to particular goods and services because urban and rural ways of living are very different to each other. As mentioned above, economic globalisation is also eroding some cultural differences in regard to values reflected in consumption. Shifting attitudes to waste will be explored later in this chapter. However, it is important to note here that while globalisation may have eroded some cultural differences it has probably increased the global gap in terms of the things that people can access and use. This, in turn, influences value in ways that are only partially reflected in economic indicators such as price and demand.

FOCUSING ON MATERIAL FLOWS

material flows refers to the fact that materials which constitute the raw materials or component parts for a product commonly travel a considerable distance before and after they are contained within that particular product.

While value cannot be reduced to economic considerations alone, it is clear that new ways to value waste economically will increase recycling and reduce long-term depletion of resources, materials and energy. Indeed some scholars have argued that the global trends, discussed above, ensure that the question of waste has become so central to the future of our economic systems that we need to rethink its role as constitutive of industrial organisation rather than simply the discarded elements.[3] This is not entirely new because the reprocessing of industrial by-products played a critical role in the development of industrial capitalism in the nineteenth century, particularly in Europe and North America. Industrialisation led to the emergence of industrial cities and hubs, partly because the co-location of different industries facilitated the use of waste from one industry as a resource for another.[4] At the same time, nineteenth-century industrialisation – particularly in the UK – emerged under conditions of minimal government regulation of working and living conditions and factory workers were forced to live and work in heavily polluted and degraded environments. Innovation may have been driven by the self-interest of the factory owners to maximise material flows for economic gain, drawing on the valuable 'resource' of a low-paid and dispensable labour force. However, neither human nor environmental health figured in their calculations.

Location continues to be a factor for turning waste materials into an economic resource. However, we have already noted that global trade is leading to a kind of swap in which resources and raw materials tend to flow from poor nations to the 'developed' ones while waste materials are flowing more freely in the other direction.[5] So while the proponents of intensified recycling have argued for the co-location of industries within 'eco-industrial' parks in order to maximise the transformation of waste into resource in a new kind of 'industrial symbiosis',[6] global waste flows are making this harder to achieve. While new and efficient industrial precincts have been established in some countries – especially in northern Europe – consumption is favouring cheap goods produced by cheap labour in relatively remote locations.

Co-location has taken a different form in East Asia where co-located industries are sucking in global flows of waste materials for 'reprocessing' rather than focus on the possibilities for local exchange (Crang *et al.* 2012). In contrast to the 'eco-industrial park' model, such industrial estates are located in regions and nations that have low standards in regard to labour market regulation or the protection of public and environmental health and the living and working conditions resemble those of nineteenth-century Europe. The sheer scale of production taking place in such industrial estates allows for innovation in design and manufacture but this comes at considerable cost to both people and the environment. The factory workers – both men and women – work long hours for low pay while others eke out a living by sifting and sorting discarded materials within the rising, co-located, dumpsites.

informal waste retrieval refers to the fact that waste materials are more commonly recycled in poor nations than in the developed world; however, the modes of exchange may be informal in the sense that they are not regulated and may not be mediated by the exchange of money.

TRACING GLOBAL WASTE FLOWS

The global trade in waste materials has long been identified as a problem and the 1992 Basel Convention on the Control of Transboundary Movements of Hazardous Waste has sought to impose new forms of international governance and control. Efforts have also been made to encourage people and organisations to use life cycle assessments to find out what can happen to things that might be discarded at the level of a household or enterprise (see Chapter 11). However, the global trade in waste is very difficult to monitor or regulate because it can involve long chains of movement and exchange in which many forms of '**informal**' or illegal activity intervene. A householder may take great care in the initial disposal of something discarded – perhaps making it a donation to a charity organisation – yet it may then enter a new commodity chain for recycled resources or materials that is profit driven and it may end up far from where it was intended.

global commodity networks refers to the fact that commodities can pass through many hands during processes of production, consumption and disposal. They enter into global networks of exchange.

Unlike flows of new goods and materials that tend to be dominated by large transnational firms, **global commodity networks** for used goods and materials are more likely to be brokered by multiple actors and appear to be much more volatile (Crang *et al.* 2012). Many things will influence the global flow of waste materials, such as different regimes for regulation or taxation. However Crang *et al.* have demonstrated that it can come down to a simple matter of categorisation, noting that the fate of used clothes imported into India will depend on whether they are categorised as clothes or rags. International trade in used clothing is restricted by trade protection laws designed to promote local manufacturing industries, however 'rags' can be processed and respun into new fabric.

waste recycling industries arise when waste retrieval becomes a formal business.

Electronic goods and materials make up the fastest growing waste stream in the world. Even more worrying is that the pathways of movement are particularly complex because electronic goods require a range of raw materials drawn from many different parts of the world and discarded products can be reprocessed and re-entered into the flow. Electronic goods and materials discarded in the developed world are more likely to be reprocessed in nations with low-paid workers and most of these nations are not signatories to the Basel Convention mentioned above. There has been an increasing flow of electronic 'waste' from more affluent developed countries to Asia, however these are not nearly as large as the waste flows between countries within the Asian region (Lepawsky and McNabb 2011). A large new industry, taking advantage of global waste flows, is arising alongside older, informal **waste recycling** practices. While the expanded industry is raising concerns about its impact on the environment and the health of those who work in largely unregulated reprocessing sites, it has become an important source of livelihood for many and it reduces the volumes of particular global **waste streams**.

waste streams has become a popular term in waste management literature because it highlights the fact that waste comes in different forms which are segregated into different pathways for disposal or treatment. The term indicates that waste does not simply disappear at the point of disposal but can enter into the dynamics of various natural systems.

e-waste is a short-hand term being used widely because the volume of electronic waste materials has grown so rapidly and alarmingly in recent decades.

The electronic waste industry in Bangladesh

Bangladesh is a destination for exports of waste electronics or '**e-waste**' from many other countries, both within the Asian region and beyond (see Figure 16.1). Bangladesh is also home to a wide range of recycling and 'reprocessing' enterprises with a recent study showing that an incredible 83 per cent of plastic waste generated daily in Dhaka is recovered and reprocessed. Approximately 200,000 people are employed in the recovery economy in Dhaka alone, and around 60,000 of these in the reprocessing of waste electronics. However, a closer look at how value is captured and profits generated highlights an extremely stratified labour force involving both formal and informal employment practices. As objects are moved from wholesalers/importers to dismantlers, they are disaggregated into their constituent materials through labour intensive activities. Table 16.1 highlights the gendered and aged divisions of labour across the sector, with the most exploitative practices occurring in the dismantling businesses which extract profit by exploiting the labour of women and children, the lowest-paid workers in the sector.

Much of the electronic waste imported into Bangladesh comes through Singapore, a key port for global trade generally, but also itself an affluent nation that generates significant quantities of electronic waste. Typically this trade is brokered by Bangladeshi importers operating in Singapore. While Singapore is a signatory to the Basel Convention, exemptions exist for materials identified as destined for 'direct reuse' or which pass tests for flammability and toxicity. Other provisions under the Basel Convention allow bilateral and multilateral trade agreements that permit hazardous waste shipments where they are 'environmentally sound' although this criterion appears open to interpretation. After importation, there are at least five pathways within Bangladesh that waste electronics may follow to recover value through extraction of materials and/or produce new forms of value as shown in Table 16.1. However, any one reprocessing business may be involved in more than one of these conduits. Lepawsky and Billah (2011) estimate that the lifespan of electronic items in Bangladesh may be double or even triple that of equivalent items in North America.

Table 16.1 Activities involved in revaluing waste electronics in Bangladesh

Activity	*Labour*	*Source of value*
Resale	No additional labour input.	Difference between purchase price and sale price.
Refurbishing	Activities that bring non-working items back into working condition, e.g. by replacing damaged components with ones salvaged from other items. Unused materials then sold to dismantlers.	Add value through labour. Sale of refurbished items domestically and internationally.

Activity	*Labour*	*Source of value*
Remanufacturing	Involves a range of innovative activities that repurpose waste electronics into different commodities in the electronics sector, e.g. CRT monitors converted to low-cost TVs and video game monitors.	Add value through labour. Sale of repurposed electronic items domestically.
Repair	Use of components from waste electronics for repair of domestic items.	Add value through labour. Fee for repair of damaged items.
Dismantling	Break apart, sort and clean items to separate useable from non-useable component parts and materials such as glass, plastics and metals. Women and children employed in this activity at the lowest rate of pay for the whole industry.	Sale of parts to domestic remanufacturing businesses, repair shops or refurbishing businesses. Sale of constituent materials to domestic manufacturing industry and as exports to regional markets such as China.

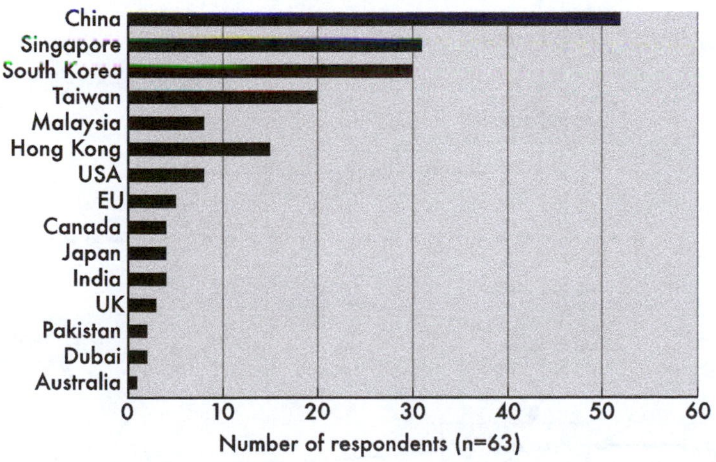

Figure 16.1 Sources of electronic waste being reprocessed in Bangladesh
Source: Lepawsky and Billah (2011)

TRANSITIONING FROM WASTE TO RESOURCE IN DEVELOPED NATIONS

Up until the 1990s the dominant mode of waste management in affluent countries has been disposal, either in the form of landfill or by incineration. However, since the 1990s there has been a new focus on promotion of resource recovery (Watson *et al.* 2008). In part, this has been driven by rising concerns about both human health and environmental pollution, although there can also be economic benefits from shifting to a more resource efficient materials economy. The key principle has been to shift from linear to circular flows, as illustrated in Figure 16.2.

industrial ecology is used to refer to the study of material and energy flows through industrial systems. The term was coined in 1989.

The rationale for the waste as resource paradigm draws on the '**industrial ecology**' discourse mentioned earlier, which seeks an integrated approach to more environmentally efficient use of resources.[7] Industrial ecology is so named because it applies the notion of ecological flows (see Chapter 9) to trace the flows of both materials and energy within the 'ecosystems' of industrial production and distribution. The analogy has been extended to talk about 'symbiosis' and the 'metabolism' of industrial processes (Graedel and Allenby 2003). Industrial material flows are represented as inputs, throughputs and outputs; each of which have different levels of environmental impact that can be measured through life

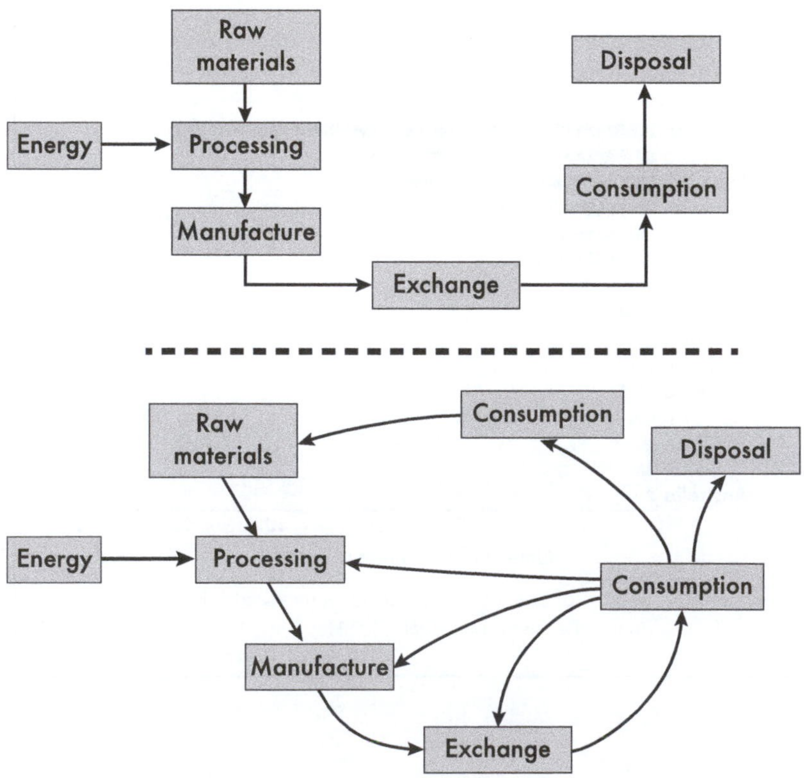

Figure 16.2 From linear flows to cycles
Source: Watson *et al.* (2008: 488–90)

cycle assessment techniques (ibid.). This has given rise to the idea of a waste management hierarchy.

Within developed nations, waste is commonly categorised in terms of three different waste streams – municipal waste, construction waste and hazardous waste – with different regimes of regulation and management applying to each stream. However, such a focus on waste streams is a downstream approach that pays little attention to the generation of waste connected with rising trends in consumption. Considerable progress has been made in linking waste back into production and multinational businesses have arisen within bulk recycling of paper, glass, plastics and metals. However, this is the easy part of the challenge because there is clear economic benefit in the efficient use of resources. The volume of waste streams can certainly be reduced by increasing recycling and by introducing more efficient production and distribution processes. However, increasing global consumption, linked with the globalisation of production, means that a *reduction* in production will eventually be needed to reduce the volume of global waste streams and this is a reality that few corporations or governments are willing to embrace. Reducing the volume of waste streams by reducing the volume of production is a difficult challenge for market-oriented economies (Watson and Lane 2011). Yet this is a challenge that must eventually be faced.

FROM REPROCESSING TO INCREASING THE LIFESPAN OF GOODS

Governments can use a combination of regulation and economic incentives to turn waste into resources and to reduce the generation of waste. As discussed above, the easiest strategy for governments to adopt in market-oriented economies is to turn waste materials back into production. Much less has been achieved in terms of moving up the hierarchy of waste from materials recycling to reuse of manufactured goods.[8] Obviously reuse – rather than materials recycling – is more common in the poorer nations of the world and in the developed world a range of welfare organisations and businesses have established a trade in reclaiming, reconditioning and retailing used clothes, furniture and household goods. However, this latter trade struggles to compete with the expanding trade in cheap mass produced new goods and there is an ongoing cultural problem in shifting public attitudes on the value of used goods.

The trade in used goods has been facilitated by the emergence of electronic trading outlets such as eBay. Most such operations have a commercial interest,

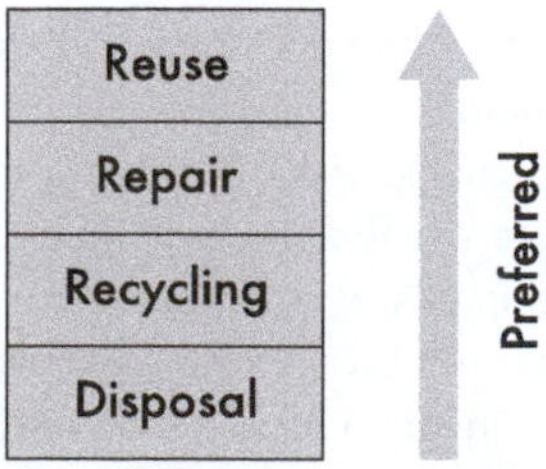

Figure 16.3 Waste hierarchy

but there are some such networks that specialise in the gifting of unwanted goods for those in need (Lane *et al.* 2009). Online networks can also help people get information on how to repair, maintain or adapt used goods and, as discussed in Chapter 3, new forms of 'collaborative consumption' are emerging. However, more could be done by governments to deliberately scale up such initiatives and to acknowledge that they make a contribution to economic activities that are not captured in a narrow index such as GDP.

In some parts of the world governments have achieved some success in getting industry associations to take more responsibility for managing the life cycle of what they produce. For example, the Australian Mobile Telephone Association has established a recycling programme for used phones called the Mobile Muster (Lane and Watson 2012) while the European Union has introduced a number of mandatory 'product stewardship' schemes, starting with an obligations imposed in 1994 in relation to packaging and dealing with packaging waste.

European Union directives have subsequently imposed new responsibilities on the manufacturers of motor vehicles (2000), waste electrical and electronic equipment (2002) and waste batteries and accumulators (2006). All these are now incorporated under Directive 2008/98/EC (Lane and Watson 2012). The emphasis is on holding producers responsible for the collection, sorting, treatment and recycling of their products once they have entered the post-consumer waste stream. In most cases, however, the reprocessing and materials recycling role is contracted out to third-party organisations that specialise in these operations and the costs of recycling are passed onto consumers through the purchase price of the goods concerned. There are few examples where either voluntary or mandatory product stewardship schemes have forced producers to take reuse, rather than recycling, seriously. However they do contribute to higher rates of materials recycling.

Food rescue

Food wastage has become a pressing concern for people with an interest in the sustainable use of natural resources and for people concerned about the global gap between the rich and the poor. A research report prepared for the Australian government (Mason *et al.* 2011) notes that much more can be done to reduce food waste before and after food products pass through the 'farm gate' but it is harder to recycle excess food once it has been prepared for consumption. Sharing cooked food within local communities is still a common practice in 'underdeveloped' nations but the practice has become less common in the developed world and a lot of edible food is entering the waste streams.

Concern about the dumping of edible food has prompted the formation of specialist food rescue organisations in a wide range of countries. In Australia alone, four impressive organisations – Foodbank, FareShare, SecondBite and OzHarvest – now operate nationally and there are similar organisations operating in other developed nations. The SecondBite organisation, for example, began as a one-person operation in 2005 but by 2013 it was operating with a staff of 100 and 600 volunteers. In 2012 it managed to rescue and recycle three million kilograms of food that would have been dumped. Food rescue organisations aim to deliver the 'surplus' food to people who might otherwise go hungry.

It is estimated that nearly 50 million people in the USA depend on government-issued 'food stamps' to put food on their table and that number has been rising steadily in recent years. The lack of a strong welfare system also means that many poor people in the USA resort to '**dumpster diving**' to collect food that is headed for the tip. Dumpster diving – known as 'skipping' in the UK – is now being promoted as an ethical practice by community groups and organisations that are simply appalled by the extent of waste. It has now reached the point where many supermarkets are willing to cooperate with 'dumpster divers' to ensure that edible food is rescued rather than dumped.

dumpster diving refers to the practice of sifting through commercial or residential waste to find useable items that have been discarded. Dumpster is a term used in North America for large waste containers and it is equivalent to the term 'skip' in the UK. 'Dumpster diving' is being used in countries that have not previously used the word dumpster.

Discussion questions

1 What are some of the factors causing an increase in the volume and complexity of global waste flows?
2 What is the difference between recycling and extending the lifespan of material goods? Which is preferable from an environmental perspective and why?
3 What are some key differences between relatively rich and poor nations on attitudes and practices relating to waste disposal?
4 What are the different pathways for revaluing electronic waste in Bangladesh?
5 What are the most promising strategies for reducing global volumes of waste streams?
6 What lessons can be drawn from historic shifts in perception and attitudes towards waste?
7 What will it take to shift attitudes to waste in developed nations?

KEY READINGS

Crang, Mike, Alex Hughes, Nicky Gregson, Lucy Norris and Farid Ahamed (2012) 'Rethinking Governance and Value in Commodity Chains through Global Recycling Networks', *Transactions of the Institute of British Geographers*, 38(1): 12–24.

Hawkins, Gay (2006) *The Ethics of Waste: How We Relate to Rubbish*, Sydney: University of New South Wales Press.

Lane, Ruth and Matt Watson (2012) 'Stewardship of Things: The Radical Potential of Product Stewardship for Re-framing Responsibilities and Relationships to Products and Materials', *Geoforum*, 43(6): 1254–65.

Lepawsky, Josh and Mostaem Billah (2011) 'Making Chains that (Un)make Things: Waste–Value Relations and the Bangladeshi Rubbish Electronics Industry', *Geografiska Annaler: Series B, Human Geography*, 93(2): 121–39.

Prior, Tim, Damien Giurco, Gavin Mudd, Leah Mason and Johannes Bebhrisch (2012) 'Resource Depletion, Peak Minerals and the Implications for Sustainable Resource Management', *Global Environmental Change*, 22(3): 577–87.

Strasser, Susan (1999) *Waste and Want: A Social History of Trash*, New York: Henry Holt.

United Nations Environment Program (2010) *Global Partnership on Waste Management* (GPWM) Framework Document (www.unep.org/gpwm/Background/tabid/56401/Default.aspx).

thematic essay

Shifting perceptions, beliefs and practices

Over time, concerns about waste have fluctuated between a preoccupation with dirt, sanitation and hygiene on the one hand and wastefulness in the use of scarce resources on the other.[9] With the advent of industrialisation and urbanisation, the scale of waste generation – and potential recycling – has changed dramatically from locally contained systems to uncontained global distribution. Of course, the time frame for this trajectory has varied between countries but the trend is the same. Where waste could once be managed locally within households or villages, now significant logistical systems are required to collect and transport waste materials from the site of generation to the site of disposal or processing, usually located on the outer fringe of cities. Some waste materials are moved globally because materials discarded in one country may have economic value based on reuse or recycling in another.

Historical studies of waste and recycling in the UK and the USA highlight key periods where there has been a shift in thinking about waste as something to be disposed of towards thinking about it as a potential resource. In the UK, for much of the nineteenth century it was common practice for domestic refuse to be collected by scavengers or 'dustmen' and taken to 'dust-yards' for reprocessing (Cooper 2008). However, by 1914 recycling was declining in the UK due to an emerging emphasis on public hygiene and the availability of incinerator technology. This trend was partly reversed between 1914 and 1945 due to wartime imperatives to use resources efficiently in the face of restrictions on international trade. Wartime governments required local authorities to implement stricter recycling measures and promoted thrift and recycling at the household scale as a patriotic obligation (ibid.).

A somewhat different story has been documented for the USA in the late nineteenth century where the rise of mass production and mass distribution systems brought about rapid changes in daily life (Strasser 1999). While recycling and remanufacturing of household discards had been a critical element within certain manufacturing industries, by the end of the century this two-way trade had given way to dominance by specialised wholesalers and waste dealers whose main business was based on processing industrial waste (ibid.: 108–9). As in the UK, the Second World War prompted US governments to promote recycling at the household level and to call for donations of scrap metal and other materials that could be reprocessed within wartime industries. However, the end of the war brought an end to the era of thrift in the USA and increasing mass production of consumer goods led to increased levels of packaging and disposability. Planned obsolescence became more prevalent and this precipitated some of the first scholarly critiques of consumerism. For example, Vance Packard's book *The Waste Makers* (1960), brought this critique to a wider public audience and this, in turn, triggered further debates about consumption and waste (Strasser 1999: 278).

Countries occupying a different position in relation to global capitalist markets followed a different kind of trajectory. For example, Hungary – one of the nations in Europe's 'eastern bloc' that turned to communism in the wake of the Second World War – has passed through three distinct waste management transitions; starting with a centrally controlled, state-run system, which gave way in the 1980s to systems driven by the capitalist economics of profit (Gille 2010). The latter was accompanied by a steady increase in the involvement of non-Hungarian organisations and interests. Gille describes the first stage – running from 1948 to 1974 – as the 'Metallic regime', characterised by an emphasis on the recovery of metals for the benefit of a closed economy in which the state was able to establish 'a vast infrastructure that collected, redistributed and ordered the reuse both of production and of consumer wastes' (ibid.: 1056). During this phase, official rhetoric was based on the assumption that all waste is infinitely recyclable or reuseable. Public discourse around potential exposure to toxins and pollutants was not permitted. The period from 1970–1985 is described as an 'Efficiency regime' in which waste is characterised in official rhetoric as a cost on production and the focus has shifted to waste reduction and reuse as steps to increase efficiency (ibid.: 1057). The current period – from 1985 to the present – is described as the 'Chemical-waste regime' in which the emphasis has shifted to end-of-pipe chemically induced liquidation of waste materials, facilitated by the privatisation of waste management services and importation of waste-treatment technologies from the west.

This brief review of historical experience in different countries shows how government policy and public rhetoric have changed over time, in response to political and economic circumstances, and indicates the potential for further change in response to future circumstances. There are some signs that urban waste mining could become one approach to sourcing rare metals for future manufacturing. However, we can also see that contemporary debates and discourses around the need to reduce waste and recycle materials are little more than a reframing of old themes, even if the scale of waste generation and the global movement of waste materials have both increased substantially. Contemporary waste governance discourses in developed countries are more strongly focused on the need for greater materials efficiency than reducing consumption, and they tend to emphasise individual responsibility for ensuring the 'public good' benefits of recycling. As with the patriotic imperatives for recycling during times of war, there is a strong moral injunction to contemporary recycling (Hawkins 2006). This new/old ethic has been internalised by many householders in affluent countries who even go beyond the waste management systems provided by government agencies to implement their own stewardship practices for reusing and recycling goods and materials within their homes and neighbourhoods[10] (Lane *et al.* 2009; Lane and Watson 2012). Studies of household practices, including scavenging bulky waste or hard rubbish collections, indicate that clothing, furniture and children's toys circulate extensively through informal networks of reuse, often involving investment in repair and maintenance. By extending the use of existing products, the rate of consumption of new goods is potentially slowed.

The act of putting out the garbage in many countries is now governed by new sets of social norms that combine with regulatory structures and infrastructure to promote what might be described as a 'new regime of waste management'; aimed at capturing waste as a resource. However, the question remains as to whether or not improvements in materials efficiency effectively challenge the overall rate of consumption of resources, or simply allow more products to be produced with the same amount of resources (Christoff 2009). According to many critics, the real problem is to be found in growth-oriented capitalist economic systems that promote ever-increasing and unsustainable levels of consumption.

NOTES

1 See, for example, Heinberg (2007); Prior *et al.* (2012).
2 Mudd (2010: 114).
3 O'Brien (2007).
4 See, for example, Cooper (2008); Desrochers (2009).
5 Moore (2012); Crang *et al.* (2012).
6 Ehrenfeld and Gertler (1997); Gibbs and Deutz (2007).
7 See, for example, Mol and Spaargaren (2006); Deutz (2009).
8 Deutz (2009).
9 Strasser (1999); Gille (2007); Cooper (2008).
10 Lane *et al.* (2009), Lane and Watson (2012). In 2012, the Australian Bureau of Statistics reported that 73 per cent of Australian households reused at least one type of item in the home, most commonly plastic bottles or containers and plastic bags.

Glossary

acceptable and unacceptable risk is a distinction commonly made in risk management literature; however, cultural beliefs play a big role in determining socially acceptable levels of risk.

addictive consumption is a widely used term that was given particular meaning by one-time chemical engineer John Ehrenfeld, who retired from academic life in 2000 and went on to become the executive director of the International Society for Industrial Ecology.

Ahern, Professor Jack from landscape architecture at the University of Massachusetts has promoted the concept of 'multiscale networks and connectivity' in a series of publications and lectures since 2011 under the title 'Safe-to-fail'.

Arendt, Hannah (1906–75) was born into a secular Jewish family in Hanover. She studied philosophy at the University of Marburg where she had a romantic relationship with her teacher and mentor Martin Heidegger. She left Germany for Czechoslovakia in 1933 and lived for a while in Paris where she worked with Jewish refugees from the Nazi regime which stripped her of her German citizenship in 1937. She moved to New York in 1941 where she worked as a leading political theorist until her death in 1975. She came to public attention when she covered the 1963 trial of former Nazi functionary Adolf Eichmann in Jerusalem for *The New Yorker* magazine.

atmosphere refers to the layer of gases that surrounds the planet.

balance sheet of project costings normally refers to a concise presentation, usually in table form, of anticipated financial costs and incomes. However, the notion of 'balance sheet' has been extended to refer to any cost–benefit analysis.

Beck, Ulrich was born in 1944 in a German province which became part of Poland at the end of the Second World War. He studied at the University of Munich where he went on to have a long and distinguished academic career. His work on the risk society was published in German in 1986 and in English in 1992.

Berry, Thomas and Brian Swimme Thomas Berry had had a long career in both western and Asian cultural and religious studies when he met Brian Swimme in 1982. He worked for 20 years as the Director of the Riversdale Centre for Religious Research and served as President of the American Teilhard Association (1975–87). Berry introduced Swimme to the work of French theologian and philosopher Teilhard de Chardin, while Swimme was able to bring his studies in mathematics and cosmology into their decade-long collaboration that resulted in the publication of *The Universe Story* (1992).

Bhutan's Gross National Happiness Index began as a casual remark by the nation's Dragon King Jigme Singye Wangchuk in 1972 when he said that 'gross national happiness' will be the best measure of the nation's attempt to modernise its economy. The idea was picked up by the nation's newly formed Centre for Bhutan Studies in 1999 and a mix of quantitative and qualitative measures have subsequently been used in the development of Bhutan's Five Year Plan.

biomimicry is a term that was coined by American nature writer Janine Benyus in a book with 'biomimicry' in its title (1997). It suggests strong benefits in learning directly from nature in designing products and processes.

bioregionalism was first promoted by environmental writer Peter Berg in the 1970s and advocated by writer/activist Kirkpatrick Sale in the 1980s. It suggests that the governance of human communities and societies needs to start with an awareness of natural systems which may be depicted with reference to watersheds, terrain and soil characteristics and dominant plant or animal communities.

biosphere is the term used to refer to the zone surrounding the planet in which living organisms can thrive. It extends from just below the surface of the planet to the part of the atmosphere which contains sufficient oxygen to sustain life.

Black Saturday refers to 7 February 2009, when temperatures of over 46°C and winds of over 120 kph combined to create fierce forest fires which destroyed 2,030 houses and claimed 173 lives in an area stretching from the edge of Melbourne to cover a range of small towns.

Blair government social inclusion agenda soon after being elected as UK Prime Minster in 1997, Tony Blair announced that his government would reduce poverty by focusing on factors which prevent some people and communities from participating fully in British society. He established a Social Exclusion Unit in his own office and continued to pursue a social inclusion agenda during his ten years as prime minister.

Blair Labour government came into being after the British elections of 1997 when Tony Blair became the youngest British prime minister since 1812. Initially seen as a breath of fresh air, the government lost popularity when it decided to support the US-led invasion of Iraq in 2003.

Bloch, Ernst (1885–1977) was the son of a Jewish railway worker who studied and taught philosophy before fleeing Germany to escape the Nazi regime in 1934. He lived in exile in the USA from 1938–48 where he worked on the manuscript for his epic work *The Principle of Hope.* As a committed Marxist he returned to East Germany (German Democratic Republic) in 1949 to take a position at the University of Leipzig. He fell out with the GDR regime over the Soviet invasion of Hungary in 1956 and was forced to resign his university position in 1957. He went to live in West Germany in 1962 where he actively supported the youth 'radicalisation' of the 1960s.

Boulding, Kenneth (1910–93) was born in England and educated at Oxford University before taking up US citizenship in 1948 to work as an economist at the

University of Michigan. As well as being a renowned economist he was a peace activist and a devout Quaker.

Bourdieu, Pierre (1930–2002) born of humble parents in southern France, Bourdieu carved out a career in philosophy, anthropology and sociology to become one of France's leading public intellectuals in his later life. His interest in anthropology – which stemmed from serving as a military conscript in Algeria in the 1950s – gave rise to his concept of 'habitus'. He initiated the argument that 'social' and 'cultural' capital are just as important as 'financial' capital for creating stronger societies.

brand power is the effective promotion of a product or service by focusing on its brand name; this has achieved 'global reach' in recent decades.

Brookings Institution is a Washington-based think-tank that specialises in social science research, especially in economics, urban planning, governance, foreign policy and global economy. It was formed in 1916.

Brown, Bob was born in 1944 in Oberon, NSW, where his father was a policeman. He became a medical doctor and worked in London before taking up a position as a GP in Launceston, Tasmania, in 1972. He fell in love with the Tasmanian wilderness and led the successful campaign to prevent the construction of a dam on the wild Franklin River in the early 1980s. He helped to establish the Wilderness Society in Australia and was elected to the Tasmanian parliament in 1983. He was elected to the Australian Senate in 1996 and became the first openly gay member of the Australian parliament.

Brundtland Report, the is the short name used for a report that emerged from the work of the World Commission on Environment and Development that was established by the United Nations in 1983.

Brundtland, Gro Harlem served three separate terms as Norwegian prime minister (1981; 1986–9; 1990–6). She was between her first two terms when she was asked by UNCED to oversee the production of the landmark report which was published by Oxford University Press in 1987 as *Our Common Future.*

business plan refers to the formal presentation of a set of goals that involves cost–benefit analysis and the reasons why the goals are achievable.

Carson, Rachel (1907–64) trained as a zoologist before becoming editor-in-chief of US Fish and Wildlife Service publications and a newspaper columnist. Before the publication of *Silent Spring* in 1962 her main publication was *The Sea Around Us* (1952).

Checkland, Peter was born in Birmingham in 1930 and originally trained as a chemist before working as a chemical engineer. He took up a position as 'professor of systems' at the University of Lancaster in the 1960s, where he developed the 'soft systems methodology' that is now in use globally.

Chernobyl nuclear plant disaster occurred in Ukraine on 26 April 1986, when a fire and explosion in a nuclear power plant killed 31 workers; it resulted in the release of radiation, affecting 500,000 people in and around Chernobyl, with radioactive particles being carried into Russia and across much of Europe.

Circles of Sustainability model was originally conceived by researchers at RMIT University in Melbourne as a four domains, rather than three sectors, model; it has been widely used in city planning in cities across the world.

climatology is a subset of atmospheric science and physical geography devoted to understanding the functioning of the Earth's climate systems.

coal seam gas refers to any deposits of gas trapped within coal seams. Efforts are increasing to tap into such deposits associated with coal seams which may not be big enough to support coal mining.

cocooning is a term that was probably coined by prominent New York-based futurist Faith Popcorn (born Faith Plotkin) in the 1990s. It refers to a tendency for people to spend more time inside their homes.

collaborative consumption refers to efforts to increase collaboration or cooperation in the purchase and consumption of goods and services; most commonly driven by the view that individual consumption is often wasteful and environmentally damaging.

communities of practice is a term coined by anthropologists Jean Lave and Étienne Wenger in 1991 to refer to the ways in which people learn particular crafts. However, it soon gained a much wider meaning and Wenger has said that it can refer to 'groups of people who share a concern or passion for something they do and learn how to do it better as they interact regularly'.

contingent valuation was first proposed in 1947 as a survey-based technique for estimating the value of non-market resources, such as benefits derived from preserving the natural environment.

coral bleaching refers to the loss of pigmented microscopic algae normally residing in coral colonies, caused by excessive heat or acidification of the sea.

cultural amenity is a term used to cover cultural facilities and the mix of cultural activities that take place in a particular area.

Daly, Herman was born in 1938 and as an academic economist he published the collection of writings *Toward a Steady-State Economy* in 1973. He worked in the World Bank (1988–94) before returning to academia. Between 1992 and 2008 he was honoured with a string of international awards for his lifetime of work on 'ecological economics'.

Darfur region war Darfur is a region that was incorporated into Sudan in 1916. War broke out in 2003 when the Sudan Liberation Movement/Army declared war on the government of Sudan over the treatment of non-Arabic communities in Darfur. A ceasefire was negotiated in 2010 and South Sudan became a separate country in 2011.

DDT (Dichlorodiphenyltrichloroethane) is a synthetic compound first produced by Swiss chemist Paul Muller in 1939. It was initially used to kill mosquitoes carrying malaria and parasites responsible for the spread of typhus during the Second World War, before being released commercially after the war for use in controlling pests in US agriculture.

deforestation refers to the removal of forests to make way for other forms of human land use.

Delanty, Gerard is Professor of Sociology and Social and Political Theory at the University of Sussex in England and editor of the *European Journal of Social Theory*. His work focuses on the implications of globalisation for the analysis of the social world.

desertification refers to a form of land degradation in which an area loses its natural reserves of water and existing forms of vegetation and wildlife.

discourse is a term used to refer to ongoing debates and dialogues on a particular topic. Contributions to a discourse can take many forms; from academic papers to public commentary and policy formulations.

Dryzek, John born in England and educated in England and Scotland before completing his Ph.D. in government and politics at the University of Maryland, near Washington, DC. He has been Head of the Department of Politics at both the University of Oregon and the University of Melbourne. He is currently Centenary Professor in the Centre for Deliberative Democracy and Global Governance at the University of Canberra.

dumpster diving refers to the practice of sifting through commercial or residential waste to find useable items that have been discarded. Dumpster is a term used in North America for large waste containers and it is equivalent to the term 'skip' in the UK. 'Dumpster diving' is being used in countries that have not previously used the word dumpster.

ecological flows is a term used in this book to refer to the movement of water, nutrients and other materials through local and global ecosystems.

ecology German biologist Ernst Haeckel coined the term *écologie* in 1866 but it takes its inspiration directly from the work of Charles Darwin on natural evolution. Although the term appealed to biologists, it struggled to establish itself as field of study until the 1920s and 1930s when Arthur Tansley, Charles Elton and Frederic Clements developed the core concepts and terminology that helped researchers make sense of complex natural systems.

ecosystem services is a term used in environmental management to refer to anything that can contributing to environmental wellbeing. It emerged from the field of 'ecological economics' as a way of ensuring that the benefits of healthy ecosystems can be factored in to all thinking about economic development.

Edinburgh's festival season occurs in August each year when a range of concurrent festivals are held; perhaps the most famous being the Edinburgh Comedy Festival.

Elkington, John (b. 1949) is an English planner and psychologist, turned sustainability consultant, who invented the 'triple bottom line' concept in 1994.

El Niño Southern Oscillation is the term used to describe fluctuations in ocean temperatures in equatorial region of the Pacific Ocean caused by the movement of warm ocean currents. El Niño refers to a relatively dry period while La Niña refers to a relatively wet period.

emergence the evolution of complex systems out of a multiplicity of interactions has intrigued philosophers since the time of Aristotle; however, its current meaning was captured well by economist Jeffrey Goldstein in 1999: 'the arising of novel and coherent structures, patterns and properties during the process of self-organization in complex systems'.

energy audits refer to surveys and analysis of energy flows for particular buildings and they are usually conducted in order to reduce energy supply requirements. They became popular after the global oil crisis of 1973.

energy generation refers to the creation or renewal of the ability to produce action.

Energy Return on Investment (EROI) is a measure of the inputs of energy required to generate energy, expressed as a ratio.

energy-driven complexity refers to the consumption of increasing amounts of energy to drive increasingly complex systems, such as modern food production systems.

entropy refers to the steady dissipation of energy across energy gradients.

environmental 'costs' include damage caused to natural systems by extraction and production processes; damage caused by the generation of streams of waste; and the less obvious costs resulting from the transport of raw materials, goods and waste.

Environmental Impact Assessment (EIA) refers to a study of all the possible environmental impacts of a proposed project to be carried out before the project begins. A requirement to conduct EIAs as a precondition for any new project was first enacted in the US National Environmental Policy Act of 1969 but the practice has now become widespread. The term Environmental Impact Statement (EIS) is often used to refer to the report of an EIA.

environmental justice is a term that emerged in the USA in the early 1980s to suggest a need to ensure that all sectors of society can have access to healthy natural environments.

Epicurus (341 BC–270 BC) was a Greek philosopher who was born in Samos, Greece. His philosophical writing focused on the pursuit of a tranquil life and he founded the Epicurean school of thought.

ethanol or ethyl alcohol – is a volatile and flammable alcohol that can be extracted from starches and sugars. It is the best known of a range of 'biofuels' which are fuels extracted from living organisms.

ethical consumption refers to a values-based approach to purchase and consumption which puts the onus on the consumer to exercise his or her choice wisely.

European Union Common Agricultural Policy (CAP) was first established in 1957 to build agricultural cooperation across Europe. Initially it focused on production but has recently focused on pricing mechanisms.

evidence-based policy was popularised by the UK Labour government led by Tony Blair in the late 1990s before being picked up by governments all over the world. It is based on the view that good policy needs to be based on rigorously researched 'objective' evidence.

e-waste is a short-hand term being used widely because the volume of electronic waste materials has grown so rapidly and alarmingly in recent decades.

Fair Trade the international fair trade movement was initiated by several Christian groups in the 1930s and 1940s before becoming part of a much bigger social movement in the 1960s. The movement was boosted by the introduction of fair trade certification in 1988. There are a number of international organisations involved in coordinating fair trade activities with the most prominent being Fairtrade International (www.fairtrade.net).

FAO Food Price Index is a measure of monthly changes in the international price expressed in terms of the average price of a basket of food commodities.

farmers' markets refers to markets at which food producers can sell the produce directly to the consumers. Although it is an ancient practice it has been consciously revived in recent times to reduce the distance between food production and consumption. There has been strong growth in new farmers' markets in the USA, Canada, the UK and Australia.

FEMA is the Federal Emergency Agency of the USA.

floodplain is the area adjacent to a river or stream from the banks of the channel to the base of enclosing valley walls.

Food and Agriculture Organization (FAO) is a UN agency that was mooted at a conference held in 1943 and formally established in 1945. Its main aim is to reduce global hunger and malnutrition and its headquarters are in Rome.

food miles refers to the distance travelled by food items or components from where they originated as agricultural products to where they are consumed as food products.

fossil fuels are fossilised plant material (hydrocarbons) that take the form of coal, oil and natural gas.

Fourier, Joseph (Jean-Baptiste) (1768–1830) was the son of a tailor who became an orphan at the age of nine. He was active in the French Revolution, jailed in the reign of terror and served in Napoleon's army before gaining distinction as a mathematician and physicist. He became famous for his work on heat transfers and he theorised the 'greenhouse effect' for Planet Earth in a paper published in 1824.

'fourth pillar' former circus strongman and founder of Circus Oz, Jon Hawkes wrote *The Fourth Pillar of Sustainability* for Australia's Cultural Development Network in 2001, which argued that 'cultured vitality' should be added to environmental, economic and social wellbeing as an indicator of sustainability. He has been pleasantly surprised by the enduring international interest in the rather low-profile publication.

fracking refers to the process of injecting water under high pressure into deep layers of shale rock in order to create fissures for release natural gas embedded in the rock into collecting wells.

functional diversity is a term used by ecologists, which refers to the level of diversity required by a biological community to make it resilient to disturbance or capable of change and adaptation.

Gaia in Greek mythology Gaia was the personification or primordial being of Earth, seen as being the mother of all. James Lovelock's way of thinking about the biosphere as a single living system came to be known as the 'Gaia hypothesis'.

Garmezy, Norman (1918–2009) was a clinical psychologist who turned from early work on schizophrenia to thinking in the 1950s about the 'protective factors' that might enable people to avoid mental illness. Having had an alcoholic mother and an absent father, and after serving in the US army during the Second World War he argued that resilience could be acquired. He was dubbed the 'grandfather of resilience theory' by *The New Yorker* magazine.

Geelong's Memory Bank was set up in July 2008 as part of a larger community art project called 'Connecting Identities'. It is a repository for a host of short 'digital stories' curated by film-maker Malcolm McKinnon.

General Agreement on Tariffs and Trade (GATT) is a multilateral agreement on the regulation of international trade that was first signed in 1947. In 1994 GATT became part of the World Trade Organization which set out to reduce international barriers to free trade.

gentrification is a term used to refer to the transformation of areas that were once clearly working class in character into areas that are better defined as being middle class.

Genuine Progress Indicator is a term that was coined by the US organisation Redefining Progress in 1995. The GPI is probably the most prominent attempt to develop an alternative to the narrow income-based GDP index. It draws on the work of a range of economists – including Herman Daly and Marilyn Waring – and appears to have been taken most seriously in Canada.

Georgescu-Roegen, Nicholas (1906–94) was born in Romania and educated in mathematics at Bucharest University. He won a scholarship to study in Paris and also spent time in London before returning to Bucharest University. He was professor of economics at Vanderbilt University in Nashville, Tennessee, where he mentored Herman Daly as a student.

Giddens, Anthony was born in London in 1936. He studied at the University of Hull, London School of Economics and King's College, Cambridge. He established his reputation as a leading sociologist in the 1970s with *Capitalism and Modern Social Theory* (1971) and *New Rules of Sociological Method* (1976).

global commodity networks refers to the fact that commodities can pass through many hands during processes of production, consumption and disposal. They enter into global networks of exchange.

Global Hunger Index is published annually by the Washington-based International Food Policy Research Institute. It combines data on undernourishment, child mortality, child 'wasting' and child 'stunting' due to malnutrition.

globalisation is often used to refer to the rise of an increasingly integrated global economy that has been taking shape since the 1980s. However, the term was probably coined by University of Aberdeen sociologist Roland Robertson in 1992, and he intended it to have a much wider meaning as the intensification of consciousness of the world as a whole.

Goodenough, Ursula (b. 1943) studied zoology at Columbia University before completing her Ph.D. at Harvard University in 1969. She was an associate professor in biology at Harvard before taking up a position at Washington University in 1978. Highly regarded for her textbooks in genetics, her 1998 book *The Sacred Depths of Nature* is considered to be the seminal text of the 'religious naturalism' movement.

Grand Renaissance Dam is under construction on the Blue Nile in Ethiopia, about 40 kilometres from its border with Sudan. When it is completed it will be the site of the biggest hydroelectricity power station in Africa.

green belt refers to an area of land within an urban area that is deliberately preserved in a natural or agricultural state. The idea of having a green 'belt' to encircle urban growth emerged in the UK in the 1930s.

greenhouse gases refers to a group of gases that have the ability to absorb and re-radiate solar energy. They include water vapour, ozone, carbon dioxide, methane and nitrous oxide, with the last three increasing in the upper atmosphere concentrations as a result of human activity.

Green Revolution refers to agricultural research and development that occurred between the late 1940s and late 1960s with the specific aim of increasing crop yields in countries where hunger is prevalent. It was led by US agricultural researchers and featured the use of synthetic fertilisers. The name was coined in 1968.

greenwashing is an adaptation of the term 'whitewashing' and it is used to refer to deceptive efforts made by producers of goods and services to convince consumers that their products have good or benign environmental impacts.

Greer, John Michael (b. 1962) a graduate of the University of Washington, Greer's prolific freelance writing and public commentary has focused on what he considers to be the impending collapse of industrial society. Although from a non-religious background he joined the Ancient Order of Druids in 995 and served as its American Grand Archdruid from 2003 to 2015.

Hansen, James was born in Iowa in 1941 and he gained his Ph.D. in physics from the University of Iowa in 1967. He was Head of the NASA Goddard Institute for Space Studies located in New York City (1981–2013).

Hawken, Paul was born in 1946 and as a teenager he followed in the footsteps of the famous US conservationist John Muir by roaming in the high Sierra Nevada range. Famous for suggesting that environmental awareness can bring about a deep and positive change in how we conceive and practise economic activity.

He established his reputation as an environmental writer with the 1983 book *The Next Economy*; his book *Blessed Unrest* (2007) was popularised by a series of public talks focusing on 'the great transformation'.

hazard exposure refers to human exposure to materials or processes that have a known potential to damage health or cause injury.

Hill, Stuart was born in England and educated in England and Canada. He worked at McGill University in Montreal before taking up the position of Foundation Chair in Social Ecology at the University of Western Sydney in 1996.

Holling, 'Buzz' (b. 1930) gained a Ph.D. at the University of British Colombia in 1957, and served in the Canadian Department of Forestry. His 1973 paper on 'Resilience and the stability of ecological systems' sparked much more interest than he could have imagined. He went on to become a pioneer of 'socio-ecological resilience', serving as the founding editor of the *Ecology and Society* journal.

Hubbert, M. King (1903–89) trained in geology, physics and mathematics at the University of Chicago where he received his Ph.D. in 1937. He worked for Shell Oil Company from 1943 to his retirement in 1964 and it was in 1956 that he made his prediction that oil production in the US would reach a peak around 1970.

Human Development Index was first proposed by Pakistani economist Mahbud ul Haq in 1990 as a way to add indicators related to health and education opportunities to the single index for per capita income. It was adopted by the United Nations in the early 1990s and uses data on life expectancy, education achievements and per capita income.

human labour replacement the age of oil led to the increasing use of machines to replace human labour in the production of food and other goods. Dependency on external sources of energy consequently grew.

human-induced climate change concern about the global warming effects of increasing emissions of CO_2 caused by human use of 'fossil fuels' have been expressed since 1824. Regular reports produced by the International Panel on Climate Change (IPCC) since 1990 have increased concerns about human-induced global climate change.

Hurricane Katrina hit the coast of Louisiana on 29 August 2005, breaking flood protection levees in New Orleans and resulting in around 1,800 deaths and the displacement of 250,000 people.

hydrosphere refers to the layer below and above the surface of the planet where bodies of water are found.

hyperconsumption is a term used to refer to excessive or non-functional consumption, which has been given particular meaning by French philosopher Gilles Lipovetsky in relation to historic trends in mass consumption.

hypoxia is a general term for low levels of oxygen; it is being used increasingly to refer to low levels of oxygen in bodies of water.

individualisation refers to the widespread observation that individual people are increasingly being expected to attend to their own needs and desires rather than look to the state, community or society.

industrial ecology is used to refer to the study of material and energy flows through industrial systems. The term was coined in 1989.

industrial farming refers to farming that relies on the intense use of machines and large-scale production processes.

informal settlement is used to refer to any settlement that has not been officially planned or sanctioned. It is considered to have less negative connotations than the word 'slum'.

informal waste retrieval refers to the fact that waste materials are more commonly recycled in poor nations than in the developed world; however, the modes of exchange may be informal in the sense that they are not regulated and may not be mediated by the exchange of money.

Intergovernmental Panel on Climate Change was formed in 1988 by two UN organisations – the World Meteorological Organization and the United Nations Environment Programme – to collate information from scientific studies of human-induced climate change. Its first report was published in 1990.

International Energy Agency is a Paris-based intergovernmental agency set up by the Organisation for Economic Co-operation and Development in 1974, following the global 'oil shock' of 1973.

International Union for the Conservation of Nature (IUCN) is an international organisation that fosters scientific research and supports the development of nature conservation projects globally. It was formed in 1948 and its headquarters are in Switzerland.

Jabodetabek is the name used for the greater Jakarta area. The name is an amalgamation of letters signifying the merging of five formerly separate municipalities and three regencies.

Jackson, Tim (b. 1957) first rose to prominence with work on 'preventative environmental management' after spending five years in the Stockholm Environmental Institute. This led to subsequent influential work on sustainable consumption. While he was serving as the Economics Commissioner on the UK Sustainable Development Commission he authored a rather controversial report that was subsequently published as *Prosperity Without Growth* (2009). As well as being professor of sustainable development at the University of Surrey he has won awards as the author of radio drama scripts performed on BBC radio.

Kelly, Petra (1947–92) was born in Bavaria and changed her name to Kelly when her mother married a US Army officer. She lived and studied in the USA (1959–70) where she was an admirer of Martin Luther King. She was one of the founders of the German Greens in 1979 and was in the German parliament (1985–90). She was shot dead by her partner, a fellow Greens politician and former army general, Gert Bastian in a murder-suicide.

keywords is a term introduced by cultural theorist Raymond Williams in 1976 to refer to words in the English language which have particular significance and enduring appeal.

Kyoto climate summit was a UN-sponsored gathering of government representatives held in the beautiful Japanese city of Kyoto in December 1997 aimed at reaching agreement on implementing the 1992 UN Framework Convention on Climate Change. Although the summit was boycotted by significant national governments – most notably that of the USA – it did agree on the Kyoto Protocol which had an initial commitment period from 2008 to 2012.

Ladakh is a region in northern India that lies between the Kunlun Range in the north and the Himalayan Range in the south. A rather remote area, it is known as the 'land of high passes'.

land use mix refers to any policy which seeks to maintain a diversity of land uses in a particular area, as distinct from segregated zoning.

Lave, Jean and Étienne Wenger are an unusual pairing in that Lave studied social anthropology at Harvard University before going to work at University of California Berkeley (UCB) while Geneva-born Wenger studied computer science before coming to work in that area at UCB. Lave and Wenger met in UCB's Institute for Research of Learning.

lithosphere refers to the outer crust of the rocky planet.

Mackenzie-Mohr, Douglas after *Time* magazine rated the first edition of *Fostering Sustainable Behaviour* (1999) as 'required reading' for anyone interested in sustainability, its lead author has risen to international prominence winning major awards in Canada and being cited in *The New York Times*.

Majone, Giandomenico was born in 1932 and educated in Italy and the USA, where he gained his Ph.D. in statistics in 1964. In 1986 he became Professor of Policy Analysis at the European University Institute in Florence.

Malthus, Thomas (1766–1834) was a prize-winning classics scholar at Cambridge University before taking his orders as an Anglican priest. He ended his career as a professor of political economy but it was his 1798 *An Essay on the Principles of Population* that has given him enduring fame. The essay – published six times between 1798 and 1826 – predicted that uncurtailed growth in human population worldwide would result in widespread famine, disease and conflict.

Margulis, Lynn was born in 1938 and gained her Ph.D. in botany at the University of California in Berkeley in 1963. She published her first theoretical work on the origins of symbiotic eukaryotic cells in 1966 while working as a young academic at the University of Boston in 1966 but she had to show fierce determination to continue this work against strong opposition. Eventually she was recognised for her role in shifting the focus of evolution to the emergence of symbiotic micro-organisms

Abraham Maslow (1908–70) born in Boston as the oldest child of immigrant parents, Maslow was deemed to be 'psychologically unstable' as a child. He studied both psychology and law and became famous for his 'hierarchy' of human needs in the 1960s.

Maslow's hierarchy of human needs was developed by the American psychologist in the 1960s. Although criticised for positing a rather inflexible relationship between diverse and intersecting needs, the concept of basic and 'higher' needs has stood the test of time.

Mason-Dixon Line was drawn up by Charles Mason and Jeremiah Dixon between 1763 and 1767 in order to resolve a border dispute between states to the north and south of the line. It has come to represent a deeper cultural divide between northern and southern states.

Massey, Doreen (1944–2016) was born in Manchester and spent much of her childhood in a council housing estate before going on to study at Oxford University and the University of Pennsylvania. She worked at the Centre for Environment Studies in London until it was closed by the Thatcher government in 1979. She went on to become a professor in geography at the Open University, retiring in 2009.

material flows refers to the fact that materials which constitute the raw materials or component parts for a product commonly travel a considerable distance before and after they are contained within that particular product.

Mathews, Freya established her reputation as an ecophilospher with the books *The Ecological Self* (1991) and *Ecology and Democracy* (1996). She was associate professor in philosophy at Melbourne's La Trobe University in 2008 and is a co-editor of the *PAN Philosophy, Activism and Nature* journal.

McDonough, William is an American architect and designer who teamed up with German industrial chemist and former Greenpeace activist **Michael Braungart** to write *Cradle to Cradle: Remaking the Way We Make Things* in 2002.

McKibben, Bill discovered a passion for journalism by becoming editor of the Harvard University student newspaper during his time at that prestigious university. He has combined his career as a freelance journalist with the position of Schumann Distinguished Scholar at the liberal arts Middlebury College in Vermont. He founded the climate change action organisation 350.org in 2007 and was called the 'world's best environmental journalist' by *Time Magazine* in 2009. In 2013 he won the international Gandhi Peace Prize.

Meadows, Donella (1941–2001) was a Harvard-trained biophysicist who taught systems dynamics alongside her husband Dennis at Massachusetts Institute of Technology (MIT). She was a member of the MIT team that undertook computer modelling for the famous *Limits to Growth* publication of the Club of Rome in 1972, with Donella named as the lead author. Shortly before she died she worked on a 30-year update of *Limits to Growth* by the same authors, which was published after her death, in 2004. She is primarily responsible for the leading 'primer' on systems thinking, published in 2008.

megacity is a term normally used for cities with more than 10 million people.

Merchant, Carolyn (b. 1936) is a well-known US-based science historian and environmental writer. Her books include *The Death of Nature* (1980), *Ecological Revolutions* (1989) and *Radical Ecology* (1992).

Millennium Development Goals (MDGs) are eight goals that were adopted at a special UN Millennium Summit held in New York in May 2000.

Millennium Ecosystem Assessment was called for by UN Secretary Kofi Annan in 2000 and the assessment report was finally issued in 2005.

Mistry, Rohinton was born into the minority Parsi-speaking Zoroastrian community of Mumbai. He emigrated to Canada in 1975 where he became a writer. His first two novels – *Such a Long Journey* (1991) and *A Fine Balance* (1995) – were both shortlisted for the prestigious international Booker Prize. His third novel, *Family Matters*, was published in 2002.

mitigation refers to attempts to reduce emissions of greenhouse gases, while climate change *adaptation* refers to action taken to adapt to the impacts of climate change.

modularity refers to the extent to which a system's components can be separated and recombined.

monocrop agriculture refers to the practice of growing a single crop in a large area, year after year.

Mundey, Jack was born in rural Queensland in 1929 before rising to prominence as the leader of the Builders Labourers Federation in Sydney in the 1960s. A member of the Communist Party of Australia he broke with trade union tradition to place a work ban on an area of bushland in a harbour-side suburb in Sydney before turning this practice into a series of 'green bans' aimed at protecting open spaces and natural heritage of the city. His ideas on combining environmental care with social justice in a 'red–green' coalition directly influenced Petra Kelly.

neo-Malthusian when Malthus's dire predictions of escalating crises did not materialise, he was widely dismissed as an alarmist and the term 'neo-Malthusian' was used to dismiss environmental writers of the 1960s and 1970s who raised new concerns about the sustainability of uncurtailed global population growth.

networks of actors/actor networks actor network theory – which is most prominently associated with the work of French sociologist Bruno Latour – goes beyond the concept of networks of human actors in that it sees a role for non-human components in such networks. However, it has deepened understanding of the behaviour of human networks.

nonpoint source pollution refers to pollution that cannot be traced to a single source. It contrasts with point-source pollution.

ocean currents can be caused by wind or by movement arising from density differences in water caused by differences in temperature or salinity.

organic farming refers to farming practices that consciously avoid using synthetic chemicals.

ozone hole refers to the annual thinning of the ozone layer over Antarctica. It was first reported in a scientific paper in the journal *Nature* in May 1985 and concern quickly arose that the 'hole' was getting incrementally larger each year. Chlorofluorocarbons (CFCs) stay in the upper atmosphere for a long time so it is hard to monitor the effectiveness of the CFC ban. However, reports published in 2013 suggested that the hole had been contained, with the 2012 manifestation being the smallest in ten years.

Paris climate summit (COP21) 2015, was the 21st meeting of the Conference of Parties to the UN Framework Convention on Climate Change and the 11th meeting of parties to the Kyoto Protocol. In contrast to the Kyoto summit of 1997, the USA and China were very active participants in the Paris summit.

Parks, Rosa (1913–2005) was born as Rosa McCauley in Alabama with both black American and Native American heritage. She suffered poor health as a child and was raised on a farm by her mother and maternal grandmother. She married NAACP member Raymond Parks in 1932 and was secretary of the Montgomery chapter of the NAACP when she triggered the bus boycott campaign in 1955.

Pearce, David (1941–2005) studied at both Oxford University and London School of Economics. He had a range of academic positions before beginning a long tenure at University College London, where he undertook his work in environmental economics. In 1989 he was appointed to the Global 500 Roll of Honour by the United Nations Environment Programme.

performance indicators are goals that are expressed as benchmarks against which actual performance can be measured.

permaculture refers to a holistic approach to the design of food producing gardens which aims to work with, rather than against, natural systems and flows. The term was coined by Australians David Holmgren and Bill Mollison in 1978; permaculture associations run training courses and offer certification for trained practitioners in many countries.

pesticide resistance refers to decreasing susceptibility of a pest population to a particular pesticide.

Petrini, Carlo (b. 1949) had been a political activist in Rome for many years before he got involved in food politics through the campaign to block the opening of an outlet of McDonald's hamburger chain near the city's famous Spanish Steps in the early 1980s. He initiated the formation of the Slow Food movement in Italy in 1986 and helped to write a manifesto for launching the international Slow Food movement in 1989.

Polanyi, Karl (1886–1964) was born in Vienna of Hungarian parents. His expertise covered economic history, economic anthropology, political economy and historical sociology. He gained a position at Columbia University, New York, in 1947 but after 1953 had to base himself in Canada after his wife was denied a visa to the USA because of her past as a communist.

Prigogine, Ilya (1917–2003) was born in Moscow just before the Russian Revolution. His family left Russia in 1921 to live first in Germany and then Belgium where Ilya became a professor of chemistry at Brussels University. He was awarded the Nobel Prize for Chemistry in 1977 for his work on 'dissipative structures' that maintain themselves in a 'far from equilibrium' state.

public policy and environmental policy public policy normally refers to policies made by government or semi-government authorities and agencies. Environmental policy refers to policies adopted by government agencies to project the natural environment but it also refers to policies adopted by private organisations to articulate their commitments to environmental protection.

ratings systems refers to comparisons made between different items, products, performances that indicate performance in relation to particular goals, such as minimal use of energy.

Regional Natural Parks (France) the first Parc Naturel Régional was set up in France in 1967, and by 2011 there were 45 of them covering 13 per cent of French territory with three million people living within their boundaries.

relocalisation refers to the suggestion that globalisation has gone too far and that people should seek to satisfy their needs and aspirations by turning more to the local context.

Repowering London is a not-for-profit organisation which aims to build on the success of the Brixton community power project to support and seek funding for similar projects in other parts of London.

renewable energy relates to using sources of energy that are in unlimited supply – such as solar power or wind energy – and which do not result in the emission of greenhouse gases.

Resilience Alliance was formed in 1999 at the instigation of 'Buzz' Holling to develop and promote the 'socio-ecological' model of resilience thinking. Based in Sweden, it publishes the influential *Ecology and Society* journal. Key figures have been Carl Folke and Lance Gunderson.

Rio+20 (2002) was a UN-sponsored summit held to mark the 20th anniversary of the 1992 Earth Summit. It had more government representatives but fewer heads of government present than the 1992 Summit and released a call to arms titled *The Future We Want*.

Rio Earth Summit (1992) was a gathering initiated by the United Nations Commission on Environment and Development for heads of state, other representatives of national governments and representatives of a wide range of international and national organisations. It attracted around 17,000 delegates.

risk exposure refers to human exposure to situations which may or may not damage health or cause injury.

RMIT University Globalism Research Centre was established in 1992, initially under the name Globalism Institute, to conduct research on sources of insecurity, community sustainability and globalisation and culture.

Rockefeller 100 Resilient Cities programme aims to encourage participating cities to address vulnerabilities to unexpected shocks (such as earthquakes or floods) and accumulating socio-economic stresses (such as high levels of unemployment). The programme began in 32 selected cities in late 2013 and reached the quota of 100 in May 2016.

Rose, Nikolas was born in London in 1947. Originally trained in biology, he studied political theory at London School of Economics. He has held senior academic positions at Goldsmiths College, University of London, London School of Economics and King's College, London. His sociological work is heavily influenced by the work of Michel Foucault.

Rutter, Michael was born in 1933 and he has been described as the 'father of child psychology' in the UK. He became professor at the Institute of Psychiatry at King's College, London, and has been a consultant psychiatrist at Maudsley Hospital since 1966.

Sachs, Wolfgang (b. 1946) holds degrees in sociology and theology from Munich University. He has worked in a range of universities in Germany and the USA and was a co-author of a highly regarded book on global development – *The Development Dictionary* – in 1992. He has worked at the Wuppertal Institute for Climate, Environment and Energy since 2009.

salinisation refers to increasing concentrations of water soluble salts in soil which can impede plant growth.

Salt, David is editor of *Decision Point*, the monthly magazine of the Environment Decisions Group at the Australian National University. He has created and produced magazines for ANU, CSIRO and Australian Geographic.

Santa Fe Institute in New Mexico was set up in 1984 by a diverse array of leading scientists including Nobel Prize-winning physicist Murray Gell-Mann. It aimed to share insights across scientific disciplines on the behaviour of complex systems in order to articulate a new 'complexity theory'.

Sarkissian, Wendy was born and educated in Canada but has spent most of her professional life in Australia. She has a master's-level qualification in English literature and town planning and a Ph.D. in environmental ethics. She has worked for 30 years as a social planning consultant in both North America and Australia.

scenario is defined by the *OECD* as a 'postulated sequence of development of events'.

scenarios mapping was initiated separately by the US military and by Shell Oil in the early 1970s to encourage contemplation of different scenarios that might evolve in the future and the particular challenges they might pose for those involved in the contemplation.

shale oil refers to the extraction of liquid hydrocarbons from shale rock; a different form of hydrocarbon to 'crude oil' or petroleum found in naturally occurring oil deposits.

Shell Oil has been working with future *scenarios* since the global oil crisis of 1973.

Social Ecology teaching and research programme at the University of Western Sydney emerged within the Agriculture School of what had been Australia's oldest agricultural college. In trying to respond to the complex needs of rural communities it adopted soft systems methodology and principles of community development.

Social Ecology model of sustainability reworks the 'triple bottom line/three sectors' model in order to bring the 'personal' into view. It was introduced into a Social Ecology teaching programme at the University of Western Sydney by Professor Stuart Hill in the late 1990s.

Social Impact Assessment emerged alongside EIA, arguably as a result of the 1969 US National Environmental Protection Act (NEPA). It is not easy to reach agreement on what constitutes good or bad social outcomes of any change and a lot of work has gone into negotiating key principles and 'variables' to be assessed for international SIA practice under the auspices of the International Association for Impact Assessment.

social inclusion became a policy orientation of the Blair Labour government after leader Tony Blair gave a famous speech titled 'Bringing Britain Together' in London in 1997. The government established a special Social Inclusion Unit. The government's ability to build a more inclusive society did not live up to Blair's rhetoric but the 'social inclusion agenda' had a significant influence on public policy in many other countries.

sociology of community the idea of community has divided western sociologists ever since Emile Durkheim criticised the seminal book on the topic by Ferdinand Tönnies in the early years of the twentieth century. There has never been a consensus on what community really means but a range of sociologists have argued that there has been a turn to community in a world of growing uncertainty.

Spaceship Earth was probably coined by US Ambassador to the UN, Adlai Stephenson, in a speech given at the UN in 1965, shortly before he died. It was made famous by Kenneth Boulding in 1966.

stakeholders are those who have a 'stake' or interest in a particular project or enterprise. The term was first used in the Stanford Research Institute in 1963.

Stern, Nicholas (b. 1946) is an Oxford- and Cambridge-educated economist who worked as a chief economist and senior vice president of the World Bank (2000–3) and as a government economics adviser (2003–7). His report on the economics of climate change was delivered to the UK government in October 2006.

Stevenson, Robert Louis (1850–94) is the author of some of the most popular classics of Scottish literature, including *Treasure Island, Kidnapped* and *The Strange Case of Dr Jekyll and Mr Hyde.* The son of devout Presbyterian parents, who expected their talented son to become a respected lawyer, Stevenson instead adopted a rather Bohemian lifestyle and made a name for himself as a travel writer.

Stiglitz, Joseph (b. 1943) is a Nobel Prize-winning economist at Columbia University in New York, who is well known for his criticism of free market fundamentalists. He has served as a chief economist and senior vice president at the World Bank.

streamwatch is a term used widely in Australia and to a lesser extent in the USA to refer to programmes aimed at monitoring water quality in streams.

sub-Saharan Africa refers to a band of countries – from Mauritania to Somalia – that are located south of the Saharan desert and north of sub-tropical forests and savannahs.

Sustainable Development Goals (SDGs) are a 2015 extension of the UN's 2000 Millennium Development Goals (MDGs) that are largely aimed to eradicate extreme poverty and disadvantage by 2015. Eight MDGs were expanded into 17 SDGs and they strongly reflect the principles outlined in the 1987 Brundtland Report.

Swimme, Brian *see* **Berry, Thomas**

Tainter, Joseph (b. 1949) was trained in anthropology at the University of California, Berkeley, before going on to become a professor in the Department of Environment and Society at Utah State University. His best-known work is *The Collapse of Complex Societies* (1990) which examined causes for the demise of several ancient societies.

Taleb, Nassim Nicholas was born in 1960 in Lebanon and educated in Paris. His extensive interests range from mathematical finance and risk engineering to various literary traditions. He lives in the USA where he has built a reputation as a talented and thought-provoking essayist.

Tansley, Arthur (1871–1955) was a student at University College London, Cambridge University and Oxford University who eventually taught botany at all three of these prestigious universities. He also spent a year studying psychology under Sigmund Freud in Vienna. Through his work on plant ecology he became an ardent conservationist.

tar sands (also known as 'oil sand') refers to loose sand that contains bitumen, which is a viscous form of petroleum.

tariffs are taxes imposed by a government on imports while *subsidies* refer to government support for domestic production.

the age of oil first coal and then oil have become the dominant source of energy for human systems since the Industrial Revolution in Europe. For two centuries, oil proved to be a readily available and cheap source of energy. However, the cost of accessing oil is steadily growing.

thermohaline circulation refers to ocean currents that are generated by differences in the density of sea water.

Thomashow, Mitchell was Chair of Environmental Studies at Antioch University New England (1976–2006). He left Antioch to take up the position of Director of Unity College Maine, and in 2011 he became Director of the Second Nature Presidential Fellows Program which aims to bring a comprehensive sustainability agenda to US colleges and universities.

Thoreau, Henry David (1817–62) was a US-based writer and philosopher who was influenced by the European Romantics and by the 'transcendentalist' school of philosophy established by his mentor Ralph Waldo Emerson. A skilled writer and public speaker, Thoreau created an enduring body of work on the joys of reconnecting with nature.

tight feedback refers to a close relationship between feedback received and the capacity of the system to adjust its performance accordingly.

tipping point a term taken from ecology, it refers to a point at which incremental changes trigger a major change in the system.

transborder pollution refers to any form of pollution that cannot be contained within national borders, or waste materials that are deliberately transported beyond the borders of the country in which they were generated.

transborder waste flows refers to the fact that waste that is generated in one nation is often transported to one or more other nations for disposal or recycling; it flows from the site of production to other parts of the world.

Transition Towns refers to an international network initiated in 2005 by UK-based permaculture designer Rob Hopkins; it aims to make particular towns or settlements much more self-sufficient in terms of energy use and food and water consumption.

triple bottom line suggests that conventional economic thinking on profit and loss needs to extend to a consideration of social and environmental outcomes of any activity or enterprise. Officially endorsed by the UN in 2007 it is sometimes referred to as People, Profit and Planet.

tsunami disaster, Sri Lanka refers to tsunami waves triggered by an undersea earthquake that occurred near Sumatra in Indonesia which travelled across the Indian Ocean to reach Sri Lanka and southern India (26 December 2004).

UN Population Division was established as a commission in 1946 and now operates as part of the Department of Economic and Social Affairs. Its key task is to produce regular demographic reports.

UNESCO emerged as an idea at a conference of national education ministers held in England in 1942. It was formalised at a UN-sponsored conference held in 1945 and by the end of 1946 it had the active support of 30 national governments.

United Nations Environment Programme was established in 1972 to promote environmental awareness and advocate for stronger environment protection policies internationally. It produces regular assessment reports and facilitates international negotiations and agreements. Its headquarters are in Nairobi.

urban form refers to the overall spatial arrangements in a city, taking into account built infrastructure and how it reflects the city's economic and social functioning.

urban heritage refers to historically significant urban buildings and infrastructure.

urban hinterlands refer to areas of land that are used to provide resources for the functioning of a city yet they are largely invisible to most city-dwellers.

urban periphery refers to the outer edges of a city, where expansion is commonly occurring. The term 'periurban' is used to refer to the zone in which urban expansion is putting pressure on earlier forms of land use.

urban sprawl refers to the tendency for cities to expand in size in a largely unplanned way.

urbanisation refers to the increasing proportion of people living in urban, rather than rural, areas.

valuation methods are techniques which aim to put a figure on values that are excluded from the dominant 'market value' framework. There is little consensus about the best approach.

Versailles, Louisiana is an area on the banks of the Mississippi River about 7 kilometres from the outer limits of New Orleans where there is a large community of Vietnamese Americans.

VicHealth is a government-funded health promotion agency in Victoria, Australia. Its innovative work has included the funding of community art work to foster social inclusion and personal wellbeing.

voluntary simplicity refers to efforts to live with less as a result of a conscious decision to avoid waste or complexity in life.

von Bertalanffy, Ludwig (1901–72) was born in Vienna and died in Buffalo, New York. Initially schooled at home he lived near a famous biologist, Paul Kammerer, who acted as a mentor. Von Bertalanffy began his university studies in philosophy and art history before turning to biology.

Wackernagel, Mathis was born in Switzerland in 1962. He gained his Ph.D. at the University of British Columbia in Vancouver (1994) and worked with his Ph.D. supervisor to develop the first Ecological Footprint Calculator. He is president of the Global Footprint Network.

Walker, Brian began his career in biology and ecology in Zimbabwe (then called Rhodesia) before completing his Ph.D. in plant ecology in Canada. He moved from South Africa to Australia in 1985 to take up the position of Chief of the Division of Wildlife and Ecology at the Commonwealth Scientific and Industrial Research Organisation (CSIRO) He has been active in the international Resilience Alliance.

waste recycling industries arise when waste retrieval becomes a formal business.

waste streams has become a popular term in waste management literature because it highlights the fact that waste comes in different forms which are segregated into different pathways for disposal or treatment. The term indicates that waste does not simply disappear at the point of disposal but can enter into the dynamics of various natural systems.

water table refers to the boundary between dry ground and ground that is saturated with water that has penetrated into the ground.

Wenger, Étienne *see* **Lave, Jean**

Wessels, Tom (b. 1951) is a terrestrial ecologist and professor of environmental studies at Antioch University in New England. His 2006 book on 'the myth of progress' was published in a second edition in 2013.

White, Gilbert (1720–93) was a rather obscure parson in an unremarkable English village before the publication of his lovingly written *Natural History and Antiquities of Selborne* in 1789. He is widely seen as the father of the 'natural history' movement in England and his work inspired many people, including a young Charles Darwin.

wicked problems is a term first coined by design theorist Horst Rittel at the University of California Berkeley (UCB) in the 1960s. Rittel collaborated with UCB urban planner Melvin Webber to develop the concept of wicked problems in regard to urban planning in a book published in 1973. The term is used to refer to complex problems that have no single, complete or trial-and-error solutions; problems which may emerge as symptoms of other complex problems.

World Bank poverty line The concept of a poverty line has been in use since the early twentieth century; in recent decades it has become popular to say that extreme poverty means people exist on less than $US1 a day. In 2006 the World Bank set the line for extreme poverty at $US1.25 a day on the estimate that this was equivalent in spending power to $US1 a day in 1996. While the World Bank draws a distinction between 'absolute' and 'relative' poverty the arbitrary poverty line adopted in 2006 has been a focus of attention.

Worldwatch Institute is an environmental research organisation in Washington, DC, founded by Lester Brown in 1974 and famous for producing an annual *State of the World* report since 1984.

Wright brothers Wilbur (1867–1912) and Orville (1871–1948) turned from manufacturing bicycles to the construction of a 'flying machine'. In 1903 they became the first humans to test the theory of flight in a heavier-than-air machine first imagined by Leonardo da Vinci 400 years earlier. They subsequently developed systems that would enable pilots to control such machines in flight.

Wuppertal Institute for Climate, Environment and Energy is an independent research centre that works with a number of German universities. Wuppertal is located in the Wupper Valley not far from the large city of Dusseldorf; the institute was set up in 1991.

Bibliography

Abram, David (1996) *The Spell of the Sensuous: Perception and Language in a More-Than-Human World*, New York: Vintage.

Adger, W. Neil and Katrina Brown (2009) 'Vulnerability and Resilience to Environmental Change: Ecological and Social Perspectives', in Noel Castree, David Demeritt and Diana Liverman (eds), *A Companion to Environmental Geography*, Oxford: Wiley-Blackwell, pp. 109–22.

Ahern, Jack (2011) 'From Fail-Safe to Safe-To-Fail: Sustainability and Resilience in the New Urban World', *Landscape and Urban Planning*, 100(4): 341–3. DOI: 10.1016/j.landurbplan.2011.02.021

Alexander, David (2013) 'Resilience and Disaster Risk Reduction: An Etymological Journey', *Natural Hazards and Earth Systems Science*, online publication, DOI: 10.5794/nhess-13-2707-2013

Ball, Phillip (2000) *H2O: A Biography of Water*, London: Phoenix (Orion).

Barbier, Edward and Anil Markandya (2012) *A New Blueprint for a Green Economy*, London: Earthscan/Routledge.

Bauman, Henrikke and Anne-Marie Tillman (2004) *The Hitch-Hiker's Guide to LCA: An Orientation to Life Cycle Analysis Methodology and Application*, Lund: Studentliteratur.

Bayliss-Smith, Tim (1982) *The Ecology of Ecological Systems*, Cambridge: Cambridge University Press.

Beck, Ulrich (1992) *Risk Society: Towards a New Modernity*, London: Sage.

Beck, Ulrich (2002) 'A Life of One's Own in a Runaway World…', in Ulrich Beck and Elisabeth Beck-Gernwheim (eds), *Individualization: Institutionalized Individualism and its Social and Political Consequences*, London: Sage, pp. 22–9.

Beck, Ulrich (2007) *World at Risk*, Cambridge: Polity.

Beck, Ulrich, Anthony Giddens and Scott Lash (1994) *Reflexive Modernization: Politics, Tradition and Aesthetics in the Modern Social Order*, Stanford, CA: Stanford University Press.

Beck, Ulrich and Elisabeth Beck-Gernsheim (2001) *Individualization: Institutionalized Individualism and its Social and Political Consequences*, London: Sage.

Beder, Sharon (1998) *Global Spin: The Corporate Assault in Environmentalism*, Devon: Green Books.

Beder, Sharon (2000), 2nd edn, *Global Spin: The Corporate Assault on Environmentalism*, Melbourne: Scribe.

Beder, Sharon (2006) 'The Sustainability Principle', in Sharon Beder (ed.), *Environmental Principles and Policies: An Interdisciplinary Approach*, Sydney: UNSW Press.

Benyus, Janine (1997) *Biomicry: Innovation Inspired by Nature*, New York: William Morrow.

Bernick, Michael and Robert Cervero (1997) *Transit Villages in the 21st Century*, New York: McGraw-Hill, chapter 2.

Berry, Thomas and Brian Swimme (1992) *The Universe Story: From the Primordial Flaring Forth to the Ecozoic Era – A Celebration of the Unfolding Cosmos*, San Francisco, CA: HarperCollins.

Blakely, Ed (2012) *My Storm: Managing the Recovery of New Orleans in the Wake of Katrina*, Philadelphia, PA: University of Pennsylvania Press.

Blewitt, John (2008) *Understanding Sustainable Development*, London: Earthscan.

Boardman, Anthony, David Greenberg, Aidan Vining and David Weimer (2010), 4th edn, *Cost–Benefit Analysis: Concepts and Practice*, Upper Saddle River, NJ: Prentice Hall.

Botsman, Rachel and Roo Rogers (2010) *What's Mine Is Yours: The Rise of Collaborative Consumption*, New York: HarperCollins.

Brown, J., W. Burnside, A. Davidson, J. DeLong, W. Dunn, M. Hamilton, N. Mercado-Silva, J. Nekola, J. Okie, W. Woodruff and W. and Zuo (2011) 'Energetic Limits to Economic Growth', *BioScience*, 61(1): 23.

Brown, Lester (2008) *Plan B 3.0: Mobilizing to Save Civilization*, New York: W. W. Norton.

Brundtland, Gro Harlem *et al.* (1987) *Our Common Future*, Oxford: Oxford University Press.

Carson, Rachel (1962) *Silent Spring*, Boston, MA: Houghton Mifflin.

Carter, Paul (1996) *The Lie of the Land*, London: Faber and Faber.

Chandler, David and Julian Reid (2016) *The Neoliberal Subject: Resilience, Adaptation and Vulnerability*, London: Rowman and Littlefield.

Chang, S. D. (1998) 'Beijing: Perspectives on Preservation, Environment and Development', *Cities*, 15(1): 13–25.

Checkland, Peter and Jim Scholes (1999) *Soft Systems Methodology in Action*, New York: Wiley.

Christoff, Peter (2009) 'Ecological Modernisation, Ecological Modernities', in Arthur Mol, David Sonnenfeld and Gert Spaargaren (eds), *The Ecological Modernisation Reader*, London and New York: Routledge, pp. 101–22.

Considine, Mark (2005) *Making Public Policy*, Cambridge: Polity.

Cooper, Timothy (2008) 'Challenging the "Refuse Revolution": War, Waste and the Rediscovery of Recycling, 1900–50', *Historical Research*, 81(214): 710–31.

Costanza, Robert (2016) 'Ecosystem Services in Theory and Practice', in Marion Potschin, Roy Haines-Young, Robert Fish and R. Kerry Turner (eds), *Routledge Handbook of Ecosystem Services*, Abingdon: Earthcan/Routledge, pp. 15–24.

Crang, Mike, Alex Hughes, Nicky Gregson, Lucy Norris and Farid Ahamed (2012) 'Rethinking Governance and Value in Commodity Chains through Global Recycling Networks', *Transactions of the Institute of British Geographers*, 38(1): 12–24.

Craumer, P. R. (1979) 'Farm Productivity and Energy Efficiency in Amish and Modern Dairying', *Agriculture and Environment*, 4: 281–99.

Crewe, Louise (2004) 'Unravelling fashion's commodity chains', in Alex Hughes and Suanne Reimer (eds), *Geographies of Commodity Chains*, London: Routledge, pp. 195–214.

Daly, Herman (1977) *Steady-State Economics*, Washington, DC: Island Press.

Davis, Mike (1990) *City of Quartz*, London: Verso.

Davis, Mike (2006) *Planet of Slums*, London: Verso.

Davison, Graeme (2004) *Car Wars*, Sydney: Allen & Unwin.

De Botton, Alain (2000) *The Consolations of Philosophy*, New York: Vintage.

De Villiers, Marq (2001) *Water: The Fate of Our Most Precious Resource*, Boston, MA: Houghton Mifflin.

Delanty, Gerard (2003) *Community*, London: Routledge.

Desrochers, Pierre (2009) 'Does the Invisible Hand Have a Green Thumb? Incentives, Linkages, and the Creation of Wealth out of Industrial Waste in Victorian England', *Geographical Journal*, 175(1): 3–16.

Deutz, Pauline (2009) 'Producer Responsibility in a Sustainable Development Context: Ecological Modernisation or Industrial Ecology?', *Geographical Journal*, 175(4): 274–85.

Dresner, Simon (2008), 2nd edn, *The Principles of Sustainability*, London: Earthscan.

Dryzek, John (2005), 2nd edn, *The Politics of the Earth: Environmental Discourses*, Oxford: Oxford University Press.

Eckersley, Robyn (2004) *The Green State: Rethinking Democracy and Sovereignty*, Boston, MA: MIT Press.

ECOTEC (1993) *Reducing Transport Emissions through Land Use Planning*, Report to the Department of Environment and the Department of Transport, London: HMSO.

Ehrenfeld, John (2008) *Sustainability by Design*, New Haven, CT: Yale University.

Ehrenfeld, John and Nicholas Gertler (1997) 'Industrial Ecology in Practice: The Evolution of Interdependence at Kalundborg', *Journal of Industrial Ecology*, 1(1): 67–79.

Etzioni, Amitai (2006) 'Voluntary Simplicity: Characterization, Select Psychological Implications and Societal Consequences', in Tim Jackson (ed.), *The Earthscan Reader in Sustainable Consumption*, London: Earthscan, pp. 109–26.

Evenson, Robert and Douglas Gollin (2003) 'Assessing the Impact of the Green Revolution, 1960 to 2000', *Science*, 300: 758–62.

Fargione, Joseph, Jason Hill, David Tilman, Stephen Polasky and Peter Hawthorne (2008) 'Land Clearing and the Biofuel Carbon Debt', *Science*, 319: 1235–8.

Flannery, Tim (1994) *The Future Eaters: An Ecological History of the Australasian Lands and People*, Sydney: Reed Books.

Flannery, Tim (2010) *Here on Earth: An Argument for Hope*, Melbourne: Text Publishing.

Folke, Carl (2006) 'Resilience: The Emergence of a Perspective for Socio-Ecological Systems Analyses', *Global Environmental Change*, 16(3): 253–67.

Folke, Carl, S. R. Carpenter, B. Walker, M. Scheffer, T. Chapin and J. Rockstrom (2010) 'Resilience Thinking: Integrating Resilience, Adaptability and Transformability', *Ecology and Society*, 15(4): 20. [Online] URL: http://www.ecologyandsociety.org/vol15/iss4/art20/

Food and Agriculture Organization of the United Nations (2012) *World Agriculture Towards 2030/2050: The 2012 Revision* (www.fao.org/docrep/016/ap106e/ap106e.pdf).

Food and Agriculture Organization of the United Nations (2013a) *The State of Food and Agriculture* (www.fao.org/docrep/018/i3300e/i3300e00.htm).

Food and Agriculture Organization of the United Nations (2013b) *Tackling Climate Change Through Livestock: A Global Assessment of Emissions and Mitigation Opportunities* (www.fao.org/docrep/018/i3437e/i3437e.pdf).

Franks, Jeremy and Ben Hadingham (2012) 'Reducing Greenhouse Gas Emissions from Agriculture: Avoiding Trivial Solutions to a Global Problem', *Land Use Policy*, 29: 727–36.

Friedmann, John (2002) *The Prospect of Cities*, Minneapolis, MN: University of Minnesota Press.

Garreau, Joel (1991) *Edge City: Life on the New Frontier*, New York: Doubleday.

Giampietro, David and Mario Pimental (1994) *Food, Land, Population and the U.S. Economy*, Washington, DC: Carrying Capacity Network.

Gibbs, David and Pauline Deutz (2007) 'Reflections on Implementing Industrial Ecology through Eco-Industrial Park Development', *Journal of Cleaner Production*, 15(17): 1683–95.

Giddens, Anthony (1995) 'Living in a Post-Traditional Society', in Ulrich Beck, Anthony Giddens and Scott Lash (eds), *Reflexive Modernization: Politics, Tradition and Aesthetics of the Modern Social Order*, Cambridge: Polity, pp. 56–109.

Giddens, Anthony (2009) *The Politics of Climate Change*, Cambridge: Polity.

Giddings, Bob, Bill Hopwood and Geoff O'Brien (2002) 'Environment, Economy and Society: Fitting Them Together into Sustainable Development', *Sustainable Development*, 10: 187–96.

Gilbert, Natasha (2011) 'Summit Urged to Clean up Farming', *Nature*, 479: 279.

Gille, Zsuzsa (2007) *From the Cult of Waste to the Trash Heap of History: The Politics of Waste in Socialist and Postsocialist Hungary*, Bloomington, IN: Indiana University Press.

Gille, Zsuzsa (2010) 'Actor Networks, Modes of Production, and Waste Regimes: Reassembling the Macro-Social', *Environment and Planning*, 42(5): 1049–64.

Gillham, Oliver (2002) *The Limitless City: A Primer on the Urban Sprawl Debate*, Washington, DC: Island Press.

Godfray, H. Charles, John Beddington, Ian Crute, Lawrence Haddad, David Lawrence, James Muir, Jules Pretty, Sherman Robinson, Sandy Thomas and Camilla Toulmin (2010) 'Food Security: The Challenge of Feeding 9 Billion People', *Science*, 327: 812–18.

Goodenough, Ursula (1998) *The Sacred Depths of Nature*, New York: Oxford University Press.

Graedel, Thomas and Braden Allenby (2003) *Industrial Ecology*, Upper Saddle River, NJ: Prentice Hall.

Graham, Carol (2011) *The Pursuit of Happiness: An Economy of Well-being*, Washington, DC: Brookings Institution Press.

Greer, John Michael (2008) *The Long Descent*, Gabriola Island, BC: New Society Publishers.

Gustavsson, Jenny, Christel Cederberg, Ulf Sonesson, Robert van Otterdijk and Alexandre Meybeck (2011) *Global Food Losses and Food Waste: Extent, Causes and Prevention*, Rome: Food and Agriculture Organization of the United Nations.

Hall, Charles and John Day (2009) 'Revisiting the Limits to Growth after Peak Oil', *American Scientist*, 97: 230–7.

Hardin, Garrett (1968) 'The Tragedy of the Commons', *Science*, 162(3859): 1243–8.

Hawken, Paul (2007) *Blessed Unrest: How the Largest Movement in the World Came into Being and No One Saw It Coming*, New York: Viking/Penguin.

Hawkes, Jon (2001) *The Fourth Pillar of Sustainability: Culture's Essential Role in Public Planning*, Melbourne: Common Ground Publishing.

Hawkes, Jon (2004) *The Fourth Pillar of Sustainability: Culture's Essential Role in Public Planning*, Melbourne: Common Ground Publishing.

Hawkins, Gay (2006) *The Ethics of Waste: How We Relate to Rubbish*, Sydney: University of New South Wales Press.

Hayward, Tim (2005) *Constitutional Environmental Rights*, Oxford: Oxford University Press.

Headey, Derek and Shenggen Fan (2010) *Reflections on the Global Food Crisis: How Did It Happen? How Has It Hurt? and How Can We Prevent the Next One?* International Food Policy Research Institute Research Monograph 165. Washington, DC.

Heinberg, Richard (2007) *Peak Everything: Waking up to the Century of Declines*, Gabriola Island, Canada: New Society Publishers.

Hill, Stuart (2011) 'Social Ecology: An Australian Perspective', in D. Wright, C. Camden-Pratt and S. Hill (eds), *Social Ecology: Applying Ecological Understandings to our Lives and our Planet*, Stroud: Hawthorn Press, pp. 17–30.

Hoffmann-Martinot, Vincent (2004) 'Towards an Americanization of French Metropolitan Areas?', Paper presented at the Department of Political Science, Universidad Autonoma de Madrid and International Relations and at the International Metropolitan Observatory Meeting, Pole Universitaire de Bordeaux, 9–10 January.

Hopkins, Rob (2008) 'Peak Oil and Climate Change', in Rob Hopkins (ed.), *The Transition Handbook: Creating Local Sustainable Communities Beyond Oil Dependency*, Sydney: Finch Publishing.

Hulme, Mike (2009) *Why We Disagree About Climate Change: Understanding Controversy, Inaction and Opportunity*, Cambridge: Cambridge University Press.

IPCC (2013) *Fifth Assessment Report* (www.ipcc.ch/report/ar5).

Jackson, Tim (2006) 'Challenges for Sustainable Consumption Policy', in Tim Jackson (ed.), *The Earthscan Reader in Sustainable Consumption*, London: Earthscan, pp. 109–26.

Jackson, Tim (2016), 2nd edn, *Prosperity Without Growth: Foundations for the Economy of Tomorrow*, London: Routledge.

Kahn, Mathew (2000) 'The Environmental Impact of Suburbanisation', *Journal of Policy Analysis and Management*, 19(4): 569–86.

Kaika, Maria (2005) *City of Flows: Modernity, Nature, and the City*, London: Routledge.

Kauffman, Stuart (1995) *At Home in the Universe: The Search for Laws of Self-Organization and Complexity*, Oxford: Oxford University Press.

Kern, Kathleen (2007) 'The Human Cost of Cheap Cell Phones', in Stephen Hiatt (ed.), *A Game as Old as Empire: The Secret World of Economic Hit Men and the Web of Global Corruption*, San Francisco, CA: Berrett-Koehler, pp. 93–112.

Koh, Lian Pin and David Wilcove (2008) 'Is Oil Palm Agriculture Really Destroying Tropical Biodiversity?', *Conservation Letters*, 1: 60–4.

Korozicz, David (2010) *Near-Term Systemic Implications of a Peak in Global Oil Production: An Outline Review*, Dublin: The Foundation for the Economics of Sustainability.

Kraemer, Claudia (2005) 'Commuter Belt Turbulence in a Dynamic Region: The Cast of the Munich City-Region', in Keith Hoggart (ed.), *The City's Hinterland, Dynamism and Divergence in Europe's Peri-Urban Territories*, Aldershot: Ashgate.

Lamb, Jonathon (2010) '"The true words at last from a mind in runs": J. M. Coetzee and Realism', in G. Bradshaw and M. Neill (eds), *J. M. Coetzee's Austerity*, Aldershot: Ashgate.

Lane, Ruth, Ralph Horne and Jenny Bicknell (2009) 'Routes of Reuse of Second-hand Goods in Melbourne Households', *Australian Geographer*, 40(2): 151–68.

Lane, Ruth and Matt Watson (2012) 'Stewardship of Things: The Radical Potential of Product Stewardship for Re-framing Responsibilities and Relationships to Products and Materials', *Geoforum*, 43(6): 1254–65.

Latour, Bruno (2005) *Reassembling the Social: An Introduction to Actor-Network Theory*, Oxford: Oxford University Press.

Lave, Jean and Étienne Wenger (1991) *Situated Learning: Legitimate Peripheral Participation*, Cambridge: Cambridge University Press.

Leakey, Richard and Roger Lewin (1995) *The Sixth Extinction: Patterns of Life and the Future of Mankind*, New York: Anchor Books.

Leakey, Richard and Roger Lewin (1996) *The Sixth Extinction: Biodiversity and Its Survival*, London: Weidenfeld and Nicholson.

Lepawsky, Josh and C. McNabb (2010) 'Mapping international flows of electronic waste', *Canadian Geographer/Le Géographe canadien*, 54(2): 177–95.

Lepawsky, Josh and Mostaem Billah (2011) 'Making Chains that (Un)make Things: Waste–Value Relations and the Bangladeshi Rubbish Electronics Industry', *Geografiska Annaler: Series B, Human Geography*, 93(2): 121–39.

Lever-Tracy, Constance (ed.) (2010) *Routledge Handbook of Climate Change and Society*, London: Routledge.

Lipovetsky, Gilles (2011) *Hypermodern Times*, Cambridge: Polity.

Lipovetsky, Gilles (2011) 'The Hyperconsumption Society', in Karin Ekstrom and Kay Glans (eds), *Beyond the Consumption Bubble*, New York: Routledge, pp. 25–36.

Lovelock, James (2006) *The Revenge of Gaia: Earth's Climate Crisis and the Future of Humanity*, New York: Basic Books.

Low, Tim (2002) *The New Nature: Winners and Losers in Wild Australia*, Melbourne: Viking/Penguin.

Macfarlane, Robert (2007) *The Wild Places*, London: Granta.

Mackenzie-Mohr, Douglas and William Smith (2006) *An Introduction to Community-Based Social Marketing*, Gabriola Island, BC: New Society Publishers.

Mackenzie-Mohr, Douglas and William Smith (2011), 3rd edn, *Fostering Sustainable Behaviour: An Introduction to Community-Based Social Marketing*, Gabriola Island, BC: New Society Publishers.

Majone, Giandomenico (1989) *Evidence, Argument and Persuasion in Policy Processes*, New Haven, CT: Yale University Press.

Marcuse, Peter and Ronald van Kempen (2000) *Globalising Cities*, Oxford: Blackwell.

Mason, Leah, Thomas Boyle, Julian Fyfe, Tanzi Smith and Dana Cordell (2011) *National Food Waste Data Assessment: Final Report.* Prepared by the Institute for Sustainable Futures, UTS for the Department of Sustainability, Environment, Water, Population and Communities (DSEWPaC), Canberra.

Massey, Doreen (2005) *For Space*, London: Sage.

Mathews, Freya (2005) *Reinhabiting Reality: Towards a Recovery of Nature*, Albany, NY: SUNY.

McDonough, William and Michael Braungart (2002) *Cradle to Cradle: Remaking The Way We Make Things*, New York: North Point Press.

McKibben, Bill (1989) *The End of Nature*, New York: Random House.

McKibben, Bill (2010) *Eaarth: Making a Life on a Tough New Planet*, Melbourne: Black Books.

Meadows, Donella, Dennis Meadows and Jorgen Randers (2004) *Limits to Growth: The 30-Year Update*, Vermont: Chelsea Green and London: Earthscan.

Meadows, Donella, Dennis Meadows, Jorgen Randers and William Behrens III (1972) *Limits to Growth*, New York: Universe Books.

Mees, Paul (2010) *Transport for Suburbia: Beyond the Automobile Age*, London: Earthscan.

Merchant, Carolyn (1992) *Radical Ecology: The Search for a Liveable World*, New York: Routledge.

Miller, G. Tyler and Scott Spoolman (2010), 13th edn, *Environmental Science*, Belmont, CA: Brooks Cole.

Mol, Arthur and Gert Spaargaren (2006) 'Towards a Sociology of Environmental Flows: A New Agenda for Twenty-First Century Environmental Sociology', in G. Spaargaren, A. Mol and F. Buttel (eds), *Governing Environmental Flows: Global Challenges to Social Theory*, Cambridge, MA: MIT Press, pp. 39–82.

Moore, Sarah (2012) 'Garbage Matters: Concepts in New Geographies of Waste', *Progress in Human Geography*, 36(6): 780–99.

Moser, Susanne and Lisa Dilley (eds) (2007) *Creating a Climate for Change: Communicating Climate Change and Facilitating Social Change*, Cambridge: Cambridge University Press.

Mudd, Gavin (2010) 'The Environmental Sustainability of Mining in Australia: Key Mega-Trends and Looming Constraints', *Resources Policy*, 35(2): 98–115.

Mulligan, Martin (2003) 'Feet to the Ground in Storied Landscapes', in William Adams and Martin Mulligan (eds), *Decolonizing Nature: Strategies for Conservation in a Post-colonial Era*, London: Earthscan, pp. 268–89.

Mulligan, Martin (2008) 'To Travel Hopefully', *Arena Magazine*, no. 97, Melbourne, pp. 19–22.

Mulligan, Martin (2014) 'On Ambivalence and Hope in the Restless Search for Community: How to Work with the Idea of Community in the Global Age', *Sociology*, 49(2): 340–55.

Mulligan, Martin and Stuart Hill (2001) *Ecological Pioneers: A Social History of Australian Ecological Thought and Action*, Melbourne: Cambridge University Press.

Mulligan, Martin, Kim Humphery, Paul James, Christopher Scanlon, Pia Smith and Nicky Welch (2006) *Creating Community: Celebrations, Arts and Wellbeing Within and Across Local Communities*, Globalism Research Centre, RMIT University, Melbourne.

Mulligan, Martin and Yaso Nadarajah (2012) *Rebuilding Communities in the Wake of Disaster: Social Recovery in Sri Lanka and India*, New Delhi: Routledge.

Mulligan, Martin and Pia Smith (2011) 'Art, Governance and the Turn to Community: Lessons from a National Action Research Project on Community Art and Local Government in Australia', *Journal of Arts and Communities*, 2(1): 27–40.

Nadarajah, Yaso, Martin Mulligan, Jodi-Anne Smith, Louise Le Nay and Christina Hindhaugh (2008) *Unexpected Sources of Hope: Climate Change, Community and the Future*, Globalism Research Centre, RMIT University, Melbourne.

Nelson, Arthur (2013) *Reshaping Metropolitan America: Development Trends and Opportunities to 2030*, Washington, DC: Island Press.

Newman, Peter and Andy Thornley (1996) *Urban Planning in Europe*, London: Routledge.

Newman, Peter and Jeff Kenworthy (1989) 'Gasoline Consumption and Cities', *APA Journal*, winter, 24–37.

Northrop, Robert and Anne Connor (2013) *Ecological Sustainability: Understanding Complex Issues*, Boca Raton, FL: CRC Press.

Norton, R. D. (1979) *City Life-Cycles and American Urban Policy*, New York: Academic Press.

O'Brien, Martin (2007) *A Crisis of Waste? Understanding the Rubbish Society*, Oxford: Routledge.

Orr, David (2011) 'Four Challenges of Sustainability', in David Orr, *Hope is an Imperative*, Washington, DC: Island Press and Springer eBooks.

Pearce, David (1998) *Economics and Environment: Essays on Ecological Economics and Sustainable Development*, London: Edward Elgar.

Perkowitz, Sidney (2001) 'The Rarest Element', in David Rothernberg and Marta Ulvaeus (eds), *Writing on Water*, Cambridge, MA: MIT Press (Terra Nova), pp. 3–14.

Pfeiffer, Dale (2006) *Eating Fossil Fuels: Oil, Food and the Coming Crisis in Agriculture*, Gabriola Island, BC: New Society.

Phipps, Carter (2012) *Evolutionaries: Unlocking the Spiritual and Cultural Potential of Science's Greatest Idea*, New York: HarperCollins.

Plumwood, Val (1993) *Feminism and the Mastery of Nature*, New York: Routledge.

Plumwood, Val (2002) *Environmental Culture: The Ecological Crisis of Reason*, Abingdon: Routledge.

Portney, Kent (1992) *Controversial Issues in Environmental Policy: Science vs Economics vs Politics*, New York: Sage.

Potschin, Marion, Roy Haines-Young, Robert Fish and R. Kerry Turner (eds) (2016) Routledge Handbook of Ecosystem Services, Abingdon: Earthcan/Routledge.

Premat, Adriana (2005) 'Moving between the Plan and the Ground: Shifting Perspectives on Urban Agriculture in Havana, Cuba', in Luc Mougeot (ed.), *Agropolix: The Social, Political and Environmental Dimesions of Urban Agriculture*, Ottawa: International Development Research Centre, pp. 153–86.

Pretty, Jules *et al.* (2010) 'The Top 100 Questions of Importance to the Future of Global Agriculture', *International Journal of Agricultural Sustainability*, 8: 219–36.

Prigogine, Ilya (1997) *The End of Certainty*, Paris: The Free Press.

Prior, Tim, Damien Giurco, Gavin Mudd, Leah Mason and Johannes Bebhrisch (2012) 'Resource Depletion, Peak Minerals and the Implications for Sustainable Resource Management', *Global Environmental Change*, 22(3): 577–87.

Rittel, Horst and Melvin Webber (1973) 'Dilemmas in a General Theory of Planning', *Policy Studies*, 4: 155–69.

Robertson, Margaret (2014) *Sustainability: Principles and Practice*, Abingdon: Earthscan/Routledge.

Rockström, Johan *et al.* (2009) 'A Safe Operating Space for Humanity', *Nature*, 461: 472–5.

Rodin, Judith (2014) *The Resilience Dividend: Being Strong in a World Where Things Go Wrong*, New York: The Rockefeller Foundation.

Rose, Nikolas (1996) 'The Death of the Social: Re-Figuring the Territory of Government', *Economy and Society*, 25(3): 327–56.

Rusk, David (1993) *Cities Without Suburbs*, Washington, DC: Woodrow Wilson Centre Press.

Rutter, Michael (2012) 'Resilience as a Dynamic Concept', *Development and Psychology*, 24: 335–44.

Sachs, Wolfgang (2015) *Planet Dialectics: Explorations in Environment and Development*, London: Zed.

Sachs, Wolfgang and Tilman Santarius (eds) (2007) *Fair Future: Limited Resources, Conflicts, Security and Global Justice*, London: Zed Books.

Sarkissian, Wendy, Nancy Hoffer, Yollana Shore, Steph Vajda and Cathy Wilkinson (2009) *Kitchen Table Sustainability: Practical Recipes for Community Engagement with Sustainability*, London: Earthscan.

Scerri, Andy and Paul James (2010) 'Accounting for Sustainability: Combining Qualitative and Quantitative Research in Developing "Indicators" of Sustainability', *International Journal of Social Research Methodology*, 13(1): 41–53.

Schnepf, Randy (2004) *Energy Use in Agriculture: Background and Issues*, CRS Report for Congress. Washington, DC: Congressional Research Service, The Library of Congress.

Sennett, Richard (2006) *The Culture of New Capitalism*, New Haven, CT: Yale University Press.

Sennett, Richard (2008) *The Craftsman*, New Haven, CT: Yale University Press.

Shiva, Vandana (2005) *Earth Democracy: Justice, Sustainability and Peace*, Cambridge, MA: Southend Press.

Slovic, Paul (2000) *The Perception of Risk*, London: Earthscan.

Slovic, Paul (2010) *The Feeling of Risk: New Perspectives on Risk*, London: Earthscan.

Solomon, Steven (2010) *Water: The Epic Struggle for Wealth, Power, and Civilization*, New York: Harper Perennial.

Strasser, Susan (1999) *Waste and Want: A Social History of Trash*, New York: Henry Holt.

Tainter, Joseph (1990) *The Collapse of Complex Societies*, Cambridge: Cambridge University Press.

Tainter, Joseph and Tadeusz Patzek (2012) *Drilling Down: The Gulf Oil Debacle and Our Energy Dilemma*, Dordrecht: Copernicus/Springer.

Taleb, Nassim Nicholas (2007) *The Black Swan: The Impact of the Highly Improbable*, New York: Random House.

Thomas, Ian and Paul Murfitt (2011), 2nd edn, *Environmental Management: Processes and Practices for Australia*, Sydney: Federation Press.

Thomashow, Mitchell (2002) *Bringing the Biosphere Home: Learning to Perceive Global Environmental Change*, Cambridge, MA: MIT Press.

Thompson, Susan (ed.) (2007) *Planning Australia: An Overview of Urban and Regional Planning*, Cambridge: Cambridge University Press.

Tverberg, Gail (2012) 'Oil Supply Limits and the Continuing Financial Crisis', *Energy*, 37: 27–34.

Ungar, Michael (ed.) (2012) *The Social Ecology of Resilience: A Handbook of Theory and Practice*, New York: Springer.

United Nations Environment Program (2010) *Global Partnership on Waste Management* (GPWM) Framework Document (www.unep.org/gpwm/Background/tabid/56401/Default.aspx).

Urry, John (2011) *Climate Change and Society*, Cambridge: Polity.

Vig, Norman and Michael Kraft (2012), 8th edn, *Environmental Policy: New Directions for the Twenty-First Century*, New York: Sage.

Walker, Brian and David Salt (2006) *Resilience Thinking: Sustaining Ecosystems and People in a Changing World*, Washington, DC: Island Press.

Washington, Haydn (2015) *Demystifying Sustainability: Towards Real Solutions*, Abingdon: Earthscan/Routledge.

Watson, Matt, Harriet Bulkeley and Ray Hudson (2008) 'Unpicking Environmental Policy Integration with Tales from Waste Management', *Government and Policy*, 26(3): 481–98.

Watson, Matt and Ruth Lane (2011) 'Mapping Geographies of Reuse in Sheffield and Melbourne', in Ruth Lane and Andrew Gorman-Murray (eds), *Material Geographies of Household Sustainability*, Farnham: Ashgate, pp. 133–55.

Wessels, Tom (2006) *The Myth of Progress: Towards a Sustainable Future*, Burlington, VT: University of Vermont Press.

White, Lynn Jr (1967) 'The Historical Roots of Our Ecological Crisis', *Science*, 155(3767): 1203–7.

Whitehead, Mark (2014) *Environmental Transformations: A Geography of the Anthropocene*, London: Routledge.

Whitmarsh, Lorraine, Safron O'Neill and Irene Lorenzoni (eds) (2011) *Engaging the Public with Climate Change: Behaviour Change and Communication*, London: Earthscan.

Wilk, Richard (2011) 'Consumption in an Age of Globalization and Localization', in Karin Ekstrom and Kay Glans (eds), *Beyond the Consumption Bubble*, New York: Routledge, pp. 37–51.

Williams, Katie, Elizabeth Burton and Mike Jenks (2000) *Achieving Sustainable Urban Form*, London: Spon.

Winne, Mark (2008) *Closing the Gap: Resetting the Table in the Land of Plenty*, Boston, MA: Beacon Press.

Winne, Mark (2010) *Food Rebels, Guerrilla Gardeners and Smart-Cookin' Mamas: Fighting Back in an Age of Industrial Agriculture*, Boston, MA: Beacon Press.

Woolcock, Michael (2009) *Towards a Plurality of Methods in Project Evaluation: A Contextualised Approach to Understanding Impact Trajectories and Efficacy*, Manchester: Brooks World Poverty Institute, University of Manchester.

Worster, Donald (1994), 2nd edn, *Nature's Economy: A History of Ecological Ideas*, Cambridge: Sierra Club Books.

Wright, Diana and Donella Meadows (2012) *Thinking in Systems: A Primer*, Abingdon: Routledge.

Xu, Yue, Gan Zhang, Jun Li, Paromita Chakraborty, Hua Li and Xiang Liu (2011) 'Long-range Atmospheric Transport of Persistent Organochlorinated Compounds from South and Mainland South-Eastern Asia to a Remote Mountain Site in South-Western China', *Journal of Environmental Monitoring*, 13: 3119–27.

Zable, Arnold (2004) *The Figtree*, Melbourne: Text.

Index

Note: Page numbers followed by 'f' refer to figures, followed by 'p' refer to photographs and followed by 't' refer to tables.